WOMEN IN THE ANCIENT MEDITERRANEAN WORLD

In this book, Guy D. Middleton explores the fascinating lives of thirty real women of the ancient Mediterranean from the Palaeolithic to the Byzantine era. They include queens and aristocrats, such as the Pharoah Hatshepsut and the Etruscan noblewoman Seianti; Eritha and Karpathia, Bronze Age priestesses from the Aegean; a Pompeiian prostitute called Eutychis; the pagan philosopher Hypatia and the Christian saint Perpetua, from North Africa, as well as women from smaller communities. Middleton uses a wide range of archaeological and historical evidence, including burials and funerary practices, graffiti, inscriptions, painted pottery, hand-prints, human remains, and a variety of historical texts, as well as the latest modern research. His volume weaves together the stories of real women, placing them firmly in the spotlight of history. Engagingly written and up to date in its scholarship, Middleton's book offers new insights for students and researchers in Ancient History, Archaeology and Mediterranean Studies, as well as in Women's History.

Guy D. Middleton completed his PhD in the Department of Classics and Ancient History at Durham University. He is the author of *Understanding Collapse: Ancient History and Modern Myths* (Cambridge University Press, 2017) and is Visiting Fellow at Newcastle University as well as a Fellow of the Royal Historical Society.

WOMEN IN THE ANCIENT MEDITERRANEAN WORLD

FROM THE PALAEOLITHIC TO THE BYZANTINES

GUY D. MIDDLETON

University of Newcastle upon Tyne

Shaftesbury Road, Cambridge CB2 8EA, United Kingdom

One Liberty Plaza, 20th Floor, New York, NY 10006, USA

477 Williamstown Road, Port Melbourne, VIC 3207, Australia

314–321, 3rd Floor, Plot 3, Splendor Forum, Jasola District Centre, New Delhi – 110025, India

103 Penang Road, #05–06/07, Visioncrest Commercial, Singapore 238467

Cambridge University Press is part of Cambridge University Press & Assessment, a department of the University of Cambridge.

We share the University's mission to contribute to society through the pursuit of education, learning and research at the highest international levels of excellence.

www.cambridge.org
Information on this title: www.cambridge.org/9781108481137

DOI: 10.1017/9781108646529

First published 2023

Printed in the United Kingdom by TJ Books Limited, Padstow Cornwall

A catalogue record for this publication is available from the British Library.

Library of Congress Cataloging-in-Publication Data
NAMES: Middleton, Guy D., author.
TITLE: Women in the ancient Mediterranean world : from the Palaeolithic to the Byzantines / Guy D. Middleton, University of Newcastle upon Tyne.
DESCRIPTION: Cambridge, United Kingdom ; New York, NY : Cambridge University Press, 2023. | Includes bibliographical references and index.
IDENTIFIERS: LCCN 2022044117 (print) | LCCN 2022044118 (ebook) | ISBN 9781108481137 (hardback) | ISBN 9781108703833 (paperback) | ISBN 9781108646529 (epub)
SUBJECTS: LCSH: Women–Mediterranean Region–History. | Women–Mediterranean Region–Social conditions. | Women–Mediterranean Region–Biography.
CLASSIFICATION: LCC HQ1137.M43 M54 2023 (print) | LCC HQ1137.M43 (ebook) | DDC 305.4209182/2–dc23/eng/20221024
LC record available at https://lccn.loc.gov/2022044117
LC ebook record available at https://lccn.loc.gov/2022044118

ISBN 978-1-108-48113-7 Hardback
ISBN 978-1-108-70383-3 Paperback

For Ellie and Charlotte

that which half emerges from the dim background of time is strangely stirring

D. H. Lawrence, *Sketches of Etruscan Places*

CONTENTS

Preface *page* ix
Acknowledgements xiv
Timeline xvi
Historical Contexts xviii

INTRODUCTION: APPROACHING WOMEN IN PREHISTORY AND HISTORY 1

PART I THE DEEP PAST 23

1 WOMEN IN CAVES 27

2 A WOMAN OF ÇATALHÖYÜK 34

3 A WOMAN OF GOZO 42

PART II THE BRONZE AGE 49

4 MERNEITH 55

5 ŠIMATUM AND KIRUM 62

6 THE WOMAN OF LA ALMOLOYA 68

7 THE PRIESTESS OF ANEMOSPILIA 75

8 HATSHEPSUT 82

9 PUDUHEPA 89

10 ERITHA AND KARPATHIA 95

11 HATIBA 102

PART III THE IRON AGE 109

12 NAUNAKHTE 113

13 HERSE 119

14 PKPUPES 125

15 ATOSSA 132

16 THE PRINCESS OF VIX 138

17 ARISTONICE 143

18 NEAIRA 149

19 PHANOSTRATE 155

PART IV THE HELLENISTIC WORLDS 161

20 OLYMPIAS 165

21 SEIANTI HANUNIA TLESNASA 172

22 TERENTIA 179

23 MARIAMNE 188

PART V THE AGE OF EMPIRE 195

24 CLEOPATRA SELENE 199

25 EUTYCHIS 206

26 ACHILLIA AND AMAZON 212

27 PERPETUA 219

28 ZENOBIA 227

29 HYPATIA 236

30 THEODORA 243

Notes 251

Select Bibliography 284

Index 289

PREFACE

In 1361–1362, the Italian writer Boccaccio wrote his *De Mulieribus Claris*, or *Famous Women* – a book, he explained in the dedication to Lady Andrea Acciauoli of Florence, 'in praise of women'.[1] This was the first book in the Western tradition to exclusively compile women's biographies – to save a record of their lives and in particular their great deeds for posterity. The book, which is still in print, consists of 106 lives of women, mythical and real, mostly drawn from the 'pagan' Graeco-Roman tradition. Arranged in chronological order, Boccaccio starts with the biblical Eve and ends with Joanna, queen of Sicily. Giving details of their origins and describing why each woman became famous, the lives are not simple factual biographies; they identify virtue and vice, assign praise and blame, and draw moral judgements.[2] Praiseworthy women are often called 'manly', whilst weak men are 'womanly'. The book provides examples for how women ought and ought not to behave, written from a male perspective.

Four decades later, in 1405, an Italian émigré to France, Christine de Pizan, also published a book of women's lives – *The Book of the City of Ladies*.[3] Although much of the material appears to derive from Boccaccio, de Pizan's work is somewhat more complex than Boccaccio's and we read in it a woman's own reaction to 'all manner of philosophers, poets and orators too numerous to mention, who all seem to speak with one voice and are unanimous in their view that female nature is wholly given up to vice'.[4] Perhaps with some irony, she explains how, through reading the works on women of so many 'learned men, who seemed to be endowed with such great intelligence' and not listening to her own judgement, knowledge, and experience, she fell into despair about herself and women in general. So many wise men could not be wrong. De Pizan prayed and three women appeared to her: Reason, Rectitude, and Justice. They persuaded her that she and the learned men were wrong, that women had lacked a true defender, and they bid her create, in 'the field of Letters', a City of Ladies – 'a walled city, sturdy and impregnable'.[5]

Christine de Pizan is perhaps the first female 'defender' of women; she argued that men had got it wrong, and she used the lives she wrote to show this. But like Boccaccio, and many more ancient authors, she is very much concerned with demonstrating moral behaviour and providing examples of it. The city is only for 'ladies who are of good reputation and worthy of praise'. At the end of her book, when the city has been built and populated, she explains that women now have 'every reason to rejoice – in a suitably devout and respectable manner', the city will 'defend and protect you against your attackers and assailants'.[6] She advises wives on how to deal with their husbands, whether good, average, or bad; advises all women to avoid gossip, jealousies, and scandalous behaviour; recommends young girls to be pure and modest and widows to be respectable. She stresses that all women, of all rank, should look out for sexually predatory men and guard their chastity – pursue virtue and shun vice. Is she simply reinforcing male views of how women should be in society, criticising men for their actions, or giving practical advice to women in general so that they can better survive in society and can undermine negative characterisations of women? The problems and the debates have not gone away.

Women in the Ancient Mediterranean World is also a book of lives, in which I try to piece together archaeological and historical evidence to tell the stories of some of the real women who lived in the Mediterranean region from the Palaeolithic to the beginning of the Byzantine Empire in the time of Justinian and Theodora. Unlike Boccaccio and Christine de Pizan, the selection does not depend on judgements of virtue or vice, on high status or on historical 'achievements'. It is not only the good, or rulers, or the elite who are worthy of remembrance, although the sources bias us to those more visible people. Also, unlike them, I have not included goddesses or mythical figures, because, whilst they may tell us something about attitudes to women and the feminine, the focus is on real women. The important principle here is simply raising the fact of these women's existence; I hope to bring to life these women in the present and where possible relate their words, bodies, images, and life experiences.

Women are still less visible in archaeology and history than men, mirroring a society that is still, in many ways, more used to considering the male as the reference point,[7] though there are plenty of researchers and plenty of books and articles seeking to rectify this. Illustrative of this bias is the story of a recently discovered Etruscan tomb from Tarquinia, an ancient town northwest of Rome. When the intact tomb was found in 2013, news of the find quickly spread through the press.[8] It was reported that the tomb held the remains of an Etruscan prince, placed on a bench along with a spear and brooches, and the cremated remains of his wife interred with him on the opposite bench. Yet, as later analysis of the remains showed, the skeleton with the spear was that of a woman of around forty, while the cremated body was that of a man.[9] The identification and characterisation, based on assumptions about sex and gender roles in which weapons are 'male' and males take priority, had been the wrong way around and were informed by long-standing ingrained prejudice.

Intellectually, I have long been aware of this androcentric bias, but when I found out that my partner and I were going to have a daughter, I realised much more viscerally just how 'male' the past still is. I wondered how she might feel hearing or reading mostly about men or a mass of 'faceless blobs', to borrow Ruth Tringham's phrase.[10] What impact would history largely without women have on a girl growing up? I know she enjoyed *The Jungle Book* much more when I read Mowgli as a girl – at her insistence; would she be more interested in history if girls and women were more visible? What impact might this awareness of women in history have on her character and personality, her identity as a woman? I did not want her to grow up thinking that history was just what men did a long time ago and that there were no 'real women', noble or normal, good or bad, in history. This book has been written in the first place for her, for when she is older and we can read it together, and now for her little sister too, and for any other reader who would like to learn a little about some of the real women of the ancient Mediterranean and how we can study them.

The women whose stories I tell – or more precisely my stories about them – have been chosen to cover a broad swath of time and space but are not used to tell a narrative history of the Mediterranean. The point is the lives themselves and, secondarily, the ways in which we can access and construct them. To some extent, the choices have been dictated by the availability of evidence or accessible research, as well as my own background, experience, and interests: Greece and Rome are there but including Aegean prehistory and non-Roman Italians; so is North Africa, Iberia, and Gozo, the Celts of France; and the Egyptians and Hittites, Levantines, Cypriots, and Mesopotamians are included too; we dig into the deep past of the Palaeolithic and Neolithic as well as historical times. And whilst there are some obvious choices that could be made about which real women to include in a book like this, I have tried to avoid too many of these and to include less well-known characters and women from a variety of social positions as well. For example, I have preferred Cleopatra Selene to her better-known mother; I find the story of the orphaned children of a deposed queen and a foreign soldier and political chancer, who grew up in exile amongst 'the enemy' and dispossessed of her inheritance – Egypt – but who ended up as a queen elsewhere, where she could celebrate her ancestry, to be both fascinating and poignant and worth exploring.

Boccaccio and Christine de Pizan relied primarily on the works of classical authors, the Bible, and writers in the Christian tradition. Each story in this book is pieced together from whatever sources are available. Archaeological, artistic, bureaucratic, iconographic, literary, and scientific evidence all play a role in uncovering the ancient person. As a starting point, sometimes we have just a name, sometimes just a body, sometimes some other aspect of material culture. Other times we may have narrative historical evidence that allows a more complete biographical sketch to be made, with the caveats that come with using such sources. The stories I tell here reflect this diversity in evidence and I hope that, as well as bringing real women of the ancient Mediterranean into focus, they will also enable readers to see how archaeologists and historians work at recreating the past. The difficulties of reconstructing ancient lives will be a recurring feature, but herein lies some of the excitement of doing archaeology and history, where we have tantalising glimpses of people and events and different interpretations of the evidence. Many stories could be told. Where possible, the words and physical existence of the women chosen will be presented, where not, other material aspects of their lives (or deaths) will be surveyed.

Constant companions and sources of inspiration in the writing of this book have been Stephanie Lynn Budin and Jean Macintosh Turfa's *Women in Antiquity: Real Women across the Ancient World* (Routledge, 2016) and Sharon L. James and Sheila Dillon's *A Companion to Women in the Ancient World* (Wiley-Blackwell, 2012), both of which contain many chapters on women in different cultures based on both material and textual evidence. Joyce Salisbury's *Encyclopedia of Women in the Ancient World* (ABC-Clio, 2001) was very helpful as were books in the Oxford University Press series 'Women in Antiquity'. Also to be mentioned are Jennifer Neil's accessible and gloriously illustrated *Women in the Ancient World* (British Museum Press, 2011) and Emily Hemelrijk's fascinating sourcebook of inscriptions touching on the lives of so many real women, *Women and Society in the Roman World* (Cambridge University Press, 2020). The first book I (and many others) read on the topic of women in the ancient world, and one to which all interested readers should turn, is Sarah Pomeroy's *Goddesses, Whores, Wives and Slaves in Classical Antiquity* (Bodley Head, 2015; first published in 1975). All of these can be heartily recommended for learning much more about real women in history – and I have learnt a great deal from them.

This book is somewhat different in scope and intent to those but owes much to them and to many other authors and researchers. I have aimed to gather together and present lives in a book that can be dipped into or read from first to last, to provide a useful introduction to the study of women in the ancient past, and a resource that can lead readers on to further study. As when writing about any subject, I have found that the more you explore the more you find, the more you think and the more you would like to share; I have tried to strike a balance in this book with the number of lives, the various social positions of the women discussed, the depth and breadth of discussion, the periods and places covered, and the style of presentation (accessible but with notes).

Finally, I make no apology for being a man doing 'women's history' or for speaking up for these 'real women'; this is human history and should be open to all students and writers regardless of sex or gender. I think this book will fill a gap on the bookshelf and I hope it will serve to foreground women in history for as wide an audience as possible. I do not claim to speak for these women but rather to draw attention to the fact that they existed and that they once lived lives of their own that are worth remembering and that we can learn more about.

ACKNOWLEDGEMENTS

This book was written for my daughter Ellie, so I thank her most of all for pushing me in this direction of study. In the final stages of preparation, my second daughter Charlotte appeared – and so the book is equally for her. For her constant support and positivity, I must also thank my partner Yoshie, without whom the work would not be possible. My family is full of strong women: I would like to thank my mother Jennifer, who brought me up, took me to ancient places, and gave me my first archaeology books; my elder sister Sarah, who has been such a positive influence; my aunt Elspeth, who lived for many years in Greece and understood my own passion for the place; and my aunt Judy, another émigré. They have shown me, throughout my life, that women are strong, capable, and resilient – I have never doubted it.

In the preparation of this book, I have been helped in different ways by many kind souls. Here, I would like to thank Sabrina Agarwal, Ellen Belcher, Stephanie Lynn Budin, Karina Croucher, Svetlana Egorova, Silvia Ferrara, Ana Delgado Herves, Despina Ignatiadou, Eva Käppel, Maria Liston, Ecaterina Lung, Caroline Malone, Meritxell Ferrer Martin, Petar Milošević, Claudia Valeria Alonso Moreno, Libby Mulqueeny, Jonathan Musgrave, John Papadopoulos, Ludivine Pechoux, Rafael Mico Perez, John Prag, Lucia Rinolfi, Jason Quinlan, Carol Stein, Simon Stoddart, and Jannis Zyganitidis, and the librarians of the Philip Robinson Library at Newcastle University.

I would also like to acknowledge the kindness and support of Miroslav Barta and Ladislav Bares of the Czech Institute of Egyptology at Charles University, Prague, where, until Brexit, I held a part-time post funded by the European Regional Development Fund project 'Creativity and Adaptability as Conditions of the Success of Europe in an Interrelated World' (no. CZ.02.1.01/0.0/0.0/16_019/0000734). This project benefitted from that association.

At Cambridge University Press, I would like to thank Beatrice Rehl for her enthusiasm and ongoing support for this project as well as all the team that saw the book through to publication, especially Aiswarya Narayanan and Trent Hancock. Thanks also to the anonymous reviewers of my initial proposal for seeing its potential and for the positive response to the final manuscript.

This work, which gathers together evidence, ideas, and comment from many sources into an original and critical synthesis, rests on the hard and often painstaking work of many researchers, often in very specialist fields; it is thanks to them that this book could be written. I hope not to have misrepresented their findings and ideas and kindly acknowledge my indebtedness to them here and in the endnotes. I would urge any interested reader to dive into the sources referenced to find out more about particular individuals, topics, or themes. Any errors and infelicities in the book remain the responsibility of the author.

NOTE on ancient names: I have tried to be consistent with names, using the most well-known or easy versions. When quoting sources, however, I have not changed the spellings of translators, which sometimes means a variety of spellings appear in a single chapter. This admittedly can be confusing, even jarring, and apologies are offered in advance.

TIMELINE

Chapter	Person	Place (modern name)	Approximate date
	Part I The Deep Past		
1	Women in Caves	France & Spain	c. 30,000 BC
2	A Woman of Çatalhöyük	Turkey	c. 7th millennium BC
3	A Woman of Gozo	Malta	c. 3rd millennium BC
	Part II The Bronze Age		
4	Merneith	Egypt	c. 3000 BC
5	Šimatum and Kirum	Syria	c. 1770 BC
6	The Woman of Almoloya	Spain	c. 1650 BC
7	The Priestess of Anemospilia	Crete	c. 1700–1650 BC
8	Hatshepsut	Egypt	c. 1507–1458 BC
9	Puduhepa	Turkey	c. 1267–1237 BC
10	Eritha and Karpathia	Greece	c. 1200 BC
11	Hatiba	Cyprus	c. C13/12th BC
	Part III The Iron Age		
12	Naunakhte	Egypt	c. 1145 BC
13	Herse	Greece	c. 850 BC
14	Pkpupes	Black Sea	c. C6th BC
15	Atossa	Iran/Persian Empire	c. 550-480 BC
16	The Princess of Vix	France	c. 500 BC
17	Aristonice	Greece	c. 480 BC
18	Neaira	Greece	c. 400–350 BC
19	Phanostrate	Greece	c. 350 BC
	Part IV The Hellenistic Worlds		
20	Olympias	Greece/Macedonia	373–316 BC
21	Seianti Hanunia Tlesnasa	Italy	c. 200–150 BC
22	Terentia	Rome	c. 98 BC–AD 4
23	Mariamne	Israel	c. 50–29 BC
	Part V The Age of Empire		
24	Cleopatra Selene	Algeria	c. 40–5 BC
25	Eutychis	Italy	c. AD 79

(continued)

Chapter	Person	Place (modern name)	Approximate date
26	Achillia and Amazon	Turkey	c. AD 100
27	Perpetua	Tunisia	d. AD 203
28	Zenobia	Syria	AD 240–274
29	Hypatia	Egypt	AD 360–415

HISTORICAL CONTEXTS

This book takes us to many places around the ancient Mediterranean Sea, and the stories told take place from the deep past of the Palaeolithic down to the early Byzantine Empire of Justinian and Theodora. As such, some kind of broader historical context may be useful, into which the lives of the women explored in the book can be placed. So, before we meet the women, a brief note about the Mediterranean region will be given, followed by a sketch of Mediterranean history concerning only the areas relevant to the book (citations refer to helpful general works). Like the book, this sketch is divided into five parts, which follow and work back from the Greco-Roman-based chronology that I am most familiar with, and which, for all it can be criticised, I think is the most accessible and helpful to a wide range of readers. These five parts are: Part I, The Deep Past; Part II, The Bronze Age; Part III, The Iron Age; Part IV, The Hellenistic Worlds; and Part V, The Age of Empire.

THE MEDITERRANEAN

The Mediterranean climate, the Mediterranean diet, the Mediterranean temperament – the Mediterranean is, in Western culture, a well-recognised unit that hangs together in our minds and conjures up many shared ideas and images. Perhaps this is a problem – a kind of orientalism in which a construct is set up by observers and critics of all kinds and takes on its own set of constructed realities. The roots of such a construction could be traced at least in part to the British Romantics and later authors and travellers who idolised the people, lands, and antique cultures of Egypt, Greece, and Rome. John Pemble has written of 'The Mediterranean Passion' of Victorian and Edwardian British, for example.[1] The view of the Mediterranean as a region in which people had more in common with each other than with those farther from the sea has been critiqued by many, including Joao de Pina-Cabral, who argues that 'the notion of the Mediterranean Basin as a "culture area" is more useful as a means of distancing Anglo-American scholars from the populations they study than as a way of making sense of the cultural homogeneities and differences that characterise the region'.[2]

Even so, the Mediterranean is a distinct unit – lands around a single sea, which not only separated communities and cultures but brought them together. As Plato said of the Greeks and the Mediterranean, they lived like frogs around a pond, with settlements planted in the west at Marseille and the east, in Egypt. Mobility has long been a feature of Mediterranean life – famous of course are the Greeks themselves and the Phoenicians and Carthaginians with whom they eventually competed. People from these cultures travelled from the far east of the sea, the Levant, to the far west, the Straits of Gibraltar. In the central Mediterranean, the Etruscans adventured on the sea for military purposes and in prehistory, the Nuraghic people of Sardinia may also have travelled far. The Romans called the Mediterranean *Mare Nostrum* – Our Sea – and their empire surrounded it. None of this is to say that the lands around the sea were or are identical – sub-regions and microregions exist, and there are, of course, inland areas too, where there may be little or no daily contact or connection with the sea.

As a region, the Mediterranean has been the subject of many histories – Fernand Braudel's *The Mediterranean and the Mediterranean World in the Age of Philip I* (English translation 1976), being a landmark work. There are more recent works that treat the whole, such as Peregrine Horden and Nicholas Purcell's *The Corrupting Sea* (2000) and Cyprian Broodbank's *The Making of the Middle Sea* (2013). Braudel focused on a very narrow period and was interested especially in the geography of the region, the difference between plain and mountain. Horden and Purcell's work travels from the early first millennium BC to beyond the turn of the first millennium BC; it emphasises Mediterranean diversity within unity and the connective nature of the sea.[3] It is undeniably important and has generated significant discussion about 'the Mediterranean'.[4] Broodbank's magisterial work surveys the region from its geological formation to the Battle of Salamis in 480 BC, with a focus on archaeology and coverage that examines many local cultures and sites around the sea whilst also maintaining a broader context. His book is inclusive in the sense that it eschews a focus on the classical regions and aspires to be a 'barbarian history'.[5] In all of these works, the Mediterranean is understood as a world in itself – a world distinctive and interconnected by the sea that defines it.

This book is not a history 'of' the Mediterranean region as opposed to history 'in' the Mediterranean region; it does not make the kind of claims, comparisons, or contrasts that might render 'Mediterranean' a problematic term, so the questions raised above can be left for others to discuss. Rather, this is a book about some of the people who lived by the Mediterranean or connected to it, broadly taken; in this case, the Mediterranean forms a convenient link between cultures and communities diverse in time and space yet connected by this important and constant feature.

INTRODUCTION

Approaching Women in Prehistory and History

In this introduction, the scene is set for the 'lives' that form the body of this book. The first thing to consider is the presence – or absence of women. This absence takes several forms: absence from the world, absence from society or parts of it, absence from culture and absence from history. The discussion then moves to misogyny and patriarchy, which in a real sense lie behind the issue of missing women but which also must be considered in theoretical terms, and matriarchy, which forms part of the story of how women came back into history and one way in which parts of human 'history' has been conceived of. The chapter then gives a brief review of attempts to put women back into ancient history and archaeology. Finally, the methods and scope of the book are described, along with the questions it addresses.

MISSING WOMEN

In 1992, Amartya Sen published a disturbing editorial in the *BMJ: British Medical Journal* in which he argued that the world was missing about 100 million women, in particular from parts of Asia and north Africa.[1] He pointed out that while more boys tend to be born around the world, girls are hardier and, given the same care, more survive. The difference in numbers must result from cultural and social factors. As Sen noted, these factors include the pervasive influence of traditional male-focused cultures, neglect of the health and nutrition of baby and infant girls, and, increasingly, sex selective abortion. Exposure and infanticide are also still practiced in some parts of the world. Eleven years later, Sen revisited the subject in another article and rather than progress found instead that little had changed.[2] Indeed, the situation may be getting worse; in India and China, amongst other countries, the increasing availability of cheap sonography is enabling more couples to determine the sex of a fetus before birth, with the result that those of the 'wrong' sex, often females, can be aborted.[3]

Although doing ancient demography is difficult, it is probably also the case that the ancient world of Greco-Roman culture – which forms the backbone of this book – was missing women too.[4] It has long been recognised that exposure was practiced in ancient Greece and Rome, although the reasons for exposure, how common it was, and its possible effects on the make-up of the general population have been hotly debated.[5] In his *Theaetaetus*, a dialogue on knowledge, Plato has Socrates – the midwife of ideas – make the following comment about how a new idea should be received, using the birth of a child as a metaphor:

> Here at last, then, after our somewhat painful labor, is the child we have brought to birth, whatever sort of creature it may be. His birth should be followed by the ceremony of carrying him round the hearth; we must look at our offspring from every angle to make sure we are not taken in by a lifeless phantom not worth the rearing. Or do you think an infant of yours must be reared in any case and not exposed? Will you bear to see him put to the proof, and not be in a passion if your first born should be taken away?[6]

As a metaphor, it relies on exposure being common-enough practice to be made sense of. The incidental suggestion here is that newborns would be assessed as a matter of course and that some infants could be considered 'not worth rearing'.

Deformity, sickliness, or weakness could be reasons for the exposure of a baby rather than its acceptance into the family.[7] One Roman-era Greek medical writer, Soranus, noted eight points to consider in judging the worthiness of a baby for rearing:

> 1) the mother should be healthy 2) the baby should be full-term 3) it should cry with vigor 4) it should be 'perfect' in all its parts 5) its 'ducts' must be free of obstruction 6) the natural functions of every member should be neither sluggish nor weak 7) the joints must bend and stretch 8) it should have the right size and shape and be properly sensitive to stimulus.[8]

Other reasons for exposing newborns could include illegitimacy, poverty – and sex. In ancient Sparta, male babies judged weak by magistrates would be tossed into a pit, but female babies were raised.[9]

Neither Plato nor Soranus were discussing girls in particular, but the view has been widespread among modern scholars, at least since the early twentieth century, that female babies were more likely to have been exposed than males.[10] La Rue Van Hook made this point about the Greeks in 1920.[11] Reasons he noted for exposing female babies included that girls were less desired as children: a girl would need to be provided with a dowry and girls could not perform military duties to defend their city. Some ancient comments support the economic argument. A comic writer from third-century BC Greece, Posidippus, penned the line, intended to be humorous to his audience, 'one rears a son even if one be poor, but exposes a daughter even if one be rich'.[12] The sentiment is also found in a first century BC papyrus from Egypt too in which a mercenary called Ilarion gave instructions to his wife to raise a male child but expose a female one.[13] Mark Golden estimates that perhaps 10 per cent of Athenian female babies were exposed.[14]

Not all infants that were exposed died or were intended to be killed directly – the choice of where to leave a new baby and whether to leave any items with it would affect its chances either way. One surviving novel from Roman times by Longus, called *Daphnis and Chloe*, has the two main characters, a boy and a girl, found as exposed babies at the start.[15] The boy, Daphnis, was found first, by a goatherd called Lamon, though Lamon was initially tempted just to take the few items left with the infant. He felt ashamed and took the baby as well. Two years later, the shepherd Dryas found the baby girl and he and his wife adopted her, bringing her up with love and affection. This is a work of fiction, but the details have to be plausible for the story to work.

A true story recounted by Roger Bagnall tells of a less happy fate for a real foundling.[16] In AD 362 a contract was drawn up in the village of Kellis, in Upper Egypt, agreeing on the sale of an unnamed girl for two solidi, a fairly low price for a slave but enough to feed a family for a year, so a not inconsiderable sum. The sellers were a married couple, Tatoup and her husband Psais, and the buyer one Tithoes, a carpenter; quite ordinary Egyptians of the period. The contract records that the girl was a foundling, an infant that had been exposed and found and nurtured by Tatoup. We do not know why the girl was sold – was this the plan all along, to raise the girl as an investment, was it opportunistic, or was it an act forced on the couple by their situation? Letters between Pliny the Younger, as governor of Bithynia, discuss individuals born free but exposed and brought up as slaves, which posed a legal problem; the fate of the Egyptian girl was not unique.[17]

Bennett argued in 1923 that there was little evidence for exposure of infants during the Roman republic or early empire, in contrast to the situation among the Greeks.[18] However, this has been strongly rejected by later scholars including Peter Brunt, who conducted a major study of Roman demographics.[19] Harris follows this view and suggests that 'the exposure of infants, very often but by no means always resulting in death, was widespread in many parts of the Roman Empire'.[20] Similarly, it is also accepted that across the Roman world baby girls may have been exposed more often than boys, as a result of a general preference for male children.

Proving that more female babies were exposed than male babies in antiquity is difficult, but such a pattern would not be unexpected and has been found in many 'traditional' societies across time and space, even into the present as Sen noted. L. S. Vishwanath has written of 'endemic female foeticide and infanticide' in parts of modern India.[21] Whether the exposure of baby girls was ever significant enough to have a demographic impact on the sex ratio of a particular population in antiquity, be it that of Athens or the entire Roman world, is unclear. We might reasonably expect differences according to urban or rural locations and to social location, as is noted by Vishwanath for India. However, it is much less controversial to assert that the practice of exposing less-valued female infants would have reinforced their lower value and have impacted social attitudes about women more widely.

Women do not go missing only because of exposure or direct killing, they also disappear due to neglect based on social and familial sex-preferences. Nowadays, 'neglect' is defined as 'circumstances when a child's basic needs or rights are not adequately met resulting in harm or jeopardy to the child's health, development, or safety' and is 'a major world health and social problem'.[22] Neglect can include a child receiving less care generally, an inadequate diet, or 'precocious assumption of adult roles and their exposure to threatening circumstances that jeopardize their healthy development'.[23] One example of how girls can suffer unequal treatment from 2021 is illustrative. Following the recent withdrawal of western troops from Afghanistan, and the increasing fragility of the Afghan economy, some parents began selling their children.[24] In one case, a baby girl was sold for $500 to provide food for the family's sons. The buyer apparently wanted the girl for his son as a wife. Why sell the girl to feed the boys? Girls can be a saleable commodity and boys take priority for parental care.

There is evidence for systematic neglect of girls in antiquity. For example, Xenophon tells us that in Athens and elsewhere in Greece women were fed less well than men.[25] This contrasted with the exceptional treatment of Spartan girls, who were better fed and physically fit through exercise. As young brides, of twelve and upwards into the teens, girls of the classical world could expect to fall pregnant multiple times to their much older husbands, which took a toll on their bodies and risked their lives in giving birth. Lauren Caldwell, who has written about Roman girlhood, quotes a passage from Plutarch, who contrasts practices in Sparta and Rome and the reasons behind them:

> Also, matters concerning the giving of girls in marriage agree with their educational system as well. Lycurgus [of Sparta] gave them in marriage

> when they were ripe and eager, in order that intercourse, now that nature was demanding it, might be the beginning of goodwill and affection, instead of the hatred and fear of those girls forced unnaturally, and also in order that their bodies might have the strength to endure pregnancy and childbirth .... But the Roman gave girls in marriage when they were twelve years old or even younger. In this way especially both body and character would be pure and chaste for the husband when he married her.[26]

Caldwell also notes a Roman epitaph for an eighteen-year-old woman called Herennia Cervilla, which may be somewhat typical. Written in the first person, but presumably in her husband's words, it says:

> To the shades below. I, Herennia Cervilla, daughter of Lucius, wife, lived for eighteen years and thirty days. With three children left behind, I ended life in pain. My dear husband, while living, set this up as a memorial to me.[27]

We do not know how her age at marriage, possibly fifteen or younger, nor how many pregnancies she had in total, but she left three living children and may ultimately have died in childbirth or due to complications.

Greek and Roman medical writers – mostlyl men, of course – did make recommendations about the bringing up of girls, including about their diet and exercise, in order to make them more ready for pregnancy and childbearing. For example, they usually recommended marriage in the later teens rather than before.[28] This 'medical' guidance for how to treat women tells us about how men wanted women to be – healthy for the purposes of marriage and reproduction with men, not necessarily for the benefit of women in and of themselves. Women across ancient societies were valued primarily for their role in reproduction.

It seems likely then, that the ancient world was missing women. And although it is dangerous to generalise from the millennium of the classical world to the Mediterranean as a whole across the swath of time and different cultures covered by this book, the Roman pattern might be indicative of traditions that existed for a reasonable period of Mediterranean history, as Roger Bagnall suggested.[29]

It should be said that none of this denies the strength of love possible in families with daughters – the relationship of Cicero to his daughter Tullia, for example, is well known.[30] Nor does it deny the value placed – by men and women – on women in the roles that society granted them. Both women and men could take pride in adhering to and fulfilling societal norms and the expectations of others, however we may judge these roles in hindsight.

Cicero's love for his Tullia, and for his wife Terentia, seems to have been reciprocated, but the sources we have are Cicero's letters, though his wife and daughter did write to him too. This position, where most of our historical sources were written by elite males, also results in missing women. As Sarah Pomeroy pointed out in the introduction to her classic book *Goddesses, Whores, Wives and Slaves* (1975; 1995):

> The literary testimony presents grave problems to the social historian. Women pervade nearly every genre of classical literature, yet often the bias of the author distorts the information. Aside from some scraps of lyric poetry, the extant formal literature of classical antiquity was all written by men. In addition, misogyny taints much ancient literature.[31]

Not only are women in a sense missing from ancient literature, they can also be found absent from modern histories. As recently as 2010, historian Susan Lee Johnson could still accuse scholars of ignoring both women's history and gender issues.[32] One recent book, which tells the story of ancient Greece in fifty lives, one of the inspirations for this book, includes only two lives of women, a poet and a courtesan.[33] Things are better than they were but not as good as they could – and should be. There is still work to do in 'putting women back in', in a variety of ways.

MISOGYNY AND PATRIARCHY

Women are missing because of cultural preferences and biases towards boys and men in traditional societies, as Sen pointed out. This may equate to a widespread and persistent level of misogyny – 'hatred of women'. Ancient Greek misogyny is well known – in particular through the infamous poem on women of Semonides of Amorgos. In his poem he casts women as the greatest evil made by Zeus. He lists different kinds of 'bad' women and their characteristics, made from different animals – a pig, a fox, a dog, an ass, a cat, a horse, a monkey. The pig-woman is fat and lives in filth, the fox-women is a contrary know-all, the dog-woman a busybody and a gossip – 'a man cannot check her with threats, no, not if in anger he dash her teeth out with a stone, nor yet though he speak gently with her'.[34] The bee-woman is the only 'good' woman – or good wife. She loves and takes care of her husband rather than spending time gossiping about sex with other women. Whether the poem is intended as humorous or serious, and whether or not it represents Semonides' own views, it gives us an insight into how some men at least could think about women in antiquity and what they thought amusing.

Misogyny is not a straightforward or blanket concept. It is not simply a case of men hating women and 'keeping them down'. As Kate Manne points out in her book *Down Girl: The Logic of Misogyny*, 'misogynists can love their mothers – not to mention their sisters, daughters, wives, girlfriends, and secretaries. They need not hate women universally, or even very generally'.[35]

We can remember Cicero and Tullia here. She suggests that male misogynists 'tend to hate women who are outspoken, among other things' and this chimes in with the sentiments expressed by Semonides about women who 'gossip' or are somehow disagreeable to men and not considerate enough to their needs. But both men and women can judge women on the basis of how much they conform to 'patriarchal norms and values'.[36]

Misogyny can be embedded and internalised even by women within a culture; as well as personal feelings or attitudes, it can comprise 'social practices and institutions'.[37] An example of this might be the tradition of female genital mutilation, which many women in the cultures where it is practiced believe is important to have performed on their own daughters and in which women themselves have often performed the cutting.[38] It might seem obvious to an outsider that the practice is harmful to girls and women – and plainly misogynistic and immoral – but that does not stop some women within those cultures approving of it, valuing it – and carrying it out. This internalisation of misogyny and its elevation to a 'norm' can help us understand the perpetuation of patriarchal cultures.

Manne wrote of patriarchal norms and values and most of the cultures in this book have been and can be considered patriarchal – political power was usually a male-dominated or almost exclusively male domain.[39] But some are less convinced by the utility of the term and traditional concept of patriarchy. Carol Meyers makes several excellent points in her discussion of the term as it relates to ancient Israel.[40] For example, if the basic unit of ancient societies was the household, and much household power in the ancient Mediterranean rested with senior women, then the concept of patriarchy clearly becomes problematic, an oversimplification and distortion of the societies in action. Political power as constructed by men was not the only power in a society. She also points out that, in organisations made up of females, they 'had their own hierarchies, independent of those in the general social systems'. Inequalities in society were based on a range of factors, economic or legal status, age, and not just sex or gender; relations between all people in society were under constant negotiation. Based on these critiques, we could ask: Who has more status, power and agency – a wealthy Roman matron of a noble family or a male slave working in a mine?

Certainly, Meyer's points must be accepted, but dispensing entirely with the notion of patriarchy may not be helpful. Pavla Miller argues that 'patriarchy ... has been a powerful organising concept with which social order has been understood, maintained, enforced, contested, adjudicated and dreamt about for over two millenia of western history'.[41] The female/male opposition may be only one intersection with which we can describe and examine an ancient society, but it is a major one, often dictating much, if not all, about an individual's life and opportunities. Misogyny and patriarchy are contexts that overshadowed and directly impacted on the lives of the women of the ancient Mediterranean.

Ancient Athens, for example, has been seen as an uber-masculine culture. Classicist Eva Keuls has even termed it a 'phallocracy', writing that

> in the case of a society dominated by men who sequester their wives and daughters, denigrate the female role in reproduction, erect monuments to the male genitalia, have sex with the sons of their peers, sponsor public whorehouses, create a mythology of rape, and engage in rampant sabre-rattling, it is not inappropriate to refer to a reign of the phallus.[42]

There was a variety of thought amongst ancient philosophers and the elite about the role and capacities of women. Plato, unusually, believed women could perform equally to men intellectually, and in his utopia could have equal rights, whereas Aristotle saw women as ruled by emotion and less spirited than men.[43] For Aristotle, women had to be ruled.[44] Later, the influential Stoics have been seen as positive about women's abilities – their capacity for virtue, for example – although they did not call for any gender equality and instead restricted women to the domestic sphere.[45]

In Greece, Spartan women perhaps had the greatest freedom and societal respect, making them odd amongst their neighbours, but how much of the stories told by other Greeks and Romans about the Spartans is true and how much a 'Spartan myth'? The same might be said for Etruscan women, often imagined as more 'free and equal' than women in many other ancient societies. In Hellenistic times, there were many famous and powerful queens – but even though 'a queen may rule in a patriarchal society' and 'enjoy the highest status,' Pomeroy writes, 'her position does not empower her female subjects'.[46]

The Roman paterfamilias is another well-known example of ancient patriarchy in action – the absolute power over a family held by its eldest male. Access to political office at Rome was also restricted to men. Never was there a female consul or an empress who ruled in her own right, no matter how powerful or historically important some individual women like Augustus' wife Livia, or in later times Galla Placidia or Theodora were. Apart from the 'rebel' empress Zenobia of Palmyra, it was only in Byzantine times that a few empresses manage to gain greater power – women like Sophia, Zoe, and another Theodora.[47] Rome was, then, a patriarchy.[48]

The overarching patriarchy of classical antiquity seems by and large uncontroversial, but this book looks further back in time too. In pharaonic Egypt, the 'gulf between the sexes' may not have been as pronounced as in the classical world, but pharaohs and officials were usually male.[49] There are a few exceptions and two of them are discussed in this book: Merneith and Hatshepsut. The societies of the Bronze Age Levant and Mesopotamia were patriarchal, with families headed by men; and the Late Bronze Age Hittite kingdom too was 'strongly patriarchal'.[50] Again, in both, there were women of power and status. Minoan Crete and Mycenaean Greece in the Middle to Late Bronze Age have been contrasted as matriarchal, feminine and pacifistic and patriarchal, masculine and aggressive respectively.[51] This very subjective and quite dubious way of characterising the Minoan and Mycenaean societies has rightly fallen by the wayside – though archaeologists do not deny that, judging by the frequency and style of their representation, women may have played an important and potentially powerful and public role in Bronze Age Crete. The Argaric society of Bronze Age Iberia has been seen, like Mycenaean culture, as a male-dominated warrior society – though some archaeologists now dispute this characterisation.[52]

Modern western society has not escaped charges of misogyny or the label of patriarchy either, despite legal equality between the sexes.[53] Caroline Criado Perez's book *Invisible Women: Exposing Data Bias in a World Designed for Men* paints a convincing picture of a society based on accepting men as the norm, the basic point of reference, with women as awkward, different, and other.[54] In part, this stems from the weight of history. Pomeroy, for example, argued that 'the rationalized confinement of women to the domestic sphere, as well as the systematization of anti-female thought by poets and philosophers, are two of the most devastating creations in the classical legacy'.[55] Ancient women may have been missing from, less visible, and less free in their own societies and then been ignored by a male-dominated modern academia and continued patriarchy – a double blow.

MATRIARCHY AND THE GODDESS

In the patriarchal world of nineteenth-century Europe, anthropology and the experience of other cultures around the world demonstrated that the family and sex-based gender roles were a matter of culture rather than nature and that the patriarchy that had been taken for granted was only one possible outcome.[56] In the grand pattern of human history, the ultimate outcome of development from promiscuous savagery – the monogamous Victorian marriage within a patriarchal society in which men dominated the public world – had to be explained.

In 1861, the same year as John Stuart Mill published *The Subjection of Women*, another book appeared, written by Johann Jakob Bachofen, a Swiss lawyer and student of antiquity. This was his *Das Mutterecht* – in full in translation: *Mother Right: A Study of the Religious and Juridical Nature of Gynecocracy in the Ancient World*. Bachofen read Greek myths with the understanding that they preserved truths about earlier times, the more so because they were collective stories, and this, amongst other personal and intellectual factors, led to his focus on women and the feminine. Bachofen presented a story of human social evolution and progress in five stages that flip back and forth between female and male power. These are: hetaerism, Demetrian matriarchy, the Dionysian age, Amazonism, and the Apollonian age.[57]

In the beginning, humans lived in groups led by strong men, 'tyrants', where children were 'sowed at random' and no one knew who their father was. Although men were dominant, power was inherited from the mother. In the next stage, Demetrian matriarchy, through their 'Amazonism', women asserted their rights to marriage and to choice of husband, transforming society into a true matriarchy in which women ruled – a gynecocracy. In his evolutionary scheme, this period was necessary for the education of men and the channelling of their powers into something constructive. Men responded in kind, bringing in the masculine and phallic age of Dionysus; men came to dominate women in marriage and lost the respect of women. The age of Amazonism saw women rebel, setting up real societies like the Amazons of Greek myth. Eller calls it 'basically matriarchy out of hand, women gone wild'; Bachofen wrote of 'man-hating, man-killing, war-like virgins' who at the same time wanted to submit to the phallic males.[58] Finally, in the Apollonian age, women realise their purpose lies in 'love and fertility and not man-hating belligerence'. Equality is achieved, oddly, through the acknowledgement of male spiritual superiority – men are the sun that lights the moon.

Although patriarchy won out with 'the permanent and complete defeat of the maternal principle' and 'the decisive conquest of women', Bachofen also believed that motherhood and female rule were central to the development of the refined human sensibilities that resulted in civilisation.[59] Cynthia Eller quotes him as follows:

> The relationship through which humanity first attains to civilization, that which serves as the starting point for the development of every virtue, the formation of each nobler aspect of existence is the model of motherhood which comes into being as the divine principle of love and unity, of peace amidst a life full of violence. By nurturing the fruit of her womb, woman learns earlier than man how to extend her loving care beyond the limits of her own self and to protect and support another creature's existence. All social progress, all devotion, all ministration to the living and respect for the dead emanates from her.[60]

Bachofen, with his confused situating of women in a grand human story, may have been more a romantic than any kind of feminist, one with a nostalgia for a world he perceived through his study and reflection. His work did not make any significant impact in itself – indeed, there was criticism of its intuitive 'methodology' – but many of its ideas have been echoed in some form by others who believe in an ancient matriarchy.[61] Other better known scholars of the period, however, such as John McLennan and Lewis Henry Morgan did take up the idea of ancient matriarchy and so a 'female' stage became built into various versions of the human story – a stage where the feminine was defeated and relegated to history by the victory of the male principle.

Somewhat earlier, another feminine-focused theory had appeared: the notion of a supreme Mother Goddess. During the Romantic movement of the early 1800s, the classical goddesses that had remained cultural symbols became more associated with nature, giving rise to the idea of 'mother nature', according to Ronald Hutton.[62] In 1849, Eduard Gerhard proposed that classical Greek goddesses originated from a single prehistoric goddess in his book *ober Metroen und Gotter-Mutter.* As other older pre-classical cultures were discovered in the Near East, goddesses seemed to take on ever greater importance and more scholars adopted Gerhard's basic idea. This provided a context for the rise in matriarchal or 'feminine' thinking.

In the late nineteenth century, anthropologist and mythologist James Frazer, author of *The Golden Bough* (1890), developed his theory that Mother Goddess worship in the Aegean and Europe derived from the Neolithic period, from pre-Indo-European times.[63] This worship was truly ancient. Jane Ellen Harrison soon 'posited the previous existence of a peaceful and intensely creative woman-centred civilization, in which humans, living in harmony with nature and their own emotions, worshipped a single female deity'.[64] Her goddess had three aspects, including the Maiden and the Mother; male gods were either consorts or sons. This ancient era of peace was shattered by the invasion of northerners who brought with them violent and warlike patriarchy.

Arthur Evans, who excavated the Bronze Age site of Knossos on Crete from 1899 also developed a belief in a strong 'feminine' character to the island's culture – owing much to Frazer and Harrison, who was a fellow member of the British School at Athens.[65] Evans' elegant and peaceful Minoans venerated a Great Goddess; young women and priestesses were frequently shown on gold rings and in fresco paintings involved in acts of worship. Goddesses themselves would appear to the women in scenes of epiphany, sometimes floating down from on high. His interpretations of Minoan society in the early twentieth century have been so influential that they continue to shape public perceptions of Bronze Age Crete: our sophisticated and feminist 'Minoans' are very much his invention.[66]

Elsewhere in the Near East, archaeologists excavating a number of sites, including Tell Arpachiyah, Chagar Bazan, and Domuztepe recognised the features of a common Neolithic culture, which they named the Halaf tradition, or just Halaf.[67] Halaf dates between roughly 6000 to 5000 BC. Figurines belonging to this tradition were identified early on as representing the Mother Goddess, for example, by Max Mallowan and John Cruikshank Rose, who excavated at Arpachiyah in 1933: 'in all of them, prominence is given to certain features which these figures were obviously intended to emphasize particularly the breasts, slender waist and pronounced navel, and steatopygous rump'.[68] The Halaf locals 'were a people worshipping the "mother-goddess"'.[69] Ancient figurines and statuettes dating back to the Palaeolithic began to be seen as representing the Mother Goddess, now the chief deity of prehistory.

In the 1950s, under the influence of Carl Jung's idea of an archetypal Great Mother, a number of other archaeological works appeared, all supporting the Mother Goddess theory: Erich Neumann's *The Great Mother: An Analysis of the Archetype* (1955), Crawford's *The Eye Goddess* (1959), and James' *The Cult of the Mother Goddess* (1959). The Jungian Neumann argued that the 'unshapely figures of the Great Mother' were the model symbols of fertility.[70] The Great Mother herself had been a constant 'inward image at work in the human psyche' and stood for 'the archetypal unity and multiplicity of the feminine nature' and even now 'determines the psychic history of modern man and of modern woman'.[71] Goddess worship was ancient and universal, a natural part of the human psyche.

Also extremely influential in the 1950s was Robert Graves' retelling, or perhaps better his reimagining, of the Greek myths. As Sibylle Ihm points out, Graves, influenced by Frazer and Bachofen, had the central idea that 'all myths deal with a universal female figure'.[72] He thought that invading Greeks from the north had brought with them to the Aegean the more masculine Indo-European culture, melding with and overlying the feminine Goddess-worshipping matriarchal pre-Greek cultures – much like Harrison. Whilst steeped in the classics, Graves' work is more 'Graves' mythology' than straight Greek myth, 'he mixes fact and conjecture in such a convincing and barely detectable way that anyone unfamiliar with the subject has to believe that all his conjectures *are* facts'.[73] That his work did not find much scholarly praise did not at all affect its popularity and impact; unsurprisingly, several of his works, Ihm notes, remain important in goddess, spiritual and feminist circles.

Greek prehistory seemed to many to supply an apparently clear picture of the transformation from matriarchy to patriarchy, with the eclipsing of the feminine and peaceful society of the Bronze Age Minoans and pre-Greeks by the masculine and warlike Indo-European Mycenaeans. This view was given especial prominence by Jacquetta Hawkes in her wonderfully illustrated 1968 book *Dawn of the Gods*. Hawkes, who was influenced by Neumann and others, thought it appropriate and natural to characterise societies along gender lines. For example, the Minoan palace at Knossos, she suggested, 'can be said to express a feminine spirit', with 'domesticity, privacy, lightness of touch and domestic amenities . . . set among gardens and flower beds' and with decoration and frescoes that enhanced 'the feminine quality implicit in the building'.[74] Mycenae's Lion Gate, on the other hand, 'expresses something enduring in the Mycenaean tradition: its aggressive masculinity and ingrained militarism'.[75] Contemporary scholars would strongly question this approach, not least for its essentialist notions of gender, but it gives a flavour of the norms of the period in which it was written.

Hawkes argued that the people of Neolithic west Asia and Europe had such a distinctive and coherent a tradition 'that it must imply a common religious belief', which flowed from east to west, with the spread of agriculture.[76] The Goddess dominated from the Neolithic through the Bronze Age and, though demoted, survived as part of later Mediterranean culture in the form of goddesses such as Cybele, Artemis, and Aphrodite – something James Mellaart had also suggested in his 1967 book about the Neolithic site of Çatalhöyük, which he had discovered in 1958, and reiterated in the 1980s.[77]

Along with Hawkes and Mellaart, the most well-known scholar in the story of the Goddess is Marija Gimbutas (1921–1994), a Lithuanian-born archaeologist and specialist in European prehistory, who worked in the 1950s at Harvard's Peabody Museum, then at Stanford, and from 1963 at the University of California, Los Angeles. Gimbutas' influential ideas about the Goddess and 'Old Europe' – pre-Indo-European Europe from the Palaeolithic to around 3500 BC – appear to have developed, and increased in intensity over several decades, from her 1974 *Gods and Goddesses of Old Europe*, republished in 1982 as the *Goddesses and Gods of Old Europe*, to *The Civilization of the Goddess: The World of Old Europe* of 1999 and the posthumous *The Living Goddesses* (edited and supplemented by Miriam Robbins Dexter, 1999).[78] For Gimbutas, Old Europe was a peaceful world infused with a feminine force, which was manifested in the widespread worship of a Goddess, portrayed in the many female figurines and in the matrilineal social system she envisioned. This world was ended, though not all at once and not completely, by the spread of the warlike Indo-Europeans, represented archaeologically by the Kurgan culture: 'the gentle agriculturalists . . . were easy prey to the warlike Kurgan horsemen who swarmed down upon them'.[79]

Firmly based on her extensive knowledge of the archaeological evidence, especially figurines and architecture, Gimbutas' interpretations of the evidence have been taken up as authoritative 'facts' about the nature of society and religion in European and west Asian prehistory, especially by some Goddess pilgrims and feminists; 'it is no accident that Gimbutas' books are shelved with feminist literature in bookshops around the world'.[80]

Amongst the evidence she interpreted as indicating the widespread worship of 'goddesses, or a goddess, in many forms' are figurines and other 'art' and architecture from Çatalhöyük and the temples of prehistoric Malta.[81] A 2016 article in the *Times of Malta* ruminates on the island's temples, the origins and presence of the Goddess – and the draw of Malta to ancient and modern pilgrims:

> Undoubtedly Malta was the foremost strong promoter of female power, reverence and mystique, as evidenced in the iconic Tarxien Temples, where the colossal seven-foot (2.13m) figure reputed to be an obese Mother Goddess, the greatest and biggest of them all ... towered over all religious symbols at Tarxien .... In this religious milieu the Mother Goddess of Fertility reigned supreme.[82]

The idea of an ancient matriarchy is an old and persistent one, but one that finds very few supporters within archaeology. Lin Foxhall has termed it a 'dead end' of feminist scholarship.[83]

Out of patriarchy have come the interlinked ideas of a long stage of history – prehistory – in which a great Mother Goddess was worshipped and where women ruled in matriarchal societies, only to be overthrown. Although these earlier contributions are no longer how we 'do' history or archaeology – making sweeping generalisations about the feminine or masculine 'nature' of societies or fitting these notions into impressionistic evolutionary schemes – these stories remain part of our mental templates of the past. They are still influential and have been part of the story of putting women back into history.

PUTTING WOMEN BACK: WOMEN IN HISTORY, ANCIENT HISTORY AND ARCHAEOLOGY

The study of women in antiquity is not new and stories about some 'notable' female figures were never lost. Many lists of notable women appeared from antiquity to the Renaissance.[84] Stories of biblical and classical women remained in circulation and formed the subject matter of late medieval and early Renaissance authors such as Boccaccio, Chaucer, and Christine de Pizan. None of these authors, however, were interested in objective history as opposed to the use of historical figures to express their own opinions on the virtues of women and provide examples for contemporaries – as well as showing off their own erudition. Histories of cities and other books published often contained chapters on women too, figures of note locally.[85]

Jane Stevenson suggests the flurry of lists appearing in the later Renaissance and early modern period reflects a societal concern with increasing numbers of educated women. She notes that these lists would provide educated women with a heritage and history of their own. In her chapter on 'learned women', Stevenson describes how in early modern Europe there were many more classically educated women, women who could read and write Latin and knew their literature, than is often thought. This is a pattern noted by Isobel Hurst for Victorian women too.[86] The educational situation for women differed depending on their location in society and the wishes of their families – and their own desires. However, women's social status and position did not depend on education in the way that men's did, so education was inevitably male-focused.

As we have seen already, women and matriarchy took their place in anthropology and connected to classical studies through myth, ancient history, and archaeology. In the late nineteenth and early twentieth century, a reader interested in women of the ancient world could consult the articles of James Donaldson of St Andrews University, which were published together as a book in 1907 entitled *Woman: Her Position and Influence in Ancient Greece and Rome, and Among the Early Christians*. Donaldson was well aware of the male bias of the ancient sources, written by men for men, and he noted that women were either subject to 'wild abuse' or 'praised to the skies' and that we should be cautious about uncritically believing anything we read.[87] His treatment is generally sensitive. Mitchell Carroll's *Greek Women*, also from 1907, was less even-handed: he suggested that 'extremism is a chief feminine characteristic' – women were either 'utterly pure and holy' or 'utterly vile'.[88] In 1914, a female scholar, Mary Sturgeon, published *Women of the Classics*, in which she focused on 'the heroines of Homer, of Attic tragedy, and of the *Aeneid* of Virgil'.[89] An alternative approach was taken by Helen McLees, who focused on epigraphy in her *A Study of Women in Attic Inscriptions*. In contrast to the grim view of the life of Athenian women given by Donaldson, she observes that 'the inscriptions, on the other hand, show that in practice there was much to render the lot of Athenian women comparatively happy'.[90] This conclusion would certainly be disputed by some – but all generalisations can be questioned and women's lives considered individually.

The American classicist Grace Harriet Macurdy (1866–1946) pioneered the study of the Macedonian queens of the Hellenistic period and 'woman-power', publishing her landmark *Hellenistic Queens. A Study of Woman- Power in Macedonia, Seleucid Syria and Ptolemaic Egypt* in 1932. Up until that point, Barbara McManus states, 'no classical scholar, male or female, had ever attempted to recover and document the lives of individual Greek women whose names are part of recorded history'.[91] Macurdy did not attempt to heroise her subjects, but she did credit them with real agency and power based on their own personalities and circumstances; these women were as political and as opportunistic as their male relatives. In 1925, Macurdy had become the first woman to give a public lecture in classics at King's College London.[92] Later in the century, more books on ancient women followed: Charles Seltman's *Women in Antiquity* from 1956 and J. P. V. Dacre Balsdon's *Roman Women: Their History and Habits* (1962), for example. The subsequent sixty years has only seen more works appear.

The first wave of feminism saw the situation of women in society change across the later nineteenth and early twentieth centuries, and a second wave of feminism reached a peak in the late 1960s.[93] This had a significant impact on the study of women in history. The new and feminism-informed study of women in antiquity emerged in the early 1970s and has grown from there, being taken up in classics and archaeology. A collection of papers published in the journal *Arethusa* in 1973 was one important landmark. It included articles on attitudes to women, women in literature, philosophy and art, sexual behaviour, and rape. Sarah Pomeroy provided a bibliography of earlier work on women in antiquity.[94] Then, in 1975, Sarah Pomeroy's classic *Goddesses, Whores, Wives and Slaves* came out. The book, with its classical-world focus, utilised textual and archaeological evidence, surveying women of all classes from goddesses, the Bronze Age and Homeric epics, through to the early Roman Empire, but it especially focused on real women rather than figures from mythology. Lin Foxhall points out that *Goddesses* represented what 'a major step forward Pomeroy and other second-wave feminist scholars made in terms of the sophistication of their historical methodologies and theoretical frameworks'.[95]

A few years later, in 1991, Pomeroy published an informal survey of forty-five ancient history, classics, and archaeology journals, finding that twenty-two had no articles connected to the study of women (the journal, *Helios*, however, had an issue devoted entirely to Roman women).[96] By this time, she could conclude that 'the study of women has, indeed, become part, albeit a very small part, of the mainstream of Classical Studies'. In the same year, her edited volume *Women's History and Ancient History* added further contributions to the growing field.[97] By 2000, Marilyn Katz was able to review eighteen recent contributions that had appeared in the space of only three years, noting that a further ten or twelve books could easily be added to her list.[98]

In archaeology, a pioneering paper of 1984 by Margaret Conkey and Janet Spector questioned current modes of archaeology and asserted that it unwittingly perpetuated a gender ideology based on contemporary assumptions.[99] One way in which this was manifest was in the notion that ancient women were 'invisible'. The problem with the notion, they wrote, is that assumptions are made about the gendered division of labour and then women and material culture; women's 'soft' material culture is seen as less visible – less durable because of its materials. A recent exploration of 'Visible men and elusive women' on summer farms in pre-industrial Sweden challenges these still active ideas, demonstrating that 'both women and men worked in both soft and hard materials, and both women and men are invisible and visible' and that 'ideals and norms, and everyday life, respectively, are different matters'.[100]

Conkey and Spector's paper did not signal an immediate change but did set the tone. In 1991, Roberta Gilchrist noted, in a paper in *Antiquity*, that 'archaeology has not been eager to address the issues, or indeed the existence of women's archaeology'.[101] In the same year, Alison Wylie also expressed surprise at why archaeology seemed to be lagging behind 'the vibrant traditions of research on women and gender now well established in most other social scientific fields'.[102] Wylie's paper appeared in a new volume edited by Joan

Gero and Conkey; their wide-ranging *Engendering Archaeology: Women and Prehistory.*[103] This book has five sections looking at the archaeology of gender, space and gender relations, material aspects of gender production, gender and food systems, and images of gender. Chapters range from deep prehistory to Sumeria and the Aztecs. The volume represents a take-off point for the study of women and gender in archaeology. In 1998, a reader in gender archaeology was published that included key papers going back to Conkey and Spector.[104] In a 2003 review, Conkey argued that feminism had 'absolutely' changed archaeology.[105] In 2009 Gilchrist's chapter, 'The Archaeology of Sex and Gender', was included in a major collection of essays in *The Oxford Handbook of Archaeology.*[106]

Now it would be an immense task to review all of the contributions to the study of women in the ancient world: books, journal articles, and web articles. But in the twenty-first century, the study of women and gender in archaeology and ancient history has flourished. Since 2010, notable contributions that are standard reference works include Sharon L. James and Sheila Dillon's *A Companion to Women in the Ancient World* (2012), Diane Bolger's *A Companion to Gender Prehistory* (2013), and Stephanie Lynn Budin and Jean MacIntosh Turfa's seventy-four-chapter *Women in Antiquity: Real Women across the Ancient World* (2016), which are excellent and wide-ranging edited volumes that contribute a great deal to the field.[107] There are also dedicated sets, including the four-volume *Oxford Encyclopedia of Women in World History* and Bloomsbury's six-volume series *A Cultural History of Women.*[108] And there are the excellent and ever-growing Oxford University Press series 'Women in Antiquity', with eighteen volumes now, and Routledge's titles in the 'Women of the Ancient World' series.

These take the exploration of women and gender far beyond the classical worlds of Greece and Rome back into Early Bronze Age Mesopotamia, the Late Bronze Age eastern Mediterranean, and beyond. Budin and Turfa's *Women in Antiquity* sets out quite programmatically to be a book about '*real* women – their bodies, names, occupations, interests, sex lives, religious functions, and legal capacities' rather than women constructed by men in myth or literature.[109] It has been a great influence on this present book.

Women are not just subjects of study; they have played an important role in Mediterranean archaeology since the early twentieth century. The British School at Athens accepted female students, though at first they could not take part in excavations.[110] In 1911, this changed, and three women joined the excavation of Phylakopi on Melos. One of these, Hilda Lorimer, went on to publish the important book *Homer and the Monuments* (1950), in which she undertook a detailed comparison of material culture revealed by archaeology and Homer's epics.[111] Reviewers of the time regarded the volume as 'excellent' and a new standard work.[112] The American archaeologist Harriet Boyd

Hawes (1871–1945) had already been excavating in Crete with Edith Hall (1877–1943). She is remembered for her discovery and excavation of the ancient Minoan town of Gournia in 1901 and its publication in 1905. Archaeology was just a part of her very eventful life full of humanitarian and political interests and other activities beyond archaeology.[113]

The English archaeologist Dorothy Garrod (1892–1968) also worked extensively in the Mediterranean. In 1925, the year of Macurdy's King's College lecture, she found a Neanderthal skull in the Devil's Tower cave in Gibraltar in 1925. In the eastern Mediterranean, she uncovered evidence for the Natufian culture and undertook important work at Mount Carmel, work she published with Dorothea Bate (1878–1951) in 1937.[114] In 1939, she became the first female Oxbridge professor – the Disney Chair of Archaeology at Cambridge; this despite the fact that Cambridge did not start awarding degrees to women until 1948. Bate, from Carmarthen, was possibly the first female scientist employed by the Natural History Museum in London in 1898; she was a pioneering archaeozoologist.

Also in 1925, Gisela Richter (1882–1972) became the curator of Greek and Roman art at New York's Metropolitan Museum of Art; she was the Met's, and possibly the United States' first female curator.[115] Richter, from London, was appointed as an assistant in 1905 to catalogue a collection of Greek vases but stayed and worked her way up. In 1917, she became a US citizen. She published many books on Greek art in her long career, including her popular *A Handbook of Greek Art* from 1959, which sixty years later is still an excellent and enjoyable introduction with its 500 illustrations. In 1944, she received an award for achievement from the American Association of University Women; in 1952, an honorary doctorate from Oxford; and in 1968, the Archaeological Institute of America's Gold Medal Award for Distinguished Archaeological Achievement. Women such as these proved beyond any doubt to society that women could, when allowed to, make significant contributions to fields such as archaeology, ancient history, art history, and classics.

Nowadays, around half of archaeologists are women.[116] However, even in a climate of increased job equality and access to education, the bullying and sexual harassment of women has been described as an 'epidemic' in archaeology.[117] High-profile female classicists like Mary Beard and Bettany Hughes have, as well as bringing good history to millions of viewers, listeners, and readers, have suffered from appalling sexism and misogyny via social media.[118]

METHODOLOGY AND SCOPE

This book is intended as a contribution to women's history, Mediterranean history, and human history; its specific aim is to put thirty 'real' women, of different backgrounds but all from around the Mediterranean, back into history, to present their lives and critically consider the evidence from which these can be reconstructed. Not all of these women have been 'missing' – some, like Olympias and Cleopatra Selene, are famous, or at least well known to archaeologists and ancient historians. Some, however, are known only from human remains, objects or images, or a combination of these. The women of this book are seen as individuals and not treated as heroines or villains, as good or bad women, or as exemplars of feminine virtue or moral rectitude; there are no goddesses or women from myths.

The approach taken in this book combines analysis of archaeological evidence, including bodies, objects and sites, epigraphy, iconography and textual evidence of various types, including texts from ancient histories to poetry; in this it is no different to many other books on the topic. Methodologically, I find the need to maintain a divide between archaeologists and ancient historians unnecessary and artificial, as will many others. For example, as a student of the Late Bronze Age Aegean and Eastern Mediterranean, the Greek Linear B inscribed tablets are an important textual source alongside the archaeological evidence of settlements, tombs, bodies, images, and objects. A consideration of these allows us to situate some women quite precisely in time and space. The Hittite and Egyptian texts of this period are also seen in combination with the material remains, allowing these cultures and their histories to be peopled by named individuals and interpreted in light of historical events. In her exploration of Sumerian women, Susan Pollock uses literary and economic texts, burials, and iconography to tell us about women and gender in different ways.[119] Alison Glazebrook and others have revealed much about classical prostitution through both texts and archaeology.[120] In other words, I work with what we have and aim to be inclusive rather than exclusive.

Women certainly appear in texts of various kinds, from labels and seals, economic texts to literary ones, including histories; literary texts especially were composed by men and may tell us about their images of women and their roles and status. Comparison of a male-authored literary text on the ideals of womanhood might contrast sharply with the reality of a woman's economic power revealed by a seal ring or public status indicated by a statue and inscription. In some cases, women authored texts of their own, but generally these were high-status women and they were largely exceptions to the rule. A great loss are the memoirs of Agrippina the Younger, great granddaughter of Augustus, wife of the emperor Claudius, and mother of Nero. No doubt there are many other texts lost that we have no idea about. But we do, perhaps surprisingly, have some texts written by named women from the Early and Late Bronze Ages. As so often in history, poorer women are often the least visible and their own voices the most difficult to hear, though it is sometimes possible. Texts and images must always be read sensitively and with concern for their contexts. Archaeology can sometimes help rectify the biases of texts by the direct study of human remains and also the spaces in which people lived and the objects that they used or had around them in life and death, though the dead too were manipulated by the living into their final rest.

The aim of this book is to locate and where possible name specific women from the Mediterranean area, and to offer a brief 'biography' of them in their historical context; thirty 'lives' are presented in chronological order from the Palaeolithic to the early days of the Byzantine Empire of Justinian and Theodora. Sometimes when we can locate a woman, we cannot know her name. In the many anonymous burials, archaeologists have given names or references to the bodies. Nameless women should not be forgotten or left out of the story, instead their physical remains and the nature and circumstances of their interment should be examined and elaborated. Even when we do have names, we may know little else about the specific individual concerned, so it is necessary to supplement the story by reference to 'women' more generally in a given time and place and to the anthropological, cultural and historical situation more widely.

Some might argue that a book that juggles 'historical' with 'prehistoric' women and the different kinds of sources that pertain to each will be uneven, disjointed or not specific enough to a particular field of study. That is as it may be, and no book will ever please all readers. The Mediterranean binds this book together, as does the focus on real women, not a specific type of evidence or a single defined archaeological culture, civilisation, or period. The aim again is to be inclusive, rather than exclusive, and this means transcending the boundaries of culture-specific archaeological and historical disciplines. Others too have approached wider Mediterranean history across significant chunks of time and space with the sea itself as the link in the chain, most notably in recent times David Abulafia and Cyprian Broodbank; it is no bad thing.[121]

This book takes a chronological approach in five parts: Part I: The Deep Past, Part II: The Bronze Age, Part III: The Iron Age, Part IV: The Hellenistic Worlds, and Part V: The Age of Empire. This scheme is chosen only for its convenience and there are biases implicit in it – a focus on Greece and Rome and the classical heritage is a product of the author's background and the impact of these cultures in later times, as well as the presence of particular kinds of evidence. But it is also true that there was a trend towards greater interconnection and integration in the Mediterranean region over time that culminated in a politically unified Mediterranean in Roman times. A brief historical introduction is given to set each part in context. The bias is tempered by the inclusion of women from non-classical cultures: Palaeolithic and Iron Age France, Neolithic Anatolia and Malta, ancient Mesopotamia from the Bronze Age to the Persians, early Iberia, Hittite Anatolia, the Levant, as well as pharaonic Egypt, for example. For classical times, I have tried to include women from a a range of locations, not just Athens and Rome. I hope to have achieved a fair enough balance across time and space. This book is not a history or description of women in these cultures generally, but a book of lives of specific women who lived in them.

Along the way, I hope to provide some insight into questions about how archaeologists and historians go about gathering, evaluating, and interpreting evidence for the lives of ancient women. This includes the use of techniques from bioarchaeology, and the study of skeletal, dental and organic remains, to the study of graffiti or literary histories. How can we go from a skeleton or a name to a whole human story? What can funerary contexts, the treatment of a body, the way it was laid to rest, and the goods it had with it tell us about the woman whose burial we are examining? How much should we believe the stories about women written in historical texts?

The women presented in this book had very different life experiences, even though most lived in patriarchal societies. The lives will, I hope, reveal something of the different backgrounds, ambitions, and activities of these women and their trajectories through life, their troubles, and triumphs. A woman of Palaeolithic France clearly had a very different life to a Bronze Age priestess from Greece or the empress Theodora, but I hope we would agree that all women of the past are worthy of research and remembrance.

PART I

THE DEEP PAST

The Mediterranean Sea as we know it was formed 5.3 million years ago, when the basin was flooded from the Atlantic via the Straits of Gibraltar – the 'Zanclean flood'.[1] Even before modern humans appeared on the scene, related hominins dwelt in the Mediterranean region.[2] Hominin stone tools dating back 1.3–1.8 million years, to the Pleistocene, have been found at Ain Hanech, Algeria, and at Pirro Nord in southern Italy.[3] Neanderthals also lived around the Mediterranean. Early pre-Neanderthal remains dating to more than 300,000 years ago have been found at Petralona, Greece, and the remains of thirteen Early Neanderthal individuals found at Krapina in Croatia, from around 120,000 years ago.[4] 'Classic' Neanderthals (70,000–30,000 years ago) also lived around the northern Mediterranean, with fossil evidence from Gibraltar, Mediterranean Spain, the south of France, Italy and the Adriatic, Greece, southern Turkey, and the Levant.[5] Modern humans appeared over 100,000 years ago, one amongst several related species of hominin, and spread into Europe perhaps 60,000–40,000 years ago.[6]

Modern humans settled the Mediterranean during the period of the last Ice Age, which lasted from around 120,000 to 15,000 years ago. Much of northern Europe was covered in ice and the Mediterranean sea level was 120 metres below its present level. Early populations were not large or settled and may have had little impact on the environment due to their hunter-gatherer lifestyle. The Palaeolithic period, from around three million years ago to around 10,000 BC, witnessed huge changes in humans, including the development of 'modern' behaviours across the Middle to Upper Palaeolithic, perhaps 50,000 years ago. Ofer Bar-Yosef notes these as follows: the appearance of prismatic blade technologies and improved weapons for hunting, including spear-throwers; the bow and arrow and boomerang; the use of antler and bone for tools and ritual items; the use of grinding and pounding tools to process plant-based foods; the use of jewellery such as beads and pendants made from a variety of materials, including shells and ivory; and the production of art in the form of figurines, portable art, and outdoor and cave paintings.[7] Into this context come the women in caves of Chapter 1.

One of the most significant changes in human history was the transition from hunting and gathering in the Palaeolithic, the old stone age, to settled agriculture – farming – in the Neolithic, the new stone age. This transformation has been termed the Neolithic Revolution and has been seen as the underlying factor that made 'civilisation' possible. Today, it is recognised that the transition (like that of the 'Palaeolithic Revolution') was more messy and it may not have been a great leap forward in terms of human health and its eventual impacts on social (in)equality.[8] Trevor Watkins argues that in southwest Asia, hunter-gatherers were becoming more sedentary before farming was adopted – agriculture became necessary later to feed these larger populations.[9] For example, there was a 'structured settlement' at Ohalo II, in the southern Levant in the Early Epipalaeolithic (23,000–15,000 BC). The inhabitants engaged in 'pre-domestication agriculture' and processed wild grass seeds, cereals, and pulses as well as hunting small animals.[10] Hunter-gatherers could and did modify the landscapes and resources that they understood.

As sedentary populations increased so settlements became more common in the Neolithic (from around 8500 BC) and monumental houses and communal buildings and sites, perhaps for ritual, also emerged, for example, at Çayönü and Göbekli Tepe. Çatalhöyük is one of the better-known settlements to have emerged at this time, where early agriculture developed alongside hunting and gathering.[11] The 'town' was occupied for centuries and was the home to the woman of Chapter 2. A 'Neolithic package' came into being, which included 'sedentism in villages, domesticated animals and grains, pottery, axes, and grinding technologies'.[12] This package spread from the Near East westwards across the Mediterranean and northwest into Europe, for reasons and in ways that are unclear and hotly debated. Was there a natural expansion or spread owing to more rapid population growth amongst farmers, a wave of advance that rippled out, migration of farmers to new lands, adoption of new behaviours and techniques by others? Whatever the how and why, between around 7000 and 5500 BC the northern Mediterranean zone became Neolithic, populated by farming communities.[13]

Seafaring too had increasingly become a part of Mediterranean life since around 10,000 BC, and the Mediterranean islands all became reachable.[14]

Although some individuals or even small groups may have managed to reach Malta earlier, the clearest evidence suggests that the island was settled fairly late, by around 5000 BC. It was probably colonised by people from Sicily, which, along with the Italian peninsula itself, bisects the Mediterranean and forms a bridge between Africa and Europe.[15] The new arrivals on Malta may have had a profound effect on the island's fauna and as Neolithic farmers transformed its flora too. The islanders instigated a 1000-year tradition of building astonishing megalithic stone 'temples' and burying their dead in subterranean chambers known as hypogea.[16] The islander we meet, from Gozo, is the woman of Chapter 3. These people were among the world's first architects and their buildings, temples that from above look somewhat like clovers, continue to amaze even in a ruined state. For reasons still unknown, the 'temple culture' of Malta ended abruptly around 2500 BC.[17]

1

WOMEN IN CAVES

One of the most exciting archaeological discoveries of modern times was made by a young Spanish girl called María Sanz du Sautuola in 1879 (Figure 1).[1] Inspired by a meeting with French archaeologist Édouard Piette in Paris, who had found various pieces of portable Palaeolithic art, María's father Marcelino had decided to carry out some excavations in the cave of Altamira, in the region of Cantabria in northern Spain. Whilst her father was working near the mouth of the cave, María went exploring further in. Soon, posterity records, she called out to her father: 'Daddy, look, oxen.' María had discovered the stunning cave art on the walls of Altamira – the first Palaeolithic cave art to be recognised in Europe. Sautuola published their findings in 1880 in his *Brief Notes on Some Prehistoric Objects from the Province of Santander*, which included his pencil drawings of the bison from the ceiling of the cave.

The cave of Altamira is decorated with coloured images of other animals too; there are deer, horses, and pigs, painted and sometimes engraved in the rock.[2] The art has recently been dated by uranium series dating, which measures the ratio of uranium to thorium isotopes in mineral deposits such as calcite overlying or near paintings, and was found to have been made over time between around 35,000 and 15,200 years ago.[3] As with other cave art sites, not only paint and engraving were used to create the images; the very contours of the rock surface played a part in the compositions.

Whilst the fantastic images of animals are the most famous examples of rock art, non-figurative signs were also created, from dots and lines to shapes such as

FIG. 1 María Sanz de Sautuola. Contributor: Museo de Altamira / Alamy Stock Photo.

'tectiforms' ('huts') and 'claviforms' ('clubs'), and were more common. A kind of 'quadrilateral sign' appears at Altamira and some nearby caves, which Paul Bahn, an expert on cave art, suggests could possibly have been made by a group of some kind.[4] What these signs mean is not known – though a recent study by Genevieve von Petzinger concludes that they did have meaning for those who painted them; they were symbols rather than doodles.[5] Interpreting symbols is not straightforward. Bahn reminds us that 'amongst the Walbiri of Australia a simple circle can mean a hill, tree, camp site, circular path, egg, breast, nipple, entrance into or exit from the ground, and a host of other things'.[6] He notes that the 'vast amount of non-figurative, abstract, or geometric marking in the caves . . . might have been just as important, if not more important, to prehistoric people' than the more recognisable figures.[7]

With Palaeolithic rock art, there has been a long tradition of assigning the paintings to male artists.[8] Kelly Hays-Gilpin has traced the assumption back to the 1870s and notes that it dominated in textbooks until the 1980s.[9] This androcentric bias is still found in specialist and popular literature and in graphic reconstructions of Palaeolithic life.[10] One book on Palaeolithic art, from 2005, suggested that most consisted of sexual graffiti, and its author concluded that, like graffiti in the boys' toilets in schools, it was made for fun by sex-obsessed adolescent males.[11] Another recent book on human evolution, from 2014, suggests that the art may have been at the centre of 'men's clubs', possibly with a religious or ritual function that may have involved shamanic trance dances; it does not explicitly mention the possibility of female artists.[12] The short National Geographic video 'Prehistory 101: Cave Art', freely available on YouTube, depicts a group of men in a cave, some preparing materials, some holding torches and two actively painting – but no women or children.[13]

Part of this gendered way of looking at Palaeolithic art is the supposed relationship of the paintings to hunting – hunting of course being a male activity linked with basic food provision and with signalling behaviour ('showing off') done whilst females merely gathered food.[14] In 1899, Francis J. Spencer and W. Baldwin Gillen published a description of the Arunta people of central Australia.[15] They described how the Arunta men created images of animals as part of rituals to increase their number. As researchers sought ethnographic parallels to explain Palaeolithic art, this view of paintings as hunting magic became popular, embraced by the cave art expert Abbé Breuil and others. So, the animals depicted in caves were identified as prey species that Palaeolithic hunters, men, sought to catch for their groups. Indeed, some Palaeolithic images do appear to depict hunting scenes or animals with arrows or spears piercing them, but very few in the overall corpus, and there are other interpretations of some of the figures or markings – some hunters may actually be birds, for example, whilst some arrows or weapons could be grass or other markings.[16]

Hays-Gilpin notes that Spencer and Gillen's assumption that only Arunta men painted and engaged in ritual activities was wrong.[17] Early male researchers would probably not have seen women's art – though female anthropologists later on did. Interviews with indigenous Australians have also confirmed that, at least in some communities, anyone, man or woman, can paint. In the case of the Vedda in the early twentieth century, women explained to anthropologists that they made paintings in caves for fun whilst waiting for the men to return from hunting; they were not ritual and not made by men.[18] Perhaps ancient hunting scenes were similarly produced, although the position of some art in inaccessible locations suggests something less casual.[19]

Was hunting exclusively a 'male' activity anyway? The recent discovery of a young female huntress from Wilamaya Patjxa in the Andes, known as WPI6, has given further evidence to the existence of 'woman the hunter'.[20] This 9,000-year-old burial, identified as female by chemical analysis of her teeth, was laid to rest with several spear tips and some mammal bones. It clearly demonstrates that hunting in the deep past was also carried out by women as well as men, at least in some communities. There is no reason that mixed groups could not have hunted together.

Palaeolithic women may have painted animals in caves; they may be responsible for some of the earliest and most impressive human painting, some of which is now known across the world. They may also have painted meaningful symbols in caves too. Certainly, there seems little reason now to assume that only men painted. But there may be a more direct route to identifying women in caves – through hand stencils, prints, and fluting marks. Hand stencils and prints have long been known at Altamira, and in 2019 the newspaper *El Pais* reported the discovery of three more painted hands there, to add to the six already known; these have been dated to more than 20,000 years ago.[21] One of these, a black handprint located far into the cave, in the Galería Final, belonged to a child of indeterminate sex. Hand stencils, prints, and flutings are an evocative survival from deep prehistory, providing a vivid link to individuals that occupied the same space millennia ago.

While Iberian Altamira faces the Atlantic, hand stencils, paintings, and fluting marks are found in Mediterranean caves too. On the Mediterranean shore, in the south of Iberia, they are found in Gorham's Cave, in Gibraltar, and the Cueva de la Pileta and Cueva de Ardales, in the Malaga region, at Cosquer and elsewhere in France, and in Italy at Paglicci.[22] Paul Pettitt and colleagues note Palaeolithic hand stencils and prints in thirty-seven caves: twenty-six in France, ten in Spain, and one in Italy (as of 2015), with most caves having only a few examples but others with many more, such as the Cosquer and Gargas caves in France.

Cosquer, southeast of Marseille, is an astonishing site, because the entrance to the cave is now almost 40 metres below current sea level – it was discovered by a professional diver named Henri Cosquer in 1985.[23] Until perhaps 10,000 years ago, the cave entrance was above sea level and the shoreline further south. The paintings were first noticed only in 1991 and dating suggests that the oldest could be around 33,000 years old.[24] A recent count of the images in the cave totals 69 hand stencils, 194 animal figures, and 240 geometric signs, as well as 2 human figures.[25] The animal figures included horses, goats, cattle, deer, and birds as well as sea creatures.[26]

Hand stencils were found in the eastern part of the cave, but finger flutings were 'found almost everywhere on the ceilings and walls of the large chamber, wherever the surface is malleable'.[27] Flutings are marks made by running fingers through the soft 'moonmilk' found on some cave surfaces.[28] Hands were stencilled in both black and red paint; and in many cases, it seems that the artists had fingers wholly or partly missing. Many explanations have been suggested for the significance of the missing fingers. One possibility is that fingers had been lost through frostbite, ill health, or accidents and the whole remaining hand was represented. Alternatively, it is possible that fingers were deliberately mutilated, perhaps for some ritual purposes. Another view is that such hand stencils are signs, perhaps like signs used in daily life in combination with or for different purposes than spoken language.[29]

Hands were one of the most popular subjects of cave painting in the form of both handprints and more commonly hand stencils; they are found throughout the world from deep prehistory of some 40,000 years ago to much more recent times.[30] The less common handprints were made simply by dipping the hand into paint and pressing it against the surface of the stone, while hand stencils involved placing the hand on the rock surface and blowing or spitting paint onto it to a hand-shaped silhouette. These techniques, learned from indigenous Australians, have been used by Michel Lorblanchet and Claude Courard to convincingly recreate hand stencils and also animals in true Palaeolithic style.[31] It is possible that the act of 'spit-painting' had a deeper meaning, since it literally involved breathing something into existence on the rock surface.[32]

It is not clear why people would make hand signs; although, as children many of us make handprints and outlines for fun and adults too have been known to photocopy their hands on the office copier. There is something satisfying in creating an image from ourselves, and some hand paintings may have been done for fun too – although we should consider the investment in creating the paint and going into the dark cave environment to make the shapes. Walker and colleagues note that the hand is 'a universally recognizable image'.[33] They identify five particular properties of hand outlines: they are unmistakably hands and unmistakably human. As such, other humans, whether of the same group or culture or not, can easily recognise hand paintings as marks left by other humans. They remain static through time and are clearly recognisable even to us after thousands of years. They also point to the hand as a 'universal point of interface' – hands reach out and touch people, objects, and surfaces, they are key to our interactions with the world outside ourselves. Hands can also serve as a scale, and by using handprints or stencils, a complex shape can be easily produced. In our visual age, an age of print and screens, the impact on an ancient person of creating and looking at an image, even a simple one, can be underestimated.

As Bahn says, without being able to ask, we do not really know what hand signs mean, but he lists the following ideas: 'they could be signatures, property marks, memorials, love magic, a wish to leave a mark in some sacred place, a sign of caring about or being responsible for a site, a record of growth, or a personal marker – "I was here"'.[34] The hand sign of Islamic and Jewish culture, the *hamsa*, often found as an amulet, is believed to bring protection and ward off the evil eye.[35] In modern times, we are familiar with hand symbols such as the 'thumbs up', 'ok', 'V', 'the finger', and the 'raised fist' and can recognise a meaning in context of use. And we often raise a hand as a greeting or farewell.

Humans are sexually dimorphic; that is, men and women tend to have certain physical differences. One of these is in women's and men's hands, which differ slightly in particular ways. One of these is size: the hands of adult males, unsurprisingly, tend to be bigger than those of adult females. In sexing handprints, this observation is of limited use – a smaller hand image could be a small man, a mature woman, or a youth. One scholar, Dale Guthrie, has argued that most cave art was made by children, especially by testosterone-full teenage boys. He analysed the hands of a modern sample population in Alaska to learn about female/male traits. Then he examined 201 handprints from French and Spanish caves and concluded that 162 were males and 39 were either women or young males.[36]

Other studies, for example that of John Manning using a modern population sample from Liverpool, have demonstrated that finger length ratio also differed by sex.[37] Manning found that women's D2 and D4 fingers (reading from the thumb as D1) had a ratio of 1.0, whereas for men it was 0.98; that is, men's ring fingers tended to be longer. If correct, finger ratio should allow the sexing of hands at all ages. This idea of measuring finger ratio of cave handprints was adopted by Dean Snow, who applied it in a study of six hand stencils from four caves in southwestern France.[38] He concluded that these were probably made by four women, a man and a sub-adult male. Snow recognised, however, that he was working with a very small sample and that his method was almost certainly not 100 per cent accurate. More recently he added twenty-six further examples from caves in France and Spain to his data.[39] The results of the analysis of all thirty-two samples showed that 75 per cent of them were probably female.

A similar approach to finger ratio has been taken by Leslie Van Gelder and Kevin Sharpe, who analysed fluting marks in caves.[40] Analysing seven sets of finger profiles from Rouffignac Cave, France, they found that five out of seven probably belonged to females, with two of those being girls of around five years of age. Their studies made use of flutings made by modern fluters of different ages as for comparison. Like Snow, Van Gelder and Sharpe are careful about the accuracy of their method, which they state may not be totally precise either in its collection of data and its analysis, but they believe it to be consistent enough to conclude that women were certainly finger fluting.[41] Emma Nelson and colleagues have recently explored the use of the palm of the hand and predicted sex accurately in over 90 per cent of their sample.[42]

Not all are convinced by these methods and their results. Patrik Galeta and colleagues, for example, have explored the accuracy of such metrics-based studies. To do this, they collected handprints of students in Bordeaux, fifty men and fifty women and measured various characteristics of their hands.[43] They found that they could successfully identify the sex of the reference population, the modern comparative data, but not other contemporary groups.

They concluded that handprint sexing studies developed using characteristics derived from modern sample populations, sometimes far away from the location of the original prints, cannot be regarded as accurate. Bahn also points to a major difficulty, the imprecision of data collection – even just measuring the prints can be difficult. In modern attempts to make handprints too, he notes that the same person can produce hand stencils that have different characteristics: 'one individual can produce very different stencils!'.[44]

However, the studies mentioned above are enough to cast doubt on the dubious idea of cave art being a male-only production. There is no reason why we should not believe that Palaeolithic women helped to create paints, finding and gathering materials and processing them, and themselves made hand stencils, prints, fluting marks, or any other paintings or engravings in caves. It is only our inherited ideas about the 'natural' roles of the sexes that makes us think otherwise.

Despite the criticisms of the hand-measuring and sexing methods, these studies have succeeded in putting Palaeolithic women into early history as active participants in cave painting, which can no longer be regarded as a men-only domain. Whatever the images of men and women's hands meant to their creators, their creation marks an important stage in human mental and cultural development. Pettitt and colleagues suggest that hand art might represent the first type of cave art and posit a link between it and the appearance later of figurative images, for example, of animals.[45] The hand stencils and prints of Palaeolithic women may have played a role in ushering in a new era in human perception and behaviour.

2

A WOMAN OF ÇATALHÖYÜK

Around eight or nine thousand years ago in southern Anatolia a young woman lived and died in the place now known as Çatalhöyük, southeast of the modern city of Konya. She was buried in a building, Building 17 of the South Area, Space 620, along with several other bodies, and found, with seventy-six other bodies across the site, by archaeologists in 2017 (Figure 2).[1] Since we have no way of knowing her name, she is known simply as F.8018 Sk (21884). It is a specific yet also anonymous memorial to the lived life of a woman who was at the very least a daughter, a neighbour, and a friend.

Çatalhöyük is situated on the Konya Plain, with the Çarşamba River flowing southwards nearby; the climate at present is characterised by hot, dry summers and cold, wet winters – it is defined as 'cold semi-arid/steppe'.[2] It was one of the first 'towns' that humans built and lived in. The early excavations were conducted by James Mellaart and his wife Arlette, between 1961 and 1965 and made famous through magazine articles and books, including the lavishly illustrated *Çatal Hüyük: A Neolithic Town in Anatolia.*[3] The town started to develop before 7400 BC and was inhabited for over a thousand years, the mud brick houses being regularly refreshed with new coats of plaster and taken down and rebuilt as needed; habitation shifted from one location to another across the site.[4] It was probably home to around 3,500 people, possibly more.

Unlike the urban spaces we are used to, Çatalhöyük developed as an organic collection of dwellings built touching each other, without streets, with individual houses entered through a hole in the roof, giving a plan something like a

FIG. 2 Feature 8018 Sk (21884) in Building 17, Space 620, Çatalhöyük. Haddow, S. D. Çatalhöyük 2017 Archive Report. 118. Courtesy of Jason Quinlan

beehive. Socialising and working may have been rooftop affairs. Indoor spaces too had a range of functions beyond just sleeping, including cooking, ritual, and craft activities. Inhabitants were buried under the floors of houses. We have to imagine F.8018 as a child running about on the roofs clambering in and out of her house and those of her friends, and climbing off the town by ladder to explore the surrounding rich countryside, a member of a bustling community. This built landscape and the environment around it are where she grew to adulthood.

F.8018's town looks like a society of equals, to judge from its buildings, which are all fairly similar in size and quality, although Mellaart initially interpreted some houses as shrines because of their more elaborate decoration.[5] Ian Hodder and Peter Pels have conducted a quantitative study of the houses at Çatalhöyük and found that the slightly more elaborate buildings, those that come to include more features such as bucrania (cattle skulls with horns), also tended to have more underfloor burials. These may have been locations for communal feasting and ritual. Perhaps they were used by kin or other types of groups cementing their familial bonds or shared interests.

Hodder and Pels call these 'history houses', where memories built up and were perhaps celebrated.[6] Sometimes it seems that body parts of dead inhabitants buried in these locations were removed and installed in other buildings, leaving some of bodies headless or armless – one human head was even plastered and possibly painted. F.8018 would have known such houses in her community and the stories associated with them and the memories they sparked would have formed a major part of her mental landscape – just as we have emotional attachments to the houses of our childhood, parents or grandparents, or to their graves, photographs, and possessions.

What was particularly striking about Çatalhöyük, and immediately apparent to Mellaart, was the town's rich 'art', especially the paintings, reliefs and anthropomorphic figurines.[7] F.8018 lived in a world of meaningful representations, pictorial and three-dimensional, observable and touchable. There are over 300 paintings on the white plastered house walls of people and animals, vultures picking at humans, hunting scenes with small human figures surrounding giant animals, bulls, stags and boars, birds and geometric patterns including chevrons, circles, lozenges, spirals and zigzags; there are also human handprints.[8] F.8018 and her friends may have printed their hands on a wall as children – one wall has fifty-seven child handprints on it.[9]

Across time, paintings were painted over and new ones composed – one theory is that the paintings may have become part of the building, not just physically but perhaps adding to the meanings and memories invested in it.[10] The physical acts of gathering raw materials and processing pigments, making brushes, and so on, might have been activities many took part in, with knowledge of sources and techniques being developed and passed down through the generations. In a recent study of the paintings, Duygu Çamurcuoğlu has concluded that painting was not a specialised activity done by 'artists' but was something many inhabitants could participate in.[11] This may explain the variety of specific details and differences between paintings within an overarching Çatalhöyük style.[12] F.8018 may have helped prepare materials and herself made art linked with daily life, ritual practice, or that was just nice to look at.

In addition to paintings, one of the most striking images from Çatalhöyük are the sets of plaster bull and ram skulls and horns, sometimes moulded onto real animal remains, set into walls, benches, and little pillars in some of the houses. Mellaart proposed that the bucrania represented a male god, contrasting with and subordinated to a goddess, represented as a humanoid figure with prominent belly button and splayed limbs; in one example, the goddess, in plaster relief on the wall, was giving birth to the bulls positioned below.[13] Dorothy Cameron, a friend of Mellaart's, later interpreted the bucrania specifically as symbols of the human female reproductive system that they resemble – womb, fallopian tubes, and ovaries.[14] Joan Relke thinks it more likely that the reproductive systems of cows, which would have been regularly slaughtered and dismembered for food by women and men from Çatalhöyük, were the generative parts being referred to by the bucrania.[15]

Ron Adams has noted examples of other societies that display animal mandibles and bucrania in Indonesia.[16] As he explains, the display of these body parts is always connected to feasting activities, which themselves can be related to events such as housebuilding or burials. In Egypt, one very early First Dynasty tomb from Saqqara has a bench all the way around its exterior, decorated with 300 bull bucrania in clay with real horns – Morris suggests these do have a royal and religious significance and that they might well be indicators of wealth.[17] F.8018 would have known of these installations and, unless there were restrictions on access to these houses, would have seen them and understood their meaning and significance.

Of the many figurines from Çatalhöyük, the best known is a female. Mellart wrote that it

> shows the goddess seated on a throne supported on either side by felines (leopards or lions?), whose tails curve up her back and curl over her shoulders. Her right foot rests on what looks like a human cranium; the area below her left foot is damaged. Her body is heavy with the flabbiness of pregnancy and with arms resting on the heads of the animals she is actually shown as giving birth to a child, the head of which protrudes from between her thighs.[18]

He placed a great importance on this figure, suggesting that 'in this "monumental" statue neolithic man has summed up his creed in a Great Goddess, Mistress of all life and death, human and animal and-judging by its findspot, a grainbin – vegetable as well'.[19] He concluded that 'if the Çatal Hüyük religion is a creation of women, one has the rare opportunity of exploring Neolithic woman's mind by studying the symbolism she used in her effort to comprehend and influence the mysteries of life and death'.[20] However, archaeologists are now less persuaded by these ideas – Carolyn Nakamura and Lynn Meskell suggest that many figurines, not always clearly female or male, could be idealised representations of maturity, abundance and age rather than sex. Elsewhere they propose that the types and number of grave goods deposited with burials also vary by age rather than sex.[21]

Infants and people of all ages received burial in Çatalhöyük, usually under benches or the floors of rooms.[22] Grave goods are generally rare, though not completely absent. One child buried in Building 1 of the North Area was wearing a necklace of 180 stone beads.[23] F.8018 was not buried with any grave goods, but her body had been covered with a layer of red, iron-based ochre.[24] Two infants were buried near F.8018. The first, F.8048, was buried with a beaded shell necklace with over forty bone and stone beads as well as perforated shells, which must surely be tender gifts from a parent.[25] The other, F.8049 was possibly buried with a fragment of obsidian deposited alongside. Another set of child remains, F.8450, has been interpreted as a foundation burial for the building. The body had red ochre around the pelvis and legs, which could have indicated a special status. The remains of a fetus, F.8047, were found buried in a basket near her too. Though it is often said that higher infant mortality prevalent in pre-industrial societies reduced parents' emotional response to the death of a child, the treatment of dead infants at Çatalhöyük suggests their recognition as people, and of communal or parental care and love. It is not clear whether F.8018 ever gave birth to any children, but we might guess that it was likely; it is at least possible that one or more of the infant burials were kin of F.8018.

The proportions of human remains found at Çatalhöyük show 'a typical pattern of natural deaths in a stable population' and there seems to be little, if any difference between the treatment of female and male dead.[26] Dead bodies may have been excarnated – left outside, perhaps on the roofs – for their flesh to be devoured by animals and to decompose in the open, something suggested by Mellaart and more recently by Marin Pilloud and colleagues.[27] There are several paintings of vultures with curved beaks 'attacking' headless bodies, and one image may show a person encouraging a vulture towards a body.[28] 'Vulture iconography' suggests that the townsfolk had a symbolic relationship with vultures, which were associated with death and the treatment of the dead. Excarnation would have had distinct advantages, not least in removing decomposing bodies from houses and the town.

Many cultures have placed a significance on the human head. Actual disembodied heads have been found at Çatalhöyük and other Neolithic sites, including Jericho in Palestine and Çayönü in Turkey. Pilloud and colleagues have identified fourteen headless bodies at Çatalhöyük; four female, three of indeterminate sex, and seven male.[29] Thirty isolated human skulls have also been found, one with plaster on it, and female remains with upper and lower limbs removed, probably before burial. This plastered skull of an adult male is the oldest known from Anatolia; it was found in the arms of a female, buried in a foundation pit of a new building.[30] Hodder explains that people dug up certain sets of remains and removed the heads, leaving cut marks on the bones, and then used the heads 'for ceremonial purposes', such as when a building was abandoned.[31] We can only guess at the meaning and significance of a physical and ritual practice that may have had great importance for F.8018 and her fellows.

In life, however, food would have been the major concern for everyone in Çatalhöyük; F.8018 would have been involved in many activities related to subsistence in her daily life, activities that would have varied with the seasons. Mellaart noted the abundance and variety of the Çatalhöyük diet.[32] Grains carbonised as a result of fires show that the inhabitants were eating emmer and einkorn wheat, barley as well as peas, lentils, and bitter vetch. Aurochs, deer, and pigs, were the main animals hunted, along with ass, sheep, and even leopards. In some communities, where males are accorded more social value, girls and women can have a poorer diet leading to worse health. However, in Çatalhöyük examination of human remains suggests that women and men generally enjoyed the same diets over the period that

Çatalhöyük was occupied and were equally healthy in terms of physical and dental health.[33]

Sonya Atalay and Christine Hastorf have presented a detailed description of the food-related activities of the townspeople in their environment, derived from archaeological, biological, and ethnographic evidence, which can provide us with a diary of a major part of F.8018's life – her mental world and what she did every day.[34] They divide these activities into five areas: production and procurement, processing, cooking, presentation, and eating. Production would include activities such as gathering, growing and harvesting, trapping, catching, and hunting, with seasonal variation in activities.

Sheep and goats may have been penned around the edge of the town. Cattle may have remained undomesticated and been consumed only at feasts or on special occasions. The paintings of Çatalhöyük show men much more often than women, and it is leopard-skin clad men who are shown in hunting scenes, so this may have been a gendered activity.[35] One of the most spectacular wall paintings from Çatalhöyük shows a red-painted bull over two metres in length surrounded by tiny human figures dressed in animal skins and armed with throwing sticks and bows. It could show either hunting or veneration of the bull, or both.[36] Even if big game hunting was a primarily male pursuit, it was probably not very important for subsistence at Çatalhöyük, though it may have had importance in other ways.[37] F.8018 and other women may have hunted and trapped smaller animals on a more regular basis.

Some foods would be eaten right away, some raw, some cooked, but the townspeople were not living 'hand to mouth' – much would have been preserved for later on, through drying, pickling, salting, and smoking. Animals would need to be butchered for eating and for preservation. Food and food storage affected the form of houses, which had ovens for cooking, as well as bins and pits and space for skin bags, baskets, and pots. Storerooms off the main rooms would have been full of produce at certain times of year, if the inhabitants were fortunate. In a good year, F.8018 would have been busy engaging with these processes and in her life would have been surrounded by these objects, things that she and her peers would have made to store the produce they generated.

The presence of ovens in the houses at Çatalhöyük suggests that much cooking took place in the home and presumably for the family group. Inhabitants cooked their foods in many ways, baking, boiling, grilling, roasting, and toasting foods.[38] Boiling was done by heating clay balls and putting them into water-filled pots, rather than boiling pots over a fire. Food was served in or on baskets, and on woven cloth mats, as well as in wooden bowls and plates; there were wooden cups and implements too. Mellaart reported that one building had contained twenty softwood pieces of tableware.[39] Food was probably served with people sitting on the floor.

Atalay and Hastorf's paper provides a rich view into the day-to-day activities of Çatalhöyük's residents and is further enhanced by illustrations by members of the Çatalhöyük Research Project. One figure illustrates the many ways of storing foodstuffs, for example.[40] Bags hung from the rafters amongst sprigs of herbs and drying fruit and baskets, pots and boxes on the floor, along with bundles of firewood. Another shows the 'indirect' boiling with clay balls, with a woman stirring the contents of watertight baskets, with a small baby held in the crook of her arm, its tiny hand grasping her necklace.[41] A third shows young and older women preparing food and serving men.[42] The pictures bring the town to life, but they also suggest that women cooked and that women and girls served the men their food. Whilst of course this may be accurate, it is possible that men were primarily responsible for cooking as in traditional Samoan culture, or that it was an ungendered activity.[43] Perhaps food preparation and cooking was a communal effort that went hand in hand with eating together. The illustrations serve to capture what would have been an important part of F.8018's life.

Does this pattern in consumption also mean that women and men also carried out the same tasks related to food production? A traditional view, supposedly 'from nature', would see men as big game hunters and providers of high calorie food and women connected with plants. Hunting is of course an outdoor pursuit. But another piece of evidence supports the idea of relative equality, at least in some areas of life, between the sexes. A number of researchers noticed traces of soot on the inside of the ribs of skeletal remains.[44] The fires in the rooms of Çatalhöyük's houses, especially important during the very cold winters, would have made the interiors smoky and this smoke would have been inhaled by those living and working in the houses. Soot was found on both female and male human remains, and built up with age, which suggests that women and men spent a roughly equal time indoors over their lifetimes.

Pounding and grinding grain is hard work and takes a toll on the body. By looking for signs of osteoarthritis in skeletal remains, in shoulders, elbows, wrists, and different parts of the spine, bioarchaeologists found that as people at Çatalhöyük grew older, more tended to suffer from osteoarthritis, which also worsened with age.[45] So whereas only 27.3 per cent of young adults (20–29 years old) had osteoarthritis, 82.8 per cent of older adults had it and while 9.1 per cent of young adults had severe osteoarthritis, among older adults it was 48.3 per cent. In all age groups, there was no significant difference between women and men, which suggests that they carried out similar types and amounts of physical activities. F.8018 and her male relatives probably obtained, processed, and consumed food together.

Can we conclude that Neolithic Çatalhöyük was an egalitarian paradise where women and men were equal? For Hodder, after years working on the site, the evidence 'suggests a society in which sex is relatively unimportant in assigning social roles'.[46] However, we should be careful not to push the evidence too far. As we can see from our own societies, in which women and men are notionally equal, and in which much of material culture might seem to back this up, there are still a host of issues connected with gender inequalities and stereotypes; these might be largely invisible to future archaeologists. At any rate, the painstaking work of many archaeologists who have studied the fabric of Çatalhöyük and the remains of its inhabitants has allowed us to find and reconstruct some of F.8018 Sk (21884)'s world on the scale of a human life.

3

A WOMAN OF GOZO

The small island of Gozo lies just a short distance northwest of Malta, in the central Mediterranean. People arrived on the islands in the sixth millennium BC.[1] In the later fourth millennium BC Maltese lifestyle changed and more complex societies were developed; this Temple Period is known for its megalithic monuments, which are often regarded as temples, and for its hypogea – caves and chambers. Over the course of this long period, many of the 'temples' were constructed, maintained and rebuilt repeatedly, suggesting a stable way of life on the islands. Around 2300 BC or sometime earlier, this lifestyle, and the Temple Period, came to an end for reasons that are unclear, and the island even appears deserted – though archaeologists will state that absence of evidence is not evidence of absence.[2] Nevertheless, the striking archaeological remains of prehistoric Malta and Gozo, the temples, labyrinthine underground complexes, and 'human' statues all continue to catch the imagination of modern people.

From 1987 to 1994, a British and Maltese team excavated a site at Xagħra, known also as the Brochtorff Circle, a large multiphase Neolithic underground burial area consisting of a megalithic circle and hypogeum (Figure 3).[3] Careful work has revealed over 220,000 human bones, which means probably more than 800 individuals were buried here over some time.[4] Although there was activity there earlier, the main period of the site's elaboration and use has been dated to between just after 3000 BC to sometime before 2500/400 BC.[5]

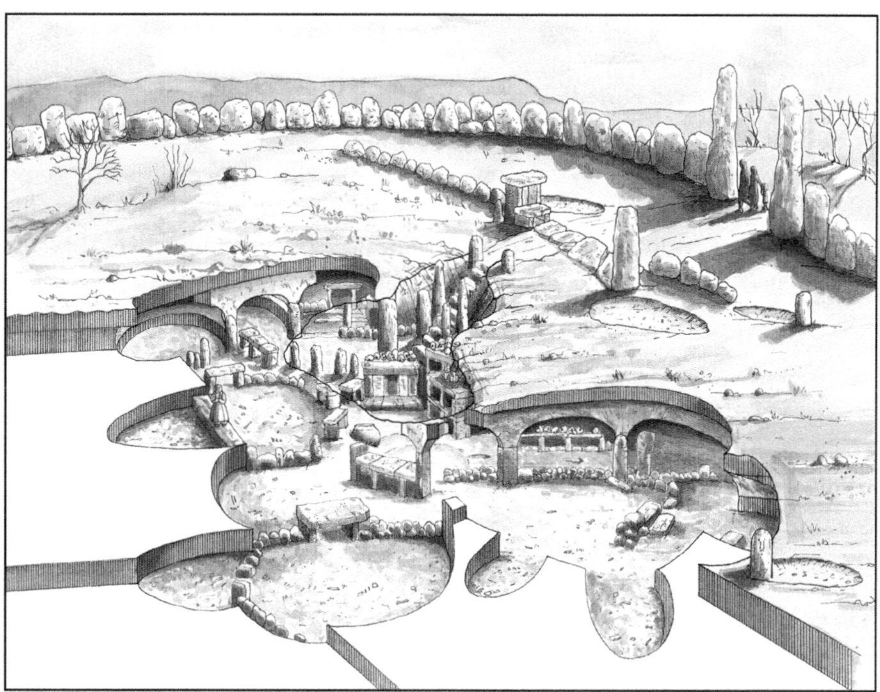

FIG. 3 Reconstruction of the west and east caves of Xagħra (the Brochtorff Circle), Gozo, and its entry. By Libby Mulqueeney after originals by Caroline Malone and Steven Ashley. The solid black line defines the area that would probably have been open to the sky. © McDonald Institute for Archaeological Research

While there were probably six thousand people buried at another site called Hal Saflieni, the human remains there were not recorded, and remains from other sites are few. This makes Xagħra the most important site currently for studying actual human remains from the Maltese temple period.[6] However, given the nature of the site, including how it was used by the people of ancient Xagħra to dispose of the dead, investigation has been difficult. This is because most of the remains are disarticulated and complete articulated skeletons are rare, though not wholly absent. It is difficult to study individuals and also to find out in depth about demography and health, although the team have attempted to do all three.

One woman buried in the 'shrine' area, in Context 1268 (100E/109N), at Xagħra has been described by Simon Stoddart and the other investigators.[7] Let us call her Person 1268. The team found her skull, arms, torso, and pelvis, along with her legs, which were crushed after her burial. Her sex was determined by several telltale features of her skull, including the prominence of the brow- or supra-orbital ridge and the size and shape of part of the jaw area (mastoid process) and confirmed by the sciatic notch of her pelvis, which is wider in a female skeleton than a male. Not all human remains are in a condition to allow this kind of determination and there can also be some ambiguity in interpreting skeletal remains; as humans we all vary in how we are made and the way we look.

Person 1268 was buried along with at least thirty-nine others, based on a count of kneecaps (patellas). The dead range in age from fetuses to the elderly, with a sex ratio of five females to six males – roughly even. Although it is not possible to gauge her age with detail, examination of parts of the skull, the vault and the lateral anterior sutures, suggest that she was somewhere between thirty-four and sixty-eight years old – quite a wide range.[8] The pelvis also suggested a mature or older woman. Bone surfaces of the pelvis tend to appear as 'ridges and valleys' in youth, then smooth out, and with aging become more granular in appearance and eventually may become arthritic and more pitted in texture.[9] Her height has been estimated from the length of her forearm (ulna) at 1.52–1.56 m.

At some point in her life 1268 had broken an arm (humerus), but it had healed well. This suggests that she must have received care, perhaps from family members and people in her community, to allow the healing to take place. What was worse for her though is that she seems to have suffered from severe arthritis. This is indicated by bone proliferation, the growth of new bone, in her middle and lower back (thoracic and lumbar vertebrae and sacrum). This was potentially both very painful and debilitating and could have made it difficult to walk or carry out daily tasks.

Person 1268's teeth also tell a story. She had a number of dental issues, including an abscess and gum disease around the left molars and right pre-molars. In her lower set, she also had gum disease, two caries, and calculus or tartar. She may have had receding gums and probably bad breath. As with her arthritis, these problems may have caused her discomfort and difficulty in daily life. Person 1268 also seems likely to have used her mouth as a third hand – much like we do today when doing chores – and this led to a particular pattern of wear on some of the teeth of her lower jaw and the corresponding upper teeth. Petra Molnar has studied 'extramasticatory dental wear' and suggests wear could come from 'basket working, stripping branches, softening sinews, cutting of pieces of meat, hide preparation, leather working' and so on, or, in some cases, just from habitually chewing on a twig.[10] Different tasks can produce different wear patterns – grooves, notches, scrapes, chips – and can impact on dental health. Age and continued wear can also erase the wear patterns from earlier in life – 1268 may have done different tasks when she was older and less mobile than when she was younger.

Person 1268 was buried with a cowrie-shell headdress. While about a thousand shell and bone ornaments were found at Xagħra, the team suggests that this might represent only a relatively small number of finished necklaces and jewellery items.[11] It might suggest that she held some special status in the community, or warranted a degree of special treatment in death, or perhaps it was just a beloved and precious possession. Islanders used a range of shells to make attractive jewellery, including limpets, murex, tusk shell, and tun shells, which had a range of colours and degrees of shininess. Shells may have been collected on purpose or obtained as a desired by-product of eating shellfish.

Another special feature of 1268's burial is that her body had been covered in red ochre.[12] The deliberate use of ochre (often used as a generic term for pigments) stretches far back into human history – Neanderthals processed, used, and transported red ochre over 200,000 years ago.[13] Ochre had a variety of uses; it was used to make cave paintings and even as an adhesive. Red ochre, in particular, has long been thought to have had some symbolic meaning associated with the dead, because it has been found on many sets of human remains.[14] In this view, red is often thought to be associated with blood and therefore with death or life. Perhaps 1268's family used this precious substance as part of their treatment of her body after she died. Other interpretations are possible though; ethnographic research shows that ochre can be used as an insect repellant, as medication taken internally or externally, for treating animal hides, and to preserve food.[15] Could the ochre have been applied as a medicine some time before she died?

The diet of 1268 and the people of ancient Xagħra has also been studied by stable isotope analysis.[16] The research suggests that the islanders did not eat a lot of fish or other marine resources but received most of their nutrition from agricultural produce and perhaps, in the earlier periods, from hunting and gathering – the amount of game and wild animals for eating probably decreased over time. Querns show that grain was processed and barley and wheat, as well as pulses such as lentils, were already grown before the Temple Period.[17]

Protein came mostly from dairy and meat and the numerous animal bones found include sheep, goats, pigs, and cattle. However, these faunal remains come primarily from the temples and cemeteries and may not represent normal daily diet – habitation sites are poorly known, though, so a good comparison is not possible. At the moment, it is not possible to conclude with certainty anything about potential sex differences in diet because the sample size of the studies is small – seven in Richards and colleagues' study and four in Stoddart's.[18] There are some differences between the individuals studied but given the number of samples the significance of this is unclear.

The Temple period, with its impressive and complex monuments and hypogea testify to a rich ritual life on Malta and Gozo through the Temple period.[19] Temple complexes were public monuments with courtyards at their entrance and various chambers within. Public rituals and feasting could be carried out outside and more select meetings, restricted to certain individuals, within. The numerous temples most likely formed the focus for local communities. Barratt and colleagues suggest that 'the monumental structures were erected as celebratory locales, where certainties of life and constrained death could be placed within a regulated tempo, and within regulated space and place, probably responding to seasonal constraints of abundance and shortage'.[20] They argue that the above-ground temples were associated with the celebration of life and the living, while the underground hypogea were associated with death: 'these enclosures effectively kept the dangerous dead and their potentially roving and perhaps mischievous spirits within a safe controlled space'.[21]

Exploring the Xagħra circle's potential alignments over the course of the year, Barratt and colleagues noted that in the early morning of the summer solstice, the two pillars at the entrance to the circle cast shadows towards the entrance to the underground area – attendants could follow the path of shadows into the underground area.[22] By contrast, the winter solstice was more significant for the temple site of Ggantija. They suggest that Xagħra's association was with death and Ggantija's with life. The islanders' culture must have been imbued with ancient traditions for which the monuments formed the focus, and meanings may have changed over time. Sites were used over a long period and were periodically renovated and modified; in the later phases, they became more complex and used more figurines but may have also been more restrictive in terms of participants. Almost certainly 1268 will have engaged with her local monuments during life, perhaps feasting with her community and visiting the dead, some of whom were probably her ancestors and relations, perhaps officiating in some way at some of the public or private rituals.

The inhabitants of prehistoric Malta and Gozo are also particularly famous for their figured statues in human form.[23] This tradition began long before the first temples, though most examples are from temples and hypogea, which suggests that they had some importance in the ritual or belief system, though exactly what is unclear. Figurines and statues may have served different functions, representing worshippers, ancestors, deceased family members or more. Isabelle Vella Gregory suggests even that 'the term human is perhaps restrictive and fails to acknowledge both the diversity inherent in this body of statuary and the possibility that these representations do not always represent humans'.[24]

One of the most enigmatic statues comes from the most complex temple site of Tarxien on Malta.[25] It was a larger-than-life size human figure, probably standing at 2.5 to 3 m in height, though all that remains of it is part of its pleated skirt, the two enormous calves and tiny feet, along with the base. Inevitably, given its size and appearance, it has been labelled as a goddess. But does it depict a female? David Trump points out that the sex of the figure, as with many others, 'is not only unemphasized but to all appearances deliberately suppressed' – perhaps the figure was neither and/or both female and male.[26] This might indeed be a deity, but we cannot rule out the possibility that it represented an actual person, whether a high status or notable person, a priestess or priest, or even a mythological founder.

Many human figures were also found at Xagħra. The most famous example is probably the small 'twin seated mother goddess', though whether that description is accurate is unclear.[27] The limestone statue consists of two 'corpulent' figures sitting on a couch, each with calves and feet like the large Tarxien statue. Each is also wearing a pleated skirt. One figure holds a small figure in its lap, which could be a baby or possibly a small statue, while the other holds a small cup. The statue was almost intact when found, with only the heads broken off; one was found and reattached. The context of the find, in the heart of the hypogeum, suggests it was an important symbolic object; it is reminiscent of the ivory statuette from Mycenae, from the Late Bronze Age (c. 1300 BC), which shows two flounce-skirted kneeling women with a baby or infant between them, which has also frequently been seen as having some religious meaning. Generally speaking, these may belong to representations of *kourotrophoi,* mothering or nursing scenes involving a divinity, which were popular in some Mediterranean communities at different times.

Vella notes that small figurines tended to be found with burials, whilst 'more elaborate' figures had a closer association with the architecture.[28] The largest human figure found at Xagħra, again skirted and with fat calves and small feet, was originally over 60 cm tall.[29] The piece had been coloured with yellow ochre in places and was finely polished. Yet the condition it was found in raises interesting questions – the statue had been completely smashed and the pieces were found spread over a wide area of the tomb. As the excavators point out, this was done during the period of use of the temple. The motivations behind this deliberate act of destruction can only be guessed at. If it was a god or goddess, was there a loss of faith by the community or did beliefs about representing the supernatural change? Did someone from a rival community smash what could have been a local symbol? If it was a representation of a specific person, did this represent the passing of the spirit or an erasure of memory? Another statue, from Tarxien, was pierced with pieces of broken shell – was this a 'voodoo doll'?[30]

Also significant in this context of physical closure is the eventual closure of Xagħra; Barratt and colleagues explain the end thus: 'After the last human interment had been placed, the ritual structures, and a number of liturgical apparatuses, appear to have been deliberately dismantled, and indeed, part of the cave system appears to have collapsed.'[31]

Thanks to the work of the team that excavated Xagħra and carefully analysed and described the material evidence, we can learn something about a woman who lived, died, and was buried more than four millennia ago on Gozo, in the central Mediterranean. Person 1268's life can be imagined to some extent as involving food and drink, sometimes in festivities and communal occasions at temples and hypogea, as involving rituals connected to the times of year and to life and death, and to her ancestors, and as involving a degree of illness, physical pain, and hardship. Whilst inhabiting very different worlds, these are all aspects of life we have in common with her.

PART II

THE BRONZE AGE

As the Neolithic Mediterranean gave way to the Bronze Age, population grew and a host of complex states appeared in Egypt, the Levant and Mesopotamia, Anatolia and the Aegean; the Mediterranean would become more connected than ever across this period. In the history of ancient Egypt, it is more usual to think in terms of 'kingdoms', 'intermediate periods' and of course 'dynasties' than the distinctions of Bronze and Iron.[1] The Egyptian state was formed in the late Predynastic period of 3200–3000 BC, and stretched 1,000 km from the Nile Delta in the north to Aswan in the south.[2] Writing also appeared at this time, used to label goods and later for royal inscriptions. In the Early Dynastic period, when the First and Second dynasties ruled, its capital was the city of Memphis, just to the south of the Delta, from where the all-powerful pharaoh ruled Lower and Upper Egypt. Egypt relied on the annual Nile flood to support its agriculture and a centralised administration and tax system was developed. It is near the beginning of the Old Kingdom that we meet Queen Merneith (Chapter 4); she was alive at a time long before the building of the great pyramids of the Fourth Dynasty pharaohs (2613–2494 BC) that we so associate with ancient Egypt, although the centralised and organised Egyptian society formed in earlier times was key in making them possible.

Somewhat east of the Mediterranean, but part of the regional milieu, lay other kingdoms of varying size and clout, including Ebla and Mari on the upper Euphrates, where archives of clay tablets have survived to reveal life in the Middle Bronze Age.[3] These states competed with and fought each other and variously came under the influence and even rule of bigger states. In the late third millennium BC, trade already went back and forth from the Mediterranean southeast down the Euphrates river to the Persian Gulf. When Sargon created the Akkadian Empire, c. 2300 BC, Mari, which was far upriver, at first managed to remain independent. Sargon's grandson Naram-Sin, however, extended the empire so that it stretched from the shores of the Persian Gulf to the northeastern Mediterranean coast, where precious cedar trees grew.

Mari survived and was ruled by governors who outlasted the Akkadian Empire; the city remained independent of the succeeding Third Dynasty of Ur, who put together the next Mesopotamian super-state and continued as a key trade artery. At the end of the nineteenth century BC, the line of governors ended and a king called Yahdun-Lim defeated seven neighbouring kings to create a new bigger state with Mari as its capital. He built canals, temples, and fortifications and also sent a military expedition as far as the Mediterranean. After an interlude under the control of Shamshi-Adad, Yahdun-Lim's heir Zimri-Lim came to power. He ruled Mari in the first half of the eighteenth-century BC, and it is in his grand palace that we meet his daughters Šimatum and Kirum (Chapter 5). Mari did not survive for much longer – it was destroyed by Hammurabi of Babylon.

The centralised Egyptian Old Kingdom fragmented into the First Intermediate Period, where local governors ruled the various parts of Egypt. Mentuhotep (2055–2004 BC) reunited Egypt once again, forming the Middle Kingdom, comprising the Eleventh, Twelfth, and partly the Thirteenth dynasties. Whilst not a period of great pyramids, it was a time in which Egyptian 'classical' literature was composed – *The Tale of Sinuhe* and other stories. 'The Middle Kingdom was an age of tremendous invention, great vision, and colossal projects' as well as a time in which there was more widespread literacy and a greater sense of the individual.[4] This period too ended with state breakdown and the Second Intermediate Period.

Following the Second Intermediate Period, Ahmose reunified Egypt (the New Kingdom – 1550–1069 BC) and founded the Eighteenth Dynasty. He and later pharaohs pushed Egyptian influence up the Levantine coast almost to Ugarit and south into Nubia. There was also contact with the Aegean and at this time Minoan-style frescoes appear in Egypt. In this Late Bronze Age Egypt, in the fifteenth century BC, we meet the Pharaoh Hatshepsut, who herself looked overseas for opportunities to enrich Egypt (Chapter 8). Perhaps the most famous of the New Kingdom pharaohs is the Nineteenth Dynasty Ramesses II ('the Great'), whose long reign lasted much of the thirteenth century BC. During his rule, Egypt would come to blows with the other major power of the eastern Mediterranean – the Hittites, under their king Muwattalli II. Fighting over influence and empire in the lands of Syria and Palestine, they faced off in the dramatic battle of Qadesh in 1274 BC.

In an Egyptian tale from two centuries later, *The Tale of Wenamun*, we hear of a woman called Hatiba, a princess of Alashiya, Cyprus (Chapter 11). Cyprus was an important centre of copper production and trade in the Late Bronze Age, notable for the ox-hide ingots that were widely exported, and Cypriot ships are thought to have carried goods and people around the eastern Mediterranean region. The kings of Alashiya (though we do not know if Alashiya comprised the whole island or just part of it) maintained diplomatic contacts with Egypt, the Hittites, and others through letters – clay analysis showing their Cypriot origin.[5] The letters may have been sent from Kalavasos-*Ayios Dhimitrios*, in south central Cyprus, a town that flourished between 1300 and 1200 BC.[6] Here we find archaeological evidence for powerful women that may ultimately have inspired the figure of Hatiba.

The Hittite kingdom, which became Egypt's great northern rival, was based in central Anatolia, with its temple-laden capital city at Hattusa (Boğazköy).[7] Its first well-attested king was Hattusili I (1650–1620 BC), whose descendants and relations ruled until around 1200 BC, when the last known king, Suppiluliuma II, disappears from history. From their city of Hattusa, the Hittite kings went on to conquer huge swathes of territory, fighting in the west as far as the Aegean and far to the south and east into Syria; they oversaw, influenced, and interfered in the politics and policies of the territories and vassal kingdoms they controlled. Politics at the heart of the kingdom were not always straightforward and there was constant infighting within the royal family – the extended family constantly grew through the generations and several kings made laws to pare it down. In 1272 BC, Muwattalli's son Urhi-Teshub became king – but after only five years on the throne, he was deposed by his uncle Hattusili III, Muwattalli's brother, and sent into exile in Syria (he even ended up in Egypt at one point). Hattusili's wife was Puduhepa, who played an important role in the kingdom in her own right, even corresponding with Ramesses II (Chapter 9).

In the Aegean, the 'Minoan' inhabitants of Crete had developed central places for feasting and drinking in the later third millennium BC and began building 'palaces', or courtyard-centred complexes, around 2000 BC, Knossos always seeming to be the most important, though by no means the only important centre – other palaces existed at Phaistos, Malia, and Zakros (and probably several other places).[8] There were probably several states on Protopalatial Crete. There were also towns such as Gournia, 'villas' and peak sanctuaries. Despite the use of the word 'palace', there is no clear indication of kingship on Minoan Crete and various suggestions have been made for how Cretan society was organised, including for the existence of influential 'high priestesses', for example.[9]

Crete was in contact with Egypt and other parts of the eastern Mediterranean – Minoan-style frescoes have been found in various locations outside of Crete.[10] Cretans are also depicted in Egyptian paintings and referred to in texts as *Keftiu*. At the end of the Protopalatial period the palaces were destroyed, but they were soon rebuilt. During the Neopalatial period, the eruption of Thera (Santorini) may have affected the island, perhaps predominantly because of ash fall in the east but also the psychological impact of the eruption, which must have been awesome. However, it was not until slightly later that there was a general destruction of palace sites, excepting Knossos, in the fifteenth century BC. It is in the context of later Minoan culture that we meet the Priestess of Anemospilia, caught frozen in a dramatic moment of history (Chapter 7).

Whilst the Minoan palace society broke down in the Late Bronze Age, the palace societies of Mycenaean Greece continued – perhaps taking advantage of or even causing the eclipse of the Cretan states.[11] The Mycenaean culture came out of the Middle Bronze Age culture of mainland Greece and in its earliest phase is known from the wealthy Shaft Graves of Mycenae discovered by Heinrich Schliemann and now, from Pylos, the famous Griffin Warrior grave.[12] Over time, some elite individuals, families, or factions managed to put together larger units, which eventually could be called states, with institutions of kingship and literate administrations, some aspects of which developed under Cretan cultural influence. Because of this, we possess some information from within, from the Linear B tablets preserved at some sites, especially Knossos and Pylos. In the Pylos texts we meet two late thirteenth century Mycenaean women from Messenia, the priestesses Eritha, and Karpathia (Chapter 10).

Contemporary with the Cretan Minoans, the Early Bronze Age Argaric culture developed from c. 2200 BC across a large part of southeastern Iberia.[13] It covered a much greater area than Crete: some 33,000 km^2 compared with less than 8,500 km^2. With elites based in hilltop sites such as El Argar and La Bastida, over the course of the next few centuries chiefdoms and state societies were formed; there may have been more variety of ethnicity, language, political organisation, and so on within the culture zone than we can easily detect from the Argaric culture package. It is at the site of La Almoloya that we meet the subject of Chapter 6, 'the woman of La Almoloya', who may have been the ruler of one such state.

The Argarics left no texts and, whereas there are fragments of Bronze Age memories in the later Greek tradition, whatever memory survived of them in later Iberia is lost. However, archaeology has revealed much about Argaric settlements, burials, crafts, and agriculture, although there are different overall interpretations and narratives. The Argaric states collapsed around 1550 BC and the hilltop settlements and the Argaric style of burial within buildings were abandoned.[14] Archaeologists have suggested that an extractive and oppressive socio-political system combined with negative health impacts of a diet increasingly based on barley and also the worsening environmental impacts of intensive agriculture in an arid area may have led to the overthrow of the system.

The collapse of the Hittite kingdom and the palace states of Mycenaean Greece, and widespread destructions in the eastern Mediterranean around 1200 BC, are a convenient point at which to mark the end of the Late Bronze Age and the very beginnings of the Early Iron Age.[15]

4

MERNEITH

Ancient Egypt has fascinated the modern west since Napoleon's campaigns took soldiers and scholars to the land of the Nile in 1798; the French and British came to blows there and many French discoveries were delivered into British possession – perhaps most notably the bilingual Rosetta Stone, which was key to the decipherment of ancient Egyptian hieroglyphics. This rather small black stone tablet can still be seen in the British Museum. The story of the discovery of Tutankhamun's tomb by Howard Carter in the early twentieth century remains a television and publishing favourite, and there have been various tours of authentic objects, including to London's Saatchi Gallery in 2019–2020; pyramids and mummies are more than ever objects of fascination and fantasy – and everyone knows the name Cleopatra.[1] But the line of pharaohs stretched back far longer than Cleopatra and King Tut – it is sobering to recall that we are closer in time to Cleopatra than she was to the first pharaohs – and there have been many other intriguing and much more ancient discoveries in Egypt.

Fans of Hollywood movies, for example, may have seen the 2002 movie *The Scorpion King*, but may not know that there really was an early ruler, from the predynastic period, that Egyptologists call the Scorpion king – he is known from an inscribed mace head, perhaps a symbol of his power, found in 1898 by James Quibell and Frederick Green in the Temple of Horus at Hierakonpolis.[2] The mace head shows the king, bigger than the other figures, with a scorpion inscribed next to him. The film is complete fantasy, though, and hardly anything is known about king Scorpion, not even his true name. When he ruled, Egypt was probably still divided at least into an Upper (southern) kingdom and a Lower (northern) kingdom, though quite possibly with a greater scattering of local rulers.[3]

At the same time, Quibell and Green also found evidence of another slightly better-known early ruler from Upper Egypt, Narmer – king Catfish; there was again an inscribed mace head and also a palette, a carved u-shaped slab of stone. One side of the palette shows Narmer wearing the white crown of Upper Egypt and smiting his enemy, a pose that was to become a standard image of all the later pharaohs of Egypt; the other side shows him wearing the red crown of Lower Egypt and inspecting the battle-fallen. His name was inscribed in a box at the top of the palette, similar to later naming practices where the royal name was written inside a *serekh* – a box representing the entrance to a palace. But 'Narmer' may not have been the king's name as such. Toby Wilkinson comments that 'Narmer' does not make sense in Egyptian, rather the symbol 'catfish' may have been, like the symbol 'scorpion', a deliberate and meaningful comment about the ruler.[4] The Narmer palette, an early treasure, links predynastic traditions – Narmer's 'name' - with dynastic ones such as the smiting pose and the *serekh* that would become fixed in Egyptian culture for millennia.

Whatever Narmer's name was, one of his strategies was to marry well and wisely. As in so many cultures, a political marriage could benefit both parties and their families and increase civil, political, and social stability by reducing friction amongst elites and regions. Narmer married a woman called Neithhotep.[5] Whilst the 'Neith' part of her name could imply that she was a northerner, Neith being the patron god of Sais, a city in the Nile Delta, it was also quite a popular element in early royal women's names. Could this have been a strategic marriage in which Neithhotep played a pivotal role in unifying the north and south, providing inside knowledge of the Delta, and mediating between north and south with her husband? Possibly. But it is also possible she was the daughter or relative of an ally (or rival) closer to home, perhaps a chief of Naqada. She may have lived in Thinis, where Narmer came from, the capital of Upper Egypt and near Abydos, but could also have lived in the developing city of Memphis, located just south of the Nile Delta, which connected Upper and Lower Egypt.[6]

Neithhotep has been associated with a major mastaba tomb at Naqada, discovered in 1896 by Jacques de Morgan, so grand that it was named the Royal Tomb.[7] It has since disappeared due to erosion and is only known from its early study. The tomb was around 54 x 27 m and built of mud-brick; the outer walls had recesses rather than being simple straight walls. Inside, at ground level, were the burial chamber and storage rooms. Although the tomb had been robbed in ancient times, some objects were still found; on these were the names of Narmer, Neithhotep, and Aha, the traditional unifier of Egypt and the first king of the First Dynasty. At first, the Royal Tomb was thought to belong to Aha, but his tomb was later found at Abydos, and so it is widely believed to be that of Neithhotep.[8] One indication of her high rank, and possibly that she ruled as pharaoh, if on behalf of her young son after Narmer's death, is the appearance of her name in a *serekh* surmounted by crossed arrows, the symbol of Neith, rather than a kingly Horus falcon *serekh*.

The First Dynasty of Egypt, from Aha on, ruled from c. 3000 to 2890 BC, several centuries before the pyramid age began with Sneferu around 2600 BC. At this time, explains Miroslav Bárta, 'a despotic form of government was asserting itself' and 'society was slowly transforming' from a land of small polities to something increasingly centralised.[9] Neithhotep had played her role in this beginning, along with Narmer, and soon another queen, Merneith, was to rule, again apparently on behalf of her young son, Den.[10] But the story of Merneith has its own peculiar mysteries that have puzzled Egyptologists.

In 1899–1900, the pioneering archaeologist W. M. Flinders Petrie was in the field at Abydos in southern Egypt. He had chosen to work there, at Umm el-Qa'ab, because previous discoveries had suggested that it was a very important site of early royal tombs. It was also a site that had suffered at the hands of earlier visitors; Petrie noted in the introduction to his publication – 'the results in this present volume are therefore only the remains which have escaped the lust of gold, the fury of fanaticism, and the greed of speculators'.[11] For an archaeologist, he ruminated, 'nothing is more disheartening than being obliged to gather results out of the fraction left behind by past plunderers'.

In an area already dug with pits by earlier excavators, Petrie's systematic clearing revealed the plan and what was left of a hitherto undiscovered tomb, given the designation Tomb Y.[12] Tomb Y was nestled amongst other royal burials – between those of pharaohs Djet and Anedjib, and behind that of pharaoh Den. Petrie found a carefully built rectangular central chamber around 9.14 x 6.4 m, with eight smaller rectangular chambers for offerings around it. This structure was surrounded by an incomplete rectangle of smaller chambers, for subsidiary burials, with the southwest corner left open for people to enter the courtyard space these created. In the central chamber, two stone stelae were found, the intact one bore the name Merneith (Figure 4). The stele was pictured in pride of place before the book's title page. 'It can hardly be doubted', wrote Francis Llewellyn Griffith in his chapter of Petrie's volume, 'that Mer-Neit . . . was a king, yet no title nor any other name for him has yet been discovered'.[13] In Petrie's list of kings at the beginning of the book, Merneith is listed as the probable fourth king of the First Dynasty, corresponding to the kings listed in ancient king-lists that give us the dynastic roll-call, albeit with a different name. Pharaoh Merneith had been discovered.

But then, four decades later, on 22 November 1946, *The New York Times* reported the discovery of a new tomb at Saqqara, in northern Egypt (south of

FIG. 4 Stele of Merneith. Egyptian Museum in Cairo. Wikimedia Commons. Photo by Walaa

Giza, Abusir, and Memphis), by Walter Emery, who had been working there since 1935. The headline read '1st Dynasty Tomb is Found in Egypt – Burial Chamber Is Believed to Be That of Queen Merneith'.[14] The article reported that the archaeologists had found a large brick chamber with some plaster still intact on the walls and that there were even the remains of a large wooden coffin – and bones. The tomb had been robbed and burned, but some pots found in the lowest levels of the excavation bore the name 'Merneith'. A seal from the tomb showed Merneith's name in a *serekh*. The tomb was large, with external dimensions of 16 x 42.6 m. A boat grave was found in the north of the area, a brick enclosure built around a real wooden boat almost 18 m in length.[15] Emery had in fact found a series of graves with boat graves, which, given their size, their architecture, and the grave goods found, led him to think that they were royal burials of the First and Second dynasties. Here was queen Merneith in Tomb 3503.

Two tombs – one belonging to a male pharaoh called Merneith at Abydos and another at Saqqara belonging to queen called Merneith; what could it mean? Was Merneith a man or a woman? Was Merneith a pharaoh, male or female, or just a royal wife or consort? Which tomb, Tomb Y at Abydos or Tomb 3503 at Saqqara was the real one?

Between Petrie's and Emery's times, advances were made in the understanding of Egyptian hieroglyphics that meant Merneith's name had to be interpreted as that of a woman – 'Beloved of the Goddess Neith'.[16] Also a seal of the First Dynasty pharaoh Den was found, which named Merneith as 'Mother of the King'. This demonstrated beyond doubt that Merneith was a woman and also suggested that she was probably the wife of the pharaoh Djet and Den's mother. But then what about Merneith's status? At first considered as a male pharaoh, her status as a female was then downplayed. Joyce Tyldesley wrote that 'instantly, on the basis of cultural expectations rather than sound archaeological evidence, Meryt-Neith was re-classified as an unusually powerful queen-consort'.[17] When Merneith was male, he was a pharaoh, a ruler, but as a woman she was only a consort. Susan Kelly also notes an inherent androcentric bias in studies of the Early Dynastic Period and concluded that 'archaeological remains suggest that Neithhotep and Meretneith possessed the major indices of Early Egyptian rulers'.[18]

The problem of Merneith's tomb was part of a wider issue about the location of the First Dynasty pharaoh's graves. There were two competing hypotheses, as summarised by Emery: (1) the tombs were at Abydos and nobles were buried at Saqqara, and (2) the royal tombs were at Saqqara and the Abydos monuments were cenotaphs or 'southern' tombs.[19] Emery believed the second hypothesis to be the correct one: that the actual royal burials were at Saqqara, though he added that 'at the present stage of our research it would be rash indeed to make any categorical statement'.[20] There were several points in favour of Emery's conclusion. One was that it would seem likely that royal tombs would be located near the new royal capital, which was at Memphis. Emery also suggests that it would be odd for pharaohs resident in Memphis to allow nobles to build tombs in Saqqara that were more impressive than their own in Abydos. Solar boats, as found at Saqqara, were restricted to the tombs of pharaohs, used by them and by gods to navigate the afterlife.[21]

This practice of having two funerary monuments may sound odd – a body can only occupy one space. But given the fact that Egypt had only fairly recently been unified, it makes sense: a monument at the capital (Memphis, Saqqara) and a monument at the ancestral city (Thinis, Abydos), itself the capital of an earlier, smaller 'state' governed by the ancestors of the First Dynasty.[22] Abydos was important as the burial place of the god Osiris.[23] Emery pointed out that Third and Fourth Dynasty pharaohs did the same; even a few later pharaohs built northern and southern tombs – with the cenotaphs at Abydos.[24] First Dynasty pharaohs will have been concerned to maintain and reinforce the integration of Upper and Lower Egypt under their rule, and one strategy may have been to present themselves in Saqqara and

Abydos, new and old centres.[25] Tyldesley has supported the idea that Abydos was the main burial site of Merneith but proposed that a second tomb at Saqqara was built as 'additional funerary monument'.[26]

Writing around a decade after Emery, Egyptologist Barry Kemp argued in favour of the first hypothesis: that the real royal burial ground was Abydos.[27] He pointed out that the attribution of the Saqqara tombs to pharaohs was uncertain because other names were also found in the tombs, the names of officials; other factors had to be considered. One key support for his view is that, when considered with their enclosures, the Abydos 'funerary palaces' were much bigger than the tombs at Saqqara. Bestock has added that the tombs at Abydos also correspond to funerary enclosures found in the North Cemetery area of the site, closer to the ancient city.[28] These enclosures may have been the forerunners of 'mortuary temples' of later pharaohs. This confirms that the 'funerary provision', as Snape expresses it, at Abydos is greater than that at Saqqara.[29]

Kemp also points out that the Abydos tombs had more subsidiary burials – the Saqqara tomb of Merneith had twenty-one but the Abydos tomb had eighty. These subsidiary burials were probably royal attendants sacrificed in order to accompany and serve their master/mistress in the afterlife, a practice that was discontinued after the First Dynasty. He suggests that it is only at Abydos that the sense of a royal entourage is created by these burials.[30] The Saqqara tombs, he argued, were not impressive enough for rulers, if they were royal the 'kingship in the 1st Dynasty must have counted for much less than the later dynasties', but he thinks it clear that they were for officials and private individuals; pharaohs were buried at Abydos.[31]

Work at Abydos in the late 1980s and early 1990s by David O'Connor has added more evidence to the picture.[32] His team discovered a series of boat graves at Abydos that date to the Early Dynastic Period – the First and Second Dynasties. He suggested that they may have originally been built for pharaoh Djer, the second king of the First Dynasty.[33] If the identification of the Abydos tombs as royal is correct, the implication is that members of the high elite, buried at Saqqara, could also have boat graves – that they were not exclusive to royalty in early times as they were later. However, the form of the tombs suggest that the Early Dynastic rulers had not yet monopolised some aspects of funerary practice that would later be exclusively royal. Traditions, after all, did change and develop over time, even if Egyptian culture became strongly conservative.

The matter of the First Dynasty burials appears to have been settled in favour of Umm el-Qa'ab, Abydos, where they continue from earlier Predynastic royal burials.[34] But why were such impressive burials allowed near the new capital of Memphis at Saqqara? It is possible that the rule of the early pharaohs was not yet tight enough to ensure a monopoly on lavish status signalling.

It is also possible that the Saqqara burials are the visible expression of the 'contract' between the ruler and high-status officials who were necessary to the exercise of power and control – royals at sacred Abydos, officials at administrative Memphis. In a different view, Ellen Morris' theory is that the Saqqara tombs were built by the early pharaohs for other members of the royal family, not that they were the tombs of officials.[35] This is what a later pharaoh, Khufu, did for his brothers, in-laws, and other relatives. Such provision would allow a pharaoh to control the location and level of display by family members who could be rivals and at the same time to represent the family at Memphis.

Neithhotep and Merneith, at this early stage of Egyptian history, may have exercised supreme power as pharaohs rather than 'just' as queens or consorts, even if they did this as regents. A regent must already have some recognised status and be thought capable of ruling in terms of their intellect, the respect they command, and their political nous. Since no pharaoh could rule alone and without support and co-operation, Neithhotep and Merneith were clearly not considered either inappropriate or incapable of rule. By the use of *serekhs* and the location and scales of their tombs, they were very much the equal of male pharaohs.

It may not be possible to write a biography of Merneith herself, or her predecessor Neithhotep; there are no words, no bodies, and no histories, but the archaeology demonstrates their existence and their importance. At the very least, it says that women in the earliest phases of Egyptian history were able to enjoy the highest status and command the greatest respect – and we remember them.

5

ŠIMATUM AND KIRUM

Arranged marriages have been commonplace through history and, according to Kennon Rider and Ann Swallow, are still the norm for around half the population of the world.[1] They can take several forms, for example, when parents and family select one or more potential marriage candidates, but the child can make a choice between them or refuse a particular individual. An arranged marriage can also be a forced marriage, in which one or both parties are given no choice in their marriage partner. In western culture, arranged marriages tend to be viewed negatively now because a cultural emphasis is placed on romantic love as the main factor in making a 'proper' or successful marriage; arranged marriages have, from a western perspective, been seen as primitive and inherently unhappy.[2] However, 'successful' or at least enduring marriages are more common in arranged marriage cultures, although this may be due to the difficulty and stigma of divorce; love may also develop in arranged marriages and is not unimportant. Marriage in these terms can sometimes be thought of as a partnership and a joint project to be worked on. It can be a way of building and cementing alliances between individuals and families, controlling property and wealth, and of producing legitimate children.

A common practice of rulers over the years has been to arrange the marriage of family members into other royal or senior houses – and this is something both parents, male and female, might set up.[3] A son or daughter might be married to the child of an ally or rival to defuse potential conflict, give status, create a strong bond, and forge a union for the next generation through shared children. Thus civil, economic, and political benefits could result from arranged marriages and these usually took precedence over feelings. In the ancient Bronze Age, the role of women in diplomacy was central and underpinned international relations.[4] Ancient Egypt was unusual in that pharaohs refused to marry off daughters to kings abroad, though pharaohs and male family members married the daughters of foreign kings.[5] We also find details about marriage practices in the cuneiform tablets, letters and documents, found in their thousands at the ancient Syrian city of Mari.[6] In these tablets, we find the story of two women of Mari, Kirum and Šimatum, whose arranged marriages were not happy ones.

Mari was located on the Upper Euphrates river, but the kingdom's reach stretched – or so its rulers occasionally liked to think – to the shores of the Mediterranean. Mari's most famous ruler, Zimri-Lim, who ruled in the first half of the eighteenth century BC, probably visited the Mediterranean port city of Ugarit, as did his father and earlier rulers.[7] Zimri-Lim had managed to win his father's kingdom back by force, with the help of the powerful Yarim-Lim, king of Yamhad, whose daughter, Shibtu, he had married.[8] As part of the marriage rites, messengers were sent from Mari to Aleppo, the Yamhad capital, to place a veil on the head of the princess.[9] Near Eastern women, at least in some kingdoms, may have had to wear veils outside the home to conform to tradition, though the evidence is very limited.[10] Mari was by this time a centuries-old city that had had its share of ups and downs; after a lull, and then something of a renaissance in the Middle Bronze Age of the early second millennium BC, the city was destroyed by Hammurabi of Babylon in around 1760 BC. That was the end of king Zimri-Lim and of the city of Mari.

As befit a king of the age, Zimri-Lim had a large family, which included 'two main wives, twelve secondary wives, and numerous concubines'.[11] According to the sources, the king was surrounded by women – he appears to have had no brothers or sons that survived, but had 'a large number of aunts, family of aunts, sisters, wives, daughters, and concubines ... and he was constantly bombarded by their letters'.[12] Among this royal family of women were two of his twenty-three or more daughters, Šimatum and the younger Kirum.

The heart of Zimri-Lim's kingdom and the home of his family was his palace. Zimri-Lim's palace, where Šimatum and Kirum likely grew up, was a site worth seeing. One tablet records a visitor's impression. It says:

> To Zimri-Lim communicate the following: thus says your brother Hammurabi (of Yamhad): The king of Ugarit has written me as follows: 'Show me the palace of Zimri-Lim! I wish to see it.' With this same courier I am sending on his man.[13]

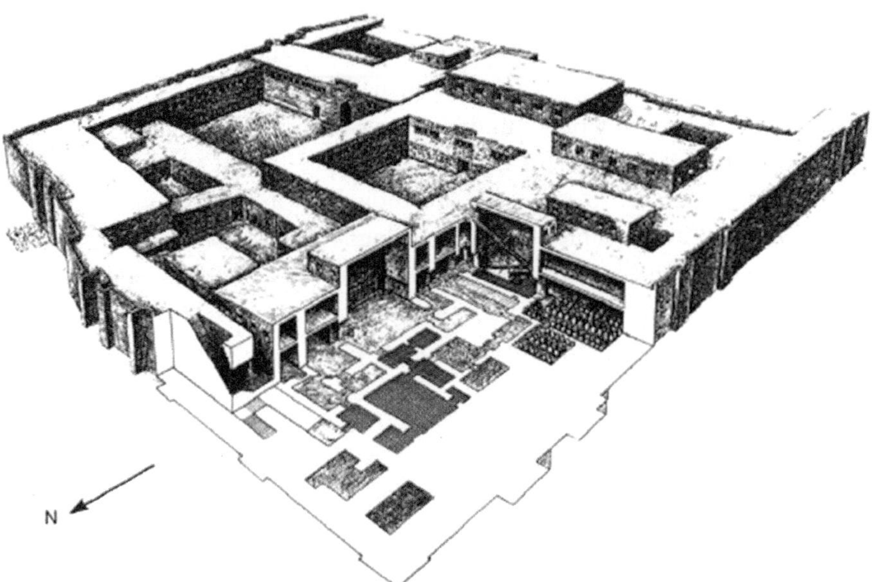

FIG. 5 Palace of Zimri-Lim. From page 38, 'Eblouissante richesse de Mari sur l'Euphrate.' Dossiers d'Archéologie 80, February 1984. Reproduced by kind permission of Dossiers d'Archéologie

Though we do not know why the king of Ugarit wanted to know about Zimri-Lim's palace (Figure 5), it could be that he wanted tips on the latest architectural and decorative styles amongst his peer kings – visits by all kinds of people, from physicians to acrobats, to other king's courts and cities were common; the Mesopotamian region and the eastern Mediterranean already formed an interconnected world.

The palace, excavated from the 1930s, was impressive. It had more than 260 rooms on the ground floor alone and its walls were as high as 12 metres.[14] It may not have been the biggest of the eastern palaces, but it was certainly very grand indeed. The palace was decorated with fresco paintings, including the famous 'Investiture of Zimri-Lim', from the wall of court 106, which shows the king (or an earlier king), worshipping the goddess Ishtar and being given the symbols of kingship, the rod and ring, by her.[15] It was the focal point for politics and royal-religious activities.

The daughters must have run around this maze, taking in the art, which included an almost life-size stone statue of a goddess that was found broken, perhaps destroyed along with the palace, and exploring and playing hide and seek. Little is known of the childhood of girls at the time, but Marten Stol notes that children 'played with skipping-ropes, dolls, knuckle-bones, bows and arrows, and practised a sort of hockey'.[16] Girls certainly played games; one badly damaged fragment of tablet states, presumably from a boy's perspective 'I can do the games of girls', which is followed by some examples. In another tablet, a goddess laments that 'I never knew the play of maidens, I never knew the romping of children'. Girls also danced to music. Some women could read and write, so there was clearly education available for a few; girls would have heard the traditional myths and stories of their culture and perhaps history too – especially for Zimri-Lim's daughters – which would have formed and enriched their worldview.

In year one of Zimri-Lim's kingship, his daughter Šimatum was married to a vassal named Haya-Sumu, king of Illansura. As part of this marriage, which was likely made to help cement ties between the two cities, a rich dowry was provided, which included gold and silver jewellery – finger and ear rings, bracelets and anklets, plus five silver and thirty bronze vases, clothing and fabric, a bed, fifteen chairs, some trays, eight attendants, including a female scribe called Šima-ilat, and eight other women.[17] The inventory is recorded on tablet ARM 22 322 (ARM stands for *Archives royales de Mari*, one of the series in which the tablets are published, the numbers indicate the volume and text).

The dowry may have marked an auspicious start to the marriage, but it is possible that Šimatum was already suffering from health problems of some kind. A tablet sent to Zimri-Lim by his ambassador, Yamsum, stated that 'the god of my lord mutilated her fingers and epilepsy is plaguing her'.[18] This was presented as a punishment for Šimatum's behaviour – slandering her father so that he 'had to face god on her account'. Lingering illness, thought to be life-threatening, might also account for why Kirum, another of Zimri-Lim's daughters was married to Haya-Sumu less than two years later. It could also have been for more practical political reasons – on one occasion, Yamsum apparently reminded Haya-Sumu, who was not always co-operative, of the honour done to him by this double marriage.

Whatever the reasons, the situation was a difficult one for the sisters, and here the tablets offer a glimpse into the personal and emotional life of a young woman of the Middle Bronze Age who experienced an arranged marriage. In one letter to Zimri-Lim, Kirum asks her father to 'set me on a queen's throne'; this is understood to indicate that she may have been being sidelined at Haya-Sumu's court or that she was somehow not being treated as she expected to be.[19] The letter also explains Kirum's desire to return to Mari 'to offer sacrifices to the gods of my father, so that I may prosper there'. Although ready to leave Illansura, Haya-Sumu was making it difficult for her – Kirum sent his written refusal to her request to leave on to her father. Haya-Sumu's reason for refusing is interesting in itself; he pointed out that if both of them were away from the city, there would be no one to take care of it – it shows that a wife could take control of more than just the household in the king's absence.[20] Kirum exclaimed to her father 'act to avoid hurting my feelings; it is upon you alone that I depend'.

Other letters are more worrying. Kirum explains in one letter that she was being effectively held captive or at least being restricted in her activities: 'In a fancy house, I am held until death, as you already know.' She then reports that Haya-Sumu said directly to her 'are you posted here as a resident-commissioner? Since I plan to have you killed, he should come, "your Star (Zimri-Lim)", and take you back'.[21] Another letter describes a murder and a cover-up – and here Mari expert Jack Sasson suggests the words may be Kirum's own – 'I swear it by my lord and by myself: he (Haya-Sumu) killed Dimri-Hammu. They say, "A lion killed him and 2 women as well.' My lord should listen to this matter.'[22] Dimri-Hammu may have been one of Kirum's servants.

Yamsum, the ambassador, reported on Kirum's situation too – how Haya-Sumu threatened to kill Kirum with a bronze dagger, if she refused to accompany him on a journey - and remarked on how dangerous he could be. He also wrote to Zimri-Lim on Kirum's behalf, explaining how she had said 'Haya-Sumu has never cared for me' and, perhaps desperately that 'since my lord (Zimri-Lim) cares nothing about me, either a woman kills herself or she jumps from the roof'. Whether she was literally threatening suicide or using a figure of speech is an open question. But Kirum repeatedly asked for help to return to Mari – even saying she was not asking for a fancy room in the palace – just a refuge.

Despite this unhappy situation, and we can only imagine how difficult it must have been for Kirum, she gave birth to a son around four years into the marriage. Šimatum had twins, a boy and a girl, but the date of their birth is uncertain. Both sisters shared a volatile husband and had royal sons; this might have complicated matters further.

Šimatum was evidently concerned about her own position at Haya-Sumu's court. In one letter to her father, she asks 'Why do they continue to slander me before my lord (Haya-Sumu)? Moreover, incredible charges (against me) are proposed in my lord's presence .... My lord (Zimri-Lim) should send me a (cylinder) seal. He must not refuse it for me.'[23] Was Šimatum also being criticised and sidelined like Kirum? The lack of writing on the cylinder seal she received in her dowry apparently opened her up to mockery over her lack of seniority, and she explained that a new lapis-lazuli seal with her name on it would prevent her being picked on in this way.

Although we might expect that the sisters would have supported each other, the evidence suggests that they did not get on. One letter reports a dispute over a gardener, presumably whose gardener he was. And in Kirum's 'captivity letter' she also states that after Haya-Sumu threatened her Šimatum then took away her remaining servants and said, 'My Star (Zimri-Lim) may do what he wishes to me, for I mean to do what I wish to you.' Kirum describes her stress – 'my life is ebbing away in constantly listening to Šimatum's words.

If my lord does not fetch me back to Mari, I shall grasp my nose and jump from the roof'. It is possible that she was desperate enough to contemplate suicide.

Eventually, the situation was brought to an end. In year ten of Zimri-Lim's reign, Kirum, who had survived in Haya-Sumu's court for six or seven years, obtained a divorce, which was performed as a ritual: '[Haya-Sumu] cut my fringes in the presence of the kings, saying, "Go away to your father's house, I have looked away from my wife's face"'.[24] Even then, Kirum complains that Šimatum poached another woman from her retainers. At least Kirum got away.

The evidence from the tablets no doubt is only the tip of the iceberg – the stories of Kirum and Šimatum, as individuals, as royal daughters, as wives of Haya-Sumu, as sisters, played themselves out over years. Being a royal daughter, married off for a father's political ends and to produce children, did not always end happily. Life with new people in a new court in a new city brought with it understandable stresses and conflicts – the reconciling of one's own personal happiness with the responsibilities of a certain position that came with birth. Was Haya-Sumu as awful as he seems? That the sisters had children with him is no guarantee that he was ever even pleasant, let alone loving – the sex was expected at least for procreation – but we simply do not know his feelings or what was behind the actions and words that have come down to us. The relationship of the sisters too was certainly strained – but was it always so? The letters of Mari give us a tiny window through which to glimpse a part of the real lives of two royal women, Kirum and Šimatum, who lived almost four millennia ago, and even to hear their unhappy voices.

6

THE WOMAN OF LA ALMOLOYA

Whilst not especially well known in Anglophone culture,[1] the Early-Middle Bronze Age Spanish Argaric culture has long been regarded as important, sometimes even 'the most important Bronze Age culture in Western Europe', on a par with the better known Aegean cultures such as the Minoans, who were busy on Crete at the same time.[2] Discovered in Victorian times by the Belgian Siret brothers, Louis and Henri, and named for the site at El Argar (in Antas, Almeria), the culture has perhaps suffered from the lack of a classical connection – unlike the Minoans and Mycenaeans there is no hint of them in later sources. Developing from around 2200 BC, the Argaric culture came to comprise several state-level polities that collapsed c. 1550 BC; this ending might have been welcomed by many, as Argaric society is thought to have been quite hierarchical and extractive, and the socio-political system it developed gladly and totally forgotten.[3]

The Argaric culture came to global attention in 2021 when Spanish archaeologists working at the site of La Almoloya in Murcia, southeast Spain, led by Vicente Lull, published a paper in the journal *Antiquity*, which reported on the discovery of the remains of a woman with a silver diadem, who had been buried under the floor of a large building (Figure 6).[4] The media immediately took up the story: the *New York Times* headline asked 'She Was Buried With a Silver Crown. Was She the One Who Held Power?' while *National Geographic* stated 'Ancient woman may have been powerful European leader, 4,000-year-old treasure suggests', and in the UK *The Independent*'s – 'Women may have

FIG. 6 Grave 38, La Almoloya, Spain. Courtesy of the Research Group on Mediterranean Social Archaeoecology (ASOME), Autonomous University of Barcelona

ruled in bronze-age Spain, burial site suggests'.[5] The exciting work at La Almoloya, some of which had already been described in an article in *Current World Archaeology* in 2015, brought another ancient woman back to life in the modern world, but the surprise at her status reflected a lingering sexism.[6]

The skeletal remains of the woman of La Almoloya, from Grave 38 (Figure 6), were found together with those of a man; both had been placed inside a large pottery jar that was buried under the floor of Room H9 of Housing Complex 1 of the hilltop town.[7] The man may have died or at least been buried very slightly earlier than the woman. Radiocarbon dating of the left femurs of both the woman and the man suggest a date of death of around c. 1650 BC, well into the Argaric period and a century or so before its end. Their ages at death, according to analysis of the skeletal remains, including the crania and pelvis, were around 25–30 for the woman and 35–40 for the man. The couple were not blood relations, but DNA analysis has shown that they had a child together – a little girl, whose body was buried under another building close by. The human remains thus tell us about a family that were intimately connected to the site of La Almoloya in the Bronze Age.

Analysis of the woman's remains revealed some indication of her physical condition and health. She appears to have had a range of congenital and inherited conditions especially related to bone development. For example, she was born with eleven ribs rather than twelve, six rather than seven cervical vertebrae, the neck bones that support the head, and she had a spinal condition, which could have caused issues with back pain, posture, and mobility. She also had an unusually shortened left ulna, the long bone of the forearm, and thumb. Whilst some of these occurring in isolation might not have caused significant health problems, in combination it suggests she was suffering from some kind of syndrome. It also appears that she had developed a lung disease of some kind, which could have been the cause of her death.

Whatever health conditions the woman of La Almoloya was suffering from, the finds associated specifically with her burial clearly mark her out as of a high status. Lull and colleagues point out that most of the twenty-nine grave goods and all of the silver objects found were hers. The silver diadem that she was wearing, with disc shape pointing downwards, over her forehead, has been picked out, unsurprisingly, as the most notable find, but there were many other valuable items. There were four circular ear tunnels, two smaller ones of gold, with embossed dots, and two larger ones of silver. Silver spirals were wound through one each of the gold and silver plugs. Six more silver wire spirals were found near her head, which were probably hair accessories. She was also wearing two silver bracelets on her left arm and a silver ring on her left hand – which matched a ring found with the male skeleton.

One of the patterns that has been observed in Argaric graves is the presence of awls or leather punches exclusively in female burials. The awl may have been symbolic of female gender and social identity – corresponding to halberds and swords in male burials. The woman of La Almoloya also had an awl – of copper with a wooden handle. The handle was finished with three silver plates. Lull and colleagues note that 'as the silver coating provides no functional advantages, these awls probably communicated social distinction beyond their association with textile production'.[8] One of the small pots found with her, a carinated cup, had also been skilfully covered in part with sheets of silver. Silver seems to have been particularly associated with high status Argaric women.

The finds associated with the woman of La Almoloya are not the only indications of her status. Burials of the Argaric culture were typically made in the floors of buildings. Grave 38 at La Almoloya was dug into the floor of room H9 in a trapezoidal building (or series of buildings) known as 'Housing complex 1'.[9] The building had a total area of around 266 m^2 and probably included an upper storey. The finds from the house include objects related to the storage and grinding of grains and to the manufacture of metal goods and textiles – Lull and colleagues point out that 'the number and variety of production processes attested significantly exceeds what might usually be expected in Bronze Age domestic contexts'.[10]

Room H9 had few finds but was special in other ways. It had a large area, of around 70 m^2, and on the north wall was a podium behind a hearth; the rest of its inner walls were lined with benches on which perhaps fifty people could sit. Because of its size and range of functions, and because of the presence of the rich Grave 38 in room H9, Lull and colleagues suggest that Housing Complex 1 can be defined as a 'palace' – and this would be the oldest known palace in western Europe. But the benched room could be interpreted in several ways. It could have been something like a throne room or audience chamber – a room where a ruler would hold court and issue commands – or it could have been some kind of council chamber where a group of equals sat together in negotiation. The presence of the burial suggests that a ruler – or ruling couple – was key to the symbolic meaning given to the building by those who built and used it. La Almoloya could well have been a royal centre, though it might have only been one among several Argaric royal centres – others including probably La Bastida, 35 km to the southwest and El Argar 150 km southwest.

Grave 38 is not the first evidence of important women in the Argaric Bronze Age of southeastern Spain. In the earliest excavations by the Sirets at El Argar in 1883–1884, four silver diadems were found – they published illustrations of these along with other grave goods in their 1887 book *Les Premiers âges du métal dans le Sud-Est de l'Espagne.*[11] Excavating at Gatas in 1886, Louis Siret and Pedro Flores found the remains of a woman who had been buried in a large storage jar, which had been covered with three stone slabs (Tomb 2).[12] Analysis of the skull suggested that she was around forty-five years old, at the time of her death. She too was accompanied by rich grave goods – she was wearing a silver headband and jewellery of silver, copper, greenstone, bone, and shell. With the body were a copper knife and a copper awl with a wooden handle. Around the handle and attached with five silver rivets was a narrow sheet of silver, 22.2 cm in length. A few other wood- and silver-handled awls are known.[13]

At Fuente Álamo, another female burial, from Tomb 9, had a similar silver headband and a copper knife and awl. This woman also had silver jewellery, including bracelets and rings, and ivory and faience beads. She was buried with a man, whose grave goods included a sword. The age of this woman is not known, but two other rich female burials, one from Fuente Álamo (Tomb 111) and another from Cerro de la Encina, were of young women, aged 16–18; the latter was buried with a man of 22–24 years at death. A number of silver headbands and now six 'disc' diadems are known, five silver and one gold, all associated with women. The Sirets identified the women with diadems as 'souveraines ou femmes de chefs' – 'sovereigns or wives of chiefs'.[14]

By their nature, precious metal crowns and diadems, plain or decorated, visibly mark out an individual as special – this is as true in the modern world, where royalty still wear or are represented (on coins, for example) wearing crowns, tiaras, and the like. In the United Kingdom, the Crown Jewels, while not often worn or seen except on occasions of ceremony, remain a symbol of the nation. In the latter case, women or men can wear the same crown, which itself is used over the generations. Lull and colleagues use the term 'emblematic object' to refer to 'a symbol that materially represents ideas or social values, demanding some form of respect or action, from submission to veneration'.[15] In the case of El Argar, there are no comparable 'male' crowns or diadems, which raises the question of whether women – and the woman of Grave 38 – were the rulers of Argaric society, distinguished visibly in life and death by their own personal silvery headgear.

The Argarics were not literate, and so to learn about their society we must rely solely on what can be gleaned from the archaeology.[16] Geographically, Argaric culture was centred around the modern-day Spanish provinces of Almeria, in eastern Andalusia, and Murcia, though it grew to encompass some 33,000 km^2; some Argaric influences can be seen across the peninsula. Already noted is the habit of making intramural burials. What also seems clear from careful analysis of the funerary evidence is that burials reflected differentiated social identities – in terms of sex and social status. When child burials become more common, the suggestion is that status had also become institutionalised and heritable. Partly on this basis, Lull and colleagues have argued for a strongly hierarchical and exploitative socio-political system, in which a relatively small hereditary elite controlled agriculture and siphoned off produce for their own benefit.[17]

Aside from intramural burials, the Argaric culture is also characterised by an increased focus on strategically located hilltop settlements – another part of Lull and colleagues' argument.[18] An early example, also investigated by Lull and colleagues, is the site of La Bastida (Totona).[19] This hilltop citadel, which may have been home to a thousand inhabitants, overlooked and presumably controlled the fertile plains below. An initial phase of occupation, with a few stone buildings, ended in fiery destruction. In its second phase, around 2025–1900 BC, the site was completely reorganised and rebuilt. Impressive fortifications and towers of around 5–6 m in height were built on substantial foundations and a large dam with a capacity of 300,000 litres of water was constructed. In phase three, 1900–1600/1550 BC, the dam was enlarged with a wall of 21 x 5 m; buildings had a range of functions, including residential, agricultural storage, and the production of metal goods and textiles. Lull and colleagues argue that La Bastida was the capital of one of several Argaric states, with a territory of over 3000 km^2.[20] These state-level societies, it is suggested, had a privileged and wealthy land-owning class that dominated society and a subordinate class producing necessities.[21]

Other interpretations of the Argaric political geography and level of complexity have been proposed. For example, Arteaga has suggested that a mega-state ruled from El Argar, with other major sites being regional centres, with other smaller sites, including forts to ensure central control on the ground, under them.[22] A completely different interpretation by Ramos Millán is that the Argaric territory was dominated by chiefdoms in which kin rather than class was key. In this view, the hilltop settlements that controlled or represented only their immediate hinterlands indicate resistance to expansionist and state-building aspirations.[23] Aranda Jiménez, Montón-Subías, and Sánchez Romero point to local differences across the Argaric culture area – for example, there are (as yet) no silver or gold headbands or diadems from inland zones.[24] It has also been proposed that the silver diadems from El Argar and La Almoloya are so similar that they were manufactured together in one workshop – like the specialised workshop found at Tira del Lienzo (7 km from La Bastida).[25] Silver was of great importance in the culture, with over 700 silver objects found – many more than are known from contemporary western Europe.[26]

Older approaches to understanding ancient Iberian culture and explaining how it changed over time were based primarily on the supposed movements of tribes and ethnic groups, such as Bronze Age immigrants from the eastern Mediterranean or later the Celts, which were assumed to be represented by particular features of the material culture or in later times described by classical texts.[27] For some time, the idea of an indigenous cultural development came second to the diffusionist idea that complexity came from the east. With more accurate dating, and changing theoretical perspectives, it has become clear that the Argaric culture was early, complex, and indigenous; unlike cultures in the eastern Mediterranean, which were often in contact, there is very little evidence for Argaric contact with cultures further afield.

Was Argaric society matriarchal rather than patriarchal – or was there equal access to political and economic power regardless of sex? Possibly. Lull and others agree that the diadems certainly do mark out high elite individuals. They speculate that women may have been 'communicative emblems of executive power' or that 'ideological legitimation as well as – perhaps – the government, lay in certain female hands'.[28] There seems no inherent reason to deny that women could have ruled rather than just that they rubber-stamped a male ruler.

Whilst the diadems indicate women of status, they do not prove that Argaric society was a matriarchy or led by women. Whilst Lull and colleagues point out the lack of male 'emblematic objects' and the deposition of fewer male grave goods, it could be the case that high status or politically charged objects were not buried with men but passed through the generations. In book two of the *Iliad*, Homer sang of the gold-studded sceptre of Agamemnon, which had been passed down to him. Sceptres and swords of state have been used over long periods of time in various parts of the world to legitimise people, institutions, or events; the Manx sword of state, without which the Manx parliament, the world's oldest surviving parliament, cannot pass laws, has been in use for over five centuries, for example.[29] By burying a woman's diadem, those laying her to rest may have been honouring her; but at the same time, the act of putting the diadem out of sight could also be signifying that her power died with her.

7

THE PRIESTESS OF ANEMOSPILIA

Some of the best-known images from Bronze Age Greece are of Minoan women and goddesses portrayed on palace frescoes and on gold rings that often show religious scenes. The enigmatic Isopata gold ring, for example, shows a number of female figures in flounced skirts, with bare breasts, who appear to be dancing outside amongst the flowers – their arms gesticulating and bodies swaying.[1] Other evidence certainly suggests the importance of dance for Minoan women – terracotta models from Palaikastro, for example, show women dancing in circles accompanied by a lyre player.[2] These images conjure up a vivid picture of life on Crete, beliefs, and practices.

On the Isopata ring, an eye floats next to the central dancer, whom the other three face, and above her, small and seemingly descending from the sky, is another female figure. Many interpretations of the scene are possible, but it is usual to see the dancers as women, possibly but not necessarily priestesses, and the small figure as a goddess descending to present herself to (or possess?) her worshippers – perhaps specifically the woman next to the eye (if it is an eye). Is the scene a record of one particular event with real Minoan women? Or does it represent an idealised image of an event – some kind of ritual – that (some) Minoan women took part in? Or is it a scene from Minoan myth? Who wore the ring and used it as a seal, and what did its images mean to them? An object sparks many questions, some unanswerable.

Another influential image is a fresco painting first described by Arthur Evans in 1901 as 'a girl' with a 'large eye and brilliant vermeil lips' and 'the usual curling hair'. This ancient woman or goddess was soon transformed into the sophisticated and 'modern' lady and nicknamed 'La Parisienne' when she was vividly described in 1902 by French archaeologist Edmond Pottier:

> What would Racine or even Euripides have said, had they been introduced to this authentic image of a relative of Phaedra? . . . Her disheveled hair, the provocative 'kiss curl' on her fore-head, her enormous eye and sensual mouth, stained a violent red . . . the mass of ribbons tossed over her shoulder in a 'come-hither' gesture, this mixture of naive archaism and spicy modernism . . . this Pasiphae who looks like an habitue of Parisian bars – everything about this work conspires to amaze us; in sum, there is something about the discovery of this unheard-of art that we find stunning, even scandalous.[3]

'Described' is perhaps the wrong word – Pottier was interpreting the image and constructing a character, a context, and a narrative around it, turning it into an object of his male gaze, sexualising it; he makes the girl both beautiful and deliberately seductive.[4] Ancient Crete was not an innocent society, the image seemed to say – its better sort mirrored in their antics the sophisticated high society of fin de siècle Paris. 'La Parisienne' has continued to captivate modern viewers – an enigmatic Bronze Age Mona Lisa. As with the female figures on the Isopata ring, we can wonder who she was or was meant to represent, whether she was a real woman or just an idealised form.

One definitely real Minoan woman was found at a site called Anemospilia, the Caves of the Wind, which was discovered in 1979 by archaeologists John and Efi Sakellarakis, who were working at nearby Archanes.[5] Located high up on the northern slopes of Mount Juktas, with views to other mountain peaks and to Knossos and the sea below, the Anemospilia site is special for several reasons. Firstly, it revealed a finely constructed but small building, which used impressive ashlar blocks, often associated with Minoan palaces, and which was plastered in white and red on the outside. The results of excavation at the site hinted at a dramatic and grisly story about the supposedly 'peace-loving' and 'sophisticated' Minoans – evidence of natural disaster and human sacrifice .

The Anemospilia site, which dates to around 1700–1650 BC, was clearly a small temple, within a *temenos* (a sacred boundary); it was built on a north–south orientation with three parallel rectangular rooms and an adjoining antechamber.[6] In plan, it resembles a building known from representations in Minoan art – the tripartite shrine. One such shrine appears on a fresco from Knossos, with a crowd of people, both men and women, gathered around it; indeed, this may represent the actual tripartite shrine, topped with 'horns of consecration', which opened onto the central court of the palace.[7] The objects found within the Anemospilia building and its layout make this religious interpretation a fairly safe conclusion and hint at how the building was used and what the woman may have been doing there.

Each room of the Anemospilia temple had a particular function and was equipped accordingly. The antechamber that fronted and connected the three cult rooms was likely used as a place where preparations were made for rituals and sacrifices. The excavators here found around 150 pots; some were for storing foods and liquids, and even textiles, some for food preparation and cooking. The east room had a stepped altar against the southern wall. A tree-branch may have been placed on the stepped altar at the back, as shown on a decorated *rhyton* from Zakros. On the benches were a variety of vessels – cups, pots, pourers, a tripod, and a wide clay dish or tray.[8] A representation on a pot from Gypsades illustrates a man placing offerings into such a vessel inside a tripartite temple located on a mountainside.[9] There were also four large storage jars in the room and two small bronze boxes were found, which may have contained some precious substance. The Sakellarakises suggest that this room was used for bloodless sacrifices and involved offerings of produce, fruits, and grains, as well as liquids and aromatic herbs and flowers.

The central room, as might be expected from the images of tripartite shrines, which show these elevated above the side rooms, was of particular importance. It housed a statue of the deity, which was originally situated on a bench next to an outcrop of unworked natural stone that may have represented the earth, nature, or some other religious idea. Unfortunately, we do not know which god or goddess inhabited the chamber; all that remained of the wooden statue (a *xoanon*) was a pair of clay feet. Between the central room and the antechamber, underneath fallen stone blocks, the excavators found the remains of a person – because of the state of the remains it was not possible to determine whether it was a man or a woman. This context immediately suggested that the temple had been destroyed in an earthquake, presumably collapsing suddenly whilst the person was fleeing; perhaps he or she had thought the quake would not be so intense or las so long and had not run out until it was too late. The person had evidently dropped a pot that they were carrying – a very fine Kamares-ware pot – vivid black with black and white swirling spirals encircling flowers and a red-spotted bull. Representations of such pots indicate that they were used to collect blood from animal sacrifices.

Interesting as these rooms are, the west room yielded more than just pottery and small finds – here the crushed remains of three more human bodies were uncovered. They were found just as they had died, killed when the temple collapsed and caught fire. In the southwest corner of the room, the farthest from the door, the Sakellarakises found the skeleton of a woman. She was found face down with her right hand held up to her head. We can guess that when the earthquake struck and the shaking began she fell, throwing out her right hand to break her fall or to protect her head from the falling masonry that crushed her. Perhaps she was taken by surprise, too shocked to run out, or perhaps she was trying to continue her task in the temple. This woman has become known as 'the priestess'.

Next to the body of the priestess was the body of a tall but slight man, aged around thirty to forty; he is known now as 'the priest'. His ring of iron on silver surely indicates a high status – in the Late Bronze Age iron was rare and precious. The excavators note that other such rings, all later in date, have only been found in supposedly 'royal tombs' – was this man a local ruler? His fine agate seal showing a man rowing a ship found at his wrist might support this conclusion. His presence at the scene suggests that what was going on in the temple was important.

The third body found in the west room was that of a younger man of perhaps eighteen. He, however, was found on an altar and in a position that clearly indicated that he had been bound and laid down on his side. A bronze blade 40 cm in length, either a knife or a lance, was found on top of him. Forensic investigation of the remains determined that he had been killed before the building collapsed – a significant amount of blood had flowed out of his body leaving the right and left sides of his skeleton different colours.

It is difficult to avoid the same conclusion as the Sakellarakises, that the man and woman had performed a human sacrifice in the west room and the other person had then carried the blood in a special pot to offer to the deity in the central room, perhaps to pour the blood onto the rocky outcrop next to the statue.[10] In this narrative, it makes sense to call the man and woman the priest and priestess, although ritual activity may not have been their main or only role in life. Might they also have been a king and his wife or daughter participating in an important ritual event? All of this happened just before a major and perhaps prolonged earthquake caused the building to collapse and catch fire. Were they sacrificing after an initial and less powerful quake to placate the gods?

Can we learn any more about 'the priestess' herself? Her teeth allowed researchers to fill in some more detail. Dental analysis suggested that she was twenty to twenty-five years old.[11] This seems a young age to die, and of course her life was cut short, but data drawn from across Crete indicates that 'peak mortality' was precisely this age and life expectancy was only about twenty eight years.[12] Her teeth, especially the front lower teeth, also had a lot of calculus, which would have given her bad breath, by modern standards, though she had no caries and had only lost one tooth.

Parts of her skull, including the cranial vault and the face, were fairly well preserved, enabling more detail to be gleaned. The investigators found that the sutures of the skull, the gaps between different parts of the cranium, were already almost or fully closed. The skull was also thicker than would be expected and osteoporosis was visible in parts. This surprised the team because it suggested a somewhat older age; they concluded that the priestess had some kind of condition that would account for this. One possibility is a haemoglobin-related condition that affects Mediterranean people: thalassemia.[13] This can bring about health problems from a very young age and can cause paleness and tiredness as well as weak bones and osteoporosis; it can lead to death at a young age. It is possible that the priestess was not a well woman.

Poor diet may also have contributed to health and dental issues and a short life expectancy amongst Minoan women, although variations in wealth and status would mean different outcomes for different women. The skeleton of an older women of around forty-five, found at Armenoi, showed little signs of having done hard physical work but did show signs of dietary stress.[14] Food shortages owing to environmental factors may have been fairly common and affected all classes, though to different degrees, and a diet made up of stored foods such as grains and pulses and little meat or fish would be low in iron and vitamins and high in carbohydrates. Puberty and pregnancy would also put stress on women's bodies, exacerbated by a limited diet. The priestess, if a high-status woman, may have had better access to more and a greater variety of food, but like the Armenoi woman could also have been affected by general shortages.

In 1987, the Sakellarakises invited John Prag and a British-based team to attempt facial reconstructions of the bodies from the Anemospilia temple.[15] Such reconstructions had already been shown to produce some fairly accurate results. Of the four, only the priestess and the priest were complete enough to work with, and the team built up from the skulls using clay to model muscles and flesh. Guiding the team was a knowledge of images of Minoan women, such as La Parisienne, which also provided guidance on possible hairstyles, though as Prag points out, the image is from two centuries later – 'but it was the best evidence we had'.[16] The finished face, he says, is not a portrait, but would have been recognisable to those who knew her (Figure 7).

The wider story of the women of Minoan Crete should also be mentioned. Since the pioneering work of Arthur Evans at Knossos, a persistent interpretation of Minoan society has been that it was dominated by the worship of a Great Mother Goddess and that Bronze Age Crete was a matriarchy. Evans himself was not entirely responsible for this; rather, a remarkable scholar, Jane Ellen Harrison, made the argument in her 1903 book *Prolegomena to the Study of Greek Religion* – Evans had met Harrison and shown her impressions of a seal with a 'mountain goddess' on top of a peak flanked by lions and being worshipped by a male figure, a temple or palace at behind her.[17] This little figure influenced her developing ideas of prehistory – as she in turn influenced his views on Minoan society.[18] Some twenty-five years later, when Harry Hall's *The Civilization of Greece in the Bronze Age* was published, a *Daily Mail* article entitled 'The mystery of Minos: Feminist society before Moses' day' mentioned Minoan Crete as 'a feminist civilization in which women were the

FIG. 7 The reconstructed face of the Priestess of Anemospilia. Courtesy of John Prag

equals of men or something more'.[19] In the 1960s, Jacquetta Hawkes and in the 1970s, Carol Thomas, were still able to characterise Minoan Crete as 'feminine', as a matriarchy, and the mainland Mycenaeans as 'masculine' and a Zeus-worshipping patriarchy.[20] Later Greek culture had its origins of the fusion of the two, though patriarchy and men eclipsed, or defeated matriarchy and women.

The inherited ideas of Evans, Harrison, and others have long cast a shadow over Bronze Age Crete and archaeologists and historians recognise Evans' effective creation of 'the Minoans' in modern times. We are emerging from this legacy now and our images of ancient Crete are changing. Nowadays, archaeologists no longer dubiously categorise or understand cultures as 'feminine' or 'masculine' – our own culture has changed and so our interpretations and characterisations of the past have changed with us. Minoan specialist John Younger nevertheless rightly points out what few would disagree on – Cretan women were very visible in Minoan society, and this surely reflects their status within Cretan society to the highest levels. If there ever was a matriarchal society in the ancient world, 'Neopalatial Crete presents the best candidate', he writes.[21] And the end of Neopalatial Crete may have seen the end of the high status of women – they are no longer represented in frescoes as before and other key material features of Neopalatial Crete that might have been associated with its particular worldview disappeared.

The evidence from Anemospilia is special in capturing a distinct sequence of events in long-ago history; it enables us to see something quite possibly very private and possibly very rare – a human sacrifice. Yet, as is usual in archaeology, there are questions still, not least why the sacrifice took place and whether it was normal or unusual. Was it because of the earth tremors that preceded the big quake that destroyed the building? Was it to do with the priestess's health? Was our Cretan lady a priestess, an attendant of the temple or could she have been a slave, or was she the older elite man's relative Did she deliver the killing wound? Who was the young man they sacrificed? Was he a volunteer, a captive, or could he even be the older man's son? And how did they feel about what they were doing? Each possible answer could lead to a different story for these people and of this event and a different interpretation of Cretan society when they lived.

The end result of the research and the Sakellarakises' find has been to reconstruct an event, to learn more about aspects of Minoan society, and to discover a real Minoan woman embedded in these contexts. Like 'La Parisienne' with her flowing locks and curls and the women on the Isopata ring, it seems very likely that this Minoan woman had also danced for the gods on the fields and mountains of Crete.

8

HATSHEPSUT

More than a thousand years after Merneith ruled Egypt and a thousand years before Cleopatra, another Egyptian woman forged a place at the heart of Egyptian politics and succeeded in making herself pharaoh, ruling as a king rather than a queen, from around 1473 to 1458 BC. Her royal name was Maatkare, but she is better known to history as Hatshepsut (Figure 8).

Hatshepsut was the eldest daughter of king Thutmose I and his wife Ahmose.[1] In time-honoured Egyptian tradition she was married to her half-brother Thutmose II, and they had a daughter called Neferure. She held the titles of 'King's Daughter', 'King's Sister', and 'King's Great Wife'. In addition to her royal titles, Hatshepsut also bore the title 'God's Wife of Amun'. Thutmose II also had a son by a woman called Isis, and when he died unexpectedly this very young Thutmose III became pharaoh. Isis was probably deemed not of sufficiently high status for the role of regent, which was assumed by the very royal Hatshepsut. An inscription from the tomb of Ineni describes this state of affairs:

> His [Thutmose II] son had risen in his place as King of the Two Lands. He [Thutmose III] ruled on the throne of he who had begotten him. His sister, the God's Wife Hatshepsut, governed the land and the Two Lands were advised by her. Work was done for her and Egypt bowed its head.[2]

The 'God's Wife' may well have felt entitled to serve as an heir to her father in her own right.[3] Inscriptions at her temple at Deir el-Bahri claim that Thutmose I did indeed choose her as his heir:

FIG. 8 Large kneeling statue of Hatshepsut, c. 1479–1458 BC. The Metropolitan Museum of Art

> Said his majesty before them: "This my daughter, Khnemet-Amon, Hatshepsut, who liveth, I have appointed [her] [ ]; she is my successor upon my throne, she it assuredly is who shall sit upon my wonderful seat. She shall command the people in every place of the palace; she it is who shall lead you; ye shall proclaim her word, ye shall be united at her command. He who shall do her homage shall live, he who shall speak evil in is blasphemy of her majesty shall die. Whosoever proclaims with unanimity the name of her majesty, shall enter immediately into the royal chamber, just as it was done by the name of this Horus [viz., by my name]. For thou art divine, daughter of a god, for whom even the gods fight; behind whom they exert their protection every day according to the command of her father, the lord of the gods.[4]

The Deir el-Bahri text might show Hatshepsut revising history in order to bolster her claims to legitimacy as pharaoh later on. It was a typical practice of Egyptian rulers to present in records what they wanted to be true, or what ought to be true, rather than what had actually happened.

Egyptologist Joyce Tyldesley, a biographer of Hatshepsut, has mapped the queen's rise to the kingship through three images.[5] In the first, a stela now in

Berlin, Hatshepsut is shown plainly dressed wearing a generic and simple crown; she stands behind her father and mother. In the second, from the Semna temple in Nubia, Thutmose III is shown as an adult receiving the royal crown from the god Dedwen and is entitled 'King of Upper and Lower Egypt and Lord of the Two Lands'; Hatshepsut here is accorded only a minor role.[6] This scene is from two years after the death of Thutmose II. But in the third image, from Hatshepsut's Red Chapel at Karnak, Hatshepsut and Thutmose III are shown almost identically, both with kilt and blue crown, both carrying a staff and ankh, and equal in size; both have male bodies. Significantly, however, Thutmose III is positioned behind Hatshepsut, as indicated by the names in the royal cartouches. Whilst still regent, Hatshepsut had already acquired the royal name of Maatkare and by year seven she had been crowned king.[7]

Much must have gone on behind the scenes to enable Hatshepsut to become pharaoh. No ruler can ascend or rule without the support of others. She must have been able to appeal to the men who supported the pharaohs, ministers, military men, local governors, and the like as a competent and legitimate ruler. Evidently, she had a clear sense of purpose in what she wanted to achieve and a sense of entitlement to it. When and how her ambitions developed is not clear, but it may have been in the early days of the regency when she perhaps realized she had a talent and a taste for rule. Later on, she was able to present events as she thought fit on the walls of Deir el-Bahri – the story of her divine conception as the daughter of Amun, her destiny to rule, and the proclamation of Thutmose I.

One of Hatshepsut's key supporters was a man called Senenmut, who for years was so closely associated with her that he was allowed to include images of himself in royal temples – something usually restricted to royalty.[8] Some earlier scholars have envisioned Senenmut as the real power behind Hatshepsut, even as her lover, but there is little evidence for either of these ideas. Their relationship does not need to be seen as one of male dominance and female passivity or sexualised in any way; it is possible for two people of the opposite sex to work successfully together and to be close allies or friends. For his service, which included being the tutor of Hatshepsut's daughter Nefurare, Senenmut was richly rewarded.

One aspect of her reign that Hatshepsut was most proud of and that she strongly emphasised was a successful expedition that she sent to the southern land of Punt in or before the ninth year of her joint reign with Thutmoses III.[9] Egypt had had some sporadic contact with Punt in earlier times. Even a thousand years before Hatshepsut some pharaohs had sent ships there, and it was known as a source of luxury goods including gold, ivory, and myrrh, all highly prized in Egypt.[10] Hatshepsut did not go to Punt herself, rather she sent an envoy called Neshy with a number of ships and troops.[11] She recorded the event in reliefs with written description on her temple at Deir el-Bahri, on what has become known as the 'Punt portico'.[12]

The location of Punt has remained something of a mystery in modern times. Somalia and the Great Lakes area of east Africa have both been suggested.[13] But it now seems clear, on the basis of the flora shown in the temple reliefs, that Punt was located in southern Sudan or Eritrea, down the western Red Sea coast, and was reached by ships setting sail from the port at Mersa Gawasis, where some remains of sea-going ships have been found along with many inscriptions mentioning Punt.[14] To get to the port from the Nile valley would have involved an arduous trek of around 100 miles east over the desert.

The reliefs show the different stages of the journey, beginning with five ships setting off on their voyage and eventually the party being met in Punt by its king and queen, Perehu and Eti, and their children. Perehu is depicted as a slender bearded man wearing bracelets and Eti as an 'obese' woman, whose physical form, so different to the Egyptian ideal, was emphasised. They also show the local Puntite's dwellings as reed-built huts on poles entered via ladders and some of the exotic flora and fauna.[15] There must have been observers on the expedition who were tasked with recording what Punt was like precisely so that it could be recorded for posterity later on.

The Egyptians brought with them necklaces, axes, and daggers: 'every good thing from the court' to offer and exchange. The Puntites' gifts too are shown in the relief, being loaded into the Egyptian ships. The accompanying text lists these:

> The loading of the ships very heavily with marvels of the country of Punt; all goodly fragrant woods of God's-Land, heaps of myrrh-resin, with fresh myrrh trees, with ebony and pure ivory, with green gold of Emu, with cinnamon wood, *khesyt* wood: with *ihmut*-incense, *sonter*-incense, eye-cosmetic, with apes, monkeys, dogs, and with skins of the southern panther, with natives and their children. Never was brought the like of this for any king who has been since the beginning.

On the safe return of the expedition, the goods were presented to Hatshepsut, who first of all offered a share to the god Amon. The reliefs show the various goods being weighed out and counted and the text describes how Hatshepsut herself took part in this while her assistant Thutiy kept a tally; the god Thoth kept a tally for Amon. Whilst there probably would have been a very public show of the expedition's return and a viewing of its treasures, all of this record need not be taken as literal truth. For example, the claims that the king of Punt came to Egypt to give the 'tribute' and that Hatshepsut became overlord of Punt seem typical pharaonic bluster. Nevertheless, there is a strong association of Hatshepsut with Punt and its rich gifts to her, and in turn her gifts to Amon. The text goes:

> Her majesty herself, is acting with her two hands, the best of myrrh is upon all her limbs, her fragrance is divine dew, her odor is mingled with Punt, her skin is gilded with electrum, shining as do the stars in the midst of the festival-hall, before the whole land. There is rejoicing by all the people; they give praise to the lord of gods, they laud Makere [Hatshepsut] in her divine qualities, because of the greatness of the marvels which have happened for her.

In addition to foreign adventures that yielded exotic riches and showed Egypt as commanding the respect of distant peoples, Hatshepsut also engaged, like all other pharaohs, in the building and restoration of temples, both to ensure the correct relationship with the gods was maintained and to show her piety and power. Her own memorial temple at Deir el-Bahri, where her memory was to be preserved for eternity, was the exceptional Djeser-djeseru, the 'holy of holies'.[16] This temple complex was excavated by Edouard Naville and the Egypt Exploration Fund from 1892 with further work since 1961 undertaken by a Polish-Egyptian team, who have partially restored it.

For Egyptians, tradition was important and art and architecture were generally conservative, but at Deir el-Bahri the architects 'broke with the tradition of copying recognized prototypes and designed an original and innovative building', although it did take some inspiration from the nearby but smaller temple of Mentuhotep II.[17] It is quite possible that Hatshepsut was closely involved in the design process, along with expert architects, and that her vision is expressed in the grand temple's architecture and its artistic programme.

The temple, with its multiple colonnades rather than the usual blank external walls, stood in the bay of a natural amphitheatre of rock, which rose up in cliffs behind and to the sides of the temple, giving a spectacular impression. This positioning was used to maximum effect as visitors approached the temple on a causeway some 37 m wide, which was lined with stone sphinxes. It had three courtyards, each higher than the last, with the first being the biggest by far, and visitors used a series of ramps to reach the colonnaded upper court, with its mortuary chapel of Hatshepsut and shrine of Amon at the end of the processional route.

Although we see the complex area as sandy and dry now, the first courtyard was planted as a garden, with exotic trees brought from Punt. This was done to please her 'father' the god Amon, who had commanded the Punt expedition take place, and stresses Hatshepsut's achievement and own connection with Punt. Hatshepsut explains all of this to her senior courtiers, and her words are recorded as follows:

> I will cause you to know that which is commanded me, I have hearkened to my father that which he hath – commanding me to establish for him a Punt in his house, to plant the trees of God's-Land beside his temple in his garden, according as he commanded. It was done, in order to endow the offerings which I owed. I was [not] neglectful of that which he

> needed ... I have made for him a Punt in his garden, just as he commanded me, for Thebes. It is large for him, he walks abroad in it.

As Betsy Bryan points out, 'Hatshepsut's trade mission to Punt was promoted in Egypt as a major diplomatic *coup*'.[18] The pharaoh would have understood well that such an expedition could, if successful, be politically advantageous at home. It seems that trade with Nubia, just south of Egypt, also increased around this time, and the goods received, again including gold and ivory, began to be illustrated in private tombs. In the north, there were missions to Lebanon, for timber.[19] Egypt in Hatshepsut's reign, she suggests, was largely at peace, enabling its wealth to be directed by the king to her numerous building projects all through the land.[20]

Delegations of Keftiu also began to be shown in tombs, for example, in the tomb of Senenmut, which suggests contact with Minoan Crete and the Aegean. Supporting this idea, but much more surprising than representations of tribute-bearing foreigners in tombs, was the discovery of Minoan fresco paintings in Palace F at Tell el-Daba, in the Nile delta, which probably belong to the period of Hatshepsut and Thutmose III's joint rule.[21] These were not only Minoan in theme but also executed in the Minoan way. The technique used, painting on hard lime plaster, turned out to be inappropriate for the mud-brick building materials used in the palace, which shrank and caused the fresco to crack and fall; it was later removed and dumped. Manfred Bietak notes that 'in this palace decoration there are no representations of Egyptian royal emblems, only motifs and symbols typically associated with the palace of Knossos, such as bull acrobatics and the maze pattern'.[22] Did Knossos lend out its craftspeople to foreign notables, as was common practice in the ancient Near East? Or was this palace used by an important figure – perhaps an important woman – from Knossos?

It is unclear what the Egyptian people as a whole thought of Hatshepsut – whether they cared if a woman was pharaoh or not. But a piece of graffiti from one tomb at Deir el-Bahri might indicate at least some people's opinion – it shows a woman wearing a king's headdress being penetrated from behind by a man. The image has been interpreted as Hatshepsut and Senenmut, but this is a guess, and even if correct does not necessarily indicate any view on the legitimacy of Hatshepsut as a female pharaoh. As Joyce Tyldesley observes, it only proves that 'the ancient Egyptians enjoyed smutty gossip as much as any other people'.[23]

Hatshepsut died on the tenth day of the sixth month of the year 22 of her reign and what happened to her body is unclear.[24] No body was found in her looted tomb – just a box with her cartouche containing a mummified liver or spleen. It is possible that Hatshepsut ended up in a different tomb and there are several possible bodies that could be hers.

Despite what could be called a very successful reign, Hatshepsut's memory suffered.[25] During the latter part of Thutmose III's thirty-three-year sole rule, an effort was made throughout Egypt to erase her name and images wherever they were found. This would not only effectively remove Hatshepsut from history – but also end her 'afterlife'. Was this Thutmose's revenge at being sidelined by a woman for two decades? Probably not – as Tyldesley points out, if Thutmose really wanted her out of the way, he could, as head of the army, have deposed Hatshepsut years earlier. And, if his feelings were so strong, why did he then wait until late in his reign to attack her memory? As it is, the erasure was 'sporadic and haphazard' – because of this we still have the evidence we have. Thutmose III's actions may simply have been to rebalance history, putting himself before the queen-regent. Hatshepsut was a successful politician and ruler, who thrived in a world dominated by men; she deserves to be remembered as one of history's great female leaders.

9

PUDUHEPA

The Hittite state started small, as one of a number of competing kingdoms in Anatolia.[1] Under a series of rulers from the early king Hattusili I, around 1650 BC, it grew to become a regional superpower, expanding from its north-central Anatolian heartland, with political and economic interests drawing its attention southeast to the Mediterranean coast, Syria, and the older kingdoms in the area, and also westward to the Aegean.[2] Its capital at Hattusa, the fortified residence of the Hittite kings, modern Boğazköy, became a splendid city of temples, testament to the rulers' commitment to the gods and the rituals necessary to win their favour and avoid incurring their displeasure.[3]

Early in the thirteenth century BC, Muwatalli II took the gods from Hattusa and moved them and his court to a more strategic location further south – the city of Tarhuntassa.[4] This relocation placed him nearer to the Levant, where he was building up to a conflict with the mighty kingdom of Egypt in the grey zone between the two powers; the mighty battle of Qadesh, which took place in 1274 BC. Muwatalli's foe was the Egyptian pharaoh Ramesses II, Ramesses the Great, who dominated Egypt for much of the thirteenth century, ruling from 1279 to 1213 BC. Both sides claimed victory, but the advantage seems to have gone to the Hittites.[5] It is with these events in the background that a woman called Puduhepa became powerful and influential as the wife of the Hittite king Hattusili III, who ruled for three decades from c. 1267–1237 BC, and as the mother of his successor Tudhaliya IV.[6]

Puduhepa was born perhaps a few years later than Ramesses, around 1300 BC, in the land of Kizzuwatna in southeastern Anatolia; by birth she was a Hurrian. The Hittite state was multi-ethnic and multilingual and the Hurrians were one people among many living in Anatolia; they had their own language and traditions.[7] The land of Kizzuwatna had, for a time, been the equal of Hatti, but it later fell under the political and cultural influence of the Hurrian kingdom of Mitanni.[8] There had been a long rivalry between the Hittites and Mittani, which ended with Hittite conquest around 1340/1330 BC.[9] Much like Greece and Rome, though, Billie Jean Collins suggests that 'although the military victory was Hatti's, the cultural one appears to have belonged to the Hurrians, as Hurrian cults and practices infiltrated deep into the Hittite heartland'.[10] Puduhepa played an active and important role in these developments, which for the polytheistic and religiously minded Hittites would not have been insignificant.[11]

How Puduhepa and Hattusili met is recorded in a Hittite document called the *Apology of Hattusili III*, in which the king explained his past actions. After the great battle of Qadesh, the victorious prince Hattusili, the king's brother, set out to return from Syria to Hatti. On his way back, travelling through Kizzuwatna, he visited the city of Lawazantiya, a city where Ishtar – Hattusili's protective goddess since his childhood – was worshipped. There he met Pentipsharri, the priest of Ishtar and clearly an important man in the city.[12] Pentipsharri's family may have hosted Hattusili and undoubtedly the priest would have assisted him with his religious observances. Hattusili also met Puduhepa, Pentipsharri's teenage daughter, who was herself a priestess of Ishtar. Whilst in the city, according to the story, Ishtar came to Hattusili in a dream and told him to marry Puduhepa.

We can speculate about the nature of the meeting and the marriage and whether it was a product of love or politics, or both. Perhaps Hattusili really did dream of marrying Puduhepa; after all, both had a special relationship with Ishtar that could have brought them together and that suggested a natural bond. With the Hittites as with many other ancient peoples, dreams were an important means for gods to make their wishes known directly to mortals.[13] Hattusili's *Apology* mentions that Ishtar gave the pair the love of a husband and wife and that children followed in turn. Though these are Hattusili's formally expressed sentiments, the pair's long partnership also suggests that the marriage worked out well for both parties. It incidentally tells us that love in marriage was a blessing or a normal expectation amongst the Hittites and that marriage was not just for the sharing of property or production of legitimate children.

Puduhepa probably did not foresee that she would one day be queen because Hattusili was not meant to become king – he took the throne as a usurper. As the king's brother, he had enjoyed great power and status, effectively ruling the northern parts of the kingdom, possibly including Hattusa, when Muwatalli turned his attention south; he was also honoured as the chief of the king's bodyguards.[14] When Muwatalli died around 1267 BC his son Urhi-Teshub became king, ruling as Mursili III.[15] Hattusili, his uncle, proclaimed himself a loyal subject and undertook important works, such as rebuilding the city of Nerik, an important religious centre, which had been destroyed years before. He had power and influence – perhaps too much. Soon the young king Mursili set out to reduce the threat he may have felt by progressively diminishing Hattusili's power. After years of treatment that he may have felt both humiliating and provocative, Hattusili rebelled and civil war followed; Mursili lost the fight and fled overseas to Egypt and the court of Ramesses.

One source that tells us this version of events is a prayer composed by Puduhepa, which parallels a similar prayer made by Hattusili and Puduhepa together.[16] In the *Apology*, Hattusili claimed not only that he had been provoked but that Ishtar had sent dreams to Puduhepa saying Hattusili would be king. Puduhepa surely supported Hattusili in his actions – and if we take the dream story at face value, it could even be suggested that Hattusili made his treasonous bid for power at Puduhepa's 'inspired suggestion' as much as his own will. With the fallout from Hattusili's usurpation playing out over the next few decades, Puduhepa may well have shaped the destiny of the Hittite Empire, perhaps even contributing to its eventual demise.[17]

As queen, Puduhepa seems always to have played a prominent role in state affairs in her own right. In 1259/8 BC, some years after Qadesh, an 'Eternal treaty' was agreed upon between the Hittites and Egyptians. This was recorded on silver tablets and versions of the treaty survive on clay tablets from Hattusa and on the walls of the Temple of Karnak in Egypt.[18] The Egyptian text describes how the silver tablet received in Egypt was sealed on one side by Hattusili and the other by Puduhepa, 'great queen' and 'daughter of Kizzuwatna'.[19] She co-sealed other treaties too, which testifies to her status – her word carried weight internationally.[20]

Puduhepa also corresponded directly with Ramesses II about the marriage of one of her daughters to the pharaoh, probably before the treaty was sealed. In itself, it is remarkable that a woman could take part in this usually masculine club, the 'brotherhood of kings', but in the letter, she also shows herself to be perfectly assured and even able to put Ramesses in his place; the pharaoh wrote to her as an equal. The letter is too long to quote in full but was written in reply to a terse letter of Ramesses who was complaining of the delay in sending the princess to him.[21] Puduhepa makes various excuses, one of which was that the Egyptian delegation arrived in Hattusa in winter, at which time she could not send a dowry (of 'civilian captives, cattle, and sheep'), and another that a treasury (possibly) in Hattusa had burnt down and had also been depleted by the deposed king Urhi-Teshub (Mursili) – she adds caustically 'since Urhi-Teshub is there, ask him if this is so'. She also points out, whilst apologising for causing any unintended offence to Ramesses, that 'Egypt and Hatti will become a single country' and that Ramesses will become her son-in-law.

A hope on the Hittite side, albeit wishful thinking, would have been that any son born of the marriage would become a half-Hittite pharaoh, though Ramesses would have had his own perhaps very different plans for his succession.[22] The princess, whose Egyptian name was Maat-Hor-Neferure, was given the title of queen-consort.[23] However, this was probably an empty gesture and in any case she had a daughter, not a son, by Ramesses, which did little for her position. She lived in Ramesses' capital for a while before being retired to the wives' palace at Medinet Gurob, where Flinders Petrie found a laundry list belonging to her. She may have died young as no more is heard of her. Another Hittite princess, and later maybe even a third, were dispatched to Egypt, all possibly by arrangement of Puduhepa.

Puduhepa also wrote to Nefertari, a prominent wife of Ramesses. Her letter does not survive, but Nefertari's reply does. Puduhepa had written to enquire about the queen's health and the state of the peace between Hatti and Egypt and their two husbands. She received a reply, though it is extremely formulaic and may not have been composed by Nefertari personally.[24] After the very standard greetings and wishes, the letter lists greeting gifts from the queen to Puduhepa including a 'very colorful' gold necklace and twelve linen garments.[25] Was Puduhepa hoping to find an equal in the Egyptian queen? Was she disappointed with the reply she received?

Another indication of the position of Puduhepa is the relief carved into the rock at Firaktin (Figure 9). In this scene, Puduhepa and Hattusili are offering libations; she to the goddess Hepat and he to the Storm God.[26] The couple are dressed the same way as the gods they are worshipping.[27] Puduhepa is shown on the same scale as the king and they are shown at their devotions in parallel; in the hieroglyphic inscription she is described, as on her seal, as 'great queen, daughter of Kizzuwatna, beloved of the deity'. The relief visibly indicates her position as equal of her husband.

Also surviving are some prayers composed by Puduhepa for Hattusili, who suffered various ailments throughout his life; these indicate both their close relationship, Puduhepa's care for her husband (and for herself), and the importance of religion in their lives. In one prayer, the queen is inspired by a dream to seek divine help for her husband's bad feet. The text goes:

> A dream of the queen: Somebody said again and again to me in a dream: 'make a vow to the goddess Ningal as follows: 'If [that] disease Fire-of-the-Feet of His Majesty will pass quickly, I shall make for Ningal ten [?] *talla* [oil flasks] of gold set with lapis lazuli!'[28]

FIG. 9 Relief showing Puduhepa seated, taking part in a ritual. Source: Wikimedia Commons. Photo by Krähenstein. CC BY-SA 3.0

A longer prayer seems to relate to a more serious illness, which the queen surmised might have been caused by their personal or political enemies:

> If Hattusili is accursed, and if Hattusili, my husband, has become hateful in the eyes of you, the gods; or if anyone of the gods above or below has taken offence at him; or if anyone has made an offering to the gods to bring evil upon Hattusili – accept not these evil words, O Goddess, My Lady![29]

As mentioned above, Puduhepa was influential in modifying the religious life of the Hittites – at least at an official state level.[30] The Hittites had accrued many gods, and across the empire many gods of the different peoples had to be dealt with officially. Puduhepa encouraged a process of syncretism between Hurrian and Hittite religion to make dealing with the gods easier. Gods and goddesses of certain kinds were grouped together and some explicitly identified with each other. In her prayer, Puduhepa identifies the goddess Hepat with the Hittite Sun Goddess of Arinna and the Storm God of Nerik with her divine son, whose city Hattusili had rebuilt:

> O Sun-goddess of Arinna, my lady, queen of all the lands! In Hatti you have yourself the name Sun-goddess of Arinna, but the land which you made, that of the cedar, there you gave yourself the name Hepat. I,

> Puduhepa, am your long-time servant, a calf of your stable, a [corner]-stone of your foundation. You picked me up, my lady, and Hattusili, your servant, to whom you married me, and he too was attached by destiny to the Storm-God of Nerik, your beloved son.[31]

The queen was also responsible for commissioning, from the court's chief scribe Walwaziti, a new version of the text for the *hisuwa* festival, a nine-day religious celebration, which was based on original tablets from Kizzuwatna.[32]

Hattusili died around 1237 BC but Puduhepa retained her influence for a long time to come, through the reign of her son Tudhaliya IV (c. 1237–1209 BC). One clear indication of this is that she appeared with her son on some of the royal seals.[33] Early in the reign of Tudhaliya, she played a judicial role in a case of the wilful damage of a ship, ordering compensation to be paid to the ship's owner in Ugarit.[34] The pronouncement was made in a letter to the king of Ugarit and she used her own seal and also the king's title, 'My Sun'. This indicates that she was acting with the full authority of the king, something she may have inherited from her position as Hattusili's queen. In continuing to wield significant power, Puduhepa may have made an enemy of Tudhaliya's wife, and a faction may have tried to remove her from power.[35] It might have succeeded, but only temporarily. Puduhepa's last letter dates from 1215 BC.[36] Though we do not know exactly when she died, it is likely that she lived to be ninety or more years of age – enjoying the last flourishing of Hittite power.[37]

Puduhepa was not the only powerful Hittite woman in their history. An important position at the top of Hittite society was that of *tawannana*, which was granted to a royal woman, usually the reigning queen.[38] While it may have started out as primarily a religious office, which gave its incumbents great visibility at festivals and in the religious life of the kingdom, the *tawannanas* often wielded much more power – and the office was held for life. Inevitably, some *tawannanas* seem to have attempted to exercise power to follow their own plans, which clashed with the policies of the kings. About one, Hattusili I proclaimed that 'in future, let no-one speak the *Tawannana*'s name .... Let no-one speak the name of her sons and daughters. If any of the sons of Hatti speaks them, they shall cut his throat and hang him in his gate'. A Babylonian wife of Suppiluliuma I also became a powerful and influential *Tawannana*, somewhat notorious for her lavish lifestyle and 'foreign' habits.

At the top of a patriarchal society, Puduhepa exercised significant real power and influence and commanded respect across the eastern Mediterranean to the Hittites great rivals, Egypt. Partly, her authority rested on the position of her husband, but a great deal of her activity must have been due to her own personality and initiative; she was able to act in her own right and not only as the royal wife. She was truly both a 'formidable consort' and 'the most powerful of all Hittite queens'.[39]

10

ERITHA AND KARPATHIA

Late Bronze Age Greece was a partly literate place. The Minoans had used a hieroglyphic script and a type of writing we call Linear A, which remain undeciphered, but the Mycenaeans, or at least the authorities associated with some of the palaces, wrote on clay tablets in Greek using the Linear B script. These Linear B tablets, accidentally preserved in fires, were first translated by Michael Ventris in 1952 and then published as a corpus in co-operation with John Chadwick.[1] Tablets continue to be found even now, extending our knowledge of Mycenaean Greece. None of them record history, literature or poetry, nor are there any lists of kings, but the information they do contain is nevertheless precious.

Over the last seventy years, Aegean archaeologists have managed to squeeze much information from the tablets about the Mycenaean world, or at least parts of it – the bulk of the texts come from the two palaces of Pylos and Knossos. For example, the texts, as working administrative documents, tell us bits and pieces about the palace economy, social structure, religion, feasting, military equipment, what palaces produced and who produced things for them. Recently, research has turned to what the study of individuals named in the tablets can reveal – there are some five thousand men named in the documents and two thousand women – and a full study of women in the tablets has been written by Barbara Olsen, filling a glaring gap in the research to date.[2]

Many Linear B texts tell us something about women's lives in Mycenaean Greece; for example, some record the existence of groups of female slaves, or 'dependent labourers', and their children. Whilst some of these women came to Pylos from the Messenia region, others came or were brought from the eastern Aegean and the coastal regions of western Anatolia.[3] Mycenaeans, according to Hittite documents, definitely had some military and political interests in the region and Millawanda, later Miletus, and its environs, may have been governed by Mycenaeans for some time.[4] Whether these women were captured in raids, were prisoners of war, were gifts from one lord to another, or arrived by some other mechanism, we do not know, but that they worked for and were supported by the Pylos palace we do know. They were involved in various aspects of textile manufacture, including spinning and weaving, as well as grinding flour and received rations from the palace.[5]

Jorrit Kelder and Marco Poelwijk have suggested, at the other end of the social hierarchy, that one tablet (PY Ta 711) from Pylos may provide us with the name of the Pylian queen – *Pu2-ke-qi-ri*.[6] This person was involved in a ceremony in which the king appointed a local governor, a *da-mo-ko-ro*. *Pu2-ke-qi-ri* has usually been assumed to be a man but Kelder and Poelwijk argue that this is not at all certain. There is no reason a queen should not have been present at and involved in such a ceremony or recorded in the related texts. They admit this is speculation, but it is correct to question the assumption. The Linear B documents can be frustrating in the details they omit or obscure – so much would have been known by the documents' users – the name of the king of Pylos, for example, did not need to be written as opposed to just *wanax*, king. Mycenaean specialists suspect it may be *E-ke-ra2-wo* (Enkhelyawon), but this is based on the amounts of land held by various people.[7] The royal couple may have carried out some duties together and could have also had distinct areas of responsibility, perhaps in their religious roles.

Between slaves and the queen, other women are visible in the Pylos tablets, including women who performed religious duties as priestesses or in other roles (Figure 10). Two of these active in Pylian society around 1200 BC were *E-ri-ta* or Eritha and *Ka-pi-ti-ja* or Karpathia.[8] The tablets referring to them taken together present something of a puzzle – but also provide a window onto a complex and dynamic world c. 1200 BC, which is largely hidden from view.

Eritha appears on several tablets, sometimes by name and sometimes by title; she was the main priestess of Sphagianes (*pa-ki-ja-ne*). Unfortunately, there is no description of Eritha's religious duties, as the palace had no interest in recording these. They do record that she was in possession of 'slaves', which indicates her special status as usually only men held slaves in the palace records. Two of these are mentioned by name – a man called Tetreus (*Te-re-u*) (PY Eb 1176) and a woman called Eratara (*E-ra-ta-ra*) (PY En 609). These two possess

FIG. 10 Female head from Mycenae – goddess, priestess? National Museum of Archaeology, Athens, Greece. Source: Wikimedia Commons. Photo by Orizan. CC BY 2.0

some plots of land of their own, which leads Olsen to suggest that the title 'slave of the priestess at Sphagianes' refers to people officiating in the cult rather than unfree people.[9] Whatever the precise meaning, that Eritha was senior to people with their own land holdings confirms her high status.

Another tablet (PY Ae 303) states that Eritha held other slaves:

> At Pylos, 14+ female slaves of the priestess on account of the sacred gold.

This enigmatic statement could refer to the assignment of 'staff' by the palace to work under Eritha in her religious office to distribute gold, in raw or finished form, to various divinities.[10] Another tablet, PY Tn 316, may support this interpretation. It records the assignment of people and goods to various divinities at Sphagianes. This included a gold vase and a woman to Potnia, 'The Lady', the same to Posideia, a female version of Poseidon, and similar gifts to divinities in the Shrine of Poseidon at Pylos, including Diwia, the female version of Zeus.[11] An earlier reading of this text was that it indicated human sacrifices, which is possible, but an allocation of staff also makes sense.[12]

Another context in which Eritha appears concerns land holdings.[13] In modern western culture, we have quite definite ideas about property and land ownership, and we can 'hold' or 'possess' them in a number of ways, which are enshrined in cultural and legal traditions. These seem obvious and natural to us but attitudes to land and property can differ across cultures. Olsen reminds us that 'how the concept of "property ownership" was understood or governed in the Mycenaean world remains largely an open question'.[14] But it seems that, as Thomas Palaima explains, the giving of parcels of food and land 'on which food could be grown are the major ways palatial centres and village communities compensated individuals for labor and other services'.[15] We must imagine how the palace itself acquired the lands it could then give away; perhaps some allotments were temporary. Then as now, there could still be disputes over rights and responsibilities connected with land.

The tablet in question is PY Ep 704, which is part of the E series of tablets about land holdings in the Pylos kingdom. In Olsen's translation the text says:

> Eritha the priestess has leased a plot of communal land from the *damos*, so much seed: 38.4 l. wheat
>
> Eritha the priestess has and claims a freehold holding for her god, but the *damos* says that she holds a leased plot of communal land, so much seed: 374.4 l. wheat

The precise meanings of some of the related terms in the original Greek are still debated, but two types of land holding were *ke-ke-me-na* land, communal land that was held from the *damos* – from 'the people', perhaps meaning a village community or 'public' land – and *ki-ti-me-na* land – held from named individuals.[16] Also relevant are the terms *o-na-to* – leased – and *e-to-ni-jo* – freehold.

As can be seen from the tablet, Eritha held some land from the *damos*. But a second and much bigger plot of land was the subject of a dispute. Eritha claimed that it was her land, or at least land belonging to the god that she was responsible for, but the *damos* held that it was leased from them. Leased land came with concomitant obligations to be performed for the owner by the holder. Leasing and obligation of this kind is known from other Bronze Age cultures and from feudal societies (even in modern societies, without being 'feudal', tenants often have some obligations to landlords, such as paying local property tax, taking care of the garden, and basic property maintenance).

The tablets do not record any resolution to the dispute between Eritha and the *damos* – it is not clear whether the palace would have been interested in recording one. Indeed, in this dispute, it is not clear whether the palace would have had any power or right as an institution to intercede. What exactly was their concern in the case? It is interesting to wonder what kind of 'legal' traditions there were in Pylos and the Mycenaean Greek states, as surely precedents for resolving disputes or actions deemed 'wrongful' had been incorporated into the state apparatus in some form. Decisions and influence probably came from the king or local ruler or governor, or village council, depending on the nature of the matter. For many years, the palaces were thought to be like spiders at the heart of an economic, political, and social web, yet Eritha's story tells us that there were forces at work in society outside the palace authority, and sometimes these involved women of high status who were in charge of property. Another tablet suggests that Eritha may also have been able to lease out land, perhaps again due to her religious role, but again confirming some of her independent capacities.[17]

The evidence does not tell us how Eritha obtained her position as priestess. One possibility is that she was a member of the royal family. But it is equally possible that the temple sphere existed outside of direct palatial control. It may well have developed in tandem with the political developments taking some Mycenaean societies towards statehood. Susan Lupack has argued for an expanded understanding of Mycenaean society not as palace-centred but with the sanctuary sphere and the *damos* playing important independent roles; in other words, Mycenaean states were societies with multiple sources of tradition and authority.[18] Eritha might have been from a local aristocratic family; perhaps the duty was handed down to her. The tablets we have seen, though, do show that the palace was involved or interested, and this must be significant. Was the palace overseeing a royal woman in her religious role, 'doing its duty' by the traditional cult areas and their officials, or attempting to influence and control these institutions by getting involved with them?

Besides Eritha, the Pylos tablets record another figure with a role in Mycenaean religion: *Ka-pi-ti-ja* or Karpathia. Karpathia appears on PY Ep 704, after Eritha, as holding two plots of communal *ke-ke-me-na* land. But it appears that she too was involved in an ongoing dispute, as the tablet records that she did not fulfil the obligations related to them.[19] Cécile Boëlle-Weber has observed that Karpathia and Eritha appear on many tablets together and even that Karpathia may have had a higher status, due to holding more land.[20] She is designated as the *ka-ra-wi-po-ro*, which is translated as 'key-bearer', and it is thought that she would have been the official in charge of keeping the keys to a sanctuary at Sphagianes.[21] However, it is not clear whether all the references in the tablets to unnamed key-bearers relate to Karpathia, so she may not have held more land than Eritha.[22]

What was a key-bearer? Such a role is referred to in the *Iliad*, where, in book 6, a Trojan woman called Theano, a priestess, holds the keys to unlock the temple of Athena. In that scene, the Trojan queen Hekabe wants to make an offering to Athena, so she descends into a basement store-room and selects a rich embroidered robe; she and her women then process to the temple, where Theano opens the door, takes the robe, and places it reverently on the statue's knees. The women 'all crying loud stretched out their arms in prayer', and Theano herself delivered their petition to the goddess – asking for the Greek hero Diomedes to be weakened and promising twelve young heifers in return. Could Karpathia's role have been anything like this?

A variety of religious or cult sites are known from Late Bronze Age Greece, usually indicated at least by figurines of various kinds and altars.[23] Some are found within palatial citadels, for example, the Cult Centre complex at Mycenae, located just below the palace on the hilltop; at Pylos there seems only to be a small shrine in the palace complex, though there could be a yet-to-be-revealed sanctuary in the Lower Town. Other locations for religious rites include caves, urban, or open-air sites such as Kynortion Hill at Epidauros, which was in use for centuries. Ritual activity also took place in locations outside of palatial areas, though palace elites may still have sought involvement with them, as with Delphi and other 'pan-Hellenic' sanctuaries of historical times. For example, it is now clear that religious rituals took place in Megaron B at Eleusis in Attica, site of the later mystery cult.[24]

Many of the religious sites of Mycenaean Greece would have predated the palaces, which in any case only appeared in a few locations but would, nonetheless, have become linked with palaces over time. Sphagianes may have been such a site. The sanctuaries would not have looked like the Archaic or Classical temples that we are familiar with, nor need they have looked like Minoan sanctuaries, but they did have some functional similarities. They were sites where animals were sacrificed and liquid libations poured and where incense may have been burned; they also received donations of precious metals such as gold and bronze and other items, such as textiles and foodstuffs.[25] As Joan Connelly points out, ancient Greek temples accrued goods and materials over time, becoming like museums and treasure houses, which made the key-bearer's role, in historical and potentially prehistoric Greece, both practical and symbolic, representing 'considerable authority within the sanctuary hierarchy'.[26]

In later times, Connelly remarks, 'the surest signifier of feminine priestly status in visual culture is the temple key'.[27] Women dedicated bronze, stone, and clay statues of themselves holding keys, and such images also appeared on grave reliefs. Votive keys of silver or bronze, sometimes of considerable size (one from a temple of Artemis in Arcadia was more than 40 cm long) were dedicated by some women – one was presented by a woman called Stratonike to Artemis on Delos. It is unclear whether the role of key-bearer survived the collapse of the Mycenaean palace system or whether it reappeared with the architectural, economic, and social developments of early historical times. Regardless of that, Karpathia's role must have carried a high status.

The Linear B tablets we have do not preserve the words of Eritha and Karpathia or provide the biographical details that would enable us to sketch narratives of their lives; we do not know whether they belonged to elite families or even the ruling house, or were selected from local girls, whether they were young or old, married or single at the time the tablets were written. They appear to us only in their relationship with the palace, though they were clearly known beyond it. Although we do not know the location of Sphagianes, and so cannot place Eritha and Karpathia physically in the religious landscape, it seems likely that these important women would have visited the palace at Pylos. Perhaps they or their families had houses in the town. The way in which the very 'matter of fact' Linear B tablets mention them shows, without any literary flourishes or authorial bias, their special status at the end of the Late Bronze Age in Greece. This status may well not have originated from the palace authorities of Pylos but may have come from the traditional religious practices in Messenia, which were recognised by the palace elite. Equally possible is that the ruling house of Pylos, as it had expanded as a state, attempted to harness the power and influence of the religious sector by placing family members in influential positions, as we know happened in other early societies. Who knows what happened to these important women when the palace at Pylos was burned and the kingdom came to an end c. 1200 BC – were they somehow able to continue in their religious roles or did these too disappear with the palace?

11

HATIBA

Once upon a time there was an Egyptian man, a priest, by the name of Wenamun.[1] Wenamun was sent by his lord Herihor to fetch wood from Lebanon to build a sacred boat for the god Amon-Ra. Sailing north with his captain Mengebet, he landed at Dor and was entertained by Beder, its prince. His good fortune soon changed and after a series of misadventures, including being robbed by his own crew and attacking a ship belonging to the local Tjeker people of Dor to replace his lost wealth, he ended up at Byblos. Here prince Tjekerbaal felled the trees to provide Wenamun with the timber he wanted. Soon the Tjeker that Wenamun had robbed caught up with him. The prince of Byblos would not arrest Wenamun but instead asked him to depart so that the Tjeker could catch him at sea themselves. However, the wind blew him off course all the way to a coastal town on the island of Alashiya (Cyprus). The story continues thus, in Wenamun's voice:

> Then the town's people came out against me to kill me. But I forced my way through them to where Hatiba, the princess of the town was. I met her coming from one of her houses to enter another. I saluted her and said to the people who stood around her: 'Is there not one among you who understands Egyptian?' And one among them said: 'I understand it.' I said to him: 'Tell my lady that I have heard it said as far away as Thebes, the place where Amun is: "If wrong is done in every town, in the land of Alasiya right is done." Now is wrong done here too every day?'

> She said: 'What is it you have said?' I said to her: 'If the sea rages and the wind drives me to the land where you are, will you let me be received so as to kill me, though I am the envoy of Amun? Look, as for me, they would search for me till the end of time. As for this crew of the prince of Byblos, whom they seek to kill, will not their lord find ten crews of yours and kill them also?' She had the people summoned and they were reprimanded. She said to me: 'Spend the night . . .'.

If we take the story at face value then a town in Late Bronze Age or Early Iron Age Cyprus was ruled by a princess, a powerful woman who saved Wenamun from the mob that would kill him and punished those who had threatened him. The author of the tale includes Hatiba's words, though the text is incomplete – a tantalising 'what happened next'. . . .

This story is recorded in an Egyptian text called *The Tale of Wenamun*. The reference to Herihor, ruler in the south, and Smendes, the 21st Dynasty ruler based at Tanis in northern Egypt or in Memphis, situates the story in the eleventh century BC – Smendes ruled from 1069–1043 BC.[2] This period, known as the Third Intermediate Period, was a time when Egypt was internally divided and had less international clout than it had in previous times, a situation that is clearly reflected in the story.[3] Egyptian culture continued to thrive, though, without any historical break. Whatever was going on in Egypt, for us, the interest is in whether there really was an Alashiyan princess called Hatiba ruling an Early Iron Age town.

There are no archaeological or internal historical sources from Early Iron Age Cyprus that prove the existence of a ruler called Hatiba, and so the starting place is always *Wenamun*. Since the papyrus and story was originally published in 1897, scholars have reacted in various ways to the text: the date of the text and its genre and level of truth or historicity have all been questioned. Benjamin Sass has studied the reception of *Wenamun* through the twentieth century.[4] He explains that whilst the setting of the story in time is quite clear the date of its composition is less so. It has been placed as early as the 20th Dynasty and as late as the 22nd Dynasty, in the reign of Sheshonq, after 945 BC. The genre of the text is also not clear. Sass writes that in modern times the story was often taken to be an actual report of real people and events, though it tended to be accepted as a literary version of a report. Others, however, thought it a total fiction. Opinion then shifted back to the idea that it was an official document because of the non-literary language it contains. Now, according to Sass, the text is seen primarily as a literary work that makes selective use of an 'official' style for effect. When considering just what type of document the story is, we should note the find context of the papyrus – a small library rather than an official archive.

Wenamun clearly has a narrative, but is it just a story, perhaps a comedy, about an unfortunate Egyptian abroad? Sass argues that the real or underlying message of the story is to highlight Egypt's weakness. During periods of weakness Amon cannot be worshipped properly and his power overseas is reduced. He suggests it was a later composition that contrasted the strong rule of Sheshonq, during which Amon could be worshipped properly with the earlier weakness of the fragmented Egypt. The details of the Levant, he notes, would square with the archaeology of the places mentioned at the time.

So where does that leave us with *Wenamun* as a historical source? It is possible that the events and names – the whole episode – are just made up, Wenamun, Mengebet, Beder, Tjekerbaal, and Hatiba could all be completely fictional and the events never happened. A middle position might be that there was some real detail, perhaps characters or settings, without the narrative itself being 'true'. Or were these real people and the story basically true? Miriam Lichtheim commented that, 'whether or not the report reflects an actual mission, it depicts a true historical situation and a precise moment', while Bernard Knapp admits that he regards 'Wen-Amun as a historical person' and that 'even if his tale is fictitious, and dates some 150 years after the events it relates, the information it contains on Alashiya must have been based on someone's experience of visiting the island'.[5]

About Hatiba and Alashiya, *Wenamun* can only take us so far – and not very far at that. Archaeology, however, can certainly reveal more about the real women of ancient Cyprus. Louise Steel writes that we 'have a wealth of archaeological evidence which can give us unique insights into women's material experiences – we can explore the things they made, used, wore, exchanged, lost, and broke on a daily basis, the spaces they lived, loved, worked, and slept in, and the tombs where they were finally laid to rest'.[6] One Cypriot tomb in particular hints at the possible existence of women like Hatiba and gives some credence to the detail of the Egyptian tale.

The site of Kalavasos-*Ayios Dhimitrios*, in south central Cyprus, is situated by the Vasilikos river and only a few kilometres from the sea, with good farmland around and sources of copper nearby. In the later Bronze Age it developed as a planned town and flourished in particular between 1300 and 1200 BC.[7] Excavations and geophysical investigation have revealed several parts of the town, including the Northeast Area, which seems to be the locus of elite activities. One of the most significant areas had a 'massively constructed' monumental building with fine ashlar masonry, Building X, which lies at the north end of a north–south road through the site.[8] This building had a row of rooms on the east side, a central square, reached through the entrance at south, and two rooms full of storage jars on the west and northwest sides.[9] These jars appear to have contained olive oil and had a combined capacity of over 50,000 litres. In addition to oil production and storage, Building X may have functioned as a venue for feasting, evidenced by animal bones and imported tableware, an administrative centre for the town or even region, as suggested by sealings, and possibly as a residence for an elite family, who may have lived on an upper floor. Around Building X, a number of tombs were found, including Tomb 11 in the street to the west of the building.

Tomb 11 is important in part because it was undisturbed and intact.[10] Within the tomb, three young women and a number of young infants were laid to rest. One woman, referred to as Skeleton 1, was around 19–20 at time of death; she had been placed on a bench on the west side of the tomb and the other two women, one 21–24 (Skeleton 2) and the other 17 (Skeleton 3), were placed on the east bench. Whilst Skeleton 1 was found articulated, the other two were disarticulated and scattered, some smaller bones being on the floor, some long bones being paired up – sometimes lower limbs with upper ones; the skeletons also appeared to be incomplete. It seems that at some point some of the bones had been deliberately manipulated in some kind of ritual.

In addition to the adult women, the bones of four infants were found on the floor of the tomb; a three-year-old and three young infants or fetuses. The baby teeth of the child were found on one of the benches. The bones of the three younger infants were found amongst fish and bird bones and may originally have been deposited in a basket, which disintegrated. An additional adult and infant skeleton were found in a niche in the entrance passage of the tomb.

The tomb was materially wealthy – one of the wealthiest known from prehistoric Cyprus. Skeleton 1 was buried wearing various items of jewellery, including six gold earrings, four gold spirals, which might have been hair accessories, two gold signet rings and two silver toe rings. Six gold earrings were also found with the women on the east bench. One interpretation of this wealth is that it was part of the women's dowry – but that assumes it was controlled by her male relatives and was not her own, as well as that she was married. Goring has noted that these 'sets' of gold earrings (another set was found in a burial at Enkomi) appear to conform to an ancient Cypriot standard of around 10.8 grams.[11] It is possible that the jewellery doubled as a kind of convertible currency, although it is evident from the signs of wear that it had been worn.

Particularly interesting are Skeleton 1's two gold signet rings, which both bear the same four-character inscription in Cypro-Minoan writing system (Figure 11). There is only one other such ring, in silver, known from Cyprus (again from Enkomi). Known from throughout the eastern Mediterranean and Near East, signet rings and seals were used to seal or authorise documents and goods and were visible signs of an individual's economic power and status. A stone stamp seal was also found in Tomb 11.

FIG. 11 Pair of inscribed gold rings from Kalavasos: *Ayios Dhimitrios*, Cyprus. Courtesy of Silvia Ferrara

The Cypro-Minoan writing system was in use on Cyprus from the Late Bronze Age to the Early Iron Age (sixteenth–eleventh centuries BC).[12] However, it remains as yet undeciphered – there are only around 200 inscriptions and no bilingual inscriptions have been found to help; so we do not know what is written on the rings. It is tempting to suggest that they are inscribed with a name, and it has been suggested that it would have been the husband of Skeleton 1. However, Steel rightly points out that this is an unnecessary assumption, which implies that women were illiterate and unable to control wealth for themselves.[13] The simplest idea would be to suggest that they do bear the name of the woman who wore them and that she used them in an economic role that encompassed ownership (or oversight) and distribution of goods within the Alashiyan socio-economic system. Another possibility is that the rings were heirlooms of her family, but they were taken out of circulation at her demise. Even if the inscription is not a name, or not her name, her possession of the rings in death still likely reflects her economic power and social status in life.

So, who were these women found in Tomb 11 and how did they die? The combination of material wealth, gold, silver, and also many local and imported ceramics, glass and ivory, the nature of the finds, and the location of the tomb, which suggests a deliberate association of the women with the important Building X, all imply that the occupants of the tomb were women of elite status. One intriguing line of enquiry as to who they were concerns the diplomatic letters sent from Alashiyan rulers to rulers in Ugarit in northern Syria and in Egypt. Goren and colleagues have physically analysed the clay of these letters and have concluded that they most likely come from Cyprus.[14] They also suggest that the clay may have come from the region of Kalavasos-*Ayios Dhimitrios*, which might in turn suggest that it was the capital of the Alashiyan polity. It is possible then that the women of Tomb 11 were part of the ruling family of Alashiya (we do not know whether Alashiya was the whole or just a part of ancient Cyprus).

All three of the women were young, and given the presence of infants, it is plausible to infer that they may have died in pregnancy or childbirth, or sometime after, perhaps of complications. However, it seems unlikely for all to have died at the same time – and along with a three-year-old. A letter from some time earlier mentions a plague in Alashiya, which could have carried away many people, but none is recorded in the few texts from this later time. Some analysis of Skeleton 1 suggests she may have sustained an injury to her hand, which resulted in some degenerative joint disease, but this need not have been fatal.[15] It might be the case that the remains were interred at different times – a family tomb that was used exclusively for women and infants of a particular elite or ruling family over a period of time.

The very suggestion of a town ruled by a woman might have been a joke in *Wenamun* – an inversion of Egyptian norms. Hatiba might have been invented as an exotic character in a funny story of misadventure – whatever ultimate purpose or message that story had. But perhaps the Egyptians did know something vaguely about the existence of powerful women in the far-off land of Alashiya, in the middle of the sea. Perhaps the name Hatiba even referred to a real woman that had lived at some point, even if the story of Wenamun itself was not literally true. The archaeological evidence from Late Bronze Age Kalavasos-*Ayios Dhimitrios*, perhaps especially Skeleton 1 of Tomb 11, suggests that there were powerful women in Alashiya, and this might be as close as we can get to the reality of Hatiba

PART III

THE IRON AGE

Whilst the end of the Late Bronze Age was marked by destruction around the eastern Mediterranean, much remained and continued. In Greece, life continued without palace states and in Anatolia and northern Syria, small Neo-Hittite states appeared or continued from earlier times, retaining much of Bronze Age culture.[1] Egypt did not collapse c. 1200 BC – it did not lose its independence until centuries later when it fell under Persian control.[2] In Egypt, we find our first 'Early Iron Age' woman, Naunakhte, a woman alive in 1145 BC in the small town of Deir el-Medina (Chapter 12).

In Greece, the Mycenaean material culture faded away by 1050 BC and Protogeometric culture faded in.[3] The earlier part of this period has often been called 'the dark ages'. There were no cities and no states either – Greece may have been a land of relatively small-scale societies, albeit there was still some contact with overseas. Nichoria, Lefkandi, and Athens are all important sites for these periods of Submycenaean and Protogeometric Greece.[4] Lefkandi is known in particular for the huge apsoidal building of stone and mudbrick, which dates to around 950 BC; the building covered the graves of a cremated man and uncremated woman and four horses. Some of our most famous images of ancient Greece come from this time – the large geometrically decorated pots, later often with funerary scenes on them, used for elite burials. Around c. 850 BC, in the Geometric period, Herse, the Rich Lady of Athens, was buried (Chapter 13).

Greeks became increasingly outward-looking, engaging in trade with others around the Mediterranean and later founding colonies and settlements overseas, where they interacted with people of other cultures.[5] In the west, in the Celtic/Hallstatt lands of the south of France, Phocaean Greeks founded Massalia (Marseilles) near the mouth of the river Rhone around 600 BC.[6] Celtic people took advantage of the availability of Greek goods, which became increasingly prominent in the aristocratic culture of their elites. Between the north-flowing Seine and the south-flowing Rhone, well positioned to take advantage of trade routes between the two, was the important and possibly 'urban' site of Mont Lassois, or Vix, where we find the subject of Chapter 16, the so-called Princess of Vix.[7]

Pkupes, the subject of Chapter 14 is both Mediterranean and not. Pictured on a painted Athenian pot of the sixth century BC, this 'Amazon' and her sisters were an integral part of Athenian culture, part of the Athenians worldview.[8] In myth, the Amazons had even invaded Athens and had been present and active in the eastern Mediterranean. In their own right, archaeology has demonstrated the reality at the heart of Amazon legends, that warrior women really existed in an 'Amazon' culture to the north of the Black Sea region – a region to which Greece had become increasingly connected.

In the east, a number of powers existed and interacted with the Greeks – the Lydian kingdom of Croesus, for example, who ruled from 560 BC. Croesus' Anatolian kingdom even incorporated some Greek states on the Aegean coast of Anatolia.[9] In a grave miscalculation, partly influenced by an ambiguously worded oracle from Delphi suggesting that if he attacked the Persians a great empire would fall, Croesus attacked the Achaemenid Persian kingdom and was defeated. The Persians had, from their initial heartland in southwestern Iran, become a power to be reckoned with under Cyrus II (559–530 BC), who conquered an empire stretching from the Mediterranean to India. He founded as a new capital the city of Pasargadae, with its lavish palace and gardens. To advertise his status, he adopted the modest title 'king of the world, great king, mighty king, king of Babylon, king of Sumer and Akkad, king of the four quarters [of the world]'. With the defeat of Croesus, the Greek city states of western Anatolia became part of the Persian Empire.

Cyrus' son Cambyses II (530–522 BC) later added both Cyprus and Egypt to the empire. Then, in 522 BC, Darius became king, in dubious circumstances. During his rule, in 499 BC, some of the Greek states of western Anatolia revolted – and were supported by the Athenians. The Persians responded by reconquering them and then invading Greece with the intention of punishing the supporters of the revolt – especially Athens.[10] However, against all the odds, Athens and soldiers from Plataea defeated the Persians at the Battle of Marathon in 490 BC. Darius died and his son Xerxes became king; in 480 BC he set out to attack Athens and her allies, including Sparta. Whilst the Persians won at Thermopylae, they were defeated at Salamis and then Plataea and beat a retreat. Xerxes' mother, Darius' wife, was the queen Atossa, who is the subject of Chapter 15.

Also in the context of the Greco-Persian wars, we meet Aristonice, a priestess at Delphi, who responded to the questions of Athenian delegation (Chapter 17). In the late sixth century BC, Athens had undergone quite radical political reform under Cleisthenes, and as democracy developed a culture of rhetoric and disputation ensued, marked by political speeches, speeches in court, and discussion and debate in the assembly. The importance of dialogue is embodied in the activities of Socrates and the dialogues composed by his pupil Plato. Surviving the Peloponnesian War, Athens returned to democracy in the early fourth century BC and from this period we have the case of the trial of Neaira (Chapter 18), which we know about from the speeches of the Athenian orator Demosthenes, though the speech was probably by Apollodorus. Also in Greece around the mid-fourth century, we find Phanostrate, a doctor, in Chapter 19.

12

NAUNAKHTE

In the third year of pharaoh Ramesses V, c. 1145 BC, an Egyptian woman called Naunakhte, who lived in the workers' village of Deir el-Medina (Figure 12), went to her local court to explain her final will.[1] It was her express wish to disinherit some of her eight surviving children, sons and daughters, because they had failed in their duty to care for her in her old age. In her words:

> I am a free woman of the land of Pharaoh. I raised these eight servants of yours, and I outfitted them with everything that is usual for people of their character. Now look, I have become old, and look, they do not care for me. As for those who put their hands in my hand, to them I will give my property; [but] as for those who gave me nothing, to them I will not give any of my property.[2]

An elderly woman of around eighty years of age, Naunakhte would have given her statement orally in front of a panel of fourteen men, her fellow villagers, and probably her husband and grown up children too, where it was recorded for posterity by two scribes in a text that is now known as P. Ashmolean Museum 1945.97.[3] This and three other papyri, along with other textual evidence, enable us to learn something of her and her family's lives and of the society of the village she lived in.

Naunakhte's statement is immediately interesting for it sets out her status as a free Egyptian woman. Unlike the city-states of Greece and Rome, there was

FIG. 12 Deir el-Medina, Egypt. Source: Wikimedia Commons. Photo by Didia. CC BY-SA 3.0

no concept of 'citizenship' in Egypt, though there was a clearly very hierarchical society with pharaoh at the top.[4] Egyptian women theoretically were equal under the law with men, rather than the property of the male head of the family as in some other Mediterranean cultures, although they did not hold public offices. Women of all classes were able to bring cases to law themselves, although most cases were brought by men (and more by men against women, rather than vice versa).[5]

The text also tells us that despite high rates of infant mortality Naunakhte raised eight surviving children, whom she 'outfitted' for life – presumably meaning that she gave them a fair start in life in terms of education, opportunity, support, and so on. For this, she expected that her now grown-up children would support her in her old age. This was an important responsibility in Egyptian society – as another 'wisdom text' from the village observes 'Do not satiate yourself alone when your mother is destitute'.[6] Finally, it makes clear that Naunakhte owned her own property and is able to set the terms of who should inherit it. In this case, the record lists those cut out:

> List of her children of whom she said, 'They will not share in the division of my one-third, but only in the two-thirds (share) of their father.'
>
> the workman Neferhotep
> the lady Menetnakhte
> the lady Hentusenu
> the lady Khatanebu
> As for these four children of mine, they will [not] share in the division of all my property.

As we can see, the four children mentioned would only inherit from their father's share of property. However, Naunakhte also states that these four children will not share in any of the property of her first husband Qenherkhepeshef or that of her own father. However, her sons Maanakhteef, Qenherkhepeshef, and Amennakhte, and her daughters Wasetnakhte and Menetnakhte would inherit from her; Menetnakhte, she clarified, would be given only a partial inheritance.

Naunakhte's will suggests how complicated things could get with regard to property and inheritance even at the village level, amongst people with far less property than the pharaohs or elites we often implicitly think about when we think of ancient Egypt. Naunakhte inherited from her father, and that property remained hers even when she was married. She also inherited from her first husband, who was for four decades the senior scribe in Deir el-Medina, a man with his own library of texts, who also carved more than two hundred graffiti around the Valley of the Kings.[7] Qenherkhepeshef was in his fifties when he married the twelve-year-old Naunakhte; he may also have adopted her before he died, ensuring her inheritance from him.

Child marriage was not unusual in Egyptian society, as in many ancient traditional societies – especially those with a concern for ensuring the virginity of the bride. Nowadays, although child marriage is illegal in many societies, it remains common in various parts of the world, for example, in some sub-Saharan African countries. According to UNICEF, 21 per cent of young women around the world were married under the age of eighteen.[8] Child marriage can have numerous harmful effects on the girls affected, including psychological and physical impacts.[9] We do not know how the young Naunakhte viewed her impending marriage to a much older man; marriage at a young age was something she would have been familiar with and that she knew she would have to do, and it had perhaps happened to older friends. We do not know whether or not she was fearful, resigned, or enthusiastic.

Qenherkhepeshef, as senior scribe, had some status in the town. He probably taught Naunakhte to read and write and she in turn taught her children in turn, which would have gained them some status in the town too – even though people in Deir el-Medina were generally more literate than those in typical Egyptian villages. Naunakhte may have felt some satisfaction with being matched with an important man and with being able to learn reading and writing from him. Naunakhte named a son of her second marriage, to Khaemnun, after her first husband, and passed on his library to another Amennakhte, and, after he died, to another son, Maanakhteef.[10] Perhaps their relationship was at least amicable, possibly it was happy.

Deir el-Medina was not exactly a typical Egyptian village – it was a state-owned village of some sixty-eight houses, perhaps five hundred inhabitants, which was populated by men who were employed to build and decorate the royal tombs of the Valley of the Kings and their families; it was not a village of farmers and could not support itself.[11] In return for their work, the villagers received rations from the state, with a diet that included bread and beer, fish and vegetables, and occasionally meat.[12] Although they were state employees, the villagers do seem to have done a lot of private work too, generating extra wealth by the use of their skills: carpenters making furniture, sculptors and painters decorating private tombs.[13] The village endured for over four centuries, with these skills being passed down through the generations.

The men were expected to put in eight-hour days, working and sleeping away from the village and returning for their day off, although workers were, probably with a nod and a wink from their managers, known to stretch out their weekends to two or three days.[14] But for much of the time, Deir el-Medina was a village of women and children, and, as Lesko writes, 'while the men were away, it seems logical that a lot of decision-making would fall to the village wives and that they would take a strong role in the community as well as household management'.[15] This might be one reason why the women of Deir el-Medina appear to have had a relatively high status.[16]

Marriage was expected to be a partnership, with the husband and wife supporting each other. Not all wives lived up to the ideal. One text presented by Deborah Sweeney contains the complaint of a man, Amunpahapy, whose wife failed to look after him when he was ill, instead travelling to the countryside and also collecting, for herself, his state pay.[17] As a punishment, she was cut out of his will and forbidden to approach Amunpahapy's house, on pain of a beating. Not all husbands were ideal either; Sweeney also presents a text that may refer to domestic violence, though the text is fragmentary. Women could sue men for wrongful behaviour just as men could sue women. If a marriage was too unhappy, divorce was straightforward (marriage itself seems to have been just moving in together) and property divided up equitably.

Women in Deir el-Medina presumably often received their household's rations and decided how it would be used until the next delivery came. With grain being provided by the state, women would grind it and make bread, using small ovens in their homes, and brew beer. Another role of women was to make clothes – spinning and then weaving flax and making linen garments from the cloth. To help out, the state also provided female servants, who would work in a house for several days, helping with grinding the grain and other tasks.[18] Sweeping the house out and keeping it tidy would also take up time – not to mention looking after any children. Women could also work for profit outside the home, keeping animals, trading; one woman who worked as a wet nurse is recorded as receiving a payment equivalent to three month's pay for a workman.[19] As perhaps one of the better off of Deir el-Medina, Naunakhte may have had help in her day-to-day tasks and in looking after her children.

Steven Snape, in his account of Deir el-Medina, has discussed the possible gendering of spaces in the town's houses.[20] The houses, entered through wooden doors from the street, had a fairly uniform design with four main areas, a 'front room', 'living room', a 'transitional' space, and a kitchen; occupants could also use the roof for various purposes, including sleeping. The most obviously 'gendered' room was the kitchen, which was the rearmost room. These contained an oven, a mortar, and a kneading trough and were roofed only with matting to let out the smoke and provide shade. The location of the kitchen, he suggests, could indicate the domestic seclusion of women; drawing a parallel with modern Egyptian houses, guests could have been entertained only in a front room while some areas of the house remained family/female only.

However, almost half of the houses have a 'box bed' structure in the front room, and these were painted with images usually associated with women – the god Bes, for example. These have been interpreted by some as 'birth beds' and to suggest that women gathered in or were present in the front room – the most public room – and not removed from the male gaze. Lesko suggests that 'a sexual interpretation in its most comprehensive sense, encompassing the procreative and erotic, the maternal and nurturing sides of female life, seems to apply to the box bed paintings'.[21] The presence of Bes, though, may refer to a more general protection of the household. Snape reminds us that spaces can be used flexibly and that the 'box bed' structures probably had 'several layers of function and meaning'.[22] In any case, given the other evidence of their activities, it seems very doubtful that the women of Deir el-Medina led particularly secluded lives.

Koenraad Donker van Heel has pieced together many strands of evidence to tell the story of Naunakhte and her family.[23] For example, he suggests that Naunakhte may have lived with her first husband in House NE VIII at Deir el-Medina, which gives her a physical location in the town. He also draws on the textual evidence to show how Naunakhte and other women in Deir el-Medina could have fun – they could hold and attend parties.[24] A number of parties are mentioned in the texts and the villagers seem to have been quite concerned with noting down who attended and how much food and drink they brought with them. This attention to detail could be due to the importance of reciprocal gift-giving in ancient Egyptian society. Donker van Heel notes that there are several references to members of Naunakhte's family attending parties – her daughter Hentusenu, who had a daughter named Naunakhte, and at the same party her sister Menetnakhte and her daughter Tapaipu. Some of her sons were also recorded as party guests, as was Khaemnun, their father.

After the elderly Naunakhte died, her property was claimed by the beneficiaries of her stated will and part of the process was again recorded – two copies survive, and perhaps there were more, for each beneficiary's records.[25] We can imagine the grown-up children visiting the house and taking their share. Her son Neferhotep, one of the children disowned, appears to have contested the will later on. Donker van Heel suggests that he was the black sheep of the family because the texts imply he had repeatedly come to his mother for help but squandered it – and then on top of that, he had failed to take care of her in her old age.[26] Her son Qenherkhepeshef, however, was singled out for special treatment – he also received a bronze bowl. This may have been because he agreed to give his father a 'pension'.[27]

With its wealth of textual and archaeological evidence, Deir el-Medina offers a unique window on life in New Kingdom Egypt; as Snape comments, 'nowhere else in ancient Egypt – or perhaps the ancient world – can we take a named, non-royal individual and examine their house, their tomb and their relationships with other named individuals'.[28] Naunakhte was not a queen or a princess, she was not what archaeologists would usually term a member of the 'elite', though through her first marriage, her literacy, and relative wealth, she probably had some standing in the village. She lived in Egypt, in the eastern Mediterranean, at a time better known for the collapse of states and for widespread destruction and war, yet her own life in this special community gives us plenty of drama on a much more human scale.

13

HERSE

In the first few hours of a new digging season in Athens, 14 June 1967, archaeologists started to excavate the area to the north of the Areopagus, the Hill of Ares, which lies to the northwest of the Acropolis.[1] Just 15 cm down, Evelyn Lord Smithson wrote shortly afterwards in an article in the journal *Hesperia*, the earth began to reveal a new burial – the upper rims of several pots appearing through the dirt. As the archaeologists explored further, they uncovered the whole burial pit with a large belly-handled amphora some 71 cm in height with various other smaller items of pottery in it. The type of amphora indicated that the burial was that of a woman, designated AA 302, who had been cremated around 850 BC. She has become known to archaeologists as the 'Rich Athenian Lady'.

This part of Athens, which much later became the agora of the classical city, its civic centre, had been used for burials since the Late Bronze Age.[2] Through the Mycenaean collapse of c. 1200 and its aftermath, which may not have affected Athens very much, and the so-called 'dark age', the people living in the area buried their dead here. From around 900 BC, there was a burial of a cremated man of around thirty-four years of age, reckoned to have been a warrior, in a pot with a 'killed' iron sword wrapped around its neck and other iron implements, weapons and tools.[3] A burial of a woman from the same period had contained a pair of small clay 'feet' or 'booties', the purpose or meaning of which is unknown but could possibly be some kind of reference to her own or her children's problem feet.[4] The Rich Athenian Lady's burial was part of this ongoing tradition.[5]

These and the Rich Athenian Lady's burials predate the adoption of the alphabet in Greece at around 775 BC and she lived long before Homer and Hesiod, the famous poets of the end of the eighth century BC, though the oral tradition of epic poetry may have been in full swing.[6] The Greek worlds they inhabited existed long before the city-state era and Athens' heyday of victory against the Persians, of Socrates and Plato, Aristophanes and Euripides, the democracy and the empire. But it is much less common now to refer to this period as a dark age and it is now recognised as an important period in its own right – termed the Early Iron Age. It is traditionally divided up into pottery-based subdivisions of Submycenaean, Protogeometric, and Geometric, and after that come historical times.

After the collapse of the highly hierarchical Mycenaean society, an ethos of greater egalitarianism may have prevailed, explaining in part the more modest material culture of the period, but as population grew and contacts with the eastern Mediterranean increased in intensity again, across the ninth and eighth centuries, differences in wealth and status reappeared, with an associated increase in craft practices to supply fine goods for the upper classes, such as jewellery and painted pottery.[7] Whilst individual households remained the basic social and economic units, aristocratic lineages appeared, called *genos*. Aristocratic culture involved, according to Dimitri Nakassis, 'control of arable land, feasting, warfare, trade and metallurgy'.[8]

Still, Geometric Athens in the days of the Rich Lady may have been a collection of villages or even just 'concentrations of homes' rather than a city as we would imagine.[9] Athens perhaps did not exist as a state and the formal union between Athens and the wider region of Attica had not yet happened. Athenian traditions from later times certainly projected back the idea of kingship as a major part of Athens' past, with a continuous line of kings and then magistrates starting with Kekrops in the Late Bronze Age and, from the twelfth century, supposedly, ruled the Medontid kings and leaders descended from the Messenian refugee Melanthos.[10] However, the tradition is not necessarily historical. Both Herodotus' *Histories* and Aristotle's work *The Athenian Constitution* really show how little the later Athenians seem to have known for certain about Athens before the early seventh century and the first 'real' (if hazy) events and characters: the attempted coup by Cylon and the reforms of the lawgivers Drako and Solon.[11]

The style of burial of the Rich Athenian Lady, with the bones of cremated individuals placed in pots, was part of a long tradition of 'trench and pit' burials, which went back to Protogeometric times.[12] A trench was dug with a pit in it into which the pot containing the cremation was placed. The remains of the cremation pyre were swept into the trench, where more goods might be deposited. Finally, the pit was filled with earth and covered with a slab.[13] If this sounds like a rather subdued or even grim form of burial, we have to remember the ceremony and experience that attended it, from the bringing and placing of the body to the treatment of the remains and the objects deposited. It may well have lasted more than a day. Some kind of feasting accompanied the funeral – careful analysis of the animal bones found, which included goats and cattle, suggests that there was more than 70 kg of meat available.[14] This would have been enough to feed several hundred people well and it testifies to the wealth and importance of the Rich Lady and her kin.

Modern day cremations are performed out of sight in gas ovens at 900° C and incineration is complete in less than an hour and a half.[15] The cremation of the Rich Athenian Lady would have taken place in public and it would, at a couple of hundred degrees less, in open air, have taken perhaps five hours or so for the body to be reduced to bones. Maria Liston, who has used pig corpses to explore how early Greek cremations worked, found that it took around six to seven hours to cremate a 95 kg pig; the Rich Lady probably weighed somewhere less than 70 kg.[16] Liston and Papadopoulos also suggest that some 120 kg of hardwood fuel would have been needed for the fire, another sign of the wealth and resources of the Rich Lady's family.

Fire visibly transforms the organic parts of a body burnt on an open-air pyre into dust and ashes in front of a watching audience and leaves the bones, which can be collected afterwards. Tim Sørensen and Mikkel Bille remind us that fire has been a special element across human cultures and emphasise how the experience of a cremation would have involved seeing 'fire and flames' that 'would change appearance over several stages during the cremation process'.[17] Different elements of the pyre and the body would set alight at different times and burn at different rates – kindling, logs, hair and flesh; smoke would rise, and the fire would change in intensity and size, eventually itself dying out into glowing embers – even the smells and the fire's sound would have contributed to the experience of a cremation. Perhaps the fire lasted all night. When the fire finally died, the Rich Lady's remains were gathered with extreme care to be placed in her jar and placed in the pit with the other items.[18]

Evidence of the Rich Lady's wealth may additionally come from the grave goods. One of the pottery vessels found was a small chest, 25 cm in height by 44 cm long and almost 10 cm wide, which had five onion-shaped additions on its lid. These were interpreted by Smithson as model granaries, which accompanied a larger independent model granary also placed in the grave.[19] From this piece, in particular, Smithson made an ingenious argument, that the five granaries represented directly the wealth of the Rich Lady's family.[20] In early Athens, men with a certain amount of wealth were eligible for the highest offices as basileus (king), polemarch (general), and archon (chief magistrate). These were the *pentakosiomedimnoi*, the 'five-hundred-bushel men'. Perhaps the five granaries represent measures of a hundred bushels of grain, which would have reminded all present at the funeral of her elite status. Smithson concluded that 'it is not impossible that she, herself, was an archon's wife' – perhaps the wife of Arriphonos, a king thought to have ruled in the mid-ninth century BC, according to the much later king list of Kastor of Rhodes.[21]

Other scholars have argued that these ovoids are more likely to represent beehives, and Isabelle Martelli suggests that honey was linked with the production of expensive purple, which itself was linked with textile production.[22] The miniature chest recalled real chests that would have contained textiles. However, Sarah Morris and John Papadopoulos point out that ancient Greek beehives were cylindrical and placed on their long sides, not ovoid. Funerary chests like these possibly did indicate family sources of wealth; others show cattle or later horses.[23] The focus on grain in Rich Lady's grave goods might have been especially notable in an economy that was shifting from a focus on cattle to an increased emphasis on grain, although the handles of the amphora she was buried in were in the shape of cattle heads – old wealth.

Inside the belly-handled amphora, the archaeologists found various items of jewellery, including a necklace made with over a thousand beads of faience, which may have been Phoenician in origin.[24] There were also three gold rings, with decoration including lozenges, zigzags, and dots, and a pair of very fine elaborate gold filigree earrings with pomegranate finials, an ivory disk and two ivory stamp seals, a pair of bronze fibulae ('safety pins'), and three straight pins.[25] Seals had not been made in Greece since the Late Bronze Age and may indicate that the Rich Lady had some economic power in her own right – whether that be related to grain, cattle, craft production, or overseas exchange. The gold earrings, in particular, have been identified as outstanding examples of craftsmanship, since they employ the techniques of filigree and granulation, which had also been lost after Mycenaean times.[26] Although now earlier work is known from burials at Lefkandi, Smithson was right in suggesting they 'imply a far more intimate association of Greeks with orientals' than had been thought at this stage in Greek history. Smithson thought the jewellery had probably been worn by the deceased at her *prothesis*, her laying out, as it had not been burnt.

What of the physical remains of the Rich Athenian Lady? The human bones, examined initially by J. Lawrence Angel in 1967, were determined to belong to a woman aged between twenty-four and forty years old.[27] With advances in forensic techniques over the subsequent decades, Maria A. Liston, a specialist in human remains, decided to re-examine the Rich Lady's remains.[28] Several parts of the surviving bones, the pelvis and ribs, show that the woman was probably in her thirties when she died, and possibly up to forty. She was perhaps 155 cm and likely weighed less than 70 kg. She was fine-boned with a skull that is 'almost childlike', but her wisdom teeth had appeared.[29] It also appears that she was in good physical condition at the time of death, at least in some ways. Her bones showed no signs of wear from hard work such as grinding grain or carrying water and likewise she had not developed the greater muscle mass associated with performing these and other laborious tasks; her joints were even free from or age-related wear and arthritis. What this suggests, Liston and Papadopoulos conclude, is that the Rich Athenian Lady very probably was a woman of high status, who did not have to do any heavy work herself and could live a fairly leisurely 'low impact' life.[30]

One of the mysteries about the grave was the presence of the smaller neck-handled amphora, common for male burials but remarked upon as odd in a female grave. It was possible that it contained an infant male burial, but it appeared to be too small and examination of the contents revealed only animal bones.[31] However, Liston's re-examination showed that the tiny bones of an infant were indeed present, mixed with the bones of sacrificed animals; some of the bones, the leg and pelvis, were clearly human. The remains of a baby would have been destroyed in the cremation, which strongly suggests the fetus was unborn and protected by its mother's body; the Rich Athenian Lady was pregnant when she died.[32] Unfortunately, because the baby is so young, it is not possible to conclude whether it was female or male. Could it be that the Rich Lady died from complications in her pregnancy?

Whoever this woman was, this care for her remains and those of her unborn child surely indicates the depth of feeling at their passing. Almost all of the Rich Lady's bones, including small bones, were present in her burial. 'The extraordinary care with which the Early Iron Age Athenians gathered her cremated remains', Liston remarks, even 'led to the preservation of most of the facial structure'.[33] The survival of much of the facial bone structure and skull enabled the team quite ingeniously to attempt a facial reconstruction, using modern forensic techniques.[34] Where parts were missing, a mirror image of the other side was used, and for the missing parts of the lower jaw (mandible) that of another woman with near identical measurements provided a model. To obtain details of musculature and soft tissue depth, data from a large sample of women was taken to provide measurements for twenty-one points of the face. Because H 16.6 was pregnant, data from heavier women were used. The details of the face were then penciled in and a neutral hairstyle added along with the earrings from her grave. Liston, Houston, and the team had given the Rich Athenian Lady a face again, after almost three millennia (Figure 13).

The story of the Rich Athenian Lady has more recently taken on yet another dimension. Maria Roussou and her colleagues recognised that story-telling could be an effective and powerful way of bringing archaeological sites 'to life' for visitors, going beyond presenting descriptions and information. So, with a team of archaeologists, designers, and IT specialists working together, they developed a prototype app to tell visitors stories that would engage them

FIG. 13 Reconstruction of the face of the Rich Athenian Lady, by Graham Houston from M. A. Liston and J. K. Papadopoulos. "The 'Rich Athenian Lady' Was Pregnant: The Anthropology of a Geometric Tomb Reconsidered," Hesperia 73 (2004), p. 22, fig. 13. Courtesy of the Trustees of the American School of Classical Studies at Athens

'in an emotional journey to the past'.[35] One story they chose to tell was that of an imaginary woman, Glauke, who mourns the death of her beloved older sister – a beautiful sister who had had a kind husband, a comfortable life, who loved her nephews and nieces but who had no children of her own. Glauke's fond memories are mixed with pain and regret; the burial gifts she sees are 'not just for her sister but for the creature too. The one that bears no name. The one that lead her to death'.[36] And even though it is imagination, they give the Rich Lady of Athens a name: Herse.

14

PKPUPES

The Amazons are one of the best-known peoples of antiquity – though long thought to be mythical. They appear in book three of the *Iliad*, from the later eighth or seventh century BC, where they are given the epithet 'a match for men'; the word 'Amazon' is still used to refer to fierce or powerful women. The Amazons were warrior women who legend had it would cut off a breast to enable them to better use their bows – the fifth-century BC Greek historian Hellanikos thought 'Amazon' could be read etymologically as 'a', 'without', 'mazos', 'breasts' (*mastos* in Greek).[1] Others thought it could be read as without 'barley', 'maza', and referred to the fact that Amazons did not farm in the way that civilised settled people would. In *Airs, Waters, Places*, the physician Hippocrates recorded that Sarmatian women burnt the right breast of their baby girls to divert power into their right arms – making them stronger fighters. Such myths about these exotic women in a society where 'proper' gendered roles were reversed abounded amongst the Greeks and Romans, Amazon specialist Adrienne Mayor tells us. An alternative and possibly more likely origin for the name comes from old Iranian 'ha-mazon' – 'warriors'. But it may be fruitless to search for meaning in the name – what would a future etymologist make of 'American'?

Amazons were generally placed by the ancient Greeks on the northern and eastern coasts of the Black Sea, the lands known as Scythia and Sarmatia (centred on modern Ukraine and beyond). The Scythians consisted of a variety of peoples and tribes that inhabited the region; some farmed whilst others were nomadic or semi-nomadic.[2] Amazons were particularly associated with Sarmatians and Sauromatians. In book four of his *Histories*, Herodotus tells an origin story of the Sauromatae. He explains that the Greeks took three shiploads of Amazons prisoner, but the Amazons got free and killed their captors. The ships were blown to the Scythian lands of Lake Maeotis (the Sea of Azov), where the Amazons seized horses and began raiding. A group of local Scythian men wanted to have children with these strong women and eventually the two groups came together, paired off, and the Amazons learned the Scythian's language. What happened next tells us much about the Amazon attitude – at least as it was recounted by Greeks.

The Scythian men said, 'we . . . have parents and property. Let us give up our present way of life and return to live with our people. We will keep you as our wives and not take any others'. The Amazons responded to the offer by saying:

> We and the women of your nation could never live together; our ways are too much at variance. We are riders; our business is with the bow and the spear, and we know nothing of women's work; but in your country no woman has anything to do with such things – your women stay at home in their waggons occupied with feminine tasks, and never go out to hunt or for any other purpose. We could not possibly agree.

The Amazon counter-offer was that 'if, however, you wish to keep us as your wives and to behave as honourable men, go and get from your parents the share of property which is due to you, and then let us go off and live by ourselves'. The men accepted and also agreed that as a new people they should move away from the lands they had raided to the northeast. Thus, Herodotus explains:

> ever since then the women of the Sauromatae have kept to their old ways, riding to the hunt on horseback sometimes with, sometimes without, their men, taking part in war and wearing the same sort of clothes as men . . .. They have a marriage law which forbids a girl to marry until she has killed an enemy in battle.

The Amazons knew about and rejected the aspects of behaviour most closely associated with women's lives in contemporary society, so the stories tell us.

Many languages were spoken in Scythia, and some Scythians would have been bi- or multilingual. One people, the Geloni, lived a settled life in a town of wooden houses, temples and walls, amongst the pastoral Budini people, but spoke a different 'half Scythian, half Greek' language. The Romeyka language of Pontus may be its descendent.[3] Herodotus tells us that the Geloni were the descendents of Greeks who fled their coastal cities during times of trouble. The Greeks founded numerous cities around the Black Sea coast and knew

Scythians at first hand – the Athenians even hired Scythians as a city 'police'.[4] We cannot dismiss their stories of the region and its people, though equally we have to admit that not everything reported may be accurate or true.

Three of the most famous mythical Amazons in the classical tradition were Hippolyte, Antiope, and Penthesileia. The story of Hippolyte involved the Greek hero Heracles, who travelled across the Black Sea to Pontus to obtain the Amazon's golden girdle, on the orders of king Eurystheus.[5] Heracles was well received by the Amazons, but a misunderstanding led to conflict between the Greeks and the Amazons and Heracles killed Hippolyte. Some versions of the myth have the two attracted to each other, but certainly one sculpted relief from a fifth-century BC temple at Selinous shows Heracles quite brutally holding Hippolyte by the hair and standing on her foot – the better to deliver the death blow. Theseus, according to some, accompanied Heracles and abducted Hippolyte's sister Antiope, luring her onto his ship and then setting sail before she could escape.[6] As Mayor notes 'abduction and rape would be in character for Theseus, who was a serial sexual predator'.[7] Penthesileia led the Amazons as allies of the Trojans when the Greeks attacked Troy; she was killed by Achilles.[8] Whilst Amazons were presented as strong, fierce, and brave, they usually ended up being killed by Greek men.

Scythians had ranged south over the Caucasus mountains and into Assyria and even to the Levantine Mediterranean coast when the Assyrian Empire was crumbling.[9] The mythical Penthesileia and her Amazons may have come from Anatolia and a number of Greek cities in Asia Minor even claimed Amazons as their founders.[10] The Trojan forces gathered for battle at the tomb of the Amazon Myrine, a hill on the plain in front of the city (*Iliad* book two). Another Greek myth held that the Amazon queen Orithyia gathered an army of Amazons and Scythians to invade Greece and destroy Athens, in revenge for Hippolyte and Antiope.[11] Thus Amazons, in a sense, lived in Athens and in Greece and nearby lands – the Athenians sacrificed annually to the memory of the brave Amazon, there were Amazon cemeteries, and even, in the far south of Greece, wooden statues of Amazonian Apollo and Peaceful Artemis, supposedly dedicated by Amazons.[12] In the mental world of classical antiquity, Amazons had a role in local history, as well as in stories of faraway lands.

The Amazons were intimately bound up with Greek identity and history and their cultural importance continued into Roman times. The earliest image of Amazons in the Greek world is on a painted votive shield from Nafplion, dating to about 700 BC.[13] It shows five figures, with the two large in the foreground and smaller figures behind each of them, and one body on the ground. The two figures on the left are bearded, and so must be men – one is often interpreted as Herakles, but this is not clear – but the large figure on the right is thought to be an Amazon. The opposing figures are in combat and brandishing weapons – the Amazon wields a spear and the male a sword.

FIG. 14 Athenian pot (c. 420 BC) showing Amazons fighting. Source: Wikimedia Commons. Photo by Marie-Lan Nguyen

The male is grabbing the Amazon's pointed hat whilst she is pushing his arm away – oddly, a bird painted above and behind the Amazon is holding her helmet plume in its beak. Perhaps this detail implies that the image is depicting a specific story or myth. Amazons appear on pottery from around Greece (Figure 14) and of pots that depict the Labours of Hercules, the acquisition of Hippolyte's girdle is the second most popular.[14]

In Greek traditions, as John Man points out, 'Amazonomachies', 'battles with Amazons', were one of the three popular 'battles with' themes, along with 'Centauromachies' ('battles with Centaurs') and 'Titanomachies' ('battles with Titans').[15] In the fifth century BC, the sculptor Phidias produced for the new Parthenon temple (and for Athens' leader, his friend Pericles) a giant ivory and gold statue of Athena 12 metres tall, armed with a spear and shield.[16] Although the original shield has not survived, descriptions and copies show that its exterior was decorated with an Amazonomachy and its interior with a Gigantomachy; a Centauromachy was depicted on Athena's sandals.[17] The metopes on the west side of the Parthenon itself also showed an Amazonachy, the Painted Stoa, in Athens' agora, which had a famous painting of a battle with Amazons (as well as with Trojans, Persians, and Spartans).[18]

Amazons also played a role in the daily life of Greeks, including Greek girls. In the highly masculine culture of ancient Greece, it could be said that there was a kind of cult of the Amazons and especially the famous Atalanta. Adrienne Mayor states that 'Amazons were featured everywhere, on women's pottery, on perfume jars, on jewelry boxes, on sewing equipment. Little girls played with Amazon dolls'.[19] This raised many questions to ponder: what kind of models were Atalanta and the other legendary Amazons for these girls, whose lives would be so different to those of the Amazons? What stories did they weave for her in their play? What did grown women, often, at least in Athens, living in seclusion, think of the free spirited and exotic women? What did the men in their drinking parties make of Atalanta, the warrior woman who decorated their drinking sets?

So far, we have been thinking of mythical Amazons and those from the stories of Herodotus, but it is now generally recognised that there were real warrior women in Scythia.[20] In the 1960s and 1970s, 'kurgan' burials in the Volga and Ural regions, ancient Sarmatia, began to be excavated, and some revealed rich burials of women with weapons and horses.[21] Over the years, many more similar burials came to light in Scythia – Valerii Guliaev notes 112 up to 1991 of which around 70 per cent were young women.[22] One burial in particular, Kurgan 16 at Akkermen (south of Odessa) has been noted as that of an 'Amazon'. Renate Rolle has described it as an intact burial 3 metres in depth, with a supine female skeleton of a young woman.[23] She was buried with a quiver, with twenty arrows, two lances, and a heavy 'fighting belt' reinforced with strips of iron. She also had 'female' items, including a spindle whorl, a bronze mirror, bracelets and pearl necklaces. What is more, her remains showed indications of trauma from fighting. She had various head injuries 'from blows and stabs' visible on the skull and also had a bronze arrowhead embedded in her knee. She may well have died in combat of some kind. As Rolle pointed out, 'this grave reinforced ... the vital importance of detailed anthropological classification. In the past, graves containing weapons, and especially heavy armour, had with few exceptions been assumed to be those of men'.[24]

In late 2019, a flurry of media reports announced the discovery of three generations of 'Amazons' found in a tomb (Devitsa V) near Voronezh, Russia, by the Don river, for example. A girl of 12–13 years old, a woman of 20–29, and one of 25–35, and an older woman of 45–55 were found.[25] Two graves had been robbed, but the older woman was buried with an elaborate gold headdress called a *calathus*, a forked arrowhead, and an iron dagger, whilst one of the 'middle-aged' women was buried with two spears, a bronze mirror, and a bracelet made of glass beads. She was also buried in a riding position. The head of the expedition Valerii Guliaev explained that 'the Amazons are common Scythian phenomenon and during the last decade our expedition has discovered approximately 11 burials of young armed women .... Separate barrows were filled for them and all burial rites which were usually made for men were done for them'.

A number of female warriors have been identified in burials in the Caucasus region, in Georgia, and Armenia, as well. Burial 3 at Jrapi, dating to somewhere in the Late Bronze/Early Iron Age, contained three individuals in a stone lined pit.[26] Skeleton 1 was identified by its hip bones as a female, and by features such as joint and tooth condition aged as 45–50 at time of death. A bronze arrow was found in her ribs and is thought to be the cause of death; her remains showed evidence of earlier healed injuries caused by being hit with a club or mace. The second woman, Skeleton 2, was younger, perhaps 16–20, and had suffered a possibly fatal blow to the head; she also had earlier healed injuries to the head. Skeleton 2 may also have been shot in the tibia with an arrow, where an arrow-sized hole remains. The women were buried with their arrows and Skeleton 1 holding a dagger. According to the osteoarchaeologists who studied the remains, the development of the women's muscles, and those of the buried man, are consistent with horse-riding. They also reflect warrior activities such as frequently drawing a bow.

In 2003, Guliaev suggested that women of a certain age and social class may have been engaged in a kind of military service.[27] This might have been a duty to protect the home when the men were away fighting. However, the literary sources suggest that Amazon women were warriors and hunters in their own right. Other than our inherited ideas about gender roles, there seems no reason not to accept that this could be the case. And we can ask why the status of these women should be seen only in relation to the activities of the male warriors.

Unlike the mythical Amazons, the bodies of real Amazons found in the ground are anonymous. But Mayor's work with David Saunders and the historical linguist John Colarusso may solve another problem.[28] Many images of Amazons on Athenian pottery have 'nonsense' inscriptions accompanying them. However, these inscriptions may be attempts to record non-Greek 'Scythian' names or words in languages such as Circassian and others from the northwest Caucasus family. They studied twenty pots and came up with a list of plausibly meaningful Amazon names. One Athenian red-figure cup from around 525–500 BC depicts Herakles and Hermes on one side, whilst on the other were Pkpupes and a group of Amazons rushing into battle on horseback and on foot.[29] Pkpupes, with its cluster of difficult to pronounce consonants, could be translated from Circassian as 'Worthy of armour'. It was painted by the Oltos painter, who himself might not have been an Athenian. The suggestion that Amazons may have been named in their own languages, or Greek approximations of them, raises the possibilities of much greater first-hand contact with Amazons and Scythians – whether on the edge of or in Scythia or in Greece itself.

Was Pkpupes a real Amazon woman, perhaps that Oltos had heard about in his hometown or from some other traveller, or was she a character from a myth not recorded? Did she grow up somewhere on the Black Sea coast, or inland, spending much of her life on horseback armed with a bow? It is at least a possibility that one of the females from the many Amazon graves bore this name or one of the others revealed by Mayor, Saunders, and Colarusso. The Amazons, real and mythologised, certainly did play an important role in the imagination of the Greeks and around the Mediterranean – and their stories of warrior women had at least some basis in reality.

15

ATOSSA

Atossa was in every sense a Persian royal woman. She was a daughter of Cyrus the Great, who ruled the Persian Empire from 559 to 530 BC, a wife of her brother Cambyses, king from 530–522 BC, one of the many wives of Darius I, king from 522 to 486 BC, and the mother of Xerxes I, 486–465 BC (Figure 15).[1] But her lasting fame in the western tradition comes from her appearances in two of the most well-known texts from ancient Greece, Aeschylus' *Persians* and Herodotus' *Histories*. Both of these works, one a tragedy play the other combining history and anthropology, present the war between the Greeks and Persians in the early fifth century BC – the wars marked by the famous battles of Marathon, Thermopylae, Salamis, and Plataea. Atossa is portrayed as a powerful woman with great influence over the men in her life.

In *Persians*, the queen is introduced by the chorus, a group of Persian elders or councillors, who open the play by expressing their fear for the fate of Xerxes and the Persian army that has gone west to invade Greece. The chorus already knows that Xerxes has gone a step too far – arrogantly bridging the Hellespont with boats so that his army could cross the sea from Asia to Europe – and has invited his own doom. The queen also reveals her own fear in reply:

> *Chorus of Persian Elders*: Look! The king's mother, radiant as the eyes of gods immortal, stands! Fall prostrate, Persians, at her feet; then rise and with one voice salute her. Hail our queen, noblest of all women in

FIG. 15 *A Persian Princess*. Artist: John William Godward. Date: 1898. Contributor: Painters / Alamy Stock Photo.

> eastern lands, Darius' wife and Xerxes' mother, hail! Mother of a god thou art, and wife hast been – unless the Fates today have turned their hands against us, and their ancient favour fail.
>
> *Atossa*: That fear is mine; I too am torn by anxious thoughts, therefore I have left the golden-furnished chamber which I shared with king Darius, to tell you my own dread . . . .

Persians was performed in Athens in 472 BC as part of a quartet of plays by Aeschylus that won first prize at that year's Great Dionysia, the festival at which tragedies were performed. The play tells of the failure of Xerxes' Persian campaign in Greece and Persian defeat in the naval battle of Salamis in 480 BC (most tragedies took on themes from mythology, so it was unusual). Atossa, the king's mother, appears as the central character – she is on stage the most, delivers the most lines, after the chorus, and, most importantly, she ties all the characters together – Xerxes, Darius, the messenger, and the chorus of Persian elders.[2] The audience in Athens, sitting in the theatre, would have seen a Persian queen, no doubt decked out in eastern finery, speaking to them about her son, the king, the Persian defeat, and the astonishing Athenian victory. What would they have felt watching this performance?

But what was the *Persians* really about – was it even a real tragedy play?[3] History, according to Aristotle, should say 'what happened', while poetry tells us the kind of things that can happen; poetry was considered more philosophical and universal. Tragedy, he says, involves the audience feeling 'pity and fear'. We can imagine the audience jubilant at the description of Salamis and the description of Athens and the Athenians, and this has led some to suggest *Persians* is an epinician, a victory poem. Can we imagine that they would have had any pity or fear for Atossa or for the Persians, from whose perspective the story is told? Aristophanes, the comic playwright of the later fifth century, suggested that it 'glorified the best achievement' and taught the Athenians 'always to desire to defeat their enemies'. How would a British audience have responded to a tragedy based on a failed German invasion of the United Kingdom in World War II, in which the story was told by Hitler's mother, just eight years after the events described?

Whatever his intention, and he may not have been thinking of provoking just one feeling, Aeschylus chose to make a Persian queen – not named in the text – the main character of his play and to put words into her mouth. While this modern reader finds the queen a sympathetic character, who cares for her son, despite his flaws, the audience may have felt that she was a very alien character – a foreign queen to whom subjects prostrated themselves, very un-Greek, speaking to them. In the male-dominated public culture of Athens, there was a feeling that respectable women's voices, and even their names, ought not to be heard (and to an extent, they should not be seen either).

Yet there are precedents in Greek culture for listening to women in public – even foreign women – in the *Iliad*, for example, where Hector's mother Hecuba laments her son's death.[4] In this emotional speech, the Greek audience of the poem are surely meant to sympathise – even with a Trojan queen; the misfortune of losing a child is universal. And of the *Odyssey*, Richard Heitman argues that the character of Penelope, the wife of the long-absent Odysseus, 'offers strikingly accurate and straightforward accounts of her own feelings, intentions, and beliefs'.[5] The *Odyssey*, then, includes a plausible female perspective and a voice, a view on the inner life of a woman (not to mention the episodes with Helen and Menelaus). Perhaps Atossa, as a character, fits in with these female characters of the Greek tradition. But Aeschylus, as an artist, may have been deliberately challenging his audience.

Nevertheless, *Persians* is a fiction, hooked around a historical event, and Atossa's lament and her conversation with the chorus, and with the ghost of

Darius, are Aeschylus' creations. We should not look to the *Persians* for the historical Atossa.

Atossa as she appears in Herodotus' *Histories*, written around 430–425 BC, is brought into his story of the Persian wars through the actions of a Greek doctor, Democedes. Democedes had been captured by the Persians and enslaved but came to the attention of Darius, who had twisted his ankle dismounting his horse during a hunt.[6] Democedes treated Darius, who made a full recovery; he was rewarded with a house in Susa and entitled to dine at the king's table.[7] Despite his new-found high status, he was in effect a prisoner and not allowed to go home. Atossa, Herodotus then tells us, developed an abscess on her breast, which burst and spread.[8] At first, she was apparently too ashamed to tell anyone, but as her condition worsened, she called for Democedes, who agreed to treat her as long as she would do him a favour in turn – she agreed. The favour was a ruse to get Democedes away from Persia and home to his native Crotona by playing up Darius. Herodotus relates what Atossa said to Darius as they were in bed:

> My lord, with the immense resources at your command, the fact that you are making no further conquests to increase the power of Persia, must mean that you lack ambition, Surely a young man like you, who is master of great wealth, should be seen engaged in some active enterprise, to show the Persians they have a man to rule them.[9]

Darius replies that he has just such a plan, to attack the Scythians, but Atossa suggests that would be too easy:

> 'Look ... what I want you to do is invade Greece. I have heard people talk of the women there, and I should like to have Spartan girls, and girls from Argos and Attica and Corinth, to wait upon me' – adding 'you have a man better fitted than anyone in the world to give you full information about Greece and to act as guide – I mean the doctor who cured your foot'.

Darius instantly agrees to invade Greece and the next day he sends on their way fifteen Persians and Democedes to reconnoitre.

The story suggests that Atossa had great influence over Darius and Herodotus goes on to make this point explicitly when discussing the rivalry over who should succeed Darius. The king had seven sons, three with his first wife and four with Atossa.[10] Before setting out on campaign, Darius had to choose an heir, and the choice was between the two eldest sons from each marriage – Artabazanes and Xerxes. On the advice of a former Spartan king, Demaratus, Darius chose Xerxes because he was born after he became king, not beforehand like Artabazanes. Herodotus makes the personal comment: 'I believe that even without this advice from Demaratus, Xerxes would have become king, because of the immense power of Atossa.'[11] On the basis of this slim evidence, much has been made of Atossa as the power behind the throne.[12]

Herodotus is an artful and entertaining storyteller – but as well as being called 'the father of history' he has also been labelled 'the father of lies'.[13] Who would know what was said in any royal bedroom? According to Malcolm Davies, who compares it with a host of other examples, the Democedes story bears all the hallmarks of a rags-to-riches folk-tale 'from which one cannot extract one or two details and privilege them with historic status'.[14] Atossa appears in the story as a woman who could and would manipulate her husband, calling into question his manliness to get her own way – to set in train the plan devised by the clever Greek to get himself home again. The story plays on common themes in Herodotus and Greek sources on Persia generally, that the queens were powerful and scheming and men were effeminate and weak (women were men and men were women), the people were soft and given to luxury, and the state was despotic – quite the opposite of the Greeks.

Alan Griffiths has pointed out that most of Herodotus' stories did come from sources of some kind, perhaps mostly oral traditions – or gossip of some kind – and were not completely invented by him.[15] But while the traditions themselves may have been circulated, they need not be historically accurate, wherever they themselves originated – in Persia or in Greece, or somewhere in between. Indeed, a lot of the detail on the Persian Empire that Herodotus presents seems to be wrong when compared to Persian sources and archaeology, as a study by Kimball Armayor has shown.[16] In the surviving Persian evidence, for example, the Persepolis Fortification Tablets, which cover part of the reign of Darius, and the Persepolis Treasury Tablets, which date from the later years of Darius to the reign of Artaxerxes I (492–458 BC), there is no mention of Atossa – although as yet the great majority of the tablets found remain unpublished.[17]

In searching for Atossa, we could almost be forgiven for supposing her to be a Greek fiction rather than a real Persian woman. Atossa is not named by Aeschylus in the *Persians* and this information was likely added by later scholars commenting on the text – after Herodotus. In the Persian sources, Lewis explains that 'it has proved distressingly difficult to find Atossa; there is no clear explanation'.[18] And Davies agrees that there is really very little evidence for Herodotus' Atossa.[19]

If Atossa is hard to find outside of the Greek imagination, the Persian sources, explored by Maria Brosius, do reveal something about real Persian women, including another probable wife of Darius, called Irdabama.[20]

Irdabama is mentioned in several texts, for example PFa 27, which records some of her instructions. It is translated as follows:

> Tell the accountants of (the place) Šullakke (the woman) Irdabama spoke as follows:
>
> 'I ordered, for Pirmakša (?) the nurseryman (?), 150 (?) *kurrima* (of) grain from my estate. And a parchment document . . . concerning (?) (the place?) Raku . . . (?), he will be making the report. Do you look at the sealed document, and do the accounting.'

Whilst perhaps not literally recording Irdabama's words, as opposed to her instructions, this text tells us several important things. Firstly, Irdabama had an estate that she could draw on to issue supplies to people, presumably in return for their services. She had staff available to make and to record such disbursements. Her estate must have been fairly sizable, because 150 *kurrima* of grain equates to about 15,000 litres, or 11,850 kilograms, which is enough grain to bake over 21,000 loaves of bread. Brosius also notes three other documents from Persepolis concerning Irdabama in which she distributed more grain, flour, loaves, and wine in three different cities, Susa, Hidali, and Persepolis. These date to 500/499 BC. Yet other documents show Irdabama as having had a large workforce of 480 workers at Tirrazziš (Shiraz?), which included men, women, and children. The documents were sealed with Irdabama's personal seal. Other royal women, such as Irtašduna, another wife of Darius, performed the same activities.[21] Evidently, Persian women of high status had resources of their own and the ability to use them according to their own wishes.

Irtašduna's name was known to Herodotus, where her name is given as Artystone; he tells us that she was the daughter of Cyrus and the favourite wife of Darius – 'who had a statue made of her in beaten gold'.[22] Irdabama too may have been heard of more widely in the Greek world. Brosius makes an ingenious argument for this, based on the idea that it was usual for royal women to have more than one name or to change their names.[23] This would make sense of the texts that appear to record Irdabama and another woman, Abbamuš, with interests in the same places. Abbamuš may be the Elamite version of the Babylonian name Apame/Apamu, and there is an Apame recorded as being part of Darius' household. One later Greek source, Arrian, records a woman called Artakama, whilst Plutarch gives the same woman the name Apama. But it seems again that little beyond the name was known. Could any of these women have been the real Atossa – or was she simply a plausible fiction?

16

THE PRINCESS OF VIX

Marc Van de Mieroop has written that 'human agency ... defines the limits of the Mediterranean world'.[1] Thus whilst not Mediterranean in a geographical sense, Iron Age Vix, in Burgundy, France, was certainly connected to the Mediterranean and to its diverse peoples and cultures. Vix is located strategically at the southern end of the northwest-flowing Seine and the northern reaches of the Saone/Rhone that flows south to the sea at Arles, near Marseilles, the site of a major Greek colony from 600 BC.[2] It is around this time that archaeologists note the adoption by many Celtic elites of the accoutrements of Greek drinking culture – the *symposion* – with its attendant cups and craters. Greek and Etruscan goods are found in greater numbers and Vix had contacts with both cultures and quite possibly Greek and Etruscan craftspeople were at work in Celtic lands.[3] Celtic mercenaries were active in the Mediterranean and Celtic people were intermarrying with Etruscans and possibly Greeks too.[4]

Iron Age Vix is famous in particular for two remarkable finds, both of Greek origin but incorporated into a native 'Celtic' context. The first is a massive cast bronze krater (mixing vessel), which stands at over a metre and a half tall and weighs more than 200 kg (Figure 16).[5] It is the largest surviving bronze vessel from the Archaic period of Greece and Christopher Knüsel has pointed out that it would take around 1,500 bottles of wine to fill the krater to the brim – conspicuous consumption.[6] The krater's neck is decorated with applique figures – crest-helmeted Greek warriors in chariots and on foot and a gorgon

FIG. 16 The Vix krater. Source: Wikimedia Commons. Photo by Ismoon. CC BY-SA 4.0

looking out from the base of each handle. There are horses, snakes, lions and other decorative motifs. The handle of the krater's lid is in the form of a woman, 19 cm in height, wearing a long dress with a shawl covering her hair, shoulders, and hanging down past her knees. Her arms and hands are held at angles in front of her, one up and one down. The second item is a massive – almost half a kilogram in weight – golden torc, or neck ring, with exquisite finely wrought winged horses before the bulbs at each end; a typically Celtic symbol of power and wealth worn by both women and men.

The krater and torc were found in 1953 in a chamber tomb dating to the end of the sixth century BC; the tomb was covered by a tumulus 42 m in diameter and 6 m high.[7] Also found were other imported metal and clay pots, jewellery including rings, bracelets and anklets of bronze and schist, and amber beads. The high-status burial is similar to several other interments, including a burial at Hochdorf in Germany and the recently discovered 'prince of Lavau', only 75 km from Vix. As a type, these have been nicknamed 'princely burials'.[8] The human remains at Vix were found in the body of a wagon, the four wheels of which rested against the eastern wall of the chamber; the krater was in the northwest corner.

René Joffroy's 1954 publication of the tomb identified the skeletal remains, which were incomplete and in poor condition, as those of a young woman, aged between 30 and 35.[9] The remains had been examined by Robert Charles, who noted their state; only the skull was in reasonable condition. The lack of weapons in the tomb perhaps contributed to the interpretation of the body as a woman. Later the remains were re-examined by M. R. Sauter and in his 1980 paper he suggested that the identification of the body as that of a woman was not certain; features used to assign sex from the cranium and poorly preserved pelvis were not conclusively female.[10] However, further physical investigation by René Langlois agreed with Charles' original conclusions, and the female identification is seen as correct by later scholars.[11] Bettina Arnold also notes that anklets, which were found in the grave, are only ever present in female burials.[12]

Another scholar, Konrad Spindler, suggested that the person was actually a transvestite priest, which explained the presence of 'female' grave goods and the lack of 'male' weapons.[13] Arnold agrees that 'the question of the possible existence of a third, ambiguous gender . . . is an important and difficult one'.[14] Such a third gender is described by the Greek writers Hippocrates and Herodotus amongst the Scythians. Herodotus refers to the 'enarees' or 'women-men', at least some of whom acted in a ritual capacity, divining the future in a way different to regular Scythian diviners.[15] Hippocrates describes them as men from the richer ranks who, after years spent on horseback, become impotent, and then dress, speak, work, and act like women.[16] However, in observations about archaeology and popular culture, Arnold, and more recently Lucy Shipley, have pointed out that it is modern androcentrism which has helped fuel doubt about the female sex of the Vix burial.[17]

So, who was this woman of Vix? Undoubtedly her treatment in death indicates her importance to her community in life. At Vix, no male burial of equal wealth has been found, and this suggests to Miranda Aldhouse-Green that 'she was once a person of exceptional importance'.[18] Was she, as Joffroy wondered, the wife of a prince, a reigning princess, or a priestess? It is quite possible that she could have been all three. Arnold considers the burial to be not only elite, but high-status elite, based on the goods it contained. Aldhouse-Green comments that 'the inclusion of a wide variety of objects, some exotic, from many different regions' could 'symbolize the woman's suzerainty over large sweeps of territory and her associations with the Mediterranean world'.[19]

Vix itself is also considered to be a 'first rank' 'princely' settlement, with a stoutly fortified hillfort at Mont Lassois, immediately to the west of the woman of Vix's grave. In the later sixth century, the plateau of Saint Marcel at the top of the fort underwent redevelopment to make it into a grand 'palatial' residence.[20] This description comes from the group of apsidal buildings in the middle of the eastern side of the plateau. The biggest of these was 35 m x 22 m and may have had an upper floor. They had painted and relief decoration on their walls and contained pottery feasting ware. Other parts of the plateau were given over to smaller dwellings, a service area, enclosures for livestock, and granaries – all important for the functioning of a ruling house and useful as a concentrated display of wealth – some of which would have come from Vix's role as a mid-point in trade between the Mediterranean and the north.[21] It seems quite possible, given the chronology, that the Vix woman may have been responsible for the development of the Saint Marcel plateau.

Women in Celtic society could be accorded a very high status. We know this is true because Iron Age Britain produced (at least) two very high status women – the queens Cartimandua and Boudica, both of whom played key, and quite different roles in dealing with the Roman occupation in the first century AD.[22] Cartimandua ruled the northern Brigantes, a sizable confederation of peoples, and was friendly to the Romans; in AD 50 she handed over to the Romans king Caratacus, who had fled to her after his defeat by the Romans.[23] Tacitus reports, as if it were a negative, that she 'divorced' one husband, the king Venutius, and married his squire. Unpopular, Venutius and the Brigantes rose up against her; the Romans rescued her. No doubt, Cartimandua, like other British rulers, had her own views on dealing with the might of Rome, now present and active across Britain, as well as wanting to know who to share her life with.

Writing of Boudica, the Roman historian Tacitus explained that the Britons 'stirred up by mutual encouragement ... with Boudica, from royal stock, a woman, as their leader – for they do not distinguish between the sexes when choosing commanders – the whole people launched a war'.[24] Quite the opposite of Cartimandua, Boudica led a violent resistance to the Romans, following her flogging and the rape of her daughters by Roman troops, which led to the burning of Colchester, London, and St Albans. Quite possibly she had already had anti-Roman views – and this may have been why her husband Prasutagus, a client-king of Rome, did not leave her half the kingdom in his will – half went to the emperor and half to the two daughters.[25] The actions of the Romans may have crystallised her feelings into the realisation that serious action was needed. Ultimately, she and the Britons were defeated – but in the United Kingdom we all still know her name. We do not know the name of the woman of Vix, or what she achieved in life, but there is no reason to doubt that she could have been a powerful and respected ruler in her own right.

Analysis of the Vix woman's skeletal remains can tell us a little bit more.[26] Measurement of her long bones gives a suggested height of around 160 cm, a little short by modern standards. She seems to have had a variety of physical issues that would have affected her appearance and movement. The first is 'wry neck', or muscular torticollis, in which the head is pulled to one side by the muscles, in this case the right side. Another problem was hip dysplasia, a problem in the formation of the hip joint, which would have led the Vix woman to walk with a 'waddling gait' – she probably would have experienced pain when walking. She may also have suffered trauma to the back of her neck, and a lesion. Her teeth showed less wear, which is often indicative of a younger age, but there was also evidence of an abscess and gum disease, indicative of an older individual; this could suggest that she had a relatively 'refined' diet. Some of the Vix woman's physical problems may have been caused by being born breech. As a member of the elite, the Vix woman may have received more care than lower status people would have had, but at the same time, it seems that she did not let her problems hold her back.

It is even possible that the Vix woman's physical appearance made her more special as an individual, as might be the case with another high-status female burial from Wetwang in the United Kingdom. The physical analysis revealed that the Wetwang woman had an extremely disfigured face, caused by a malformation of the bone near her nose; this would have resulted in 'a highly disfiguring, bright red facial growth'.[27] The grave also contained red coral and a mirror and Aldhouse-Green states that 'it is almost as though her abnormality were being celebrated'. Certainly, this Iron Age woman was also given a special burial. The appearance of both the Vix and Wetwang women seems to have been no obstacle to their high status – could it be that it helped define their position or at least contributed to their special place in the community? Some authors have noted that special physical characteristics can be linked with shamanism or ritual authority – and with special burial practices.[28] In Okinawan tradition, for example, illnesses were linked with the journey to becoming a priestess or shaman.[29] Indeed, Knüsel has argued that the Vix woman may have been a ritualist, partly drawing on Tacitus' comment that 'it is an ancient custom in Germany to consider many women to be prophets and (as superstition grows) as goddesses'.[30]

The evidence of the Vix woman in the context of her times clearly suggests her importance – and there is no reason we cannot accept her as a powerful ruler of a wealthy society in her own right. How she got her position, we do not know. Like other Celtic women, she could have had a military as well as a political role. Probably she was charismatic and undoubtedly she could count on the support of influential men in her society. She commanded great wealth and could afford to commission the production of expensive items of great beauty by the most capable Greek craftsmen, which also demonstrates her international contacts. None of this helps us fill in the personal detail of her life, her name, opinions, or experiences; there is much we cannot know about her. That she was remarkable is a message she has sent through time with the help of the extraordinary Vix krater.

17

ARISTONICE

At the heart of ancient Greece lay a small city perched on a mountainside – Delphi.[1] At the heart of Delphi was the temple of Apollo, where delegations from cities far and wide, even beyond Greece, would come for answers and advice. And at the heart of the temple was a woman, the Pythia, the priestess of Apollo and mouthpiece of the god (Figure 17). For a thousand years successive Pythias occupied this position as 'the voice at the center of the world', until the oracles eventually ran dry in the fourth century and then pagan cults were outlawed by the Roman emperor Theodosius in the AD 390s.[2] Around 480 BC, the Pythia was a woman called Aristonice. Her words have reverberated through western history.

Delphi and its oracle have many beginnings.[3] The earliest Greek tales, the *Iliad* and the *Odyssey* say a little about Delphi, suggesting the site was active and important even before 700 BC. Agamemnon consulted Apollo and was given a prophecy in Pytho, another name for Delphi and in the *Iliad* 'rocky Pytho' is renowned as rich, listed with Troy and Egyptian Thebes.[4] Hesiod's *Theogony*, also from around 700 BC, describes how Kronos vomited the stone given to him to swallow in place of Zeus – Zeus then set it up at holy Pytho.[5] The *Homeric Hymn to Apollo* tells us about Apollo and how he set up his shrine and oracle there, how the site changed from Krisa to Pytho to Delphi.[6] But the hymn, being to Apollo, does not describe the Pythia. The poet Alcaeus tells a completely different story again.

FIG. 17 The Pythia consulted by a king. Contributor: Science History Images / Alamy Stock Photo

In Aeschylus' play *Eumenides*, a Pythia herself describes the origins of the Pythia, the female oracle, as being inherited originally from the female Ge, earth, through her daughter Themis and her sister Phoebe, who gave it to her brother Phoebus, Apollo.[7] Modern scholars Bernard Dietrich and Sarah Pomeroy also both see an element of takeover by Apollo of an older 'female chthonic cult'.[8] Whatever the real origins of sacred Delphi, Apollo worship, and the oracle, it appears the site only began to rise to prominence alongside the development of the Greek states and other sanctuaries and the increasingly interconnected Greek world in the eighth century BC.[9] With it increased the importance of the Pythias.

Pythias had originally been chosen from among the young women of the region, peasant girls, Joan Connelly explains.[10] However, after one young Pythia was raped, the practice was changed to choose from women aged over fifty. These women might have already been married and had children, which made the position of Pythia of Delphi different from most female priesthoods in the Greek world, where wealthy, aristocratic virgins were more usual candidates. Aristonice, we can guess, may have belonged to a local Delphian family, not necessarily particularly well-off or politically prominent; she may well have led a normal life as a girl and young woman, have been married, and even had children before being selected as Pythia later in life. Becoming Pythia may not have been something she either expected or looked for.

At Delphi, unusually, the god spoke through the Pythia directly, without the use of lots or other signs used at other oracular sites, which could be subject to priestly interpretation – though the ambiguous utterances of the Pythia did have to be interpreted very carefully. We have around six hundred surviving oracular responses, which record the voices of some of those women chosen to serve as Pythia, albeit that these are their voices 'at work'.[11] In ancient Greece, what was in so many ways a man's world, it is surprising that a god could speak in a woman's voice and command respect and careful attention and could arguably influence the course of history at crucial moments in time.

The words of Aristonice must be counted as some of the best known from all of antiquity; they are preserved for us in Herodotus' *Histories*.[12] They were spoken in 480 BC to a delegation sent to Delphi from Athens, in the midst of the war between the mighty Persian Empire and a handful of allied Greek city-states.[13] The Athenians had defeated the Persians under king Darius at Marathon in 490 BC and now the Greeks were facing another invasion by his son Xerxes.

The Athenians wanted advice from the god on how to proceed. Aristonice's first response to the Athenians seemed to foretell their utter defeat:

> Why sit you, doomed ones? Fly to the world's end, leaving
> Home and the heights your city circles like a wheel.
> The head shall not remain in its place, nor the body,
> Nor the feet beneath, nor the hands, nor the parts between;
> But all is ruined, for fire and the headlong god of war
> Speeding in a Syrian chariot shall bring you low.
> Many a tower shall he destroy, not yours alone,
> And give to pitiless fire many shrines of gods,
> Which even now stand sweating, with fear quivering,
> While over the roof-tops black blood runs streaming
> In prophecy of woe that needs must come. But rise,
> Haste from the sanctuary and bow your hearts to grief.

The Athenian delegation were shell-shocked; a call to give up and run away was not what they had expected. Aristonice had already told a party from Argos to stay neutral and the Cretan delegation to keep the island out of the war altogether.[14] She also apparently said that if the Spartans fought, either a Spartan king or Sparta itself would fall; the forecast for the Athenians was not entirely surprising.

Delphi's biographer, Michael Scott, has discussed Delphi's apparently quite pessimistic stance; perhaps they saw the invasion quite clearly for what it was – a very real existential threat.[15] Nevertheless, a distinguished Delphian called Timon – perhaps sensing that the response given to the Athenians was not entirely satisfactory – recommended that the Athenians seek the Pythia's advice again, this time as suppliants.[16] So, bearing olive-branches, they again visited Aristonice. This time she said:

> Not wholly can Pallas win the heart of Olympian Zeus,
> Though she prays him with many prayers and all her subtlety;
> Yet I will speak to you this other word, as firm as adamant:
> Though all else shall be taken within the bounds of Cecrops
> And the fastness of the holy mountain of Cithaeron,
> Yet Zeus the all-seeing grants to Athene's prayer
> That the wooden wall only shall not fall, but help you and your children.
> But await not the host of horse and foot coming from Asia,
> Nor be still, but turn your back and withdraw from the foe.
> Truly a day will come when you meet him face to face.
> Divine Salamis, you will bring death to women's sons
> When the corn is scattered, or the harvest gathered in.

This oracle seemed milder, and the Athenians wrote it down and took it back to Athens, where it was made public. Delphic oracles were famed for their ambiguity – which is part of what made them convincing however things turned out in the end. Inevitably, though, there were disagreements in Athens over the correct interpretation of Aristonice's words. Herodotus tells us that old men thought that 'wooden walls' referred to the acropolis, which had once been surrounded by hedge, meaning that it would be saved. Others though it meant they should prepare a fleet of ships with which to meet the Persians – wooden walls. Yet the last two lines of the oracle seemed to suggest that they would be defeated in a naval battle off the nearby island of Salamis. Thus, the professional interpreters of oracles advised surrender.

One notable Athenian, Themistocles, however, argued that the oracle meant they would defeat the Persians in a naval battle – hence the oracle said 'divine Salamis' rather than 'hateful Salamis'.[17] This fitted his own policy precisely; a few years earlier, he had persuaded the Athenians to build a navy using funds from the silver mines at Laurion. In the interpretation of the oracle – and in Athens' strategy for survival – he prevailed again and as we know the Athenians went on to win a great victory at the Battle of Salamis in 480 BC; Xerxes and his Persian fleet departed.[18]

Had the Pythia amended her views after the Athenian delegation and the priests had had further conversations, perhaps ones in which Themistocles' plans were stressed? Even if they had lost, the wooden walls could then have been reinterpreted to ensure the oracle was not wrong – the wooden walls could have meant 'flee in your ships', just as the oracle had first suggested.

If we chose to, we could argue that the double-edged words of Aristonice the Pythia 'saved' western civilization from an alternative history in which

Greece was wholly conquered by the Persians. She gave the Athenians a divinely sanctioned option to flee in their ships or to fight a sea battle that they might win or lose. Aristonice (or Apollo) had very sagely left the decision open to the Athenians themselves – and was suitably ambiguous in terms of the eventual outcome.

Really, we know nothing else of Aristonice. Indeed, very little is known of any individual Pythias, despite their importance and the longevity of the oracle at Delphi. Several ancient sources state that the first Pythia was a woman called Phemonoe, but of her we know nothing more.[19] It is not wholly implausible that the first Pythia's name would be remembered, like the date of the first Olympic games, but equally she might well be a later invention. A later Phemenoe is known from a Roman poem by Lucan, *The Civil War*, in which she was consulted by a Roman general, Appius Claudius Pulcher, in 48 BC.[20] She tried to get out of giving him an oracle by pretending that Delphi no longer functioned – then made up an oracle to mollify him.

The episode is especially interesting because Lucan describes how Delphi had fallen silent over the years because kings did not want to know the future; Delphi may have functioned best when it was the centre of a world was dominated by small city-states that the city could, in some sense, mediate between. Though there were still priests and a Pythia, Parnassus had fallen silent, Phemenoe stated. Perhaps Lucan, as a poet, chose the name as a deliberate echo of the first Pythia.

In addition to these Phemenoes, we have the names Perialla, Themistokleia, and Xenokleia, and a Pythia called Theoneike. Perialla, Aristonice's predecessor, was infamous; Herodotus tells us that she was bribed to give a certain response to a Spartan embassy with regard to the royal succession.[21] As punishment, she was removed from office. According to Diogenes Laertius, Themistokleia, a priestess of Delphi, was the teacher of Pythagoras.[22] Xenokleia appeared in a myth recounted by Pausanias, denying Herakles an oracle on the basis that he had committed murder.[23] Theoneike appears much much later, in a third century AD inscription, which ironically was re-used in a Byzantine church; she is the only Pythia recorded in an inscription.[24] This should not surprise us overmuch as the emphasis in the cult would always have been on the Pythia as Pythia, though, rather than on the woman who was the Pythia.

Much thought has been given to the role, actions, and abilities of the Pythias.[25] It has often been thought, at least in modern times, that the Pythias were simply stooges, who babbled frantically and incoherently in their chamber in the temple of Apollo. Ancient sources give different pictures of what happened and why. Later sources from Roman times mention that the Pythia, when consulted, was affected by a 'breath', vapour, or wind that came from an underground chasm over which she sat on her tripod. The *pneuma*, with its 'delightful fragrance', according to Plutarch, overcame the Pythia and she delivered her oracles.[26] She was inspired or physically possessed by Apollo and, depending on the source, would either babble excitedly and incomprehensibly or speak calmly in either prose or verse.

There has long been a debate on the reality of the gaseous vapours at Delphi and whether the Pythia was, in effect, high. Littleton has argued that 'the Pythia ... in company with a great many shamans elsewhere, modern as well as ancient, achieved prophetic ecstasy through the use of hallucinogens', possibly cannabis or fly-agaric.[27] Cannabis might have been burned while the laurel leaves could have been laced with fly-agaric. As for the chasm, the French archaeologists at Delphi reported in the early twentieth century that there was no evidence for any chasm beneath Apollo's temple. Almost a century later, Jelle De Boer and John Hale identified intersecting faults below the temple and argued that hydrocarbon gases could have been released via fissures when there was tectonic activity.[28] Inhalation of ethylene has been reported to cause 'immediate signs and symptoms of intoxication, including repeated episodes of nausea, stomach spasms, paleness, light-headedness, short periods of unconsciousness, convulsive movements of ... arms and legs, and periods of apnea (cessation of breathing)'.[29] This idea of has become popular, though not all are convinced.[30]

Another part of the traditional interpretation is that whatever the Pythia did or said, the real oracles must have been composed by sober attendant male priests who 'interpreted' the Pythia for those consulting the oracle, which included embassies from states great and small. Women, especially uneducated women from poorer families, could surely never have given meaningful advice on important matters of international politics and they certainly would not have been able to deliver it in polished oracular language. Or are we underestimating the capacities of Pythias through the ages? Living at the hub that connected so many Greek states, and in a place where news and information would have gathered and been accessible, Pythias would have been exposed to contemporary politics. There seems no reason why Pythias, who would have been chosen carefully, perhaps trained to some degree, and who would have been in conversation with other Delphians, including the priests, could not speak. We should remember that for high-class prostitutes in parts of ancient Greece, knowledge and the ability to talk intelligently were attributes prized by male customers – there was nothing to say women were not able to match men in this. Maurizio reminds us that 'every ancient source without exception speaks of the Pythias (or Apollo) delivering oracles'.[31]

In ancient Greece, an androcentric world, god could speak in a woman's voice. For as long as people remain interested in the Greeks' unlikely victory against the mighty Persians, the continued survival of Aristonice's words and her name is ensured.

18

NEAIRA

Neaira was supposedly a prostitute who sold her body for sex; she was also, in our single source for her life, a courtesan, a concubine, or 'that sort of woman'.[1] These labels are pejorative ones, carrying the moral and social judgements of the male-authored ancient Greek sources – no prostitute from classical Greece has left us her own testimony. But we could also choose other terms for Neaira that would fit her at various points in her life: she was a child, a girl, a woman, a sex slave, a victim, a partner, a lover, an opportunist, a mother, and above all, perhaps, a survivor.[2] Whilst all those labels we can apply may fit, she herself, her character and emotions, her aspirations and motivations remain elusive; some are given to us by a man, Apollodorus, who is using her story for his own ends – hardly a disinterested source. Even though we lack her own words and her physical remains, her story, shadowy as it is, is still worth exploring as a life as valuable as any other and therefore worthy of remembrance and sympathy.

The only source for Neaira's life is a legal speech once attributed to the Athenian orator Demosthenes but probably by Apollodorus. This Apollodorus had a long-running and bitter feud with a fellow Athenian called Stephanos, with whom Neaira lived. In the late 340s BC he took the fifty-year-old Neaira to court in an attempt, he stated, to use her to destroy his enemy. The charge laid against Neaira was not that she was a prostitute but that she 'is an alien woman and is living as his wife with Stephanus contrary to the laws' (§16).[3] Athens had not always had such strict rules about marriage between Athenians and foreigners – the law on citizenship, by which only the child of a citizen man and woman could be recognised as an Athenian citizen, and therefore have full legal rights, had been introduced in 451/450 BC and reinstated in 403/402 BC.[4] For this crime of cohabiting with an alien woman as if she were an Athenian citizen, the law specified that the guilty woman and her property would be sold and the man fined the considerable sum of 1,000 drachmae. If it were not for this hatred between Apollodorus and Stephanos, Neaira's life story would not have survived at all, yet the speech itself may have sealed for her an undesirable fate.

Neaira lived in Athens in the first half of the fourth century BC, but her childhood was spent in Corinth, and for two years she also lived in the city of Megara. As an infant, she and six other girls were bought by a woman called Nikarete, a former slave turned madam, who 'was skilled in recognising the budding beauty of young girls' and who 'knew well how to bring them up and train them artfully' (§18). Nikarete was not interested in running any old brothel or street operation. Rather, she set up her business as a more exclusive type of prostitution, one that made the pretence that the girls were free, rather than slaves; in this trade, she could charge men more for using them.

These girls, including Neaira, were to become *hetairai*, which is often translated as 'courtesan' or 'companion', and is the feminine form of 'male friend', rather than *pornai*, 'whores' or 'prostitutes', although there is a great deal of debate and discussion about the terms.[5] *Pornai* were paid by the sex act, at prices ranging from an obol to slightly more than one drachma (which was six obols); a skilled male worker's wage can be reckoned at perhaps a drachma and a half per day.[6] Cost and earnings related to physical characteristics and skills, the young and attractive would have been able to earn more than the older women and those judged less attractive, who would only have been able to charge low fees; these women could expect to have to work more to make a living.[7] Prostitutes of varying degrees of 'quality' were therefore available to men of different economic status, not only the well-off, but also to slaves.

Pornai could be slaves or free women; some worked in brothels of varying standards whilst others worked the streets. They were given names such as 'Didrachmon' and 'Obole', both references to cash; names that depersonalised, humiliated, and perhaps even made fun of them.[8] Though hard to spot archaeologically, not least because sex work needs no special location, Building Z in the Kerameikos of central Athens may have been an upmarket brothel that doubled as a tavern and may also been a place where the women worked at textiles.[9] This blurring of the lines need not have been unusual. Building Z was a spacious single-storey building with a wide-open courtyard. Apparently, said the fourth century poet Xenarchos of Athens, it was 'possible to see [comely babes] warmed by the sun with their breasts exposed, fully naked in a row, drawn up in a battle line' and 'from these, anyone can find a

FIG. 18 Hetairai at a symposium (the Phintias hydria). State Collection of Antiquities and Glyptothek Munich. Photograph by Renate Kühling

pleasing one'.[10] Sex was widely, openly, and inexpensively available throughout classical Athens.[11]

Hetairai were different.[12] They would not only have sex or sexual contact with male customers but also attended by invitation *symposia*, exclusive male drinking parties, where they would be expected to engage in conversation as well as drinking and eating with the men – something no respectable Athenian wife could or would do (Figure 18). *Hetairai* tended to have longer-term customers and more exclusive relationships than the *pornai*, who would have to service more clients perhaps with less choice; this was the case for Neaira. They could be educated women, literate and knowledgeable – because they were given the opportunity to be. For these reasons, *hetairai*, like Pericles' 'companion' Aspasia, have often been romanticised – the latter, for example, in Walter Savage Landor's 1871 book of fictional letters *Pericles and Aspasia* – but while they perhaps had more control and better conditions than many *pornai*, there should be no illusions that they were not part of a sex industry based on ingrained inequalities of power.[13]

Neaira was perhaps lucky to have been bought for training as a *hetaira*, given that there were other fates that could have been immediately and in the longer term far less comfortable. But both *pornai* and *hetairai* aged and lost their appeal to potential customers – and their ability to command a higher price. In one comedy play, Epikrates describes the famous but aging *hetaira* Laïs thus:

> When she ... was a young chick, she was made wild by the riches .... But since she has run her course and her body is sagging, it is easier to see her than to spit. She flies off to every engagement, and she takes half a drachma in payment. She will give herself to young and old alike. Laïs has become so tame ... that she takes money right out of your hand.[14]

Epikrates and the crowd may have found Laïs' fate funny, but for Laïs herself, and for others like her, the reality of the struggle to get by in life, made harder by aging, would have been far from amusing. Epikrates' comic statement, to us, is rather tragic. The inevitable passage of time affected Neaira too.

Like Laïs, Neaira was apparently 'quite a celebrity' (§26) whilst a young woman in Corinth. But when she and Nikarete's other girls had lost their youthful appeal, Apollodorus tells us, she sold them on – Nikarete's own economic considerations were paramount. Neaira may still have been a teenager at the time. She was bought as a slave by two men, Timanoridas and Eucrates, for their exclusive use, for thirty minae, but when these men were to marry, she was offered the chance to buy her freedom at a discount, on the condition that she left Corinth. We are told that various former clients gave her money but that the bulk of the fee was provided by one Phrynion, whom she then accompanied to Athens. Phrynion evidently felt Neaira, now a free woman, owed him and that he could treat her as he pleased; we are told that

> when he came back here, bringing her with him, he treated her without decency or restraint, taking her everywhere with him to dinners where there was drinking and making her a partner in his revels; and he had intercourse with her whenever and wherever he wished, making his privilege a display to the onlookers. (§33)

At one such party, whilst Phrynion slept, Apollodorus tells us that many men had sex with Neaira while she was drunk – even the house slaves. If it happened and was not just a slander, it can be wondered whether it was consensual sex, coercive, or physical gang rape. Apollodorus seems to be trying to show Neaira as licentious, since she must have allowed herself to be used in this way even as a free woman.

The ancient Greeks had no word the equivalent of the English term 'rape', although acts we would deem to be rape and sexual violence are described in the literature and some such offences were regarded as wrong and were punishable.[15] It seems that in Athens the public treatment of these acts depended, at least in part, on how they affected and reflected on citizen men, rather than being crimes against women in their own right. For *pornai* and *hetairai*, and also for slaves and for wives, sexual violence in a hyper-masculine society may have been a common occurrence and something women themselves might be blamed and punished for. Rape in mythology was a common theme on Athenian pottery and according to Eva Keuls was an 'overriding preoccupation' of the Athenians.[16]

Neaira was not happy with Phrynion, which is not altogether surprising; Apollodorus, presumably speculating on her feelings, stated that 'she was not loved as she expected to be' (§35). She managed to escape from him, taking with her not only the clothes and jewellery he gave her, and her two maids, but also movable property from his house, and fled to Megara. She lived there for two years but apparently found it difficult to make a living. According to Apollodorus, she told the visiting Stephanos her story and he offered not only to protect her from Phrynion but also to keep her 'as his wife' in Athens and to register her two sons, fraudulently, as Athenian citizens. To what extent this is true, and these children were Neaira's but not Stephanos' from an earlier marriage, is unclear and disputed – when the court case was being heard, these two would have been adult citizens for many years.[17] Neaira's daughter Phano also came to Athens.

Once settled in Athens as 'a respectable woman living with her husband', Apollodorus tells us, Neaira went back to 'her trade' and was able to charge higher rates because of her new purported status, which Stephanos himself, who had no proper income, wanted to cash in on (§41). We hear little more of Neaira's own story from Apollodorus' speech, which turns to focus on Phano, attempting further to blacken Neaira and Stephanos' names by suggesting her own licentiousness and adultery and her two illegal and ill-fated marriages to Athenians. One of these marriages was to a man chosen as king-archon, a high and sacred office of state; Phano's position involved her performing 'rites many and solemn and not to be named' (§73). Any taint attached to Phano would have shocked the Athenians.

Apollodorus paints a deliberately lurid picture of Neaira's life – a life that stood in stark contrast to the ideal of an Athenian citizen woman; Stephanos, we are led to believe, was a terrible man and she a terrible foreign woman. Both had affronted the dignity of Athens and its rightful citizens and citizen wives and daughters. Apollodorus' motivation was, as he readily admits, not justice in our sense of the word but justifiable revenge: 'the wrongs done me by Stephanus, men of Athens ... have led me to come forward to accuse this woman Neaera' (§16). Apollodorus had had no interest in her before his clashes with Stephanos. Neaira's story, as told by him, was simply a way to ruin Stephanos; her life was a means to an end.

By the time of the lawsuit against her, Neaira was around fifty years of age and had probably been living with Stephanos in Athens for around thirty years, as, Stephanos probably claimed, a *pallaka*, a concubine. We have to assume that their relationship worked for them, whatever the precise legal situation about Neaira's citizenship status. Was it a loving relationship? There is no reason to doubt that it could have been – it is difficult to comprehend their long association without there being some affection. If the children were Neaira's and not Stephanos', this is a further reason to think he loved her, for why else would he risk passing them off as true Athenians? It is enough to suggest that Neaira may, from being a childhood sex slave and adolescent commodity, have found a degree of happiness and stability in her life with Stephanos. Of course, we do not know the outcome of the trial – perhaps there was no happy ending for the couple; Neaira may have been sold yet again.

It is ironic that two of the most famous women of classical Athens, Neaira and Aspasia, were foreign *hetairai*, yet fitting in the sense that an Athenian ideal of citizen women was to be silent and invisible, a view famously put in the mouth of Pericles by the historian Thucydides.[18] Pericles, the great Athenian democrat and hero, divorced his Athenian wife and then brought Aspasia to live with him; she even bore him a son. Pericles was, again ironically, responsible for passing the citizenship laws that Neaira and Stephanos fell afoul of.[19]

The ancient biographer Plutarch, admittedly writing some five centuries later, tells us that Pericles was attracted to Aspasia's intelligence and political acumen, though 'his affection . . . was chiefly erotic in its nature'.[20] He notes that Socrates took his pupils to visit her and that men even brought their wives to see her, even though 'she ran an establishment which was neither orderly or respectable, seeing that she educated a group of young female companions to become courtesans'. If this was the case, she had much in common with Nikarete, who had bought and brought up Neaira in Corinth. Plutarch also describes the love between Aspasia and Pericles: 'he would kiss her warmly both when he left for the marketplace and when he returned home each day'. Could we imagine such a life for Neaira and Stephanos too?

19

PHANOSTRATE

When we think of ancient medicine, we might think first of the Greek tradition beginning with Hippocrates and probably then of Galen in Roman times. Hippocrates stands at the beginning of the western medical tradition and we have a collection of texts attributed to him known as the *Hippocratic Corpus*.[1] The Hippocratic Oath, a statement of professionalism, was still regularly taken by newly qualified doctors until fairly recently, albeit in a modified form. Galen achieved fame in Roman times as an extraordinarily learned and intellectual doctor, a collector and editor of medical texts, a public performer of medicine and sometimes gruesome experiments, and doctor to the rich and famous.[2] His influence was felt deep into medieval times. Yet these are only two men in a very long tradition, and the world of health and medicine was a world in which women too played a vital, if not always so visible, role.

Going back to the Homeric epics, we can find details of the medical knowledge and practice of the Greeks and the association of these with women.[3] Early on in the *Odyssey*, for example, the young Telemachus, son of the hero Odysseus, goes to visit king Menelaos in the hope of finding out news of his long-gone father. He and his travel companion Peisistratus are welcomed by Menelaos and Helen in their palace and they talk together, the king and queen wondering about the identity of the two young men. When Odysseus is mentioned, Telemachus lets drop a revealing tear, and as the conversation continues Peisistratus reveals who Telemachus is and tells the royal couple of his difficulties at home in Ithaka. The four become sad and weep together, putting off further talk till the morning. At this point, Helen decides to ease their upset by slipping a drug into their wine 'a drug to quiet all pain and strife, and bring forgetfulness of every ill'.[4] The 'cunning drugs' she had acquired from Polydamna, 'a woman of Egypt', where 'the earth . . . bears greatest store of drugs, many that are healing when mixed, and many that are baneful'.

Later on in the *Odyssey*, we hear about the misadventures of Odysseus and his men on the island of the goddess Circe. Circe, who is described as *polyfarmakou*, 'expert in poisons', tricks the men and into their welcome meal of 'cheese and barley meal and yellow honey with Pramnian wine' she 'mixed evil drugs'.[5] Through her magic medicine, made to make the men forget their homeland, and with a tap of her wand, the men are transformed into pigs, which Circe promptly pens up in her pigsties. Odysseus replies in kind with help from Hermes, who mixes him a potion using the plant moly, which makes him immune to Circe's drugs. Tricked, she learns his identity, takes him to bed, and turns his crew back into men. Many drugs, potions, and remedies were known to the ancients, over a thousand are described in the pharmacology of Dioscorides, and in the hands of women (or men) could be helpful or harmful.[6]

One fifth century BC reference to women as physicians is particularly interesting. This is in Plato's *Republic*, where Socrates is clarifying what constitute significant and relevant differences between men and women in terms of what their abilities are and their skills could be.[7] He suggests we should agree that 'a man and a woman who have a physician's mind have the same nature' – in the same way a male and female guard dog can both be effective at guarding, though one bears children and the other does not. On the other hand, a male doctor and a male carpenter, he suggests, have different natures, though both male. Plato refers incidentally to both men and women having 'a physician's mind' – it is not a point that needs further argument or explanation; it implies that both men and women acted as physicians in fifth and fourth century BC Athens.

One such woman was Phanostrate, who lived in Acharnai in Attica, the territory of Athens, around the mid-fourth century BC. She is relatively well known because on her death she was commemorated with a grave stele on which is written: 'Midwife and doctor, Phanostrate lies here, she caused pain to none, but all lamented her death' (Figure 19).[8] The words emphasise her skill and popularity – they suggest she was effective at relieving the afflicted of their pain and that her death was a real loss to the community. The stele also has a touching scene in relief where the seated Phanostrate is shown shaking hands with a woman called Antiphile. Antiphile has her hair covered and is standing facing Phanostrate; around their feet there are children of various

FIG. 19 Phanostrate's stele. National Archaeological Museum, Athens, NAM inv.nr. Γ 993. Photographer: E. Miari © Hellenic Ministry of Culture and Sports / Hellenic Organization of Cultural Resources Development

ages. Phanostrate's womanhood and her role as a midwife, surrounded by children, are prominently shown for those who could not read.

The type of carved funeral scene on Phanostrate's grave stele is a standardised composition and the hand-shaking (*dexiosis*) is a common motif signalling emotion.[9] Where two women are depicted, it is usually mother and daughter or sisters, so perhaps Phanostrate and Antiphile were sisters; the children may have been Antiphile's, delivered by Phanostrate. Though 'respectable' women might have lived more secluded lives than men in classical Athens,[10] Lucia Nováková and Monika Pagáčová suggest that the public imagery reflects how 'private virtues' were 'beneficial for the polis as a whole. A thriving and harmonious household contributed to the prosperity of the state, which is why women on funerary reliefs were associated with the public sphere'.[11]

One of Phanostrate's successful treatments is revealed on a statue base from the sanctuary of the healer god Asklepius on the southern slope of the acropolis in Athens.[12] The dedication is fragmentary but tells us that a man called Delophanes set up the statue of Phanostrate when his wife Lysimache was helped. Delophanes may have been fulfilling a vow made by their daughter. This confirms for us that Phanostrate did indeed practice medicine and gained a public reputation for healing. Her statue would have been visible to all who came to the sanctuary and might even have served to advertise her skills.

The family and household was clearly one realm in which women were able to practice health care, as Phanostrate may have done with her own sister. Indeed, it was a responsibility for an ideal wife to care for all, including slaves, as Xenophon in his book on household management explained to his new wife:

> One of the duties that fall to you, however, will perhaps seem rather thankless: you will have to see that any servant who is ill is cared for.
>
> 'Oh no', cried my wife, 'it will be delightful, assuming that those who are well cared for are going to feel grateful and be more loyal than before'.[13]

Not every woman would have had the skills and possible training of Phanostrate, and so all well-to-do ladies might not have cared directly for the sick, but it is likely that some remedies were common or traditional knowledge and could be applied.

The inscription on Phanostrate's stele clearly describes her as both a midwife (*maia*) and a doctor (*iatros*). Midwifery was probably practiced by women on a semi-skilled and skilled basis, with experience and knowledge passed down and shared within families, households, and communities. It need not have been a full-time job in the modern sense for all. Without anything like modern health services or formal medical training, female relatives, friends, neighbours, and 'wise women' would have been the first port of call in many instances.[14]

One of the most famous midwives of classical Greece is Phainarete – famous because she was the mother of the philosopher Socrates. In Plato's dialogue the *Theaetaetus,* Socrates himself asks Theaetaetus 'haven't you heard that my mother Phainarete was a good, sturdy midwife?'.[15] He then uses midwifery as a metaphor for how he himself practices philosophy, or how he brings forth knowledge from the people he talks with. He tells us that midwives were women past child-bearing age but who had given birth; they had experience of pregnancy and labour. 'Their chants and the drugs they administer can induce labour and relieve the pains, as they see fit; can bring a difficult birth to a successful conclusion; and can bring on a miscarriage, if that is what seems best', he explains. But, in a phrase that sounds odd after this introduction, he tells us that in common with midwives, he is barren of wisdom.[16] It may be that he is stressing the value of know-how and experience over book-learning or theorising. Whether Socrates really likened himself to a midwife or this is a fiction of Plato's does not devalue the incidental details we can take from the text.

A much later source from the second century AD, Soranus, a Greek in Roman times who wrote the *Gynaecology*, suggested that the best midwives would be literate, which again tells us something about the level of education at least some men thought appropriate for women in this area. Soranus' work was presented in a simplified form in Latin by one Muscio, who states that 'I used women's words so that even ill-educated obstetrices would easily be able to understand the meaning, albeit when read to them by another women'.[17] This suggests that, in his time, some midwives were literate and others not; the situation was probably as diverse earlier on in Classical and Hellenistic times. It may be that female doctors were more likely than midwives to be literate; as Flemming notes 'medicine was a field in which written texts played an important role – as vehicles of knowledge and authority, as items of practical utility and social prestige – and the levels of literacy within the associated professions are likely to have reflected this'.[18]

The Hippocratic writings only refer to women as midwives or in relation to childbirth, but the Xenophon quote suggests a wider area of medical care could be expected from some women, even when they were not trained physicians. Referring to Phanostrate as a doctor does suggest that she had a degree of formal knowledge and we know she worked as a doctor outside the household. Again the issue of literacy comes up and there is debate about how educated and literate respectable Athenian women were allowed to be; it very likely differed according to individual circumstances.[19] A statue from Tlos in Asia Minor, from the first half of the first century BC, tells us about another woman doctor; it reads: 'Antiochis of Tlos, daughter of Diodotus, commended by the council and the people of Tlos for her experience in the doctor's art, has set up this statue of herself.' Holt Parker suggests that this Diodotus was the medical authority mentioned by Dioscorides and that Antiochis 'like many learned women of the past probably received her first encouragement and education from her father'.[20] We can but guess who Phanostrate learnt from, but on balance she is likely to have been literate and a reader; perhaps her father was encouraging.

The ideals of respectable women as silent and invisible that we find in the democratic leader Pericles' famous funeral speech in Thucydides need not always have been the reality of Athenian society as a whole. In the *Theataetus*, Socrates expected that his companion could have heard of his mother by name – and for a woman's name to be public knowledge was not entirely respectable, supposedly. Some decorated pottery of the mid-fifth century BC shows girls and women reading or with texts or learning to read.[21] Phanostrate's identity as a doctor may also have conveyed her literacy, her learnedness, and her social status to the folk of her town, as Antiochis' statue did more directly three centuries later. She too may have been held in high esteem by the people of her town. There is a contradiction in Athenian society that shows a range of values existed, not only the one in which women were silent and unseen.

If some women could read and become learned doctors, practicing at home and in the community, did they also write about medicine, preserving their practice and setting forth their theories and methods? Parker notes that Aetius quoted extensively from the books of Aspasia, who lived before 550 BC.[22] Antiochis too was cited by the first century AD Asclepiades Pharmakion.[23] Pliny the Elder cited numerous female sources. The eminent Galen cited earlier experts either by referring to their books or by making a more practical reference to their medicine or method, which might have been passed around by word of mouth or have become traditional; most women were referred to in this practical sense.[24]

Flemming notes that there are complete texts from two possible female doctors surviving – Cleopatra's *Gynaecology of Cleopatra* (and other works) and Metrodora's *On Women's Diseases*, though the Cleopatra texts appear to name the author as Theodote in some places.[25] Flemming also points out, however, a host of difficulties with the texts of both authors, which suggest caution and more research is needed before accepting them as the works of two real women. One cautionary principle involves the names of female medical authorities. Cleopatra, not the pharaoh, but sharing her name, is associated with works on gynaecology, cosmetics, and aphrodisiacs, and 'the royal status of Cleopatra certainly added potency to the medical material transmitted under her name', while for Metrodora we find that *metro* is Greek for womb and *dora* gift.[26] A third, Aspasia, is known nowhere else than in Aetius, and she shares a name with the famous courtesan of mid-fifth-century Athens. One Lais, associated with abortives, was the name of a famous Corinthian courtesan. Men may well have authored some or all of these, using the names of famous women to promote their work; the use of a female name does not seem sufficient to prove a woman was behind any particular cure.[27]

Phanostrate, though, was a real woman, attested to in public monuments; she was doubly skilled as both a midwife and doctor, and there is no reason to doubt the evidence of this, whatever the dominant masculine values of classical Athens were. As Holt Parker has observed: 'women's roles as tenders of the sick, like most of their activities, are immemorial and invisible' yet we do have 'a few glancing references' in texts and the archaeological evidence.[28] And we can see through considering the lives of Phanostrate and other women that women's role in health and healing was an important part of everyday life in the ancient world in both the private and public worlds. Phanostrate must have been a valued and respected member of the community.

PART IV

THE HELLENISTIC WORLDS

The Hellenistic period begins with Alexander the Great, the Macedonian king who defeated Persia and conquered a vast empire that stretched from Greece to India, or perhaps even with his father Philip's domination of Greece that set the scene for his son's career.[1] Although Alexander was king for only thirteen years and died in 323 BC, he left the world greatly changed and set in motion further transformations – including the spread of Greek people and culture widely around the eastern Mediterranean and further east. On his death, the empire was divided up by his generals and these new successor kingdoms formed the political arrangements of a new competitive Hellenistic world of monarchs.[2] In Egypt, for example, his general Ptolemy founded a dynasty of pharaohs that ruled till the death of Cleopatra VII. Olympias, Philip's wife and Alexander's mother, was present at the birth of this new world and played an influential role in her son's life and, for a time, in the turmoil that followed his death. She is the subject of Chapter 20.

Apart from this enormous change in the east, much was going on elsewhere in the Mediterranean. The powerful Punic kingdom of Carthage, in North Africa, was an active player in the central and western Mediterranean.[3] The Carthaginians were involved in a variety of ways with the Etruscans, Romans, Italians, and Greeks, as well as local North Africans, peaceful and otherwise; they fought a sea battle alongside the Etruscans against the Phocaean Greeks at Alalia (c. 540 BC) and made treaties with Rome in around 500, 350 and 279/8 BC. In Sicily, they developed a particular rivalry with the Greeks of Syracuse, which impacted the Carthaginian state's development and policy – a 'great war' broke out in 310 BC and Agathocles of Syracuse even invaded Carthaginian Africa, though he was ejected and peace was brokered in 306 BC.[4]

The Etruscan culture had developed over time in northern Italy. The Etruscans were an urban and literate culture, engaged with their neighbours and peoples abroad. At one impressive sanctuary on the coast at Pyrgi, connected by a 10 m wide paved road to the city of Caere inland, archaeologists found three inscribed gold tablets.[5] One was in Phoenician and was matched by one in Etruscan; these detailed the founding of the temple by Thefarie Velianus, ruler of Caere. The Etruscans were influential before and in parallel with the rise of Rome. Rome even had some Etruscan kings, such as Lucius Tarquinius Priscus. But the later story of the Etruscans is one of their eclipse and absorption into the Roman world; their own histories were lost. But archaeology has revealed important aspects of their history and lives, including most famously their funerary habits. Here, in a tomb near Chiusi, we meet Seianti Hanunia Tlesnasa in Chapter 21.

In 279/8 BC Carthage and Rome were in alliance – both facing off the Greek king Pyrrhus of Epirus. But the Carthaginians and Romans soon came to blows themselves in three wars that spanned more than a century – the First (264–241 BC), Second (218–201 BC) and Third Punic Wars (150–146 BC).[6] These devastating wars, from which Rome eventually emerged victorious, saw the destruction of Carthaginian power in the central and western Mediterranean – and eventually the destruction of the city itself. In 146 BC, the Romans also destroyed Corinth in Greece, asserting their influence there too. The Greek ancient historian Polybius observed later how in the space of fifty-three years (220–167 BC) Rome had conquered 'practically the whole known world'.[7]

The Romans were fighting in the western and in the eastern Mediterranean, and in this era of conflict with external enemies there were also conflicts within the state, between factions and families, between Rome and its Italian allies and subjects.[8] The Social War, between Rome and various states in Italy, was fought over access to Roman political rights. Begun in 91/90 BC, it resulted in massive slaughter. Whilst Rome later reached accommodation with the states it had fought, political infighting, violence, and civil war continued unabated, with figures like Marius, Sulla, Pompey, and Julius Caesar all contributing to the breakdown of the republican system across the first century BC.[9] Cicero stands out at this time, for his political and legal career, his philosophy, and his voluminous correspondence – and his death at the hands of his enemies. Supporting him throughout was his wife Terentia, who we meet in Chapter 22.

Over time, increasing Roman presence in the Hellenic eastern world and Seleucid weakness presented both opportunities and dangers. In Judaea, the Hasmoneans came to power after the Maccabean revolt of 166–164 BC against the Seleucid kings. Then, in 40 BC, because there were no male Hasmoneans left, the Roman senate, now fully able to interfere in the east, decided to make Herod, an Idumaean the king of Judaea and on his behalf they invaded Jerusalem and installed him in 37 BC.[10] Lacking a local support-base, and regarded by some as not properly Jewish, Herod would rely on the Romans for his power, and could be assumed to work towards their interests, with Judaea as a client kingdom. Herod's wife Mariamne is the subject of Chapter 23.

20

OLYMPIAS

Olympias, born around 373 BC, was the daughter of Neoptolemus the king of Molossia, a rural, inland, and not-so-important place in Epirus in north-western Greece. The region lacked the old established city-state culture of other parts of Greece, but the oracle of Zeus at Dodona, by tradition the oldest oracle in Greece, did give it some cachet and ensured ongoing contact with the rest of the Hellenic world.[1] The royal house, the Aeacids, claimed descent from the Greek hero Aeacus and from his more famous grandson Achilles – a family connection that Olympias' son Alexander (the Great) certainly took seriously.[2] Despite her origins on the periphery of the Greek world, Olympias occupied a central place in the history of the Aegean and eastern Mediterranean – and farther afield – in the second half of the fourth century BC because of her marriage to Philip II of Macedonia and her son Alexander the Great.

Plutarch's biography of Alexander describes the meeting and marriage of Olympias and Philip in 357 BC.[3] They met on the island of Samothrace in the northern Aegean whilst being initiated into the ancient mysteries there.[4] Philip supposedly fell in love with her straight away and soon arranged the marriage with Olympias' male relatives – Plutarch does not mention what Olympias thought or felt about this turn of events. This story, with its 'chance' meeting between two eligible and strategically placed royals, may be a romanticised version of what was a typical pre-arranged political marriage designed to bring political advantages to both families. Growing up, Olympias would no doubt have been aware that her future would involve such a marriage; her modern biographer Elizabeth Carney suggests that 'the personal feelings of either Philip or Olympias about each other were irrelevant both to the creation of the marriage and to its perpetuation'.[5]

Macedonian kings were polygamous, and Olympias was Philip's fifth 'strategic' wife. One source, Athenaeus, wrote that 'Philip always married in connection to a war'.[6] By marrying Olympias, he gained even wider influence over northern Greece than he already had. At the same time, Olympias, coming into the Macedonian court, had the opportunity to develop an active influence in the royal household and in Macedonian high politics – very much family-based. Olympias may have taken her most famous name when she married – her name as a child was Polyxena, which was later changed to Myrtale, perhaps in connection with some kind of religious rite; later in life she also acquired the name Stratonice – 'victory in war'.[7]

Because of their polygamous habits Macedonian kings created an ideal context for competition between wives in their own right and on behalf of, or using, their sons.[8] This atmosphere of rivalry was exacerbated by Philip's reluctance to have an officially 'favoured' wife or a designated heir. Olympias thus became attached to Philip's extended royal household when there were already four wives and at least three children, two daughters and a son, Arrhidaeus. Olympias had two children with Philip, Alexander (b. 356 BC) and Cleopatra (b. 354 BC). Relations between wives could become cut-throat when seeking furtherment or influence but need not always have been sour; between women without sons in competition, alliances and friendships may have been made – the wives had their experience and positions in common.[9]

Philinna may have been Olympias' greatest rival, at least for a few years, as she was the mother of Philip's other son Arrhidaeus.[10] However, it became clear as he grew that Arrhidaeus was not fully competent; Alexander was thus the only real contender as Philip's heir – and Olympias, his mother, will have gained in status and power because of this. Their rank and favour was advertised by Philip in very public terms at sacred Olympia, where he built an extraordinary monument – the Sanctuary of Philip (the Philippeion; Figure 20).[11] This was described by Pausanias, the Greek travel writer of the second century AD:

> The Mother's Sanctuary is inside Altis, and so is the round building called the Sanctuary of Philip, on the pinnacle of which is a bronze poppy that ties together the roof beams. This building is on the left by the exit by the Council-house. Built in fired brick with columns standing round it; Philip built it after the fall of Greece at Chaironeia. Philip and Alexander are there, and Philip's father Amyntas, all by Leochares in ivory and gold like the portraits of Olympias and Eurydike.[12]

FIG. 20 The Philippeion at Olympia. Contributor: Constantinos Iliopoulos / Alamy Stock Photo

Not only did the monument pick out Olympias and Alexander from Philip's wives and children, it depicted all five family members as 'god-like'. The statues were of ivory and gold, materials that were usually reserved for statues of gods and goddesses. The building looked like a temple and was located within a sacred boundary in one of the most holy and ancient places of the Greek world.[13] Philip is even recorded as having a statue of himself carried with statues of the twelve Olympian gods at his daughter's wedding to Olympias' brother. If not claiming actual divinity, Philip was certainly declaring an exalted status for himself, which he extended to his parents, his heir, and Olympias.

But Philip married again, twice, though this may reflect more on his political rather than emotional thinking; it need not reflect in any way on the state of his relationship with Olympias and Alexander at all, which is often said to have been strained.[14] Plutarch's story is that Philip's ardour was dampened by the fact that Olympias slept with snakes – probably a reference to her extreme devotion to particular religious cults. However, the prospect of more sons to compete with Alexander would have troubled Olympias. Several sources do agree that something happened that drove both Olympias and Alexander to leave the court for a time.

The incident they record involved a drinking party held by Philip in 337 BC, with members of the Macedonian elite, to celebrate his marriage to Cleopatra, the niece of Attalus. During the party, Attalus somehow questioned

Alexander's legitimacy as heir-apparent, possibly suggesting that Attalus meant that any child of Philip and Cleopatra would have been 'more Macedonian' and so more suitable to become king. Alexander, made angry, threw a wine cup at Attalus and may have had one thrown back at him. But Philip's reaction – possibly drawing his sword against the furious Alexander, or at least not defending him – seems to have been key. Olympias and Alexander left – Olympias back to Molossia and Alexander to Philip's enemies in Illyria.

A public reconciliation was attempted in 336 BC at a great Panhellenic festival; Philip had arranged for Olympias' brother Alexander to marry his and Olympias' daughter Cleopatra, thus confirming the importance of Olympias and their son Alexander. However, at this happy event, Philip was murdered by a former lover, Pausanias. Inevitably, it was suggested that Olympias incited Pausanias to act; Plutarch says she was 'chiefly blamed for the assassination', though he also mentions that Alexander might have encouraged him too.[15] Pausanias apparently had his own motivations: Philip failed to defend him against Attalus, who had had him gang-raped.[16] They may have been involved – but given Philip's age and the fact that he was about to go to war with the Persians (who might have been involved) it would have been a risky strategy.

Philip was dead and Alexander king. According to the writer Pausanias, when Philip died 'Olympias took his baby son, the child of Attalus' niece Kleopatra, and murdered the child and the mother together by dragging them on to a bronze oven filled with fire'.[17] But according to Justin, she killed Cleopatra's daughter in front of her before forcing her to hang herself. Carney suggests Justin's account may be the closest to the truth, since Olympias later had another Macedonian queen, Adea Eurydice, hang herself.[18] The killings were not simply crimes of passion by a spurned wife, though revenge may have been a part of it, but were rather a calculated political act, erasing a rival branch of the family who might attempt to seize the throne.[19] They would have been less remarkable had a man been responsible and were par for the course in Macedonian politics – and a culture in which vendettas and revenge were the norm.

This murder – of a young mother and child – certainly gives the impression of an ambitious and ruthless, even brutal woman. It ties in with other judgements about Olympias, for example, that she was passionate, extreme, and violent. Plutarch tells us that Olympias was an initiate and a participant in orgiastic religious rites, which were particularly associated with the northern lands[20] but was given to extremes in her worship: 'it was Olympias' habit to enter into these states of possession and surrender herself to the inspiration of the god with even wilder abandon than the others'. These could be wild occasions, involving ecstatic worship, processions and dancing, snake handling, epiphanies of the god, and possession (perhaps best brought to life in Euripides' play *The Bacchae*).[21] Into the procession and rites, she supposedly also added large, tamed snakes, 'which terrified the male spectators'.

Whilst Alexander was king and was away fighting, Olympias stayed in Macedonia, though they remained in constant contact through letters. On the basis of her son's kingship, as part of the Macedonian royal house and as a member of the Molossian royal house, she certainly occupied a position of power and influence alongside Antipater, who was left in charge of military matters, although very little is known of her activities.[22] One source records purchases of grain by Olympias and her daughter Cleopatra from Cyrene, in north Africa. They were named as individuals in a list alongside states; Antipater is nowhere similarly named.[23] The implication is that, whether acting under Alexander's instructions or not, both Olympias and Cleopatra were acting as rulers. She also made gifts to sanctuaries, a bowl at the shrine of Hygieia in Athens and golden crowns at Delphi.[24] In around 331 BC, Olympias left Macedonia for Molossia, perhaps because she and her daughter could rule there more independently away from Antipater; Cleopatra's husband, Olympias' brother, king Alexander had died and Cleopatra became regent.

Alexander died in Babylon in 323 BC and the world was thrown into chaos as his companions – the Successors – fought for control of the vast new empire.[25] Olympias' position, so tied to the career of her son, immediately became precarious.[26] There was no obvious heir, though Alexander's wife Roxane was pregnant and soon after gave birth to a boy – Alexander IV. But in Sardis, the Macedonian infantry had made Arrhidaeus into king Philip III.[27] There were two kings and one regent – Perdiccas, who married a daughter of Antipater and had rejected Cleopatra.[28] Philip III married a Macedonian princess, Adea Eurydice, granddaughter of Philip II. Perdiccas died and Polyperchon became regent; in 319 BC, he invited Olympias back to Macedonia to act for Alexander IV and to regain her position and status, bringing her back into the centre of the political life of Macedonia and the empire.[29] Quite why he did this is unclear but it was possibly due to Olympias' popularity, her special status as the mother of Alexander and wife of Philip.

This popularity is amply demonstrated by Olympias' triumphant return to Macedonia. At the head of an army went Olympias, Aeacides her nephew, king of Molossia, the infant Alexander IV, Roxane, and Polyperchon.[30] They were met in the field by Philip III and Adea Eurydice, but the Macedonian army, seeing Olympias, deserted and went over to her side. Philip and Adea Eurydice were captured and killed, and Olympias appears then to have had many of the Macedonian nobility, presumably those who had supported her enemies, killed.[31] Whilst her behaviour was presented as reprehensible, it was nothing unusual for Macedonian royalty and their conflicts, but Olympias, being a women, may have been judged more harshly in the sources. These actions may have lost her the support of many.

The impression is that both Olympias and Adea Eurydice were at the head of their armies, both, at least nominally, acting for 'their' unready kings. Olympias would have been in her fifties and at the confrontation was dressed as a bacchant; Adea Eurydice was younger and appeared as a warrior, probably leading her troops. Adea Eurydice's grandmother was Audata, an Illyrian, wife of Philip II, her mother was Cynnane, who fought in battle herself; each trained the next in Illyrian style. Whilst ancient Greek women generally did not take part in battle or lead armies, there are these 'northern' examples, and a number of other Hellenistic queens also led armies and took charge of campaigns or actions.[32]

Olympias' success was short-lived. In 316 BC, Cassander, the son of Olympias' old enemy Antipater, led his army north and took control of Macedonia. Olympias was besieged in the city of Pydna, on the coast of northern Greece and, when no support came from her allies, she eventually surrendered. Alexander IV and Roxane were taken prisoner and later killed.

Carney explains how the various sources 'differ about the context of her death, its perpetrators, and its method'.[33] In the travel writer Pausanias' version, she was stoned to death by some of the Macedonians. In Justin's, she dressed up and cowed the executioners by going out to meet them in royal clothes – they were reminded of just who she was and did not kill her. Others were then sent to stab her, and she died without crying out in a 'womanish' way. Another version, by Diodorus, has Olympias given a kind of public trial by Cassander.

To try to kill her quickly, before anyone could change their mind, he also tried to trick her into escaping – but she stayed to try to put her case. Soldiers were sent into her quarters to kill her but were also too affected by her presence to go through with it. The story goes that the families of those she had had killed were given the task of killing her. All the sources seem to suggest that the execution of Olympias was a major step, for which Cassander wanted others to share the responsibility; her reputation and the fact of who she was, Philip's wife and Alexander's mother, still counted at the end.

What happened to Olympias' body? One suggestion is that she was buried at Pydna, where she had met her death. The evidence for this rests primarily on two fragmentary inscriptions found at Makriyialos, which might, upon reconstruction by modern scholars, be read to suggest that her tomb was there and that descendants of her family lived nearby.[34] Another recent suggestion is that she was buried at Amphipolis, where in 2012 archaeologists began to excavate a major burial complex centred on the Kasta Hill.[35] The entrance to this vast construction is guarded by two sphinxes, over the doorway, and inside are two monumental caryatids. A lion, found elsewhere in a riverbed, is argued to have topped the mound. Andrew Chugg has made an argument that features of the tomb support this – the caryatids and the lion that went on top.[36]

Olympias lived through a time of momentous changes, some of them brought about by her husband, others by her son. She was very much a powerful character in her own right and was undoubtedly a powerful player in the drama of those at the top.

21

SEIANTI HANUNIA TLESNASA

In a brief article from the 1960s, Herbert Mentink wrote that 'I have yet to come upon a writer who can refrain from such adjectives as amazing, fascinating, mysterious, baffling, enigmatic, puzzling, and ambiguous when he speaks of the Etruscans'.[1] Usually this mystery extends both to their origins and language. Did they really come all the way from the eastern Mediterranean to Italy as legend had it or were they an indigenous culture that bound themselves into a wider culture? The Etruscan language, unrelated to any other European language, is represented by 11,000-odd surviving inscriptions but remains undeciphered.[2] Their tendency to luxury and debauchery, their sensual habit of removing all body hair, and their unique way of doing things from boxing to bread-making and flogging to flute music were proverbial in ancient times and made the Etruscans oddities to the Greeks and Romans, from whose viewpoints we have come to know them.[3] They were also known for their 'religious expertise', especially haruspicy, the bloody art of divination from animal innards.[4] The Roman emperor Claudius was fascinated by them and even wrote a history of them, very sadly lost.[5]

But does this image stand up to scrutiny? Etruscologist Jean MacIntosh Turfa points out that really the mystery of the Etruscans 'is in our own minds'.[6] Rather than simply following the partisan views of most classical authors when discussing strange 'others', non-Greeks and non-Romans, much can be and has been learned of the Etruscans from their own material culture, the things they made, used, looked at, and touched, from their inscriptions and even from the bodies of Etruscan people themselves. Archaeology has enabled many aspects of Etruscan history, society, and culture to be known – more so than many other essentially prehistoric societies. More archaeology-driven approaches to the Etruscans are now the norm, represented in recent scholarly and more popular books by Etruscan specialists.[7] Texts looking in on the Etruscans from the outside can now be compared and contrasted with the view from their own material culture.

One woman we can learn directly about from archaeology is Seianti Hanunia Tlesnasa.[8] She was buried around 2,200 years ago in a tomb at Poggio Cantarello near the Etruscan city of Chiusi, now in Tuscany. Her remains had been placed in an extraordinary terracotta sarcophagus on top of which there was a painted effigy, presumed to be a portrait of Seianti herself, in a reclining position (Figure 21); an inscription gave her name written right to left in Etruscan style in letters which were similar to the Greek letters in use elsewhere in Italy.[9] The sarcophagus was found in 1886, when the tomb was excavated by local archaeologist Oreste Mignone.[10] When it was first found and opened it appeared to be intact, neither robbed nor reused. It was straightaway agreed that the skull did indeed belong to a woman, as could be expected from the effigy, but her age at death was unclear and was placed roughly at mature or elderly.[11]

The chamber tomb, dug into the bedrock, was small and undecorated – there were none of the famous architectural details or tomb paintings known

FIG. 21 Sarcophagus of Seianti Hanunia Tlesnasa. © The Trustees of the British Museum

from Etruscan tombs elsewhere, such as Tarquinia or Cerveteri. Along with the sarcophagus, however, there were five silver objects hanging from the walls: a silver mirror, a strigil, a perfume bottle, a box, and a bucket or *situla.*[12] These objects have been missing since 1939 and are now known only from a photograph, the publication of the tomb, and later catalogue entries. They may have been made especially for Seianti's burial or used by her in her life. The skeleton, sarcophagus, and grave goods were acquired by the British Museum in 1887 and a century later, minus the silver set, became the subject of an intensive research project, which has revealed much about her life and her real appearance.[13]

The sarcophagus and effigy are remarkable, and it is not surprising that they have long been on display to the public. The sarcophagus measures 180 × 43 × 42 cm, with the effigy, placed on two slabs, having a height of 82 cm.[14] Made up of five clay pieces, it weighs a total of 688 kg. Judith Swaddling, part of the British Museum's Seianti project, reported that it took four men to move each piece around the museum – it must have been very difficult to manoeuvre the sarcophagus into the tomb.[15] The fired clay was covered in a white layer on which coloured pigments could be painted.[16] The front of the sarcophagus was decorated with architectural reliefs, four bar triglyph-type patterns divided by three rosettes.

The painted effigy of Seianti shows a wealthy woman reclining comfortably on a mattress, resting her left arm on a deep red–painted cushion. She is wearing a white dress with a purple border and has a veil over her head, which she is lifting with her right hand to reveal her face. Her skin is pale and smooth, her eyes dark and her lips slightly parted. In her left hand she is holding a mirror, and it seems she is captured in the act of looking at herself. She is bedecked with golden jewellery, including pendant earrings, a twisted snake bracelet, and an armband on the bicep of her stout right arm. She has on a gold necklace and on her left hand is wearing six rings. The figure is stunning for the lifelike appearance of Seianti in motion, with her figure and flowing, wrinkled clothes so well executed. Put together from clay, it is an astonishing achievement.

Seianti's skeletal remains are mostly present and have been examined carefully. They reveal a woman of around 1.54 m in height, who died aged fifty to fifty-five.[17] The cause of death could not be determined from the skeleton, but she would have been considered fairly old. Her childhood seems to have been a healthy one. The analysis revealed that Seianti had particularly strong upper legs – the femoral bones were robust and the trochanters, the areas muscles attach to, were also prominent, suggesting well developed muscles. Her upper arm bones were also robust. The plausible interpretation is that Seianti grew up as a keen horse rider and her legs grew strong from gripping the horse. We can imagine this as something she loved doing, and as a pastime that indicated her wealthy status – well off enough to have a horse to ride and the time to ride it.

Indeed, horse riding and racing were particular passions in Etruscan society.[18] According to the Roman historian Livy, one of the early Roman kings of around 600 BC – the Etruscan Tarquinius Priscus – built the first circus in Rome and imported the sports of boxing and horse racing from Etruria.[19] A most important piece of archaeological evidence about Etruscan horse racing comes from Poggio Civitate. Here archaeologists found more than sixty-five clay plaques, made locally, forming a horse racing frieze that would once have decorated the walls of a major building, possibly a temple or other civic structure, which dated to the sixth century BC. The horses are shown in motion, with individually styled manes – stiff or free flowing. The riders are quite small on the horses; they wear capes and pointed hats and have long hair, which is possibly bound or curly; they carry whips to spur on their mounts. In her presentation of the plaques, Margaret Cool Root suggests the 'small beardless jockeys' to be young men, but this does not contradict a tradition of private riding by women.[20]

When she was around fifteen to twenty years old, though, Seianti seems to have had an accident – possibly, Robert Stoddart suggests, when riding.[21] The skeletal remains show that she sustained 'an extensive injury' to her lower spine and the right side of her pelvis. In this case, it looks like the horse and rider fell and Seianti's right leg was crushed beneath the animal as it came down. During the fall, she may have hit her head on something hard, knocking out some teeth and injuring her jaw. Although she recovered and lived another four decades, the injury to her hip area would eventually have become very painful as the joint cartilage wore away, causing bone on bone contact. She probably suffered lower back pain indicated by a damaged sacroiliac joint on the right side, the area where the spine joins the pelvis.

John Lilley examined what is left of Seianti's teeth and jaws.[22] Seianti's face would have had a slightly lop-sided appearance that became more pronounced with age, which was caused by an asymmetrical mandible. Whilst this could have been caused ultimately by the suggested riding accident, it could also have been a developmental abnormality, or perhaps was caused by a later condition. Her jaw appears to have had only restricted movement; certainly later in life, she may only have been able to eat soft foods or soups and liquids. She may have jutted her lower jaw for comfort and when moving it may have made audible clicking and grating sounds; Lilley points out that she may have spoken through gritted teeth to limit painful movement. Seianti also appears to have had chronic gum disease, periodontitis, which leads to 'loss of tooth support, painful gums and suppuration from the crevices at the margins of the teeth'.[23] It might have become too painful to keep her mouth clean, which would have made the gum disease worse. Very likely Seianti suffered from bad breath.

At any rate, she had a range of oral problems and Lilley concludes that she would have had 'chronic oral pain, limited mouth opening, poor oral hygiene and repeated tooth loss'.[24]

The close examination of Seianti's remains does give us part of her biography. But can we place Seianti into a broader context? What did other ancient people know or think they knew about the Etruscans and Etruscan women?

The Etruscans have been known to non-Etruscans for a very long time – the Greek poet Hesiod mentioned 'the famous Tyrsenians, very far off' in his *Theogony*, composed around 700 BC. The Greek historian Herodotus wrote of the tradition that they came to Italy from Anatolia, and Roman poets sometimes called them Lydians, the name of an Anatolian people. Dionysus of Halicarnassus, though, around the time of Augustus, thought that they were a native Italian people. Evidently there were different traditions and opinions about the Etruscans even then – and this was not unique to them.[25]

Because no Etruscan literature or history has survived, and the Etruscan people eventually fell under the spell of ever-expanding Rome, this 'looking in' at the Etruscans from the outside has been normalised – and it certainly contributes to the 'mystery' that surrounds them. We very often see the Etruscans through the biases of Greek and Roman writers; Roman writers developed and highlighted ideas of Romanness by contrasting Roman ways with the ways of 'others', including their neighbours. As Maria Beatrice Bittarello has suggested 'Roman representations of foreign peoples often reveal the pressing need to justify attacks against them, and constantly present Rome as possessing the 'correct' cultural and religious values'.[26]

Etruscan women have also been recreated from the outside by classical authors – doubly othered by Roman men in terms of culture and gender. As noted by Vedia Izzet, one ancient text stands out; this is a description of Etruscan women found in Athenaeus' *Deipnosophistae* ('Scholars round the dinner table'), from around AD 200, but taken from the fourth century BC work of Theopompus.[27] It reads as follows:

> It is a law among the Etruscans that all their women should be in common: and the women pay the greatest attention to their persons, and often practise gymnastic exercises, naked, among the men, and sometimes with one another; for it is not accounted shameful for them to be seen naked. And they dine not with their own husbands, but with anyone who happens to be present; and they pledge whoever they please in their cups: and they are amazingly fond of drinking, and very handsome. And the Etruscans bring up all the children that are born, no one knowing to what father each child belongs: and the children, too, live in the same manner as those who have brought them up, having feasts very frequently, and being intimate with all the women. Nor is it reckoned among the Etruscans at all disgraceful either to do or suffer anything in

> the open air, or to be seen while it is going on; for this is the custom of their country: and they are so far from thinking it disgraceful, that they even say, when the master of the house is indulging his sexual appetites, and anyone asks for him, that he is doing so and so, using the coarsest possible words for his occupation. But when they are together in parties of companions or relations, they act in the following manner. First of all, when they have stopped drinking, and are about to go to sleep, while the lights are still burning, the servants introduce sometimes courtesans and sometimes beautiful boys, and sometimes women; and when they have enjoyed them, they proceed to acts of still grosser licentiousness: and they indulge their appetites, and make parties on purpose, sometimes keeping one another in sight but more frequently making tents around the beds which are made of plaited slats, with cloths thrown over them. And the objects of their love are usually women; much more, however, do they enjoy consorting with boys and striplings; and these are very beautiful, as is natural for people to be who live luxuriously, and who take great care of their persons.

Etruscan expert Larissa Bonfante notes that Theopompus has certainly exaggerated some aspects of women's activities in Etruscan society and misunderstood others but concludes that there is likely some truth in his account.[28] Indeed, as different cultures set different store by personal grooming and favour particular looks, there is no reason that Etruscan aristocrats should not have had a culture of physical beauty. Seianti's mirror and pose could support this as could the representation of her as somewhat younger and sleeker than she was at her time of death.

Paintings from sarcophagi and tombs do show Etruscan women drinking and reclining with men at drinking parties, even sharing a blanket, but these were likely husbands and wives.[29] Seianti may have socialised this way. In Greek culture, wives were excluded from such parties – the females present, if any, were *hetairai*, prostitutes and flute girls – the Etruscan practice would have been seen as bizarre and immoral by many Greeks. That Etruscan aristocrats kept mixed company does not mean that Etruscan women (and men) were having orgies or affairs willy-nilly, though the idea of this may have titillated the ancient Greek or Roman reader. Perhaps the Etruscans were more sexually open than the Greeks and Romans but what seems to come through is a society in which men and women were perhaps more openly equal and affectionate than elite Greco-Roman culture thought appropriate. A decorated bronze *situla*, a container for wine at a feast, shows a fascinating pictorial narrative of a young couple meeting and courting – the woman affectionately 'chin chucking' the man – then having sex in a number of positions, and finally the woman giving birth to their child.[30] Was this the desired life narrative of Etruscan aristocrats?

Men and women are depicted in tomb paintings as watching athletics contests together, and Theopompus thought that they exercised naked together as well. Nude male gymnastics was a central pillar of Greek culture, but Bonfante suggests that Etruscan men always exercised in shorts, and that if women did exercise, they would probably have been covered in some way too.[31] However, Ellen Millender reminds us that Spartan women do seem to have exercised and raced nude, though when wrestling wore shorts. In Sparta, this exercise had serious ritual and social associations and may have been part of a Spartan girl's transition to womanhood and marriage.[32] These ways were criticised by other Greeks, especially the Athenians, and Spartan women were judged licentious. It is unclear whether Etruscan women were similarly being judged for a real behaviour, which would have had specific cultural meanings, or were just being exoticised or stereotyped by others.

In writing about the Etruscans, who we should remember were still around in his day, Theopompus has clearly been influenced by his own Greekness in making Etruscans decadent and immoral in contrast to the respectable Greeks. In a sense, he is holding up a mirror to his Greek audience rather than writing a thoroughly evidence-based and objective history – and certainly this is how Athenaeus used him.[33] How much was Theopompus interested in accuracy and facts and how much in telling a story of strange foreigners in a distant land? Are any of his comments reflective of the life of Seianti?

Seianti's effigy has now been on display in the British Museum for more than a century and her face – as rendered by the unknown artist – has been seen by millions of visitors from around the world. Her physical remains have helped fill in details of Etruscan life. We look at Seianti now as Seianti looks at herself – in a scene of private life composed ultimately not to be seen but to be put away in her grave for eternity.

22

TERENTIA

Terentia was born around 98 BC and reportedly died aged 103, in AD 5 or 6.[1] From her name, she must have come from an old and respectable family called the Terentii; one branch, the Terentii Varrones, traced itself back to a consul of 216 BC.[2] The identity of her mother and father are not known, though her mother must have married twice as Terentia had a half-sister, Fabia (whose father must have been a Fabius), who was a Vestal Virgin. Terentia is best known by her male connection – she was the wife of the lawyer, philosopher, and politician Marcus Tullius Cicero (106–43 BC) – it is impossible to write about her without also writing about him. The couple lived in the dangerous years of the twilight of the Roman Republic and were at the very heart of the conflicts and rivalries that tore it apart. This was the era when powerful Roman warlords were already emerging to challenge the status quo, of civil war, of Sulla, Pompey the Great, and the rise of Julius Caesar.

Unfortunately, but typically, we have neither Terentia's own words or her remains from which to learn directly about her, her own thoughts and feelings, and her views on the period, its politics, or her marriage and family. Rather, we are reliant on the letters Cicero sent to her and their daughter Tullia and other sources that mention her, including Plutarch's *Life of Cicero*. The letters discuss events and situations and are essential historical sources, but they inevitably provide only a limited and second-hand picture of the person. Even so, as her biographer Susan Treggiari writes of Terentia and Tullia, 'they are . . . the only Roman women of the classical period adequately documented by private letters'.[3] This makes it important to try to engage with them despite the difficulties and inevitable caveats.

The young Terentia would have actively participated in the religious life of her home, not least during the customary transitions from infant to girl and woman.[4] This would have included the worship of the household gods, the *Lares* and *Penates*, represented by figurines that occupied a niche in the house, probably with incense, wine, and other offerings.[5] A respect for the father, the *paterfamilias*, would have been inculcated through the worship of his *genius*. As mentioned, she also had a half-sister who became a Vestal Virgin and in growing up would no doubt have been inducted into public religion as well, an area of society in which women had their own responsibilities. Religious life was not only a matter of piety, it also helped create a network of women embedded in society, which could impact on politics more widely.

As a girl, Terentia would have received an education in a variety of subjects, including the good management of a large household with lands, property, and a staff of slaves.[6] This would have required both literacy and numeracy. Beyond this domestic sphere, over which women were expected to preside, Terentia and other elite women are likely to have grown up bilingually in Latin and Greek; many nurses were Greek-speakers and Greek the language of culture. Within the household, women would have been introduced to classic works of poetry and literature to ensure they were sophisticated and refined enough to participate in elite Roman life in the company of other women and also men. Some elite women were known as writers and poets themselves, including Terentia's contemporary Clodia; and as a testament to relatively wide literacy rates, even some non-elite women were also able to write and send letters and notes.[7] Unlike in classical Athens but more like the Etruscan elite, Roman women could participate in mixed parties; as Cornelius Nepos, a contemporary writer, stated: 'what Roman is ashamed to take his wife to a dinner party?'.[8] Conversational and social skills would have been important, especially in an elite culture that valued speech, rhetoric, and debate.

However, it was important to balance developing a suitable level of sophistication with instilling proper – socially desired – morality and virtue.[9] One writer, Musonius Rufus, argued that girls should receive the same education as boys, including in philosophy, with an emphasis on four Stoic virtues: reason, self-control, justice, and courage. In this way, a girl/woman would be better able to defend her virginity and chastity and to fulfil her role as a dutiful wife and a protective mother, all of which were of the utmost importance.

Terentia would doubtless have known of a string of women from Roman tradition notable for their intercessions into politics and war, such as Hersilia, a Sabine woman who intervened in the battle between the Sabine and Roman men, who had captured her and other Sabine women and Veturia and Volumnia, the mother and wife of Coriolanus, who prevented his attack on the city.[10] In 195 BC, a group of elite Roman women organised and carried a public political protest about a law called the *lex Oppia*, introduced in 215 BC, which restricted what they could wear to funerals – to limit opulent display amongst the elite. They gathered in numbers outside the houses of the tribunes, who then repealed it. Less distant was the indomitable Cornelia, the daughter of Scipio Africanus, who defeated Hannibal, and mother of the murdered reformers Tiberius and Gaius Gracchus, and Sempronia, the wife of Scipio Aemilianus, who destroyed Carthage.[11] Cornelia was a legend in her own lifetime, living a public life as a widow, entertaining the great and good and corresponding with leading men of the age; she became an almost legendary example of an elite Roman woman – virtuous, a good mother, and undoubtedly intelligent and sophisticated too. Terentia would have seen the statue of her in Rome, set up after her death, and had her own thoughts about Cornelia – perhaps especially after her own divorce from Cicero.[12]

Terentia and Cicero married in around 80 BC, when she was eighteen.[13] Cicero may have known Terentia's family and possibly Terentia herself for some time – Cicero's cousin was a Varro and he was a friend of M. Terentius Varro, who lived near Cicero's hometown of Arpinum. Terentia's family were of a higher standing than Cicero's and richer; there must have been perceived benefits on both sides for the match to have been made, including a financial boost for Cicero, but this does not rule out the possibility of affection or love that may have existed. For Terentia, it may have been exciting to be married and a partner to a man who loved learning and who was determined to make his way in the world.

Cicero decided to study in Greece, Athens and Rhodes, training in rhetoric, an essential skill for his career in the law courts of Rome and helpful for moving into and upwards in politics too. He did not belong to an old aristocratic family – he could claim no great ancestors in his lineage; he had to work hard to progress in civic life. He made it a deliberate policy to live a public lifestyle; he made himself accessible to all callers to his house, developed a wide circle of friends and contacts, sought to win people's favour, and tried to construct a positive reputation for himself.[14] Being married and having children was an important part of this; Terentia and Cicero's daughter Tullia was born in 77 BC. Treggiari suggests that Terentia went with Cicero abroad and that Tullia may have been born in Rhodes.[15] Perhaps both Terentia and Cicero looked back on these days in old, sophisticated Greece as a happy memory.

Whilst Cicero cultivated a busy public work life back in Rome, Terentia would have ensured that their household ran smoothly, duties that would have included managing staff, supplies, and the production and acquisition of any necessities. It may have included overseeing the business generated by the various properties they owned and acquired over time, which brought in agricultural produce and other resources. Like other elite Roman wives, Terentia would have hosted parties at home for the friends and colleagues of her husband and for their wives, and from Plutarch and Cicero's comments, we can imagine her as a forthright participant in these.[16] She would have attended similar parties at the houses of others. There would also have been women-only gatherings and possibly unaccompanied trips to the countryside, as well as participation in religious festivals throughout the year. The domestic sphere, vital to the life of the family, was the charge of a wife, but Terentia would not have been closeted away as a wife from classical Athens would have been.

Of Terentia's character, some impression can be gained. Plutarch, in his life of Cicero comments that 'Terentia was never at any time a shrinking violet type of woman; she was bold and energetic by nature, ambitious, and, as Cicero says himself, was more inclined to take a part in his public life than to share with him any of her domestic responsibilities'.[17] She had domestic responsibilities, the same as any Roman wife, but she was also an active and outgoing woman; politically inclined, she may have been driven to participate on her own account and not just as her husband's partner. One means of participation was through the networks of elite women that existed; these were a means of communication between women but also between allied and rival individuals, families and groups – male society. Women made alliances and worked 'behind the scenes'.[18]

Cicero became one of Rome's two consuls in 63 BC. This was the highest office of state and his great achievement, which reflected also on his family and descendants; Terentia must have been a great help and support to him in his journey, not least by ensuring his household functioned properly. Doubtless her own knowledge of the political world, seen from the women's side, was essential. On his way to the consulship, Cicero had come into conflict with Lucius Sergius Catiline, an ambitious and corrupt member of an old elite patrician family. Catiline was aggrieved that he had not been able to achieve the consulship that he thought he was owed. He tried to win popular as opposed to traditional aristocratic support by offering the general cancellation of debts. When that did not work, he, and supposedly hundreds of other conspirators, including women they had won to their cause, apparently sought to have Cicero, the 'new man' (not from an old family) he regarded with scorn, assassinated, along with many other senators.[19] The plot failed and Catiline fled to his supporters and another rebel Manlius, who had an army at his disposal. But Catiline was defeated and died in battle, whilst the other conspirators were arrested.

Behind this story is another, involving Terentia and a woman called Fulvia. According to Sallust, the historian of the conspiracy of Catiline, one of the conspirators, Quintus Curius, was in love with Fulvia, but when she appeared cool to him, he let slip that soon he would be able to control her life completely. Fulvia questioned him further, pretending to be enjoying the evening's wine and company, and 'to please her' he revealed the whole assassination plot. Fulvia pretended to be impressed, but the next day, according to another historian Diodorus, she went to Terentia to tell her about the sinister plan of Catiline and the others. Terentia already had reason to dislike Catiline, since he had allegedly seduced her half-sister Fabia, the Vestal Virgin; though she was acquitted of the crime of unchastity, it remained a stain on her and the family's reputation.[20] Terentia told Cicero Fulvia's news, the plot was foiled, and a group of the conspiracy's leaders arrested. The network of elite women had saved the day.

Terentia and a number of other women were also involved in the further fate of the conspirators.[21] In an official role as wife of the consul, Terentia presided over the all-woman ceremony of the *Bona Dea*, the Good Goddess, performed this time at their house in Rome. This was a great moment – but then the sacred fire on the altar went out. Suddenly 'a great bright flame sprang up . . . which terrified most of the women'; 'the sacred virgins told Cicero's wife Terentia to go at once to her husband and tell him to act as he had decided to act for the good of his country, since the goddess was sending him a great light to promise him both safety and glory'.[22] Thus steeled, Cicero acted decisively. The fate of the conspirators was debated in the senate, with Caesar arguing for imprisonment and Cato that they should be put to death. Cicero marched the condemned prisoners through the city to the place of their execution, a grim subterranean stone vault, where they were strangled. Cicero had prevented a putsch, saved the day, and become the defender and saviour of Rome – all with the help and support of Terentia.

The next year, 62 BC, something else happened at the *Bona Dea* rites, this time being hosted at Julius Caesar's house by his wife Pompeia.[23] Plutarch tells us that a bold young noble called Clodius snuck into the rites dressed as a female musician, with the aid of a girl of the household, apparently with the aim of seducing Pompeia.[24] He was caught, however, and brought up on charges. Because of the scandal, or perhaps with some other motivation, Caesar divorced Pompeia. Clodius and Cicero had once been friends, but now Cicero had exposed Clodius' false claim that he had been out of Rome at the time of the rite. According to Plutarch, he did this to get on Terentia's good side. Terentia was against Clodius because she thought his sister Clodia wanted to marry Cicero, and that they were arranging this through a go-between, one Tullus, a close friend of Cicero's. Plutarch explains that 'Terentia's suspicions were aroused by the way in which Tullus kept on visiting and paying attentions to Clodia, who lived close by; and since Terentia had a violent will of her own and had gained the ascendancy over Cicero, she urged him to join in the attack on Clodius and to give evidence against him'.

Clodius was acquitted, but angry at Cicero he set about turning as many people as possible against him.[25] In 58 BC, Clodius, now holding office as a tribune, passed a law against those who had executed a citizen without trial – precisely what Cicero had done with Catiline's allies. Cicero's career and influence nosedived and he was forced into exile; Clodius condemned him, forbade anyone to shelter him, and had his property confiscated and sold. Plutarch records that Clodius had Cicero's villas burned and his house in Rome was demolished and a temple to liberty built on its ruins.[26] Terentia's life became increasingly complicated as a result of her husband's drastic change of fortunes, which she herself had partly caused. Possibly she was ill and probably she was in a constant state of anxiety.

In several letters written to Terentia and the family, Cicero explained his feelings and responded to news coming to him – from them and from others. The letters reveal the strong love that existed within the family, and Cicero's respect for his wife, his fears for her health, as well as his gratitude, his guilt, and his shame in failing her. They reveal Terentia's circumstances, feelings, and actions too, what she endured and how she behaved. In a letter from April 58 BC, which Cicero wrote from Brundisium, he worries for Terentia 'a sick woman, physically and spiritually exhausted' but also rests his hope in her work on his behalf 'if there is any hope of my return, you must build it up, and help in the campaign'.[27] His letters stress the burden he was placing upon her, and she rose to the challenge.

In April, Cicero did not know whether Terentia had been stripped of their or her own property and exhorts her to 'bear up with all the dignity you can muster'. A letter from October discloses money worries; Cicero wrote that 'what grieves me is that in your unhappy and impoverished state you should be contributing to any unnecessary outlay... I beg you, where expense is concerned, let others bear it who can, if only they will'.[28] In a letter from November, he is shocked to hear that Terentia plans to sell a row of houses to raise money.[29] Thinking of his young son Marcus, and the family's resources, he implores Terentia not to use her own money but to seek help instead from friends.

Terentia may also have lived in fear for herself at this time. The October letter reveals that she had apparently even been forcibly physically removed from the Temple of Vesta, where she had taken refuge with her step-sister or other women she knew, to the place where the tribunes met, to be interviewed – or humiliated – by Clodius.[30] This and other sources, by their language, suggest threats and even violence towards Terentia, Tullia, and little Marcus, and to Cicero's son-in-law Piso, who was apparently kicked by the consul, his own relative, when he was putting forward Cicero's case to him.[31] It seems Cicero found this out in a letter from a friend; perhaps Terentia did not want him to increase his worry, and quite possibly she took pride in her own resilience.

A fourth letter, from November 58 BC, shows how much work Terentia was doing in her husband's absence; Cicero states again that 'I know that a large share of this burden rests on your shoulders'.[32] Trying to win support for her husband amongst the great and good in Rome, she advises him on who to thank for their help; he openly acknowledges that he is acting on her advice in his letters to these friends. Terentia was also concerned for Cicero's physical safety and offers to join him, and he assures her of his safety; he asks, though, that she stay in Rome to continue working on his behalf. Cicero requests that Terentia continue to keep him up to date of what is happening with the case: 'all I ask is that you write me the most comprehensive and detailed account'. The letter affirms that Terentia was fully engaged in the struggle to return Cicero safely to Rome, a true partner to her husband. Eventually, the Senate recalled him and he returned, met at Brundisium by his darling little Tullia ('Tulliola') and in Rome by crowds of well-wishers; but after such a series of events, it may have been very difficult for both Terentia and Cicero to adapt to life together again.

The marriage of Terentia and Cicero lasted some years more, in which Terentia arranged two more marriages for Tullia.[33] It continued to have ups and downs, with the couple working together after Cicero's return to politics and plenty of affection shown in the sources. Cicero chose the wrong side when Rome became further divided, siding with Pompey, who was defeated; Caesar pardoned him for his part, but his position was precarious.[34] Cicero may have joined in against the wishes of Terentia and Tullia, as implied in another letter, written as he set out to join Pompey; Claassen notes that 'Cicero sometimes appeared extremely irresponsible in his treatment of his family'.[35] Tullia's marriage to Dolabella, a supporter of Caesar, which was arranged by Terentia and Tullia, may also have caused difficulties – Dolabella had a very poor reputation and the marriage ended in divorce. Tullia died in 45 BC, after giving birth to a son (Figure 22).

Cicero's letters to Terentia shrank in length and became more formal, less affectionate and it could be that their relationship was becoming more perfunctory; Terentia and Cicero had been through a lot and must in some ways have been exhausted.[36] The last surviving letter of Cicero to Terentia, of 47 BC, seems very curt.[37] It simply informs Terentia to prepare their villa at Tusculum for the arrival of himself and guests and ends with a 'farewell' and the date and place of writing – no affectionate words, as had once been normal. Even if written in haste, the tone is different. Then, in late 47 or early 46 BC it seems Cicero initiated a divorce. Plutarch tells us that Cicero brought the trouble in his private life on himself. He states that Cicero:

FIG. 22 Terentia and Cicero receive news of their daughter Tullia's death (c. 1500). Source: National Library of the Netherlands, Netherlands. Public Domain.

> considered that she [Terentia] had neglected him during the war; she had allowed him to set out without sufficient means for his journey; and even when he got back to Italy he did not find her any kinder to him. Though he waited a long time at Brundisium, she did not come there herself; and when his daughter, a young girl, made the long journey, she failed to provide her with a proper escort or sufficient money for her expenses. In fact, she had actually stripped Cicero's house of everything it possessed and had incurred a number of large debts besides. These, certainly, are the most plausible reasons given for the divorce.[38]

But Plutarch also explains that Terentia denied all of these charges and suggests her denial was believable because Cicero soon after married a very rich young woman, Publilia. Terentia apparently thought it was because he fell in love but one of Cicero's freedman claimed it was a marriage made for gain – to solve Cicero's never ending money problems. Mark Antony used this to publicly criticise Cicero for divorcing Terentia. Cicero may have become unhappy with Terentia, but Terentia may equally have been unhappy with Cicero, perhaps because of his constant need for money and the trajectory of his political career, which had brought him and by extension the family into danger.[39] As Treggiari points out, Terentia might have thought herself better off without Cicero, able to manage her own affairs and finally to live in peace.

It is possible that Terentia married again, as a later source has it, to the historian Sallust, who wrote the history of the conspiracy of Catiline. There would have been a twelve-year age gap between them – Terentia being the elder, in her fifties. For this reason, it has been thought unlikely. But Sallust could have been a catch, with his successful military career and intellectual interests, while Terentia, with her knowledge, experience, and wealth could equally have appealed to him. It may be more likely though that Terentia, like Cornelia, remained a once-married woman, an honourable status, a woman who had been a dutiful and loving wife, who had borne and raised her children properly and who had taken part in some of the high intrigue and dangerous political machinations of Rome in the Late Republic

23

MARIAMNE

Helen of Troy is remembered by posterity for her beauty and for causing strife amongst men – hers was the face that launched a thousand ships. But Helen was a figure of ancient Greek myth. Mariamne, the queen of Judaea, was equally known as a beauty and as both a cause and victim of conflict, but unlike Helen she was very real; her story too, though, 'in the course of time ... became a legend', with Boccaccio, Voltaire, and Byron, amongst others, retelling it in much later times.[1]

The tale of Mariamne is known to us primarily from the histories of the ancient Jewish historian Josephus, who was born around AD 37. Josephus, a Jewish aristocrat and leader, fought against Rome but then went over to them, the winning side.[2] As a reward, he was granted Roman citizenship, a pension, and a house in Rome – the emperor Vespasian's old house; he never went back to Judaea. In his leisure at Rome, he wrote two major histories in Greek: the *Jewish Wars* and the *Jewish Antiquities*. The first covers the period of AD 66–70, the unsuccessful Jewish revolt against the Romans, and the second is a history of the Jews going back to creation, which Josephus wrote to show the antiquity of the Jews and to educate the Greco-Roman world about them.[3] The accuracy of his accounts has often been debated and it is clear that he was not simply a disinterested recorder of facts. His own opinions and biases run through his work, which served in part to shore up his own position in Rome.[4] When we read about Mariamne, we should not forget that we are encountering Josephus' Mariamne, presented consciously and deliberately to the reader in the context of the work.

Mariamne was born around 50 BC and lived as a contemporary of the famous Cleopatra VII of Egypt, Mark Antony, and the emperor Augustus. She came from an old royal dynasty, the Hasmoneans, and was the granddaughter of king Hyrcanus II.[5] The Hasmoneans were descended from Mattathias and belonged to a priestly family by which the men were entitled to become the high priests of the Jewish temple in Jerusalem and Jewish leaders.[6] They had been instrumental in winning Judaea its independence from the Seleucid kingdom in the Maccabean revolt of 166–164 BC, and in maintaining it, with Roman help, after that. In the recent past, between 76 and 67 BC, Judaea had been ruled by a Hasmonean queen, Alexandra (Shelamzion/Salome), in her own right.[7] This Alexandra was Mariamne's great grandmother.

We can well imagine that Mariamne was brought up in full knowledge of her family's central place in Judaean history; she may have seen her great grandmother, in particular, as something of a role model and as an example of what was possible for a royal woman in Judaea. Mariamne's mother, another Alexandra, was an equally strong character, always pushing her family forward. This understanding of what royal woman could be and do would also have been bolstered by the activities of Cleopatra in nearby Egypt. Several comments by Josephus suggest that Mariamne was indeed very proud of her status and demanded that others acknowledged it.

As a descendent of Mattathias, then, Mariamne had a rich heritage in terms of her family history; but as a first-century BC Judaean, she also had a rich and diverse cultural heritage. She was probably multilingual, like Cleopatra, and would have spoken and been literate in Aramaic, Hebrew, Greek, and possibly Latin too. Jewish culture was old and had its own heroic and sagacious figures, as Josephus sought to demonstrate in *Jewish Antiquities*. She would have known the stories of ancient Jewish queens and other women, such as Bathsheba, the wife of David and mother of Solomon. Yet in the wake of Alexander the Great, many aspects of Greek culture were transplanted and adopted across the east, including in Judaea.[8] History-writing in the classical style was one aspect of this – Josephus himself writing in Greek even though Jews had begun writing histories in the tenth century BC, long before the classical Greeks or the Romans.[9] Many of the later Hasmoneans bore Greek names, which would have fitted them into the Hellenistic world they inhabited.[10] Gruen has written of the 'enormous' repercussions of this meeting of cultures: 'the encounter of the Jews with the language, literature and learning of the Hellenic world created a cultural revolution'.[11] Mariamne was heir to the Hasmonean line and to both Jewish and Hellenic cultures.

Josephus tells us nothing about Mariamne's birth and childhood; such details were not relevant to his narrative. Rather, she comes into Josephus' histories as a character in the story of Herod, her husband. The two were betrothed in 42 BC though not married until 37 BC, after Herod had been declared king of Judaea in 40 BC and with the Romans had taken Jerusalem by force. Herod had already been married to a woman called Doris, from Jerusalem, with whom he had a son called Antipater, but he divorced her (though their son was to come back into the story later on). Mariamne's Hasmonean pedigree was impeccable, and this was useful to Herod, who was not Judaean but Idumaean and regarded as something of an outsider. Undoubtedly, this was a political marriage – as Josephus notes, it gave Herod a connection to the earlier Hasmonean kings.[12] The pair had probably known each other for some time since Herod's father had served Mariamne's grandfather Hyrcanus.[13]

Mariamne may have had mixed feelings about the marriage. On the one hand, she might have been pleased with the powerful position it put her in and felt that this was her due. Becoming queen must have felt like a natural step, even if it was as Herod's wife. Were she to have children, there would be a good chance that her family would continue to rule and the Hasmonean line would survive, although there was Herod and Doris' son to worry about. The couple did manage to have children: two daughters and three sons, Alexander and Aristobulus, who were educated in Rome, and a third son who died there. On the other hand, she might have disliked Herod, perhaps intensely. In itself, a sexual relationship is no guarantee of personal affection in a marriage; even sharing children need not create an emotional bond between the parents, especially not in a politically motivated union. However, Josephus does suggest, in places, that the couple did, at least sometimes, have a loving relationship. It may be that the relationship started off well but spoiled over time, ending, as we shall see, with implacable hatred from Mariamne and violent anger from Herod.

Several times, Josephus tells us about Herod's great love and affection for Mariamne, but his portrayal of this is of an unhealthy love. Explaining why Herod brought up their children in royal style he wrote that, apart from because their mother was royal and Herod king, 'a more compelling reason was his passionate love of Mariamne, which every day consumed him more fiercely'.[14] In Josephus' view, this passion blinded 'him to the calamities that his beloved was bringing upon him'. Mariamne, he reports 'hated him as passionately as he loved her' and for good reason – he had killed Hyrcanus after welcoming him back to Judaea from Parthia, and after being persuaded to make Mariamne's brother Aristobulus high priest had him killed too, drowned at a party.[15] Josephus intimates that the tall and handsome (and Hasmonean) Aristobulus appeared to be too popular with the people when he had appeared publicly fulfilling his sacred office; thus he presented a serious risk to Herod's rule.[16] Mariamne, Josephus suggests, was to become a major source of trouble for Herod.

After the murder of Aristobulus, Alexandra wrote to Cleopatra asking her to persuade Mark Antony to punish Herod, a move that illustrates how high-status women of the Mediterranean world could maintain relationships with one another and affect politics. In 35 BC, Herod was requested to visit Mark Antony, the Roman who had backed him earlier. Herod went off and was not at all sure he would return to Jerusalem. He left Joseph, his uncle, in charge but secretly requested that if he were killed, Mariamne should immediately be executed as well. Josephus explains 'for that he had a tender affection for this his wife, and was afraid of the injury that should be offered him, if, after his death, she, for her beauty, should be engaged to some other man'.[17] He was even worried that womaniser Antony would fall in love with Mariamne – Josephus paints us a picture of a madly jealous and murderous Herod. Was Herod really obsessed or is this merely Josephus' spin to present Herod as weak and imbalanced?

According to the story, Joseph often talked to Mariamne and Alexandra of Herod's kindness and affection for them, something that must have rankled. One day he let slip Herod's secret plan. Mariamne and Alexandra saw this not as evidence of love but rather as indicative of Herod's poor treatment of them; they felt 'that they could not escape destruction, nor a tyrannical death, even when he [Herod] was dead himself'.[18] The women became even more suspicious and fearful of Herod and worried for their lives.

Alexandra, when she heard a rumour that Herod had been executed by Antony, made her own plan. She wanted Joseph to help them flee to the Romans – partly because the beautiful Mariamne would charm Antony and his followers, who could install them as rulers of the kingdom themselves.[19] Given that a queen had ruled Judaea before, this was not far-fetched – both Alexandra and Mariamne may have been ambitious. The plan was shelved when it was confirmed that Herod was alive, but Herod's sister Salome and their mother Cypros took the opportunity to inform on the Hasmonean women to Herod. Their motivation, according to Josephus, was their ill will to Mariamne. He tells us that 'when they had differences with one another, Mariamne took great freedoms, and reproached the rest for the meanness of their birth'.[20] Mariamne's attitude of superiority to others in the family and her willingness to speak openly, which are plausible characteristics, made her enemies.

Salome intimated that Mariamne and Joseph had become too close in his absence and that Joseph had revealed Herod's plan to her. Herod confronted Mariamne, who strenuously denied it. According to Josephus:

> being overcome with his passion for his wife, he made an apology to her for having seemed to believe what he had heard about her: and returned

> her a great many acknowledgments of her modest behaviour: and professed the extraordinary affection and kindness he had for her. Till at last, as is usual between lovers, they both fell into tears, and embraced one another with a most tender affection.[21]

The two went to bed, apparently, but as Herod professed his love Mariamne, she retorted that leaving orders for Joseph to kill her was a strange way to express his fine feelings. For Herod, this seemed proof that Mariamne and Joseph had indeed been too close – that Joseph would otherwise not have revealed his secret plan. Joseph was put to death. Josephus also tells us how Herod wanted to put Mariamne to death too, but he 'was restrained from doing any rash thing to her, by the love he had for her'.[22] Imagining she had a role in stirring up trouble, he had Alexandra taken into custody. Herod was shocked at Mariamne's words to him and this feeling was to stay with him; he felt both 'vehement affection and jealousy'. If there is any truth to the story, what was Mariamne's motivation in speaking as she did – was she genuinely upset and disturbed by the extreme behaviour of Herod, who at once said he loved her but was also able to order her death? Did she feel compelled and confident to speak out without imagining there could be consequences – or without caring?

In 30 BC, Herod had to visit Octavian, who had defeated Antony and Cleopatra, in Rhodes to make his peace with him. He left Salome and Cypros at Masada but Mariamne and Alexandra at Alexandrium – again with orders to kill them if he was killed.[23] The family – the four women in particular – could not stand to be together. It seems as if political factions had developed around these two pairs of women, and another around Doris and Antipater.[24] Alexandra and Mariamne felt that they had been unfairly imprisoned and were again worried about the order to kill them, should Herod be killed, this time revealed by one Sohemus. Mariamne started to speak up about her situation – Josephus tells us that she now 'openly declared' how 'it was an unsupportable task to live with' Herod any longer, 'without concealing her resentments'.[25]

On his return this time Herod was happy, having made friends with Octavian, and went first to Mariamne with the good news 'preferring her before the rest, on account of his fondness for her, and the intimacy there had been between them' but Mariamne did not stay silent.[26] Rather, she spoke plainly to Herod that she was not at all happy for him, that she was sorry for his success, and that she grieved at it. His response was more confusion:

> he took this so ill, and yet was so unable to bear it, in account of the fondness he had for her, that he could not continue long in one mind; but sometimes was angry at her; and sometimes reconciled himself to her;

> but by always changing one passion for another, he was still in great uncertainty.[27]

Later, he called Mariamne to his bed chamber. She came but refused his advances and again reminded him of his murder of her grandfather and brother. This time he was almost driven to violence. His sister Salome saw an opportunity to instigate her own conspiracy. Sending a cup-bearer with wine to Herod, she had him tell the king that Mariamne had prepared the drink with a love potion and that he was not sure what it was. Herod, suspecting poison, had Mariamne's eunuch tortured for information, but he knew nothing. Mariamne was put on trial and given a death sentence, but Herod put off the execution, still preferring to keep her alive. But 'Salome and her party laboured hard to have the woman put to death. And they prevailed with the king to do so, and advised this out of caution, lest the multitude should be tumultuous'.[28] Mariamne, and later her mother, two scions of the Hasmonean house were dead. Herod killed his and Mariamne's adult sons some years later.

Mariamne's heritage and upbringing may have given her the sense that she could speak freely and openly in her marriage to Herod. However, she may have pushed the limits of what Herod would tolerate. Josephus thought that she treated Herod too haughtily because he loved her so passionately that she thought she could get away with it; he concluded that she did not quite realise that Herod was the ruler and she his subject.[29] Nevertheless, he thought her 'a woman of excellent character' – a contrast to Herod.[30]

The portrait of Mariamne in Josephus *Jewish Wars* and *Antiquities* is not disinterested biography but is part of the author's reflection on Herod and the Herodians. Although recounting many of Herod's successes, Josephus mixes the personal, emotional and political and uses the chaotic and spiralling situation in Herod's family and the king's emotional instability and indecisiveness to paint a picture of him as a weak and unstable man, unable to control himself or the women of 'his' family.[31] Attacking a man via his relationships with women was a common rhetorical strategy.

Is there anything of the real Mariamne salvageable? The characterisation, as far as it goes, rings true – whatever the truth of the events and private words that Josephus recounts. Mariamne comes to us as a proud and perhaps overweening woman, very aware of her status and willing to talk down those she perceived as lesser – a woman whose love for her Hasmonean family and shock at her husband's murder of them never left her, a woman who was troubled by her husband's apparent obsessiveness over her. Mariamne's excessive pride may have been, in part, an understandable response to a feeling of being trapped.

FIG. 23 Mariamne Leaving the Judgement Seat of Herod. Artist: John William Waterhouse. Date: 1887. Wikimedia commons. Photographer: Art Renewal Center.

The story of Mariamne and Herod survived the centuries in Europe as a favourite tragic tale. Mariamne has been the subject of numerous plays, including Elizabeth Cary's *The Tragedy of Mariam*, of 1613 and Amélie Rives *Herod and Mariamne* (1888); operas, poems, and novels such as Voltaire's 1725 *Hérode et Mariamne*; and recently Angela Hunt's *King's Shadow* (2019).[32] In 1887, J. M. Waterhouse, painter-extraordinaire of classical and antique scenes, exhibited a sumptuous painting of Mariamne, on the way to her execution, which went on to tour the world and win a number of prizes (Figure 23).[33] As Simon Goldhill observes of Waterhouse's masterpiece, 'the body language . . . eloquently captures this distorted world of fear, plotting, and danger'. The characters avoid looking directly at one another and 'the breakdown of trust in the court of Herod is vividly embodied'. Mariamne's own story 'is crisscrossed with rumors, false accusations, and the power of corrupt communication in the environment of the eastern court'. It is a fitting illustration of this woman's life and its end.

PART V

THE AGE OF EMPIRE

Out of the chaos of the later years of the Roman Republic, a time when the city's influence nevertheless continued to expand around the Mediterranean, came order in the form of Julius Caesar's nephew Octavian, who would become the emperor Augustus in 27 BC. The last man standing in the bitter and bloody civil conflicts, he defeated Mark Antony and Cleopatra, who had dominated the eastern Mediterranean. They left alive their three children, including a daughter Cleopatra Selene, who grew up in Rome, in the house of the emperor, and who later ruled in Mauretania with her husband Juba, as clients of Rome (Chapter 24).

The dynasty of Augustus, the Julio-Claudians, continued to rule through Tiberius, the son of Augustus' wife Livia, Caligula, Claudius, and Nero, whose reigns and characters are so vividly brought to life by the historian Suetonius. The last Julio-Claudian emperor was Nero, driven to suicide AD 68. After a brief period of instability, the general and former consul Vespasian established the short-lived Flavian dynasty, consisting of himself and his sons Titus and Domitian.

Vespasian ruled from AD 69–79 and died only a few months before the eruption of Vesuvius and the destruction of Pompeii and Herculaneum, in the Bay of Naples, which stunned the Roman world.[1] An eyewitness report of this survives in a letter of Pliny the Younger, whose uncle tried desperately to mount a rescue mission by sea. But the destruction also preserved a snapshot of first-century Roman life for archaeologists – buildings and paintings and even the graffiti written on the walls of the town by its inhabitants. It is here we find the enigmatic Eutychis (Chapter 25). The emperor Titus responded to the tragedy at Pompeii with funds and government agents to co-ordinate relief in the region. Titus' brother Domitian succeeded him, and it is in his reign, or slightly after, that we meet the gladiators Achillia and Amazon (Chapter 26).

In these early centuries AD, the new religion of Christianity was spreading. The reasons for the success of Christianity in antiquity have long puzzled scholars, and a number of factors can be mentioned. One is the general openness of polytheists to religious ideas, another is that monotheistic ideas could already be found; in two ways, then, Christianity was already familiar. Another popular idea has been the importance of a 'personal relationship' between the individual and god – although this could be found in pagan cult too. Possibly more important are the emotional and moral elements, including a focus on love and acceptance within the community of worship of believers, men and women, of different social classes – a different belief in how to live the best life. In a society of vast inequalities, this, and the reward for faith of an eternal life in heaven, may well have appealed to many who had little in the world. There is no simple answer. In the context of the spread of Christianity and the state's responses to it, we find a young woman from North Africa, called Perpetua (Chapter 27).

The light of the empire's golden age of the second century AD sputtered out in the third, an age of crisis which was marked by civil and 'foreign' wars and an epic turnover of short-lived emperors, often military men raised to the purple by their armies.[2] The Sasanian Persians under Ardashir and then the great Sapor, who ruled from AD 239–270/3, undertook to reconquer former Persian territory and make inroads into the Roman Empire, which prompted military responses from the Romans in turn. In AD 243, Gordian III pursued the Persians almost to Ctesiphon, where he was killed and his army defeated; Sapor recorded this victory in an inscription at Naqsh-i Rustam.[3] Philip was made emperor and came to terms, paying a huge sum to the Persians. In AD 252, Sapor destroyed a Roman army of some 60,000 followed by numerous conquests; in AD 260 he defeated an army of 70,000, captured the emperor Valerian and took thirty-seven cities of the eastern empire.

There was a flurry of unrest in the Roman Empire and local leaders took control to restore order when the imperial power was incapable. In this context, Septimius Odainathus, Roman senator and leader of Palmyra, came to the rescue, himself defeating Sapor and pursuing the Persians back to their capital Ctesiphon – saving the eastern part of the Roman Empire.[4] But his death led to the rise of his wife Zenobia, who went to war with Rome; we meet her in Chapter 28.

The Roman Empire survived, transformed, put back together by Aurelian (AD 270–275) and then reformed by Diocletian (AD 284–305), but the increasing popularity of Christianity caused other challenges – including the creation of new values and identities and a clash of world views. Eventually there were Christian emperors – the first being Constantine (AD 306–337), who took the sign of the cross to victory on his soldiers' shields at the battle of the Milvian Bridge and who moved the imperial capital east to Byzantium, now Constantinople. Despite this 'official' change, the Roman world remained a melting pot of beliefs and practices for some time. In the ancient and venerable city of Alexandria, famed for its library and tradition of learning and philosophy, the diversity and challenges can both be seen. The city had a mixed population of Greeks, Jews, Egyptians, along with Romans and others; pagans and Christians could be found there. Through the fourth century, the city became riven by social and religious divisions as Christians and pagans clashed. The philosopher Hypatia, who we meet in Chapter 29, lived through these times – and died in them; her life and death have often been used to represent the waning of Hellenism, the traditions and thought-world that consciously derived from ancient Greece, and the ultimate eclipse of classical life.

The empire was divided in two on the death of Theodosius in AD 395, with his son Honorius in the west and Arcadius in the east. In the fifth century, the western empire fragmented as migrating groups set up their own states within its borders.[5] Rome was sacked in AD 410 by Alaric and his Visigoths. The Vandals and Alans set up a kingdom in what had been Roman North Africa. But the eastern empire ruled from its capital of Constantinople, now referred to as the Byzantine Empire, remained intact and only fell in 1453. In the sixth century, the empire was ruled by Justinian AD 527–565 and his wife Theodora (Chapter 30).[6] An ambitious ruler, Justinian attempted the reconquest of the western empire, defeating the Vandals and having some successes in Italy – not that the Italians all welcomed this. Our attitudes to Justinian's reign, and his and Theodora's personalities and motivations, have been thoroughly influenced by the historian Procopius, who, in addition to writing a mainstream history of Justinian's wars, left us his scathing *Secret History*, which purports to tell the real, behind the scenes story. With the death of Theodora, our journey through the lives of 30 real ancient Mediterranean women comes to an end.

24

CLEOPATRA SELENE

The name Cleopatra has an immense resonance in western culture, conjuring up images of romance, intrigue, actress Elizabeth Taylor, and the clash between ancient Egypt and the rising power of Rome.[1] She is indelibly linked with some of Rome's most powerful men: Julius Caesar, Mark Antony, and Octavian, who would become Rome's first emperor. We might think of a young, exotic, and beautiful queen being rolled out of a carpet in Caesar's presence, or clutching an asp to her breast to take her own life. That Cleopatra is rightly famous, occupying the Egyptian throne at what in hindsight was a pivotal point in Mediterranean history – if she and Antony had defeated Octavian then things might have turned out very differently indeed. A Hellenistic-style monarchy would have continued to rule in the east and, if Antony had consolidated himself in Rome as well, the two states may have been combined: Antony and Cleopatra's empire. The 'what ifs' are intriguing. Less famous but no less interesting in terms of her position and the life she lived is that of Cleopatra's daughter with Antony, Cleopatra Selene (Figure 24).[2]

Cleopatra Selene was one of three children born to Cleopatra and Antony – born into the highest echelons of society in a world of conflict, danger, and opportunity. At the time of her birth in around 40 BC, her mother was the ruler of Egypt, the latest scion of a dynasty descended from Alexander the Great's general Ptolemy. Her father had been Julius Caesar's right-hand man and then became leader of one of the factions vying for power after his assassination in 44 BC. This was just the latest phase of civil war at Rome,

FIG. 24 Coin of Cleopatra Selene and Juba II. Courtesy of Roma Numismatics Ltd., Auction XVIII, 29/09/2019, Lot 516. www.romanumismatics.com/

but the conflict impacted the whole of the Mediterranean – the period 49–30 BC has called by Josiah Osgood an 'age of world war'.[3] After 44 BC, Rome was held by a triumvirate of Antony, Caesar's heir Octavian, and Lepidus. They ushered in a period of terror – killing off enemies in proscriptions – and then defeated Caesar's assassins at the battle of Philippi. Dividing up the empire between them, Antony went east to raise money in the richest and oldest kingdoms and provinces. Then in 42 BC he met Cleopatra, who, as an eastern ruler that had failed to support the triumvirs, had been summoned by him to his court at Tarsus.[4]

Whether or not Antony and Cleopatra ever got married 'officially', there is no doubt that they soon went all in in their relationship, which clearly blended politics and love, to the extent that Octavian could twist the relationship into a propaganda tool to use against Antony and to boost his own position in Rome.[5] One indication of this blending is found in the status that Antony gave his children by Cleopatra (he had four other children by two other wives). In 37 BC, Antony, leaving Rome and sending his pregnant wife Octavia (Octavian's sister) back there, recognised his twin children by Cleopatra and the couple renamed them Cleopatra Selene ('Moon') and Alexander Helios ('Sun'). At this point, he also gifted Cyprus and parts of the east to Cleopatra – without the approval of Rome.

A few years later, when little Cleopatra Selene and Alexander Helios were around six years of age, a great ceremony was held by Antony and Cleopatra in Alexandria – the occasion, described by Plutarch and Cassius Dio, has become known as 'the Donations of Alexandria'.[6] Plutarch describes how two golden thrones were set up on a silver dais, for Cleopatra and Antony, with three more for the children. Antony declared Cleopatra Queen of Kings and his sons Alexander and Ptolemy to be Kings of Kings. He distributed lands to each, and Cyrenaica in North Africa and possibly Crete to little Cleopatra Selene. In reality, the lands were not in his gift, some were already Roman provinces with rulers and others were yet to be conquered; even so, coinage was issued for Cleopatra Selene in both areas.[7] Cleopatra senior was dressed as Isis and Antony may have appeared as Dionysus, giving the occasion a religious veneer that emphasised the almost divine status of the couple and downplayed Antony's Romanness.[8] The children were part of this new world.

Prior to the Donations, Antony apparently also celebrated a kind of triumph in Alexandria, presenting the spoils of his latest campaigns to his queen. This too may have been twisted in its reporting back at Rome, where it caused shock – a triumph was a ritual victory procession held in Rome, not elsewhere. Whether a proper 'triumph' or not, it likely indicates Antony's eastern focus; it and the 'donations' indicate Antony's eastern focus. If we recall that hundreds of senators left Rome, which was under the control of Octavian, and joined Antony in the east, the prospect of an 'eastern empire' of some kind seems less fantastical; and at this stage, Rome's imperial phase under Octavian-Augustus was far from being the inevitable outcome. Little Cleopatra's destiny would surely have been to be married off when old enough, possibly to cement a strategic alliance or to support her brother Alexander – such sibling marriages had been common in the Ptolemaic dynasty.

What did Cleopatra Selene make of these events? Probably she was too young to take in the wider significance of the 'donations' ceremony, but at the same time, being at the centre of such a fabulous, rich, and public 'family' event would likely have been a lasting memory. Perhaps it was a formative moment for the young girl. No doubt Selene was brought up to know that she belonged to an ancient and wealthy dynasty and that she occupied a certain place and status in the world. Whatever promise there seemed in those days, that world came crashing down after Antony and Cleopatra were defeated by Octavian at the Battle of Actium in 31 BC – or rather they fled, abandoning their navy and large land army. In 30 BC, Octavian invaded Egypt itself, taking Alexandria. Antony killed himself, and later, after meeting Octavian and failing to make any favourable settlement with him, so did Cleopatra. Aged only ten, then, Cleopatra Selene lost both her parents and the future that they had sought to secure for her and her two brothers.

It might have been expected that Octavian would do away with Antony and Cleopatra's children; his potential rival Caesarion, the son of Julius Caesar, was killed later on. However, he did quite the opposite. Octavian held a triumph in Rome in 29 BC, in which he paraded a statue of Cleopatra clutching an asp. Cleopatra Selene and Alexander Helios were there too – Cassius Dio wrote that they were 'part of the spectacle and a trophy in the procession'.[9] He notes that Octavian rode behind them. However, a victory monument from Nikopolis ('Victory-town', near Actium) contradicts this; it appears to show the triumph and a young boy and girl of the same age, who can only be Cleopatra and Alexander, riding in a chariot with Octavian, who holds out an olive branch – a symbol of peace.[10] For Octavian – later Augustus – the virtues of clemency, justice, and piety were an important part of his public image and (to whatever extent was practical in the circumstances) his own moral outlook.[11] Treating the children of defeated enemies well was an illustration of this – and numerous foreign children were represented on his Altar of Peace (the Ara Pacis) in Rome; it also provided a pool of potential 'friendly' rulers that he could use later on.[12]

After incorporating the children in his triumph, Octavian delivered them into the care of his sister, Antony's Roman wife, Octavia. Octavia was part of Octavian's own household at Rome and the two siblings were certainly close; she was promoted as an ideal Roman matron – a model of virtue appropriate to Octavian's public morals.[13] She took in Antony's son by his first wife and raised all the children with her own and Antony's two daughters, as well as looking after her three other children from her first marriage.[14] Indeed, the household of Octavian was full of captive royal children that could be brought up as little Romans. Sources such as Plutarch and Cassius Dio describe Octavian in very positive terms as 'a loving and caring surrogate father'.[15] Thus, from an Egyptian princess of Macedonian heritage – a half-Roman one – little Cleopatra Selene was, from the age of around eleven, brought up at the heart of Octavian's emerging imperial Roman Empire.

Cleopatra Selene would have spoken Greek as her first language, but, like her mother, was probably multilingual. In Rome, she would have found other Greek speakers but must have learned or improved her Latin too. As with some other girls of elite households, she would have received some – and perhaps a very good – education. This would have included reading and writing and other skills necessary for running a household. Octavian's daughter Julia, around the same age as Cleopatra Selene, was tutored by a very well-paid grammarian called Marcus Verrius Flaccus; it is possible Selene was his pupil too.[16] Julia was remembered even in much later times for her learning. Octavian's household fairly bustled with cultural and intellectual figures of the day, including the poets Horace and Virgil, and, with the formation of the new Palatine library, it must have been hard to not to be caught up in the atmosphere of learning.

Whilst in Octavia's care, Cleopatra Selene would have come to know a young man called Juba, the son of King Juba I of Numidia in North Africa. Somewhat older than Cleopatra Selene, he had been brought up in Rome since 46 BC, when his father had been defeated by Julius Caesar.[17] The western provinces had been relatively neglected for some time, and in 27 BC Augustus (the name/title Octavian was given) went west to Spain, taking Juba with him. As part of the reorganisation of the region, Augustus decided to set up Juba and Cleopatra Selene as rulers of Mauretania, a large part of western North Africa.

In 25 BC, the two were married in Rome, Cleopatra aged fifteen and Juba twenty-two. As senior royals of North African origin, who had grown up in

Rome as part of the 'first' family, they were perhaps an obvious choice to install as friendly, pro-Roman rulers. The marriage was celebrated by a Greek poet Krinagoras of Mytilene, who wrote:

> Great neighbouring regions of the world, which the Nile, swollen from black Ethiopia, divides, you have created common kings for both through marriage, making one race of Egyptians and Libyans. Let the children of kings in turn hold from their fathers a strong rule over both lands.[18]

The poem, in somewhat exaggerated terms, clearly suggests that Cleopatra and Juba were regarded as the new joint rulers of Mauretania, both being descended from kings. It also implies an expectation for the continuation of their own new royal line. This, of course, as all would have known, would be an arrangement surviving under the gaze and in the interests of Rome.

Cleopatra Selene's modern biographer Duane Roller notes that while she ruled in Mauretania for around twenty years, 'there are few details about her life at the royal court beyond what can be extrapolated from its material culture and the activities of her husband'.[19] But the material culture does reveal an interesting pattern that suggests Cleopatra was powerful and able to act and to rule in her own right and that she placed importance on her own Ptolemaic heritage and the memory of her mother.

One indication of her status and individual power is that she minted coins in her own name, as 'Queen Cleopatra', which appeared alongside Juba's own coinage.[20] As joint rulers, they also issued a joint coinage; Cleopatra with her Greek legend appeared on one side and Juba with his Latin legend on the other. Coinage, as material culture that would carry a message through the population, emphasised the couple's unity and dynastic aspirations and their individual power, status, and cultural affiliations.

Whilst some of Cleopatra Selene's Mauretanian coins provide a portrait, others depict a crocodile between her name and 'queen'. This motif was, according to Jane Draycott, probably chosen specifically for her by her mother, and it was used on coins of 37–34 BC in Cyrenaica and Crete when she was given those territories by her father.[21] After Egypt was annexed, Octavian then issued some of his own crocodile coins with the legend 'AEGVPTO CAPTA' ('Egypt captured') split over and under a crocodile. Clearly, he was announcing his triumph, but perhaps he was also indicating that he had quite literally captured Egypt, in the person of the young Cleopatra. In any event, when queen of Mauretania, Cleopatra Selene quite deliberately chose to use proudly (and perhaps defiantly?) the crocodile as her own sign once again.

Cleopatra Selene is also styled 'daughter of Cleopatra' on some of her coins, while the Egyptian goddess Isis, who her mother identified with, is also represented. A temple to Isis was also built in Cleopatra Selene and Juba's capital Iol-Caesarea, as part of the extensive renovations of the city when it became their royal seat.[22] No doubt this was done to recall her mother and to keep her memory alive and even, in a sense, to keep her present and visible to her daughter. It seems that Cleopatra Selene also commissioned portrait sculptures of herself and her mother for the city, and imported sculptures from Egypt, including some pieces more than a thousand years old, to give Caesarea an Egyptian flavour. Various elements, then, suggest Cleopatra Selene's sense of identity was bound up with her mother and her Ptolemaic Egyptian ancestry.

Cleopatra Selene's words are lost to us, even if we know something of her life. However, there are a number of surviving images of her, from different times in her life and from different kinds of contexts. Mentioned already is the relief sculpture from Nikopolis, showing Cleopatra Selene and her brother Alexander Helios as children riding in a chariot with the victorious Octavian. Egyptologist Giuseppina Capriotti has argued that an earlier image from Egypt, a statue of two children found at Dendera in 1918, shows Cleopatra Selene and Alexander Helios.[23] The two children are shown embracing, standing in the coils of a snake and holding snakes in their free hands. The girl has a crescent moon on her head, while the boy has a sun-disc on his. The girl has a hairstyle typical of Ptolemaic women – the 'melon coiffeur'.

Two other images stand out. One is a life-size marble head of a mature woman found near the royal palace in Caesarea.[24] The head was exceptionally well executed, with attention given to the shape of the mature face, the prominent lower lip, and melon coiffure hairdo held back by a diadem. Whilst sometimes identified as Cleopatra Selene's mother, it has some significant differences in face and hair to her images that suggest it really is Cleopatra Selene. It may date to her later years, in the final decade BC.

The second is the so-called Africa dish, from the Villa della Pisanella, at Boscoreale, which was buried in the eruption of Vesuvius in AD 79. This silver dish, some 22.5 cm in diameter, is dominated by the central figure of a mature woman. Draycott argues that this woman is none other than Cleopatra Selene.[25] She has individual features that suggest the image is not a goddess, nor does she look like any of the imperial family. The hook nose and thick neck suggest a Ptolemy, whilst the elephant scalp cap suggests Africa more broadly rather than Egypt alone. She also holds a snake in one hand and a moon-topped cornucopia in the other, which recall her mother and her own name. The cornucopia itself is decorated with a bust of Helios, the sun god – but also Cleopatra Selene's brother. Other images on the dish associated with Heracles recall the claimed ancestry of both Mark Antony and Cleopatra. Whilst not a direct portrait, and presumably manufactured after the death of Cleopatra Selene, it shows a continued interest in her and her story. It is fascinating to wonder what significance the dish had for its owners in imperial Italy.

We do not know the circumstances of Cleopatra Selene's death, though it is thought she died sometime in the final decade BC. She was probably buried in the mausoleum at Tipasa, east of Caesarea, where Juba would later be buried. The mausoleum is a massive circular stone tumulus over 100 feet high. The cylinder with its sixty engaged ionic columns is set on a square base and topped with a stepped cone. It may date from c. 100–50 BC, although some suggest it was built by Cleopatra Selene and Juba when they took the throne.[26] The design of the tomb harks back to the tomb of Alexander in Alexandria. If it was built by Cleopatra and Juba, it may again betray an emphasis on her Hellenistic heritage. If it was built at the same time as, or shortly after, the Mausoleum of Augustus in Rome, itself influence by Alexander's tomb, then it would also reflect contemporary links with Rome – and the Hellenistic influence on Rome.

Cleopatra Selene died a queen and ruler, but her and Juba's new North African dynasty was not to last, even though they appear to have had four children, boys and girls.[27] One daughter is recorded on an inscription (possibly two) in Athens, but her name is unknown – it might well have been Cleopatra. Another, a Drusilla, recorded by Tacitus as a granddaughter of Cleopatra and Antony, seems more likely to have been a descendant rather than a daughter of Cleopatra Selene. An elder son may be pictured on Augustus' Altar of Peace at Rome, possibly even with Cleopatra Selene. Based on his appearance, he would have been born in around 20 BC but probably died before his father in AD 23/24.

Their son Ptolemy, named for Cleopatra's illustrious royal ancestors, did become king after the death of his father and ruled for over fifteen years. He came to an unhappy end when he was executed by Caligula during a visit to Rome. The unstable Caligula may well have felt inferior to Ptolemy, whose name and pedigree went back over three centuries to Ptolemy and Alexander the Great. And, as Roller explains, Ptolemy 'had been acting with increasing independence, issuing gold coins and assuming triumphal regalia'.[28] Ptolemy was also something of a military success, unlike the Roman emperor. Whilst Ptolemy may have been a part of the extended Julio-Claudian family, that would be no protection from Caligula.

Whilst we have little with which to piece Cleopatra Selene's story together, her turbulent childhood, her adolescence spent at the heart of Augustan Rome, and her love for her mother and her interest in advertising and promoting her Ptolemaic heritage – somewhat more impressive than her husband's – can give us a sense of her character. Although ties with Rome were strong, she perhaps had a sense that she was quite rightfully queen of a large part of North Africa. As Roller justifiably states: 'Cleopatra Selene was the most important royal woman of the early Augustan period'.[29]

25

EUTYCHIS

Eutychis' name appears in a graffito on the entrance to the House of the Vettii at Pompeii, the ancient Roman town destroyed by the eruption of Mount Vesuvius in August AD 79, along with a price; it reads: 'Eutychis, a Greek lass with sweet ways, 2 asses' (Figure 25).[1] On the face of it, it looks like an advert for sex – a calling card for a female prostitute of Greek origin to attract, presumably, male punters.[2] Over 11,000 inscriptions have been found at Pompeii and this one is not by any means the only one referencing sex and the sex industry.[3] The sex trade was a normal part of the hustle and bustle of many ancient cities. More than 100 female prostitutes are known by name from Pompeii; 'prostitutes were', explains Robert Knapp, 'quite literally, everywhere'.[4]

Disarmingly simple, this brief graffito rather invites many questions. Who was Eutychis? How old was she? How did she end up in Pompeii? How did she become a prostitute? Who wrote the graffito mentioning her and why? And what was her relationship, if any, with the House of the Vettii and its occupants? It seems safe to accept that the text does refer to a real person, or the graffito would be pointless, but how much more can we know about Eutychis and her life?

To begin with, was Eutychis this woman's real name? The name is Greek, which could indicate that she was an imported slave rather than a local woman, but it has been argued that Greek names or the use of Greek writing or language do not necessarily indicate ethnically Greek people.[5] Southern Italy

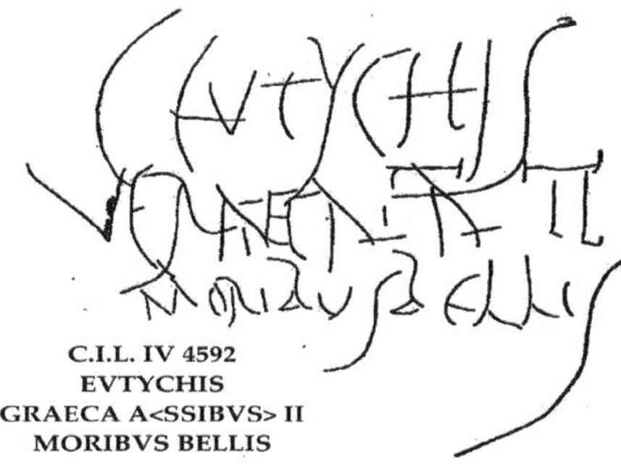

FIG. 25 Graffiti from Pompeii naming Eutychis. Source: Wikimedia Commons

had been Hellenised for centuries and was even known to the Romans as Magna Graecia, or Great Greece, so even if she was Greek she may not have been particularly 'foreign'. It might be that the name still added an element of exoticism supposed to appeal to would-be customers. 'Eutychis' could be translated as 'lucky'; it could have been her birth name, given by parents or perhaps more likely was a working name for sex work, chosen by herself or given by a pimp, or, if she was a slave, it might have been given to her by her owner.

It was not uncommon to give ironic or supposedly humorous names to slaves – a dehumanising aspect of slavery that reflected the stark inequalities of power and status between owner and owned. Orlando Patterson commented that 'the changing of a name is almost universally a symbolic act of stripping a person of his former identity. . . The slave's former name died with his former self'.[6] 'Lucky' might have been a particularly cruel choice of name that brought amusement to some. For Eutychis, it possibly emphasised and compounded her feelings of powerlessness; but at the same time, the name could have helped differentiate between aspects of her daily life and her own 'inner' identity – it could well have helped her maintain a separate sense of herself as herself.

Whether or not she was Greek, it is possible that she was trafficked as a sex object, or at least in part as such. The capture and enslavement of women, and their use for sex, went back a long way and was enshrined as a practice in Homer's epics the *Iliad* and *Odyssey*.[7] In the Hellenistic and Roman Republican periods, piracy and warfare were key sources of slaves in the Mediterranean – Roman expansion filled the slave markets.[8] Many slaves would have been born into slavery, but across the empire, there may still have been tens or even hundreds of thousands of slave sales each year.[9] Slave traders that specialised in prostitutes appear to have been unpopular figures – but that belies the ubiquity of the practice.[10] A slave could be sold multiple times – one comment, albeit about ancient Athens, refers to a woman called Pythionike as 'thrice a slave and thrice a prostitute'; her life may have been a particularly difficult one.[11]

Is it not too much to assume that Eutychis was equally powerless? Possibly – but arguably it is reasonably safe to assume she was. One of the stock characters of early Roman comedy was the *lena* – the madam – who prostituted girls, sometimes their own daughters, because of poverty.[12] If Eutychis was a freeborn woman, it is likely that she would only have turned to prostitution from a lack of other options to support herself, for example, if she was widowed and had no other support network to turn to. Desperation in a society where poverty and destitution were commonplace would have pushed vulnerable people down avenues they may have preferred not to venture down. Women who work as prostitutes do not necessarily do so for long periods but can slip in and out of the business when they need to; Eutychis might similarly have worked as a prostitute only once or only occasionally. If she was a slave, then powerlessness was a given; her master would have had total authority over her, including the power to compel her to perform sex work for his profit.[13]

Powerlessness is also suggested by research on contemporary prostitution. Sex work is very rarely a positive choice for a woman; the pervasive 'happy hooker' myth really is a myth.[14] One very grim example from the Roman world, from Bulla Regia in North Africa serves to remind us of the fear, subordination, and violence that women could be forced to live with. It consists of the skeleton of a woman with a lead slave collar around her neck; its inscription read 'This is a cheating whore! Seize her because she escaped from Bulla Regia'.[15] There is no sugar-coating the facts this evidence represents. The collar itself probably dates to the fifth century, the Christian period, and suggests that the spread of that religion did little to change some of the most exploitative aspects of Mediterranean life and society.[16] A complete emotional contrast is found in a gold bracelet found outside of Pompeii, which bears the message 'From the master to his slave girl' – but this is the 'master' speaking, not the 'slave girl'.[17]

The price of 2 *asses* on the Eutychis graffito is low, the cost of a loaf of bread, and might be indicative of Eutychis' age or attractiveness, or her desperation – it could have been set by herself or her pimp or owner. It is possible that Eutychis was primarily a domestic slave of some kind but that her owner rented her out when she was not busy with other things to bring in some extra income. Potentially she could even have been being punished for something. In Apuleius' novel *The Golden Ass*, we read about a young woman called Charite, who had been kidnapped by bandits. Caught trying to escape, one of the bandits suggests selling her to a brothel or pimps in a nearby town – 'seeing her servicing men in a whorehouse will be sweet revenge for you', he says to the men.[18] Whilst some prostitutes worked in brothels and some from inns or taverns, others, perhaps the most vulnerable, worked outside in the open streets – Sarah Pomeroy points out that our word 'fornicate' comes from the

Latin word for 'arch'.[19] The low price might indicate that Eutychis was one of the latter.

Some slave prostitutes in antiquity managed to save money and buy their freedom and some even worked their way up to managing brothels themselves. An inscription from Italy shows this, with Vibia Calybe managing the brothel of another woman, Vibia Chreste.[20] The inscription is unique in openly showing off a direct link with the sex-trade, but though she is called a 'madam', its emphasis is on how Vibia Calybe 'earned her own money without cheating others'.[21] There was, at least in elite male literature, an idea that female prostitutes were scheming, greedy, wily, and dishonest – Ovid wrote that 'ten mouths with as many tongues wouldn't be enough for me to describe the scandalous tricks of prostitutes'.[22] The reputation did not stop men using them. It is not clear whether Vibia Calybe's case was rare or normal, but it is worth pointing out that it also demonstrates how women aided and abetted the sex-industry and the exploitation of other, presumably younger and more vulnerable women. It is possible that even if Eutychis started out as a slave, she too could perhaps have bought her freedom eventually; however, freedom in poverty could exacerbate vulnerability.

Returning to the city of Pompeii, some scholars have argued that its urban space can be divided into zones – areas where morally questionable or 'deviant' behaviour such as sex work went on and areas that were respectable.[23] These zones, however, might not reflect Roman ideas and could just have been better locations for the sex trade. Although scholars argue about how to define a brothel, and some argue that there was only one 'real' purpose-built brothel in Pompeii, the Lupanar[24], Pompeii seems to have had at least thirty-five built locations where sex was for sale; sex could be sold outside of brothels in baths, bars and taverns, public outdoor spaces, as well as the punter's home.[25] It seems that sex for a price was readily available throughout the city. With this in mind, what might the relationship be between Eutychis and the House of the Vettii?

The House of the Vettii, in the north-western part of Pompeii, close to the Vesuvian gate (Region 6, Block 15), was one of the largest houses in Pompeii.[26] It was an atrium-style house, in which the visitor would, from the porch, be able to see through the front door, through the atrium with its square pool, to the colonnaded garden. The garden had fountains and bronze and marble sculptures, and the house was decorated with many now famous paintings of mythological scenes.[27] One painting in particular has caught the modern gaze – this is a painting of the god Priapus, weighing his giant phallus on a pair of scales against a bag of money.[28] Two money chests were positioned in plain sight just through the front door, on opposite walls to the left and right. Two bronze seals found near one of the chests are generally agreed to give the names of the owners of the house, Aulus Vettius Restituti and Aulus Vettius Conviva, often presumed to be brothers and thought to be wealthy freedman.[29] Conviva seems to have been an *Augustalis*, a fairly prestigious priesthood usually held by ex-slaves, with office-holders being chosen by the town council.

Given the presence of the Eutychis graffito at the front door, is the simplest explanation to accept that Eutychis was a prostitute (full- or part-time) working from the House of the Vettii? Does the Priapus connote a link with sex that would support this? Priapus can refer to fertility or plenty as much as sex; but although often taken as a comic figure, he can also be associated with sex and male sexual aggression and violence.[30] Priapus was a guardian who would threaten to punish thieves by raping them.[31] The meaning of the Priapus painting in the House of the Vettii may be mainly protective – but sexual violence is there too.

A little room (room *x*) in the house has caused some discussion concerning its relationship with sex. This room, tucked away behind the kitchen and with no other access but through it, was decorated with three sexually explicit and non-mythological paintings. Thomas McGinn has noted that this kind of decoration is usually found in slave quarters, separate from the owner's and more public areas.[32] When such areas had separate access, they may have functioned as brothels or sex cubicles, he suggests, but when they did not this function seems unlikely. Unless we believe in the upper-class Roman notion of vulgar freedmen, like Petronius' Trimalchio in the *Satyricon*, it seems unlikely that the Vettii would want punters walking through the house to visit the little room behind the kitchen, so this was not likely to have been a place of business for Eutychis.[33]

John Clarke has suggested that this room was reserved for the cook and that it was a kind of 'gift' to the cook, with the decoration 'reminding him of the pleasures of the lupanar', or brothel.[34] He argues that the Vettii valued their cook highly, taking as a parallel the esteem that the coarse and greedy freedman Trimalchio had for his chef – the genius behind his extraordinary and excessive dinner-party cuisine. McGinn, on the other hand, suggests that rooms like room *x* were private sex clubs; the decoration was intended to create a brothel-like atmosphere for its users to enjoy.

It seems doubtful that sex was being sold from room *x* of the House of the Vettii, but the Vettii may have been having sex with slaves or prostitutes there, distanced from the main public and private parts of the house. Perhaps Eutychis was one of the domestic slaves used in sex parties, and perhaps she also worked as a prostitute outside of the house, either on her own terms or pimped by the Vettii.

But, what if we are completely wrong in our speculations, plausible as they are? McGinn has pointed out that the graffiti from Pompeii that appear to name prostitutes might not do so at all – or at least not necessarily in all cases.[35] It is quite possible that some of the graffiti are slurs of one kind or another – much like subway or public toilet graffiti in western cities. Apart from being presented publicly as a prostitute, another aspect of the insult might be the low prices advertised – the woman being named is not just a prostitute but a cheap prostitute, available to the lowest sort of man for money. If this is right, some of the names could refer to 'respectable' women and might have been written by jilted lovers or favourites, or just spiteful people. Creating a list of prostitutes from the graffiti, as McGinn notes, might simply be reproducing the casual misogyny of some Pompeiian males (or jealousy of females?). Eutychis, then, might not have been a prostitute at all, in any sense; she may have been a house slave in the House of the Vettii – or she could even have been part of the family; or perhaps she had nothing to do with the house.

The Eutychis graffiti, simple and obvious as it appears, is not so easy to interpret, and thus it is not easy to find Eutychis, the real woman behind it. But highlighting one graffito in this way can allow us to ask questions and generate possible answers and possible stories; this is one way towards recovering the real lives of past people. Eutychis' life could have been so many things, and her own feelings about it could have varied greatly depending on her own character and expectations. But in outlining the options, we should be careful not to try to 'rescue' our notional Eutychis or sanitise her story, making it more hopeful than it probably was. Being a prostitute in the Roman world in many cases, and certainly for the most vulnerable and desperate, would have meant a truly horrendous existence, compounded by the associated shameful stigma of the work and a lack of hope that things would get better.

26

ACHILLIA AND AMAZON

It is a warm dark night in the great city of Rome. You are squeezed with your friends into the terraces of one of the most impressive buildings of the Roman empire, the Colosseum, lit by the flickering light of hundreds of torches, part of a crowd of thousands of city-dwellers eager and ready to be entertained. Everyone knows the emperor Domitian (ruled AD 81–96) always puts on a good show, but there is to be nothing ordinary about tonight's bloody spectacle, for the emperor has laid on not only a performance of gladiators but this time female gladiators.[1] As the women troop out, sword-arms clad in armour, shields at the ready, and bare-chested, a thrill runs through the massed ranks of the shouting crowd. Tonight would be a night to remember.

Gladiators throughout the Roman world, west and east, captured the ancient imagination, with some gladiators becoming popular celebrities, winning fame and fortune; there were even 'fan clubs' dedicated to favourite fighters.[2] Graffiti from Pompeii shows that fans paid close attention to the combatants, the fights, the statistics, and to details such as handedness.[3] Children had gladiator toys to play with. In his *Satyricon*, Petronius describes the eager anticipation of a display put on by one Titus – the character Echion remarks enthusiastically: 'we're due to have a marvellous show three days from now . . . it won't be wishy-washy; there'll be something worth watching . . . it'll be a butcher's shop for the whole amphitheatre to see . . .. He's already lined up several freaks, and a woman who fights from a chariot. . .'.[4] Whilst some were interested in the skill, others were perhaps more interested in the violence and the kill. A study of skulls from a mass grave of gladiators discovered in 1993 in Ephesus, in Asia Minor, showed numerous instances of cranial trauma – injuries that healed and injuries that occurred around the time of death – inflicted by swords, shields, tridents, javelins, and the hammer traditionally used to dispatch losers.[5]

Gladiators have equally captured the modern imagination, female gladiators the most – it was major news when a body from Roman times was discovered in London and eventually suggested by archaeologists to be the remains of a female gladiator, although this identification is not at all certain.[6] One reason for the fascination is that the idea of a female gladiator seems to many essentially transgressive – socially sanctioned violence has most often belonged to the masculine domain. This is much like the controversy over and ambivalent reception of women's boxing today, which, despite having a long but hidden history, has only fairly recently (and not unanimously) become 'normalised'.[7] Women's boxing has been around since the eighteenth century, and female gladiators were active in Roman society for a long time, perhaps two centuries or more; repeated legislation to ban them is found from Augustus to Septimius Severus. Another reason for the fascination with female gladiators is that the evidence for them is so limited; they are mentioned in only a few fragments of ancient literature and the archaeological evidence for them is limited.[8]

It is first important to remember that whilst gladiatorial combats were enjoyed throughout the empire by enthusiastic spectators, and the role appealed to some members of the Roman-era elite, including the emperor Commodus, being a gladiator was not considered an 'honourable' profession for men, let alone for women. Public performance and the selling of oneself were inherently disgraceful in Roman elite morality. The Roman orator Calpurnius Flaccus declared that 'no one of the people is lower than a gladiator'.[9] Being a gladiator carried the same social and legal stigma as other 'disgraceful professions' like acting and prostitution, rendering the person *infamis*, without moral standing and certain legal and political rights.[10] This ambivalence was well described by the Christian writer Tertullian:

> Take even those who give and who administer the spectacles; look at their attitude to the charioteers, players, athletes, gladiators, most loving of men, to whom men surrender their souls and women their bodies as well, for whose sake they commit the sins they blame; on one and the same account they glorify them and they degrade and diminish them; yes, further, they openly condemn them to disgrace and civil degradation.[11]

Whilst there could be benefits for successful gladiators – some gaining wealth, and/or living long enough to retire comfortably, and some joined up voluntarily, signing away many of their personal rights, many gladiators were forced into the role. This could happen because they had been found guilty of some crime or owed money, had been captured in battle, or were a slave sold into a school or show. Spartacus, who led a slave revolt in the late 70s BC, had deserted from the Roman army, been caught, and sold as a slave to a gladiator school in Capua owned by one Cornelius Lentulus Vatia.[12] Others were forced into the role through having no other choice of how to make a living. And of course, whatever skills training imparted, many would have suffered injuries and would have died early.

Presumably based on actual cases, a law of AD 19 stated explicitly that the male and female descendants and relatives of senators or those of the equestrian order should neither be hired out by others for the arena or hired themselves, even if they offered themselves for service, whilst freeborn men under twenty-five and women under twenty should also not be engaged to perform.[13] The reasons given included making a mockery of the social order to which they belonged. In AD 200, a show took place involving women, which resulted in highborn women in the audience being ridiculed in some way; as a result, women were banned from the arena by the emperor Septimius Severus.[14] It may be that strictures against female gladiators were aimed primarily at elite women's behaviour rather than lower class women, though the lack of a specific term for female gladiators could possibly be taken as indicating that they were out of the norm.[15] But just how frequently women appeared in the arena as gladiators during imperial times is a matter of debate – given the relative invisibility in the sources it could have been commonplace and so not worth highlighting or alternatively only mentioned infrequently because it was rare.[16]

One Roman author, the satirist Juvenal writing in the first half of the second century AD, composed a vivid passage referencing female gladiators in his notoriously misogynistic sixth satire on women; its intent is to entertain and perhaps to moralise – or to entertain through the moralising rant of a stock conservative Roman.[17] He wrote:

> Why need I tell of the purple wraps and the wrestling-oils used by women? Who has not seen one of them smiting a stump, piercing it through and through with a foil, lunging at it with a shield, and going through all the proper motions? – a matron truly qualified to blow a trumpet at the Floralia! Unless, indeed, she is nursing some further ambition in her bosom, and is practising for the real arena. What modesty can you expect in a woman who wears a helmet, abjures her own sex, and delights in feats of strength? Yet she would not choose to be a man, knowing the superior joys of womanhood. What a fine thing for a husband, at an auction of his wife's effects, to see her belt and armlets and plumes put up for sale, with a gaiter that half covers half the left leg;

> or if she fights another sort of battle, how charmed you will be to see your young wife disposing of her greaves. Yet these are the women who find the thinnest of robes too hot for them; whose delicate flesh is chafed by the finest of silk tissue. See how she pants as she goes through her prescribed exercises; how she bends under the weight of her helmet; how big and coarse are the bandages which enclose her haunches; and then laugh when she lays down her arms and shows herself to be a woman! Tell us, granddaughters of Lepidus, or of the blind Metellus, or of Fabius Gurges, what gladiator's wife ever assumed accoutrements like these? When did the wife of Asylus ever gasp against a stump?[18]

In this passage, 'Juvenal-as-satirist' – for his poetic persona need not be representative of his own views – describes the shocking behaviour of some upper-class young women of the period, who dared to train and fight in public like or as gladiators. Their behaviour was shocking because it went against traditional gender expectations – women behaving like men – and was doubly outrageous because these were upper-class women, presented in the poem as the granddaughters of old noble families. The last point is emphasised by contrasting the shameful behaviour of these young noblewomen with the more appropriate behaviour of the lower-class wife of the famous gladiator Asylus.

But for all the opprobrium heaped on these women by Juvenal, and perhaps by many others in antiquity (even those who may anyway have watched enjoyed such spectacles), we can read the poem as revealing of women who presumably did rejoice in their physical strength and skill, who took going through 'the proper motions' seriously, who trained hard and acquired the right kit for their activities. Juvenal and other men may have disapproved and mocked, but that says little about the inner world of those women themselves. At the same time as revelling in these 'masculine' pursuits, Juvenal comments that such women also displayed excessively delicate and 'feminine' characteristics. The contrast has a poetic and rhetorical effect but need not be false in principle, given that any individual's personal identity can be complex. Whilst the traditional public culture of Roman antiquity, masculine as it was, may have remained the dominant ideology, expressed and reinforced in a variety of ways over centuries, this masks such 'alternative' identities but should not erase them.

Achillia and Amazon were two female gladiators whose existence we know unambiguously from a famous marble relief of the first/second century AD from Halicarnassus, an old city on the west coast of Asia Minor (Figure 26). It is unlikely that these were their real names; gladiators, just like modern-day wrestlers, often adopted stage names, whether anonymous everyday names, names like Felix, (happy/lucky) or Asiaticus (the Asian), ironic names like Florus (Blossom), or names drawn from history and myth.[19] In the eastern

FIG. 26 Achillia and Amazon. Female gladiators on a marble relief from Turkey. © The Trustees of the British Museum

empire, gladiator named as Dareios and Cyrus recalled powerful Persian kings.[20] Achillia brings instantly to mind the Greek hero Achilles, whilst Amazon of course suggests the mytho-historical warrior women of the north – in myth Achilles had fought with and killed the Amazon Penthesileia during the Trojan War, as the audience would have known. It is quite possible that the women were involved in a dramatic and violent recreation of this famous combat.

The relief shows the two women in poses of action, facing off against each other. Each is armed with a sword and has the sword-arm heavily armoured; the figure on the right appears left-handed, as she holds her shield in her right hand and sword in the left. Bare-chested, like most male gladiators, and clothed in loincloths, they carry rectangular body-sized shields, wear greaves, and their helmets are shown in the lower register. Achillia and Amazon were *scutarii*, shield-carriers, and seem closest to *provocators*, who were armed with short swords.[21] The relief explains that they were granted *missio*, which means that they were released from the combat to fight again another day – either because they had fought to a draw or because the loser had fought well enough to be reprieved.[22] Combats where fighters were well-matched and could show off their skills were appreciated, and participants could survive, although some 'fights' put on were little more than glorified executions.[23]

The relief begs questions. It was not a typical funerary monument set up by retired gladiators, in which they might record their earlier popularity or achievements, or dedicated by comrades, friends or family.[24] So the logical conclusion is that it commemorated the occasion it records and the two combatants involved. Dunkle suggests that it could have been dedicated by the sponsor of these particular games as a public reminder of a memorable show, although such reminders usually took the form of public paintings or household mosaics.[25] Another possibility is that the relief was set up in a gladiatorial training school, to inspire other fighters.

Or could it be that Achillia and Amazon together paid for the relief to be made and set up to commemorate their own 'epic' combat? If they belonged to the same school in Halicarnassus, then they probably knew each other and were comrades, rivals, and perhaps friends. Whilst being a gladiator was certainly dangerous and violent, comradeship and friendship from the barracks may have been a valued benefit for otherwise vulnerable people thrown together in such circumstances.[26] An inscription suggesting this was set up to a young gladiator in Rome by his troupe: 'To well-deserving Macedo, novice Thracian gladiator, of Alexandrian extraction,' it reads, 'the whole troupe of Thracian gladiators raised this monument. He lived 20 years, 8 months, 12 days.'[27] The Halicarnassus relief raises possibilities that go beyond just demonstrating the existence of these two women.

That the women are depicted bare-chested has suggested to some there may have been an erotic element to the spectacle of female gladiators. This may be so. Certainly, evidence suggests that male gladiators were, or could be, or wanted to be, objects of female lust. A graffito from Pompeii, for example, records: 'Celadus the Thracian gladiator. Girls think he's magnificent.'[28] But Dunkle proposes that it indicates equality with male gladiators – and that for men, fighting bare-chested was equated with courage.[29] Nudity can and could have multiple meanings as understood by the nude person and by those looking on. Whilst public performance and nudity could be taken as a sign of the 'availability' of the performer, already part of a disgraceful profession, nudity could also, especially in the Greek east, be associated with the heroic and the athletic. Spartan girls had, albeit unusually, trained in the nude.

Juvenal wrote that women who trained for the arena went through 'the proper motions', and, whilst his remark may be comic in intent, we can credit Achillia and Amazon with this positive motivation to play their roles with due seriousness and attention to the traditions and rules. They may have taken pride in this, whether or not any spectators perceived their partial nudity in other ways. Whilst their sponsor may have considered the erotic effect of their performance, Achillia and Amazon may have had other understandings of what they were doing.

Without any more evidence, we cannot say where Achillia and Amazon were from, and whether they were 'respectable' women fighting voluntarily or women who had been somehow forced into the arena. If the former, they would probably have suffered social disapproval from some quarters, and by signing away their rights would have put themselves at risk in a number of ways, but they would have done so knowingly. If the latter, they joined many others coerced into a dangerous and disgraced profession, with only a slim chance of long-term survival and a happy ending. Though in a way even more on the periphery of 'respectable' society than male gladiators, female gladiators like Achillia and Amazon nevertheless had the possibility of obtaining a certain kind of glory and also within their schools had an opportunity for pride and comradeship, neither of which should be dismissed as unimportant in life, especially in the world of the most vulnerable in society.

27

PERPETUA

In AD 203, a young mother was killed by animals in the amphitheatre of Carthage in North Africa on the orders of the local Roman authorities.[1] She died alongside other members of her small religious group, men and women, apparently confident in the knowledge that she was about to enter heaven. This woman was called Vibia Perpetua and she was a Christian; she left us part of her story in a text called *The Passions of Perpetua and Felicity* (Figure 27). The text gives us a fascinating insight into the mind of a young Roman woman caught up in the power of her beliefs. It also reveals much about the workings of Roman society, especially those times in which people came up against the system. Here we will explore who Perpetua was and how she ended up dying in this terrible way.

In its first centuries, Christianity, whilst attracting increasing numbers of followers, provoked confusion and hostility among others. The emperor Nero singled out Christians to blame for Great Fire of Rome in AD 64.[2] Enough was said about their habits, which were supposed to include cannibalism and sexual immorality, to make them suspicious and an easy target.[3] In AD 110, Pliny the Younger, governor of Bithynia, wrote to the emperor Trajan about how he should deal with Christians of 'every rank, age and sex' in his province, who were present in both town and country.[4] Trajan responded that Christians should not be hunted out and should be forgiven if they repented but punished if they did not. Persecution, however, became part of early Christian identity as did the older Jewish notion of martyrdom, dying for

FIG. 27 Perpetua. Mosaic from Basilica di San Vitale, Ravenna, Italy. Source: Contributor / Alamy Stock Photo.

one's beliefs. As Robin Lane Fox has argued 'the most excellent Christians in the early Church were neither the virgins or the visionaries. They were the Christians whom pagans put to death'.[5]

Martyrdom was an important element of early Christianity, in which men and women died for their beliefs and for their identity.[6] It is not the case that the Roman authorities were constantly seeking to root out Christians or destroy Christianity wholesale, but there were areas in which the two sets of beliefs, expectations, and practices collided – with fatal consequences if neither side would compromise or back down. For some early Christians, a culture of martyrdom became valid and even attractive. Non-Christians, on the other hand, were astonished and repulsed by voluntary martyrdom, where an individual could have avoided death through some simple action; they saw it as a form of suicide. But for Christians, the stories of the martyrs became a core part of their culture and lore; they inspired faith and guided behaviour. Glen Bowersock explains that 'the personal sufferings of martyrs and saints created a wholly new literature that was as exciting to read as it was edifying'.[7] This new and growing body of literature combined fact and fiction and acquired authority from its attention to detail. Cults of martyrs grew up and their relics were collected and venerated.

To some contemporaries, it appeared that Christians had a thirst for death – one story, from the reign of Commodus, tells of a group of Christians in the province of Asia who offered themselves up to a local governor to be executed; no one had sought them out or accused them of anything, but they nevertheless wished to be killed for their beliefs.[8] The Christian writer Tertullian, from Carthage in Roman North Africa, used this story to threaten the governor – what if 'thousands and thousands of men and women of every age and rank' give themselves up for execution – how could the city of Carthage possibly survive?[9] Tertullian may have exaggerated his numbers, but by AD 256 most of the towns in the two provinces of North Africa must have had a bishop, since one source records that 130 of them attended an important church meeting. Christianity had taken root early on in Carthage and North Africa.

Tertullian's speech dates to the early third century AD and takes us to a prosperous and Romanised North Africa. Here, in February or March AD 203, Perpetua, along with a number of other Christian women and men, were publicly executed in the amphitheatre at games being held to celebrate the birthday of the emperor's son Geta. They were to be killed by wild animals for the enjoyment – and edification – of the crowd.[10] We are fortunate to have the Latin text called *The Passions of Perpetua and Felicity*, which tells the story of Perpetua's arrest, incarceration, and martyrdom. The anonymous 'editor' of the text, whose own notes preface it, tells us that part of it is her own account 'as she left it, written in her own hand and in accordance with her own understanding'.[11] This then may offer us a first-hand account of the experiences and feelings of a young North African woman arrested and sentenced to death for her religious beliefs.

It is not clear where in North Africa Perpetua came from or lived; her own text does not tell us. One tradition from outside of *The Passions*, from a version in Greek and from a later text called the *Acta Perpetuae et Felicitatis*, is that she and her group may have come from the small town of Thuburbo Minus.[12] This city was around thirty miles southwest of Carthage and was the provincial capital and main metropolis. The town was founded around AD 14, on the Bagrada River, as a settlement for veterans of the Roman army: this was one means of Romanising a province and paying off demobilised troops. It became wealthy from agriculture, providing grain for the city of Rome. It was well appointed too, with an aqueduct bringing in water and with its own amphitheatre. However, Thomas Heffernan has argued that since there is no mention of Perpetua coming from the city in the earliest texts, and that although Perpetua and her group may indeed have been arrested in Thuburbo Minus, it is more likely that they came from Carthage.[13] At least the milieu is reasonably clear, even if the details are not.

Roman Carthage by Perpetua's time was a multilingual mix of indigenous North African, Punic, and Greek and Roman cultures.[14] It was a wealthy port city with a forum, a large circus, and baths almost as big as those in Rome itself; the amphitheatre too was almost as big as Rome's Colosseum.[15] Christianity may have come to Carthage from Rome, from Alexandria, or from the east, or may have grown up amongst some members of the Jewish community in the city – or perhaps, as Barbara Gold suggests, arrived many times in different ways.[16] In this way, it might have attracted different kinds of people, forming perhaps several groups not all necessarily with exactly the same outlook or practices or demographic make-up; there were, after all, many kinds of 'Christianity' in early Roman Christianity.[17] Adam Becker suggests that 'Perpetua and her comrades were a sub-group within a sub-group, that they were Montanists who were drawn to prophesy and martyrdom'.[18] There were no churches yet, no Christian architecture, so for Perpetua and her fellow Christians communal worship and meetings took place in private homes – house churches or *domus ecclesiae*.[19]

The editor of *The Passions*, whose comments preface Perpetua's text, give us a sprinkle of biographical information. Perpetua was 'a woman well born, liberally educated, and honorably married, who had a father, mother, and two brothers .... She had an infant son still at the breast and was about 22 years of age'. If we believe this, then we can surmise that Perpetua belonged to the wealthier part of society, though not its highest echelons. She would have had a degree of education befitting a girl of her status, including reading, writing, and the skills of household management.[20] Of her family, she and her brother were catechumens, who would have been receiving instruction in Christianity prior to baptism; they had a teacher called Saturus, who also gave himself up to the authorities. The father was not a Christian, but the mother and others may have been. The emphasis on family might be there because many women of Perpetua's age would not have had a living father – and to add further weight to her story.[21]

The editor gives no more information about the husband and Perpetua does not mention him in her account. Roman girls might marry from age twelve, but Perpetua might have married considerably later, perhaps at eighteen to twenty.[22] We can only speculate as to why this was. At no point do the husband's family ever claim custody of Perpetua's son. Kate Cooper has suggested that the infant might have been born out of wedlock or with a partner who was unsuitable or who left her for some reason, possibly (but by no means definitely) her religious views, which could have developed in a way he disapproved of.[23] There might well have been no husband and that certainly would not have been 'respectable'.

The story in *The Passions* begins with Perpetua and other catechumens in her group having just been arrested, and it then moves through a series of episodes. There is the initial imprisonment, then their transfer to a military prison, the first of Perpetua's visions, which are discussed below, their public trial in the forum, and another vision. The group are then transferred to a second military prison where they were put in the stocks, and Perpetua has a third vision. Then, on the day before the executions, she has a fourth vision. After Perpetua's diary the visions of Saturus are also given. The editor then tells the story of another young woman called Felicity and described the day before the execution and the grim contest itself.

One important aspect of Perpetua's account is her relationship with her father. The whole story is coloured by his entreaties to her and her refusal to obey him. Her first statement is that 'while we were still with the prosecutors, my father, because of his love for me, wanted to change my mind and shake my resolve'. She argued that as a Christian she could only be called a Christian. Her father 'angered by this name threw himself at me, in order to gouge out my eyes'. He left, taking with him 'the arguments of the devil' – arguments intended to get her to change her mind. By attempting to dissuade her from her public declaration of Christianity and the path that would take her down, the father was tempting her from what she understood as the right thing to do.

In Roman families like Perpetua's, the father was the ultimate authority (the *paterfamilias*) and would have expected to be respected and obeyed. However, Perpetua was adamant in refusing her father's demands and pleas not once but several times, when she was first imprisoned, before her hearing, and again at it. His depth of despair at her fate and attempts to persuade her to change her course are graphic and moving. He pleaded with her to have pity on him, to think about her brothers, her mother, her mother's sister, and her own son 'who will not be able to live without you'. He accuses her of behaving out of pride and reminds Perpetua that her behaviour would have repercussions for all of them – 'if you are punished, none of us will be able to speak freely again'. He begged at her feet and addressed her as lady rather than daughter. She again refused him, and he departed in 'great sadness'.

Then at the public hearing we see a throng of people and Perpetua's father with her baby son: 'offer the sacrifice. Have pity on your baby,' he said, dragging her from the step. Even the official in charge of the case, the procurator, Hilarianus, says to Perpetua: 'Spare the gray hair of your father, spare your infant son, offer the sacrifice for the health of the emperors'. To which she replied, 'I will not'. Then he asked: 'Are you a Christian?' – 'I am a Christian', she replied. Hilarianus condemned the Christians to the beasts. Her father tried again, and this time the procurator, running out of patience, had him thrown to the ground and beaten. Perpetua had been given the chance to go free if only she would burn incense to the health of the emperors and deny her Christianity.

Perpetua was not insensitive to her father's suffering or to the potential trouble she would be causing her family were she to be found guilty and executed. But however much she loved him, she could not obey; it was a matter of conscience. Perpetua is thought to have been a Montanist Christian, like Tertullian, who rejected the biological family in favour of the religious one that they were a part of. Her inner struggle between blood and spirit comes out in the narrative, for example, when she remarks that after their first argument after her arrest she was 'freed' from her father and 'refreshed' by his absence over the next few days. She may have chosen her fate, but that does not mean it was easy for her to endure.

Imprisonment itself was terrifying for her. After the first stage of custody, possibly a kind of house arrest somewhere where her father could visit her, the little group were moved to a military prison, where they would be held until the games.[24] Perpetua wrote, 'I was terrified because I had never before known such darkness. Oh cruel day! The crowding of the mob made the heat stifling; and there was the extortion of the soldiers'. Her arrest, imprisonment, trial, and death all seem to have been public spectacle, which must have added greatly to the strain of the situation. Perhaps there was also a performative element of the road to martyrdom that she drew strength from.

Perpetua's little baby boy was with her in prison: 'I was consumed with worry for my infant in that dungeon' she explains. Two deacons from Perpetua's church, Tertius and Pomponius, were able to arrange that the prisoners be moved, albeit temporarily, to a better part of the prison. After being moved, Perpetua was able to nurse her son who was 'weak from hunger'. It might have been that, in her distress in prison, feeding her baby became difficult. At this point, Perpetua gave up her baby to her mother and brother to look after, but being separated was also difficult: 'I endured such worry for many days, and I arranged for my baby to stay in prison with me. Immediately I grew stronger, and I was relieved of the anxiety and worry I had for my baby.' She explains that 'suddenly the prison became my palace, so that I wanted to be there rather than anywhere else'. Perhaps she had found a new strength, though it is difficult to see anything positive in the situation for her son.

After the trial, though, when the prisoners 'returned cheerfully' to prison, Perpetua's father would not return her son to her this time (it is unclear how the son ended up with the father) – but Perpetua found a further message in this: 'as God willed, the baby no longer desired my breasts, nor did they ache and become inflamed, so that I might not be tormented by worry for my child or by the pain in my breasts'. Any maternal feelings that she had had would, conveniently, no longer distract her from her own journey of faith towards the martyrdom that was in sight. Any guilt she felt was gone. Perhaps Perpetua's milk would not come because of the stress she was under or her diet. If so, she may well have interpreted this according to her own religious narrative. Or perhaps it is a literary device to deflect criticism from Perpetua for abandoning her baby.

Key to *The Passions* are the four visions of Perpetua, mentioned above. These mark out the fate of the prisoners and Perpetua herself and enabled them to become resigned to it – or even embrace it. The visions provide support to Perpetua's own identity as an 'out' Christian and clearly made her feel special and 'chosen'. In the first vision, there was a bronze ladder with iron weapons attached and a serpent at its bottom. Perpetua's teacher Saturus climbed it first and called down to her to climb carefully and watch not to get bitten by the serpent. Stepping on the serpent's head and climbing up, Perpetua reached heaven. This the group interpreted as a sign that they would indeed suffer and die. Her second vision was of her dead brother, Dinocrates, who had died horribly of a face cancer, aged seven. In the vision, he was unable to reach up high enough to drink from a bowl of water. This was interpreted as a sign to pray for him, which she did. In the next vision, Dinocrates no longer had his facial disfigurement, just a scar, and was 'clean, well dressed and refreshed', drinking from the inexhaustible bowl of water. The visions of Dinocrates seem to suggest the power of prayer to save a tormented soul.

The final part of Perpetua's narrative tells of her fourth vision, in which the deacon Pomponius leads her to the amphitheatre and into the arena. There, rather than beasts, an ugly Egyptian appeared with his supporters to fight her, whereupon she was stripped and transformed into a man, her handsome male followers oiling her/his body. A giant man then appeared, carrying a trainer's wand and a green branch with golden apples; he exclaimed 'this Egyptian, if he defeats this woman, will kill her with the sword, but if she defeats him, she shall receive this branch'. A detailed fight scene, which suggests Perpetua (if indeed she wrote the account) was no stranger to the games, sees Perpetua defeat the Egyptian; the trainer gives her the branch and says 'Daughter, peace be with you' and then she began to walk toward the Gate of Life. Her interpretation of this vision was that it was really the devil that she would be fighting in the arena.

On the day of the games – 'the day of their victory,' the prisoners went 'joyously' to the amphitheatre, 'as if going to heaven' and 'Perpetua followed, with a shining face and a calm step, as a wife of Christ and darling of God ... the intensity of her stare caused the spectators to look away'. They were dressed up in the costumes of pagan gods, but Perpetua, we are told, resisted this, saying 'we came here freely, so that our freedom might not be violated, and we handed over our lives so that we would not be forced to do anything like this. We had this agreement with you'. Perpetua began singing a hymn as the group were whipped along a line of gladiators. She and Felicity were stripped naked and wrapped in nets to be given to a wild cow (a female animal was chosen to match their sex), but the crowd reacted to the sight of 'a delicate young girl' and Felicity who 'had recently given birth ... her breasts still dripping with milk'. The pity or outrage extended as far as putting unbelted robes on them to cover their bodies.

The cow attacked them and Perpetua was thrown down first. Perpetua modestly rearranged her gown and pinned her hair up. She helped up Felicity, who had been crushed. Perpetua, possibly in a state of shock or 'so deep in the spirit and in ecstasy', the text says, did not at first realise she had already been thrown to the cow. The injured Christians were thrown into a part of the arena where they could be finished off, but the crowd demanded they be brought back into the middle of the arena, so they could see the death blows. 'The martyrs got up unaided and moved to where the crowd wished them to be.

First they kissed each other so that the ritual of peace would seal their martyrdom, The others, in silence and without moving, received the sword's thrust . . . Perpetua, however – so that she might taste something of the pain – screamed out in agony as she was pierced between the bones. And when the right hand of the novice gladiator wavered, she herself guided it to her throat.' The next line suggests that 'perhaps such a woman, feared as she was by the unclean spirit, could not have been killed unless she herself had willed it', which takes us back to the idea of martyrdom as a kind of suicide.

The issue of whether Perpetua actually wrote the account has been much debated.[25] How could she have written such an account in prison – where would she have obtained the writing materials? Did she leave notes? Did she dictate or tell her story to a visitor? Or did someone write the whole account on her behalf, as her experience could be imagined, filling in the details from their own knowledge of events? Jan Bremmer and Marco Formisano conclude that we cannot really know: 'in the end we cannot be wholly sure to what extent we have access to the *ipsissima verba* [the very words] of this remarkable young woman'.[26] The balance of opinion seems to be that the text is, at least in some sense, 'authentic', at least in that the martyrdom happened as described. Perhaps some of the details are true and the interpretations are also Perpetua's. In any case, *The Passion* offers an insight into how the Roman Empire worked on the ground, how the law and civic society functioned, and what happened to the condemned; it offers a plausible story, complete with emotions and motivations, of the disintegration of a family and the experiences and feelings of a Christian woman in the pagan empire. It remains vivid and moving.

28

ZENOBIA

In AD 272, the Roman emperor Aurelian defeated his eastern enemy, the empress Zenobia of Palmyra (Figure 28). As befitting a victorious Roman general, he celebrated an immense triumph in Rome, which is recorded in the *Historia Augusta* as a 'most brilliant spectacle'.[1] In the procession, there were three richly bejewelled chariots from the east, two from Palmyra, one a gift from the king of Persia, and Aurelian's own chariot, drawn by four stags, which had once belonged to the king of the Goths. There were elephants, tigers, giraffes, elk, and two hundred other 'tamed beasts ... from Libya and Palestine'. There were 800 pairs of gladiators, bound prisoners from sixteen different peoples, northern, eastern, and southern, including some 'Amazons' – Gothic women who had fought against Rome. The various peoples held placards identifying their nations for the watching crowd. And of course, there were the political prisoners – Tetricus, a Roman who had set up his son, also present, as emperor in Gaul, wearing outlandish Gallic trousers. Then there were some of the great and good of Palmyra, 'and there came Zenobia ... decked with jewels and in golden chains, the weight of which was borne by others'. The people of Rome and the senators also took part in the procession and days of games and shows followed.

We might think it natural that Zenobia's execution would follow such an elaborate display of Roman power, but despite setting up her own independent empire, fighting the Roman emperor, and losing the war with Aurelian, Zenobia and her children were allowed to live on near Rome, in a house at

FIG. 28 Coin of Zenobia. Classical Numismatic Group, Inc. www.cngcoins.com/

Tivoli. She might even have remarried in her retirement. Her children married into the Roman elite and Zenobia's descendants are recorded in Rome for some time.[2] Being a woman may ultimately have saved Zenobia's life.

The main historical source for Zenobia is the Latin *Historia Augusta* (*HA*), which is a book of lives of emperors, would-be emperors, and other notable people, from Hadrian to Carinus. As Ronald Syme has written 'it is the sole Latin source of any compass surviving as evidence for more than a century and a half of imperial history (117–284)'.[3] The life of Zenobia is included in the book entitled 'The Thirty Pretenders' (*Tyranni Triginta*) and is the longest single 'life' in that section. In there too is a much briefer life of her husband Odainathus and their two sons Herennianus and Timolaus. Oddly only the *HA* mentions these sons; Odainathus' known son and heir was called

Vaballathus. Zenobia also appears in the lives of various emperors, including Gallienus and Aurelian. There are no substantial Palmyrene or eastern sources surviving, just a few traditions, and we must recall the 'outsider' Roman perspective that permeates the *HA*'s descriptions of Zenobia.[4]

The *HA* does not tell us about Zenobia's birth, but she was probably born around AD 240/241.[5] The young Zenobia, whose combined Roman and Palmyrene name was Septimia Bat-Zabbai, grew up in Palmyra, Tadmor in the local language, which had grown to become a populous, cosmopolitan, and wealthy city on the back of its oasis and fresh water springs and its agricultural productivity.[6] Its central location connected trade between east and west, which included precious silk and spices coming from the east; as ships of the desert, camels were held in high regard. Many Palmyrenes grew rich as merchants and the city became very fine, with colonnaded streets, a theatre, sacred precincts, and temples, such as the temples of Bel and Nebu; the Great Colonnade ran through the city. The architecture was heavily Greco-Roman in style. Growing up in the city, Zenobia would have taken part in the numerous religious and public festivals in the yearly round. As Nathanael Andrade eloquently describes, the physicality of Palmyra, its water, its smells, sounds, and sights 'dominated her all her sensory experiences', and the city's traditions shaped her understanding of the world.[7]

Pat Southern has explained some of the difficulties of understanding Zenobia's origins. It is possible that she was the daughter of a Palmyran leader called Julius Aurelius Zenobius Zabdilah, who had fought with the emperor Severus Alexander against the Persians – her son Vaballathus also had the Roman name Julius Aurelius.[8] However, several Palmyran inscriptions describe her as the daughter of Antiochus – one Antiochus led a rebellion after her defeat, although this could equally have been a younger son. Some Arab sources suggest she was the daughter of a tribal chief of the 'Amlaqi. Of her mother, nothing is known. To be a suitable wife for Odainathus, the leading man of Palmyra, it seems safe to conclude that she came from a suitably prestigious and powerful family. They married in around AD 257/258 and their son Vaballathus was born in AD 258/260. She may have taken the name 'Septimia' from her husband, whose Roman name (he was a citizen too) was Septimius.

As a child, it is not clear whether Zenobia received any formal education, though she learned to read and write and possibly trained in such skills as playing music and singing.[9] However, her apparent interest in mythical and historical women could indicate that she received a broader education, which included some history and literature, or that she had been a curious child asking questions – or both. As an adult, Zenobia employed a Roman rhetorician Cassius Longinus, supposedly as a tutor in Greek letters, but his appointment was partly also about affirming an elite identity and boosting the cultural capital of herself and her court.[10] We should expect that Zenobia's cultural background was Palmyrene in the first instance, but in adulthood she tried to develop a much wider cultural framework. The *HA* explains that she traced her descent from Cleopatra and the Ptolemies and took the famous women Dido and Semiramis as models.[11] He adds also that she drank from jewelled and golden vessels that had once been Cleopatra's. This all may be true but could be an easy way for the author of the *HA* to characterise her as an overly ambitious, clever, and dangerous 'eastern' women – very un-Roman.

Palmyrene was probably Zenobia's first and most natural language, since she is supposed to have written a letter in Palmyrene to Aurelian that Cassius had to translate into Greek, but the *HA* explains that Zenobia was multilingual.[12] She knew Greek and read Roman history in Greek rather than Latin. Her reading in Greek may have been good, and her Latin reading poor, but perhaps she was not as confident writing in Greek. She could speak Latin but was hesitant to do so, but apparently she brought up her sons to speak Latin primarily. The *HA* also claims she spoke Egyptian very well and composed a history in the language. Bringing up her sons Herennianus and Timolaus as primarily Latin speakers, if indeed this was the case, would have been a practical and political choice by Odainathus and Zenobia; Timolaus did so well that he became a famous Latin rhetorician (though as mentioned, he is unknown out of the *HA*).[13] In a bustling place like Palmyra, multilingualism must have been fairly normal.

Inscriptions in the city show that there were statues of Zenobia in Palmyra, though they are no longer present. Southern suggests a statue would probably not have been a real portrait but an idealised representation – perhaps with the typical 'strong, firmly outlined features, and large almond-shaped eyes gazing dispassionately into the middle distance'.[14] As with other Palmyrene statues of women, such as 'the Beauty of Palmyra', she may have been shown wearing an embroidered headband and jewelled 'turban', covering her hair.[15] Jewellery was an important part of the display, with women wearing large pendant earrings, necklaces, and bracelets; 'all display of finery seems to be concentrated in their jewellery and headdress'.[16] The *HA* suggests that when she made public speeches, 'it was in the manner of a Roman emperor ... wearing a helmet and girt with a purple fillet, which had gems hanging from the lower edge, while its centre was fastened with the jewel called cochlis, used instead of the brooch worn by women'. The *HA* tells us (of course) that Zenobia was beautiful:

> her face was dark and of a swarthy hue, her eyes were black and powerful beyond the usual wont, her spirit divinely great, and her beauty incredible. So white were her teeth that many thought that she had pearls in place of teeth. Her voice was clear and like that of a man.[17]

The Roman east was not a peaceful place in the third century – many wars were fought between the Romans and the Persians. In AD 252 the Persian king Sapor destroyed a Roman army 60,000 strong, a victory followed up by numerous conquests; in AD 260 he defeated an army of 70,000, captured the emperor Valerian and took possession of thirty-seven cities of the eastern empire. Palmyra was not taken but the Palmyrenes must have had to fight hard to defend their home. In this context of east-west conflict, Zenobia's husband Septimius Odainathus rose to power in the middle.

Odainathus was born around AD 215/220 and was to have a stellar career until his eventual murder in AD 268. A Palmyrene with Roman citizenship inherited from his grandfather, he was not born an emperor or even a king, but he succeeded in working his way into power and using it effectively – the *HA* and some modern historians even credit him with saving the Roman Empire. By AD 252, a bilingual Palmyrene/Greek inscription from Palmyra describes him as leader of the city, and elsewhere he is described as a Roman senator – he shared these titles with his son, which suggests he was thinking in terms of hereditary powers and position.[18] By AD 258, under Valerian, he had achieved consular status.[19]

When Valerian was captured by the Persians, Rome was thrown into further turmoil, fighting the Persians and each other. Amongst the Romans, Gallienus came out on top, with Odainathus supporting him. The *HA* states 'and so Odaenathus was made emperor over almost the whole east'.[20] Whilst his precise legal position and imperial titles in Roman terms are unclear, he had in Palmyra been recognised as 'king of kings', a title with real significance in the east; he was undoubtedly the de facto ruler of the eastern empire.[21] Despite his power, though, there is no indication that Odainathus sought to break with Rome; he seems always to have worked within the Roman imperial system and allowed Gallienus to nominate officials in the east.[22] Then, in c. AD 267/268, Odainathus was murdered; the date, location, perpetrator, and reasons for his assassination differ by source.[23] It could have been a Palmyrene rival, a Roman or Persian assassin, or even a family member – or a some combination of those. Zenobia, now a widow, buried her husband in the tomb he had built for himself.[24]

Although no doubt there is much we do not know, there seems to have been surprisingly little trouble in the transfer of power to Zenobia and the ten-year-old Vaballathus.[25] In one version of events, Odainathus' murderer was handed over to the army, which then elected Zenobia and Vaballathus to govern. They may well have been with the army when Odainathus was killed, as they had accompanied the army before. Winning the support of Palmyra's military would have been essential; she clearly had connections and supporters in the army, in particular perhaps two generals Zabdas and Zabbai.

These generals had both been given the first name Septimius as a reward for their support of Odainathus.[26] Perhaps reflecting the importance she placed on being a visible and physical presence amongst the army, the *HA* states that she often rode a horse rather than riding in a carriage, that she often walked with her foot-soldiers and that she drank wither her generals. Indeed, it records that she was thought both hardier and braver than her husband – who was very much a man of action. Zosimus, a historian writing in the early sixth century AD, too states that she 'had the courage of a man, and with the assistance of her husband's friends, acted in every respect as well as he had done'.[27] Were these compliments – perhaps double-edged observations of how unwomanly, in a Roman sense, she was?

The *HA* states that Zenobia 'proceeded on the death of her husband . . . to cast about her shoulders the imperial mantle; and arrayed in the robes of Dido and even assuming the diadem, she held the imperial power in the name of her sons'. However, Zenobia did not immediately set herself up as an independent ruler and rival of Rome. Since Vaballathus was a minor, Zenobia ruled as regent on his behalf; he had several of his father's titles already, including 'king of kings', which was only meaningful in an eastern context and was not 'separatist'. No contestable Roman titles were claimed and Vaballathus and Zenobia seem to have been accepted as rulers by the various Roman governors in the east; she did nothing to disturb the status quo.[28] As wife of Odainathus and mother of Vaballathus Zenobia, probably not yet thirty, had ended up in an extremely elevated position within the empire.

At first, Zenobia continued the policies of Odainathus; maintaining the Palmyrene army, building forts, and defending against Persian attacks – all of which would serve to maintain Palmyra's status and its trading economy. But in AD 270, she used her military power to extend Palmyran rule south through Arabia to Egypt and northwest into Anatolia. An army reportedly 70,000 strong of Palmyrans, Syrians, and others, commanded by Zabdas, invaded Egypt, defeated its Roman army, and occupied Alexandria. After some instability, the prefect Probus was defeated; initially, the Egyptians, not knowing what to do, issued their civil documents without referring to any ruler, but by AD 271 they had begun to label them in the name of Vaballathus and the new emperor Aurelian. Zenobia had created a Palmyran empire.

The reasons for Zenobia's expansionist decisions are unclear. Andrade notes that Gallienus' successor Claudius II sent an army against her in AD 269/270, which was defeated, and suggests that Claudius may have been part of a group of Gallienus' supporters involved in the murder of Odainathus.[29] With Rome against her, expansion may have been a strategy for survival, or an opportunistic response to win an empire for her son. She may have thought that it would give her more bargaining power within the imperial project rather than seriously wanting to secede from it. At the same time, there were other attempts to split off chunks of the empire – Postumus formed a Gallic Empire, run in Roman fashion, in the west from AD 260, which Zenobia's contemporaries Marius and Victorinus, and then Tetricus I and II ruled.[30] This tendency to division, which suggests the difficulty of maintaining sole rule of such a huge bloc in the face of potentially more effective local governance, would eventually be incorporated into imperial policy by Diocletian, who divided the empire into an eastern and western half, each with a senior and junior emperor.[31]

Yet Zenobia presented her domain and Vaballathus' position as subordinate to Rome and the emperor, at least initially. The ships full of Egyptian grain essential to the survival of the city of Rome were not stopped. Some coins minted in the east showed Aurelian with a radiate crown, labelled Augustus, whilst Vaballathus was shown only with a laurel crown.[32] In what was undoubtedly a careful policy of Zenobia's, Vaballathus claimed neither the title of Caesar nor Augustus. With their victories, coins showing Aurelian and Vaballathus paired as 'harmonious busts' appeared and Vaballathus was also given Latin titles such as rex, consul, imperator, and dux Romanorum – but they went no further.

The nuance may have been meaningless for Aurelian, who presumably came into power with his own agenda, one in which neither a hereditary dynasty of Palmyran rulers of the east nor a Gallic empire in the west figured. He gathered an army in Byzantium in the winter of AD 271/272. In response to this, Zenobia now made the decision to claim the title of Augustus for the young Vaballathus and for herself, which is recorded on milestones in Arabia and Palestine.[33] Zenobia now minted new coins, in a Roman style with Latin or Greek legends, showing Vaballathus as Augustus with a radiant crown and herself as Augusta (or *Sebaste* in Greek), looking like a typical third-century Roman empress.[34] Septimia Zenobia Augusta and Vaballathus, now grandly titled the Imperator Caesar L. Julius Aurelius Septimius Vaballathus Athenodorus, Persicus Maximus, Arabicus Maximus, Adiabenicus Maximus, had finally claimed the purple.

The historian Zosimus tells us that as Aurelian's army advanced through Anatolia, many cities went over to him.[35] Zenobia waited at the major eastern city of Antioch. In a major battle outside the city, Aurelian's cavalry retreated, tricking the Palmyran heavy cavalry into pursuing them. When the Palmyrenes were exhausted, the Romans turned and slaughtered them. Zenobia, along with the general Zabdas and the remnants of the army retreated to Emesa. At Emesa, the Romans were again victorious and proceeded to besiege Palmyra itself. Zenobia fled eastward on a camel but was caught crossing the Euphrates and brought back to Aurelian. The emperor put her and her supporters on trial and, according to Zosimus, Zenobia claimed she had 'as a simple woman' been manipulated by the men around her; Cassius

Longinus was executed and others too, on the basis of Zenobia's accusations.[36] Was this Zenobia's defence? Was it a calculated strategy, playing on Aurelian's reputation for mercy? Or had she been manipulated by men of the Palmyrene elite, perhaps including Zabdas and Zabbai?

Being a woman may have saved Zenobia's life. Both Zosimus and the *HA* suggest that Aurelian was uncomfortable with the idea of having fought and defeated a woman, because it could be seen, in a sense, as unmanly; a woman could not be a serious threat.[37] The *HA* relates a letter to the senate, supposedly by Aurelian, in which he defends his actions – stressing Zenobia as a powerful woman and worthy adversary, 'how wise in counsels, how steadfast in plans, how firm toward the soldiers, how generous when necessity calls, and how stern when discipline demands'.[38] It even suggests Odainathus' victory against the Persians was down to her and that 'such was the fear that this woman inspired in the peoples of the East and also the Egyptians that neither Arabs nor Saracens nor Armenians ever moved against her'. He did not put her to death, it says, because she effectively preserved the eastern empire for Rome.

But how much of the *HA's* Zenobia is real? *The HA* is one of the most frustrating and puzzling sources for Roman history; notoriously unreliable, it blurs the lines between history and fiction, with invented characters, letters, poems and speeches, and made-up sources.[39] It revels in 'scurrilous gossip, rumor-mongering, and character assassination'.[40] Even its six named authors are an invention – it is now generally agreed that a single author was behind the whole collection.[41] It is possible, as Ronald Syme has argued, that the *HA* was intended as entertainment or that the author was simply having fun.[42] Perhaps we should judge it as clever amusement rather than bad history.

One intriguing suggestion about the *HA*'s life of Zenobia has been proposed by Diederik Burgersdijk, who suggests that it was a kind of inversion of a much older satirical and famously misogynistic poem on Roman women by Juvenal.[43] The poem targets wealthy married women in particular, with the explicit purpose of persuading Juvenal's friend Postumus not to marry. He luridly describes their supposed cruelty, extravagance, gluttony, greed, use of Greek, interference in legal matters, lack of chastity, learnedness, lustfulness, participation in open conversation with men, pride, superstitiousness, unfaithfulness, and unfeminine, manly behaviour. Whether or not the poem represents Juvenal's own views, it shows us by antithesis how respectable women were expected to be.

In the *HA*, Zenobia, in contrast, is presented as a model of chastity: 'such was her continence, it is said, that she would not even know her husband save for the purpose of conception. For when once she had lain with him, she would refrain until the time of menstruation to see if she were pregnant; if not, she would again grant him an opportunity of begetting children'. After her defeat, in Rome, the *HA* says 'she lived with her children in the manner of a Roman matron'. Her appearance was the opposite of how Juvenal described ugly women, though she had darker rather than pale skin, as was the Roman ideal. Possibly Zenobia's insistence on learning and using Latin, and on having her sons use it, is a contrast with Juvenal's Roman women insisting on using Greek. She also kept eunuchs, a criticism of Juvenal's, but these were old rather than the young ones of the women in Rome. Zenobia drank and talked with men, specifically kings and generals are mentioned, but this was for political reasons, to get the better of them, rather than for pleasure. Whether the author did have Juvenal in mind, an elite readership may well have seen a reflection.

The fall of Zenobia was followed by the destruction of Palmyra, which was relieved of its territories and its walls; east–west trade caravans travelled via Nisibis instead. It was not completely abandoned though; Aurelian built a temple and Diocletian built baths there. Zenobia's old rivals ruled an increasingly Christian community, which even had a bishop. In the sixth century, the historian Procopius tells us that Palmyra was almost completely deserted and that Justinian refortified and garrisoned it. We do not know what Zenobia's retirement was like – whether she dwelled on her grand achievements, even if they had not lasted, how she felt about her new life, which must have been one of comfort and relative security and some notoriety. Whilst Zenobia had landed on her feet, Palmyra had fallen very far.

29

HYPATIA

> There was a woman of Alexandria named Hypatia, daughter of the philosopher Theon, who made such attainments in literature and science, as to far surpass all the philosophers of her own time . . .. Some of them [Alexandrian Christians] entered into a conspiracy against her; and observing her as she returned home in her carriage, they dragged her from it, and carried her to the church called Caesareum, where they completely stripped her, and then murdered her with shells. After tearing her body in pieces, they took her mangled limbs to a place called Cinaron, and there burnt them . . .. This happened in the month of March during Lent, in the fourth year of Cyril's episcopate, under the tenth consulate of Honorius, and the sixth of Theodosius.[1]

This is the story told by Hypatia's near contemporary Socrates Scholasticus (c. AD 379–450) in his *Ecclesiastical History*, which Hypatia scholar Maria Dzielska tells us provides 'the most important and most valuable intelligence' about her life.[2] Hypatia was killed in AD 415 in the city where she was born and lived her extraordinary life.[3]

Hypatia is one of the most romanticised female figures from the ancient world. Her image as the last in a long line of Greek philosophers and scholars stretching back centuries is similar in some ways to that of the fourth century Roman emperor Julian – a pagan schooled in the Greek classics fighting the implacable forces of Christianity. This sense of an ending of the world of antiquity with the death of Hypatia is certainly the image promoted in Catherine Nixey's excellent 2017 book *The Darkening Age: The Christian Destruction of the Classical World*, which retells the story of her murder by a mob of Christian *parabalani* – 'reckless ones' or in Glen Bowersock's words 'Christian terrorists'.[4]

Hypatia's story, and that of the tipping point between classical antiquity and Christian late antiquity and the early medieval period also inspired Alejandro Amenábar's movie *Agora* (2009), in which we see the Christian mobs running riot in Alexandria, destroying venerable pagan statues and books, what was left of the famous Library housed in the Serapeum, and finally killing the beautiful virgin philosopher herself, portrayed with dignity by actress Rachel Weisz. Of course, parts of this epic and beautiful film are fictionalised, modified, or added for dramatic effect, but many aspects of it are based on the historical record.[5] Both of these retellings have added weight to the myths that have grown up around Hypatia and they sit within a tradition that stretches back through modern times some three centuries.

One early portrayal of Hypatia was written by John Toland and published in 1720 in a book entitled: *Hypatia: or, the history of a most beautiful, most virtuous, most learned, and every way accomplish'd Lady who was torn to pieces by the clergy of Alexandria, to gratify the pride, emulation, and cruelty of their archbishop, commonly but undeservedly titled St. Cyril.* Toland extolled Hypatia's fine character, inextricably linked with his idealisations of the female gender, calling her 'the glory of her own sex' a woman 'without the least blemish' and 'numberless perfections ... beauty, innocence, and knowledge'. Later he remarks that she was 'a charming mind in a charming body' and that men should forever be ashamed that it was men who killed her.

Toland's version of the story too is based on the ancient sources, and was fairly well received when it appeared, although some saw it as an attack on the church and on Christianity itself.[6] Indeed, the French philosopher Voltaire later adopted Hypatia explicitly for the purpose of critiquing the established religious order. She also served as one of Edward Gibbon's examples of how Christianity destroyed the ancient world – a theme revisited in Nixey's book. In his words, 'the murder of Hypatia has imprinted an indelible stain on the character and religion of Cyril of Alexandria'.[7] Quite apart from historical interest, Hypatia had become a character that enabled modern authors to 'articulate their attitude toward Christianity, the church, its clergy, the patriarch Cyril, and so on'.[8] But it was later on, in the mid-nineteenth century, that 'the literary legend of Hypatia reached its apex'.[9]

In English, her fame increased through Charles Kingsley's popular historical novel, *Hypatia*, first published in 1853. His Hypatia was a romantic figure, beautiful and intelligent, chaste but with many male admirers, and she disapproved of Christianity. In the book, Philammon asks Hypatia 'why ... do you so dislike Christianity?' Hypatia replies:

> because it denies itself to be one of those many methods [of finding truth or perfection], and stakes its existence on the denial; because it arrogates to itself the exclusive revelation of the Divine, and cannot see, in its self-conceit, that its own doctrines disprove that assumption by their

> similarity to those of all creeds. There is not a dogma of the Galileans which may not be found, under some form or other, in some of those very religions from which it pretends to disdain borrowing.[10]

Of course, after a long build-up to her inevitable fate, Kingsley's Hypatia dies a horrible death at the hands of Alexandria's Christians, stripped naked as she tried to fight off and was dragged by the *parabalani*, 'those hell-hounds', to the church. In a last moment her strength shines through:

> She shook herself free from her tormentors, and springing back, rose for one moment to her full height, naked, snow-white against the dusky mass around – shame and indignation in those wide clear eyes, but not a stain of fear. With one hand she clasped her golden locks around her; the other long white arm was stretched upward toward the great still Christ.[11]

Hypatia the novel was labelled 'immoral' by the church and by some Oxford academics: Lewis Carroll was shocked by some of the anti-Christian remarks in the book, and Tennyson thought the description of Hypatia's death distastefully gruesome.[12] Ruskin stated that 'the story of *Hypatia* is the most ghastly in the Christian tradition, and should for ever have been left in silence' – glossed over, forgotten. Despite these reactions, the novel was very popular and reprinted for many years; apparently it was Queen Victoria's favourite Kingsley novel.[13]

The novel also inspired controversial paintings – Charles Mitchell's 1885 *Hypatia*, shown at the Grosvenor Gallery, showed a young nude Hypatia resting on a Christian altar, illustrating the scene from Kingsley's novel quoted above. In the theatre too it inspired a play by G. Stuart Ogilvie and Max Beerbohm Tree, which in 1893 ran to 104 showings at London's Haymarket Theatre.[14] The scenery was designed by Sir Lawrence Alma-Tadema, the great Victorian painter of scenes from antiquity, and was regarded as a central pillar of the visually stunning production.[15] The film *Agora*, made more than a century later, is a recognisable descendent of this Hypatia tradition (Figure 29).

But what of the 'real' Hypatia? In recent years, scholars have again tried to reconstruct her life and disentangle the real woman from the idealised symbol of womanhood or the classical world invented by male scholars and writers, ancient and modern, critically and sensitively examining both her life and intellectual contributions.[16] The ancient sources are few and not particularly detailed – sometimes just a sentence or two; all are men and most focus on Hypatia's death. Many are at some remove in time from Hypatia. Socrates Scholasticus, quoted above, was a contemporary of Hypatia and devoted a short chapter to her in his *Ecclesiastical History*. What makes his chapter even more valuable is that his own teachers in Constantinople included Helladius

FIG. 29 Charles William Mitchell, *Hypatia*, 1885. Possibly illustrating Charles Kingsley's novel. Wikimedia Commons. Public domain

and Ammonias, both non-Christians who had been teachers and priests in Alexandria in Hypatia's time; they would clearly have been aware of her.[17]

Socrates and the other sources tell us that Hypatia was the daughter of the philosopher Theon. Theon was a famous scholar, best known for his mathematical works, which included commentaries on the *Almagest* of Ptolemy, a work on astronomy, and an edition of Euclid's *Elements*, on geometry.[18] The tenth-century Byzantine *Suda*, a kind of encyclopaedia of the ancient world, also contains an entry on her, which tells us that 'she was not satisfied with her education in mathematics by her father but also gained knowledge of philosophy'.[19] Socrates states that she followed Plato and Plotinus and both sources mention her as a popular teacher in the city 'expounding in public to those willing to listen on Plato or Aristotle or any other philosopher' (*Suda*), 'many of whom came from a distance to receive her instructions'. Philostorgius states that she was known for her ability in maths and in astronomy and 'reached an excellence far above her teacher'.[20]

Hypatia's students would have been predominantly well-off young men – a public education not being appropriate for women – even if she did speak in public to wider audiences too. How did her students feel towards her? Some of the sources emphasise Hypatia's beauty and virtue: 'though naturally modest and fair-minded, she remained unwed, and she was so exceedingly beautiful and fair of form that one of her colleagues fell in love with her' says the *Suda*. Damascius' *Life of Isidore* agrees that she was beautiful and remained a virgin. Both sources tell the story, true or apocryphal, that when her student proclaimed his love for her, she flung a bloody menstrual napkin at him and said 'It is this you love, young man, not beauty'.[21]

More important than that story as a source are the letters sent to Hypatia by her former pupil Synesius and the letter in which she is mentioned. His letters address and refer to her with respect, affection, and even love. In one letter, dictated from his sickbed where he lay in grief following the death of his children, he addresses her thus: 'may you receive it in good health, mother, sister, teacher, and withal benefactress'.[22] In another, to his brother, he asks: 'salute for me the most holy and revered philosopher [Hypatia], and give my homage also to the company of the blessed who delight in her oracular utterance'.[23] Hypatia and some of her students shared a close and lasting bond.[24] The letters also reveal areas of Hypatia's practical mathematical and scientific expertise.[25] In one letter to Hypatia, Synesius asks her to supervise the production of a hydroscope and in another, to one Paeonius, he sends an astrolabe, commenting that 'it is a work of my own devising, including all that she, my most revered teacher [Hypatia], helped to contribute'.

One of Hypatia's key works appears to have been devoted to Ptolemy's *Almagest*, the text her father had also worked on.[26] In the opening inscription, Theon wrote: 'Theon of Alexandria's commentary on the third [book] of the Mathematical Syntaxis of Ptolemy, the edition having been prepared by the philosopher, my daughter, Hypatia.'[27] She is also recorded as having written a commentary on the astronomical *Canon*, Diophantus' *Arithmetic*, and a commentary on Apollonius' *Conics*.[28] Quite what she did is unclear, but possibly she was concerned with making classic texts and difficult maths more accessible to students, which would tie in with her positive reputation as a teacher.[29]

Hypatia is also recorded as having played a role in the public life of Alexandria, an area generally reserved to men: 'on account of her self-possession and ease of manner, which she had acquired in consequence of the cultivation of her mind, she not infrequently appeared in public in presence of the magistrates. Neither did she feel abashed in coming to an assembly of men' states Socrates Scholasticus.[30] Damascius records that she was 'wise in practical affairs and motivated by civic-mindedness' and 'came to be widely and deeply trusted throughout the city'.[31] This public role was not unique to Hypatia, it was part of the perceived role of philosophers, who were ideally seen as people who would offer disinterested advice, even to those of high rank.[32] Hypatia's learning and demeanour, and probably the fact that her status and contacts made through teaching brought her into contact with elite males, meant she was able to fulfil this role, despite being a woman. It seems she advised at the highest levels of Alexandrian society, including Egypt's governor Orestes.

However, the sources agree that Hypatia's political life played a role in her death. They suggest that she got caught up in the feud between Cyril, the powerful archbishop of Alexandria and Orestes. Orestes was a Christian but tolerant of non-Christians, whereas Cyril was more dogmatic. Hypatia was a pagan and her circle consisted of non-Christians, Christians, and Jews. Socrates Scholasticus also says 'for as she had frequent interviews with Orestes, it was calumniously reported among the Christian populace, that it was she who prevented Orestes from being reconciled to the bishop'.[33] Damascius reports that Cyril was jealous of Hypatia's popularity and influence, saying he was piqued by the sight of all the visitors to her house.[34] Because of this, Damascius says, Cyril plotted her murder – as described at the outset of this chapter. From the sources available, we cannot be certain.

Hypatia may have offended Cyril, but John of Nikiu also gives an idea of what some less educated Christians may have thought of Hypatia:

> she was devoted at all times to magic, astrolabes and instruments of music, and she beguiled many people through [her] satanic wiles. And the governor of the city honored her exceedingly; for she had beguiled him through her magic. And he ceased attending church as had been his custom.[35]

Were there any precedents for Hypatia's career? As a female philosopher, Kathleen Wider argues, she was far from unique in the ancient world - 'there were women involved with philosophy throughout ancient Greek history'.[36] In his *History of Women Philosophers* of 1690, Gilles Ménage counted sixty five – just for the Hellenistic period.[37] In Alexandria itself, a female mathematician called Pandrosion was active a couple of generations before Hypatia and may have been something of a role model for her.[38] Pandrosion seems to have pioneered some innovative mathematical methods, though came in for criticism by Pappus, another mathematician of the time and most likely a rival, for whom we have to thank for knowledge of Pandrosion's existence. Although modern mathematicians have demonstrated that Pandrosion's methods work, her legacy was short-lived; unlike Hypatia, she has dropped out of history.

Upon her death in AD 415 Hypatia may have been sixty years old, if she was born in AD 355, as both Dzielska and Watts agree; not the beautiful young girl of the myth but an older woman, a venerable thinker, teacher, and adviser.[39] She had been born into the beating heart of Alexandrian and Hellenic learning at a time when there was heated conflict between and within religious groups not only in the city but throughout the empire. Laws forbidding 'pagan' (that is 'traditional') sacrifice had been passed by the emperor Theodosius in AD 381 and again in AD 391 and the most famous Serapeum temple in Alexandria, which Hypatia would have known well, was destroyed in AD 392 by the bishop Theophilus.[40] This Theophilus was a devout anti-pagan, who had already mockingly paraded pagan cult objects through the streets of the city.

It is hardly surprising, given the turn of history, that Hypatia has become a symbol of reason versus dogmatic religious fundamentalism and of a romantic past that linked her time back to the pre-Socratics. But if we can learn a lesson from her real life, it is perhaps not only to admire her obvious intelligence and wisdom but to admire her 'tremendous personal talent, sheer force of will, and ... determination to live her life philosophically', and the strength and resilience that she showed in facing the daily struggles that enabled her to win and maintain her position as a pre-eminent woman in a male-dominated world.[41]

30

THEODORA

Theodora is a woman about whom we are supposed to believe the worst. She has the misfortune to have become one of the main subjects, alongside her husband, the emperor Justinian, of one of the most famous, accessible, and lurid texts from antiquity: *The Secret History*, by Procopius. *The Secret History* is a book that has defied classification; it is not exactly a history and not exactly a biography – in Byzantine times, the writer of the *Suda* labelled it both a comedy and an invective. Peter Sarris, in his introduction to one translation, rightly calls it 'vitriolic' – with 'carefully calibrated pieces of character assassination aimed at the Emperor and his wife'.[1] 'Our' Theodora is fundamentally entangled with Procopius' own vision of his times revealed in *The Secret History* and to approach her we must approach him too.[2]

Procopius, born around AD 500 in Caesarea, Palestine, was a well-educated man who knew his classics, adopting in his *History of the Wars*, which described Justinian's major wars against the Persians, the Vandals, and the Goths, the classical style of Thucydides, who wrote almost a thousand years earlier.[3] His *History* seems accurate when it can be checked against other sources of the time.[4] Probably from a well-to-do family in a fairly bustling port city, the seat of the local governor, he trained in law and in the AD 520s became a legal adviser to the general Belisarius, who he accompanied on various military campaigns in Italy, North Africa and the east. He spent a good portion of his life amongst the high and mighty and lived in Constantinople from the AD 540s until his death in the AD 550s or 560s. Procopius, then, was well-placed to write his *History of the Wars* and his *Secret History* must also derive from his inside knowledge of the upper echelons of the eastern Roman world of Late Antiquity and his opinion of its members.

As Procopius tells it, Theodora came from a humble background. Her father Acacius worked for the circus as an animal keeper; he was the Master of Bears for the Green faction in Constantinople. After he died, leaving a widow and three young daughters, Theodora's mother remarried. However, the Greens soon replaced the family in their role as animal-keepers. Desperate, without any livelihood or means, the mother armed the girls with wreaths and displayed them as supplicants to the Greens in front of the whole circus crowd, hoping for mercy – but to no avail. The Blues, though, whose Master of Bears had just died, took the family on in the same role. As the daughters, all attractive, reached maturity, the mother put them on the stage – they became entertainers and prostitutes, shameful professions that were intertwined in the Roman imagination.

Procopius appears to revel in the lewdness of his tale. He tells us that even when she was too physically immature to have vaginal sex with a man Theodora would have anal sex with poor men and slaves out of doors and in a brothel. When she reached puberty, she became a low prostitute (the term Procopius uses refers to the lowest rank of foot-soldier) because she lacked any distinguishing skills like playing a musical instrument or being able to dance: 'she just sold her youth to passers-by, working with nearly her entire body'.[5] According to him, she habitually got naked in public and displayed her body sexually, was sexually adventurous, promiscuous, engaged in group sex, engaged in sex acts with animals in public, and was sexually insatiable. Once hired as a companion by a man called Hecebolus, who had been appointed governor of the Pentapolis, five cities in Libya, she was later dismissed and relied on prostitution to work her way around the eastern Mediterranean back to Constantinople. She was also, he writes, malicious, witty, and indomitable, ready with a comeback and given to laughing out loud in public. *The Secret History* paints the young Theodora as the opposite of a respectable Roman woman – whilst giving his reader plenty of gossip and titillating detail; this Procopius gives us to illustrate Theodora's character before she met Justinian and before she became empress.

Back in Constantinople, Justinian fell for Theodora – although we do not know how the two met – and she became his mistress.[6] The two were still not able to marry, however, because the current empress did not approve of Theodora at all and also because the law forbade men of high rank from marrying actresses or prostitutes, even ones that had given up the trade. When the old empress died, Justinian changed the law and they then married, probably around AD 522–523. This turn of events would seem to reflect a loving relationship that they both wished to make respectable.

Then in AD 523 both Justinian and Theodora were raised to patrician status by the emperor Justin. This, Procopius says, gave her both wealth and influence and was a mark of imperial favour. David Potter has explained just what was involved in this change of social position, which was not just a bureaucratic exercise but involved very public ceremonies and celebrations.[7] Theodora would have been formally presented to the emperor and other dignitaries, senators, and courtiers, where she would be given written confirmation of her new status. Then she would have been introduced to the leaders of the Blues and Greens, who would acclaim her. After that, she would have been taken to Hagia Sophia to put on the clothes of a patrician.

Justinian is vilified in *The Secret History* as a demon, not even human – as monstrous as his father.[8] We are told how in one meeting a respected person reported seeing Justinian's head disappear as he paced the room; another saw his face transform into a featureless lump of flesh. His inhumanity was also to be measured in his behaviour and ruination of the empire. Justinian's biggest mistake, Procopius emphasises, amongst a catalogue of errors and evils, was to choose Theodora as his wife, when he could have picked any of the empire's most noble, properly brought up, modest, and chaste virgins. Theodora was 'the common bane of all mankind . . . double-dyed with every kind of horrible pollution and guilty over and over again of infanticide by wilful abortion'.[9] Theodora too was supposedly accompanied by demons as a young prostitute and she apparently dreamed of one day marrying the Head of the Demons. Theodora as empress, Procopius spells out for his readers, was powerful, manipulative, implacable, vengeful, avaricious, terrifying, unforgiving, and cruel.

The Theodora we meet in *The Secret History* is a hate-figure, repugnant, barely a human being and certainly the opposite of what a respectable Roman woman, and especially an empress, should be, but to what extent is she real? One scholar, Leslie Brubaker, has argued that *The Secret History* is not a history at all but rather 'a successful piece of fiction, a brilliant parody on the imperial panegyric'; she concludes that 'it tells us nothing about Justinian and Theodora'.[10] Brubaker's argument is an interesting, if controversial one. She suggests that the book is an upside-down imperial eulogy in which Justinian is unmanly and Theodora unwomanly, both demonic, and as a pair a disaster for the empire.[11]

The form *The Secret History* follows, Brubaker argues, inverts the standard Greek model of imperial panegyric formulated by an earlier scholar Menander, which began with praising the emperor's family and noting any miracles that accompanied his birth, listing the emperor's achievements and actions in war and peace, comparing him favourably with previous emperors, and then noting the prosperity of the times. Menander added the advice that appropriate details could be freely invented. In *The Secret History*, instead of recounting all of these positives in praise of the emperor, Procopius recounts a barrage of negatives to damn him for posterity in what Clive Foss has called 'a venomous pamphlet of dubious merit'.[12] If the primary aim was to damn Justinian, the catalogue of Theodora's shortcomings could simply be invention and never intended to record or reflect literal truth. Even if both Justinian and Theodora were the targets, we should wonder how much was distorted or exaggerated or just made up for Procopius to make his point.

In his *History of the Wars*, Procopius tells the story of the Nika riots, an episode of civil unrest and violence in Constantinople in January AD 532 in which Justinian was in danger of being deposed; quelling the riot by force resulted in the deaths of perhaps 30,000 people.[13] At one point, before ordering the troops in, Justinian apparently contemplated flight and on this occasion, Theodora is supposed to have said:

> As to the belief that a woman ought not to be daring among men or to assert herself boldly among those who are holding back from fear, I consider that the present crisis most certainly does not permit us to discuss whether the matter should be regarded in this or in some other way. For in the case of those whose interests have come into the greatest danger nothing else seems best except to settle the issue immediately before them in the best possible way. My opinion then is that the present time, above all others, is inopportune for flight, even though it bring safety. For while it is impossible for a man who has seen the light not also to die, for one who has been an emperor it is unendurable to be a fugitive. May I never be separated from this purple, and may I not live that day on which those who meet me shall not address me as mistress. If, now, it is your wish to save yourself, O Emperor, there is no difficulty. For we have much money, and there is the sea, here the boats. However consider whether it will not come about after you have been saved that you would gladly exchange that safety for death. For as for myself, I approve a certain ancient saying that royalty is a good burial-shroud.[14]

Theodora argues against fleeing, but it could be said that she was not appealing to Justinian's better nature here or even displaying courage. Quite the opposite. This Theodora is desperate for her husband – and herself – to hang on to power. It is interesting that the vacillating Justinian is set on his path of action by his wife; this too is part of Procopius' criticism of the pair; the weak and unmanly Justinian must follow his wife's lead. But are these really Theodora's words – or anything like them? Did this event ever actually take place? Given that it appears in the *History of the Wars*, a published and not a secret work, there is possibly some truth to it.[15]

Speeches played an important part in classical historical writing and modern scholars have debated their veracity, form, and use for years.[16] In an oral culture, speeches were important, and in written history they allowed writers to break up a narrative with dramatic or informative interventions by real historical characters. Speeches could be used to explain the motivations of the actors, present opposing arguments about what was happening or what should be done, or even to consider wider moral or political issues. Thucydides, whose example was followed by many other historians, including Procopius, explained his own method for using speeches in his work. He tried to remember and to find out what was actually said, but given the difficulty of this, would also include the sort of thing that was likely to have been said in the circumstances – what was appropriate. The speeches might have contained some things that were said, but they were his own literary works, composed by him and fitted into his own selective history.

For Procopius, writing in this tradition, we can expect speeches to have similarly been his own products that may or may not contain anything really said in actual speeches given. Ralph-Johannes Lilie has noted that the ancient saying Theodora uses, about royalty being a good burial shroud, was slightly modified by Procopius, so that it referred to their royal rule, rather than to tyranny, as it had originally; he suggests that educated readers would have noticed this subtle slight to the imperial couple, being compared to tyrants.[17] It is probably also significant that it is Theodora, a woman, who advises the uncertain Justinian to stay, which makes Justinian, who takes her advice, look weak. The speech is plausible, but that does not make it a true historical record of who said what and why. Mischa Meier has argued that the whole description is a literary artefact, a conclusion that Lilie agrees with.[18]

Taking Procopius out of the picture, as Foss has done, and reconstituting Theodora from other sources, suggests a very different woman.[19] One major aspect of Theodora appears to have been her religiosity. She possibly built or was certainly involved in the construction of the church of St Sergius and Bacchus in Constantinople. Its dedicatory inscription states: 'May he [Sergius] increase the power of the God-crowned Theodora whose mind is adorned with piety, whose constant toil lies in unsparing efforts to nourish the destitute.'[20] Caring for the poor and weak was another of her concerns. Together with Justinian, she built several poorhouses. One ancient source, John the Lydian, devoted a book to her charitable acts.[21]

Procopius may have been right about the facts of Theodora's origins and early years, although he may have replaced her motivations, stark necessity transformed into morally reprehensible lewdness; this might be borne out by some of her later attitudes and actions. As empress, she showed a special degree of concern about the treatment of women generally, as Procopius himself notes in *History of the Wars*, in a story in which Theodora forced an errant husband to return to his wife, that her 'nature always led her to assist unfortunate women'.[22] Perhaps, in her view, women deserved better treatment from their husbands and from men in general.

Theodora was also concerned with actresses and prostitutes. At one point in *The Secret History*, Procopius explains that Theodora 'made it her business to devise punishments for sins of the flesh'. She gathered up 500 prostitutes from the city, 'women who sold their services in public at three coppers, just enough to keep body and soul together' and sent them, apparently unwillingly, to a convent called Metanoia (Repentance).[23] As Foss explains, the imperial couple did close the brothels of Constantinople in AD 528 but gave to the women affected new clothes and made Metanoia a place of refuge and forgiveness; they also refunded losses to the prostitutes' masters.[24] Another law of 535 AD got rid of the men who procured prostitutes, some of whom were women sold into the trade by poor families, and another in AD 537 released prostitutes from their profession.

How out of work prostitutes were supposed to make ends meet is unclear, but Theodora and her husband's moral and Christian beliefs may have influenced these actions, which they presumably did in order to right what they saw as wrong. It is hard not to think that Theodora's own experiences might have inclined her to help less fortunate women, as she saw fit, though it does not prove anything about her early years. Procopius could even present good, or at least well intended, deeds as evil.

Procopius has dominated the western tradition about Theodora since the discovery of the text of *The Secret History* in the Vatican Library and its publication in 1623; at that time, some of the more explicit parts of the work were omitted but soon became available.[25] Presumably, this legacy would please him greatly. But before that, there were other more positive traditions about Theodora that had survived. In the early fifteenth century, Christine de Pizan related one in *The Book of the City of Ladies*, though the name Antonia rather than Theodora is used.[26]

Here, Justinian and Antonia are presented very romantically as a couple in love. Out walking from Constantinople one day they took their rest under a tree, Justinian with his head in Antonia's lap. As he slept, she saw a vision, which, 'being a wise woman', she understood would mean Justinian, one of the emperor Justin's officials, would one day become emperor. As he woke:

> She spoke to him most sweetly, saying to him: 'My dearest heart, I love you and have always loved you: being the master of my body and my affection you know this full well. Since no lover who is so adored by his lady should refuse her anything she asked him, I want you to grant me a favour in return for my virginity and the love which you have received from me .... The favour which I ask from you is that when you are emperor, you will not scorn your lover, the poor Antonia, but will faithfully take her in marriage to be your honoured companion who will rule at your side.'[27]

The two exchanged rings. Sure enough, not long afterwards Justin died and Justinian was elected emperor; he took the army and attacked Persia. When he came back victorious, Antonia sought him out in the palace. With her identity hidden, she asked for justice – a man had promised to marry her and they had exchanged rings. Justinian said that the law required the man to fulfil his vow and asked if she had proof. Then 'she took the ring off her finger and held it out to him, exclaiming, 'Noble emperor, I can certainly prove it with this ring. See if you recognize it.'[28] Justinian did indeed recognise the ring and stuck to his promise, whisking Antonia off to the palace to be 'decked in finery' and then marrying her.

The eastern tradition has also been much more positive and led in February 2000 to Theodora's beatification in the Syrian Orthodox Church.[29] Theodora was regarded as Egyptian by Egyptians and Syrian by Syrians and was thought to be 'the faithful child of a faithful priest', as Potter writes.[30] She was staunch in her religious views and kept to them, even though they differed somewhat from those of Justinian. This made her popular with like-minded Christians – and unpopular with others, like Procopius. She was beautiful, of course.

Theodora is a puzzle. Brubaker states that 'in Theodora, Procopius created the perfect anti-woman' and it is true that she remains notorious because of him and through the easily available translations of *The Secret History*.[31] But we

FIG. 30 Theodora on a mosaic from the Basilica di San Vitale, Ravenna. Courtesy of Petar Milošević/CC BY-SA Wikipedia

also have a Theodora who was popular, was loved, and who was a religious and moral woman who tried to do good in her society. She lives in one of the most famous images from late antiquity – a powerful queen with her court, royal and religious, in the mosaic on the walls of the Byzantine church of San Vitale in Ravenna. If nothing else, the puzzle of Theodora, a circus girl who became empress, teaches us not to believe everything we read (Figure 30).

NOTES

PREFACE

1 Boccaccio. (2011). *On Famous Women*. Translated by G. A. Guarino. New York: Ithaca Press.
2 See chapter 3 of Franklin, M. (2006). *Boccaccio's Heroines: Power and Virtue in Renaissance Society*. London: Routledge.
3 De Pizan, C. (1999). *The Book of the City of Ladies*. Translated by R. Brown-Grant. London: Penguin.
4 De Pizan (1999), 1.1.
5 De Pizan (1999), 1.3.
6 De Pizan (1999), 3.19.
7 Recently documented in Criado Perez, C. (2019). *Invisible Women: Exposing Data Bias in a World Designed for Men*. London: Vintage.
8 Shipley, L. (2015). 'Leaping to conclusions: Archaeology, gender and digital news media'. *Antiquity* 89, 472–477.
9 Pinna, A. (2013). 'E' di una donna lo scheletro trovato alla Doganaccia'. *Viterbo News*. Available at www.viterbonews24.it/news/e-di-una-donna-lo-scheletro-trovato-tomba-etrusca-nviolata-_30573.htm; Weingarten, J. (2013). 'How a prince became a princess'. *Zenobia: Empress of the East*. Available at http://judithweingarten.blogspot.com/2013/10/how-prince-became-princess.html.
10 Tringham, R. (1991). 'Households with faces: The challenges of gender in prehistoric architectural remains'. In Gero, J., and Conkey, M. (eds.). *Engendering Archaeology: Women and Prehistory*. Oxford: Blackwell, pp. 93–131.

HISTORICAL CONTEXTS

1 Pemble, J. (1987). *The Mediterranean Passion: Victorians and Edwardians in the South*. Oxford: Clarendon Press.
2 de Pina-Cabral, J. (1989). 'The Mediterranean as a category of regional comparison: A critical view'. *Current Anthropology* 30(3), 399–406; Goddard, V. A., Llobern, J. R., and Shore, C. (1994). 'Introduction: The anthropology of Europe'. In Goddard, V. A., Llobern, J. R., and Shore, C. (eds.). *The Anthropology of Europe*. Oxford: Routledge, pp. 1–40.
3 Abulafia, D. (2003). 'Introduction: What is the Mediterranean?'. In Abulafia, D. (ed.). *The Mediterranean in History*. London: Thames and Hudson, pp. 11–31.
4 For example, Algazi, G. (2005). 'Diversity rules: Peregrine Horden and Nicholas Purcell's The Corrupting Sea'. *Mediterranean Historical Review* 20(2), 227–245; Nixon, L. (2002). 'Reviewed Work(s): *The Corrupting Sea. A Study of Mediterranean History* by P. Horden and N. Purcell: *The Mediterranean in the Ancient World* by F. Braudel, R. De Ayala, P. Braudel and S. Reynolds'. *The Journal of Roman Studies* 92, 195–197; Horden, P., and Purcell, N. (2005). 'Four years of corruption: A response to critics'. In Harris, W. V. (ed.) *Rethinking the Mediterranean*. Oxford: Oxford University Press, pp. 348–375.
5 Page 25, Broodbank, C. (2013). *The Making of the Middle Sea: A History of the Mediterranean from the Beginning to the Emergence of the Classical World*. London: Thames and Hudson.

INTRODUCTION

1 Sen, A. (1992). 'Missing women: Social inequality outweighs women's survival advantage in Asia and north Africa'. *BMJ: British Medical Journal* 304(6827), 587–588.
2 Sen, A. (2003). 'Missing women – revisited: Reduction in female mortality has been counterbalanced by sex selective abortions'. *BMJ: British Medical Journal* 327(7427), 1297–1298.
3 Gellatly, C., and Petrie, M. J. (2017). 'Prenatal sex selection and female infant mortality are

more common in India after firstborn and second-born daughters'. *Journal of Epidemiology and Community Health* 71, 269–274; Hewitt, G. (2011). 'The unstable future of a world full of men'. Phys.org. Available at https://phys.org/news/2011-10-unstable-future-world-full-men.html.

4 Pages 227–230, Pomeroy, S. B. (1995). *Goddesses, Whores, Wives and Slaves*. New York: Schocken Books.

5 Grubb, J. E. (2013). 'Infant exposure and infanticide'. In Grubb, J. E., Parkin, T. and Bell, R. (eds.). *The Oxford Handbook of Childhood and Education in the Classical World*. Oxford: Oxford University Press, pp. 83–107; Schmitz, W. (2013). 'Exposure of children'. In Bagnall, R. S., Brodersen, K., Champion, C. B., Erskine, A. and Huebner, S. R. (eds.). *The Encyclopedia of Ancient History*. Chichester: Blackwell, pp. 2604–2605.

6 Page 105, Patterson, C. (1985). '"Not worth the rearing": The causes of infant exposure in ancient Greece'. *Transactions of the American Philological Association (1974–2014)* 115, 103–123.

7 Patterson (1985), 113.

8 Quoted in Patterson (1985), 114.

9 Pomeroy (1995), 36.

10 Page 626, Krause, J.-U. (2011). 'Children in the Roman family and beyond'. In Peachin, M. (ed.). *The Oxford Handbook of Social Relations in the Roman World*. Oxford: Oxford University Press, pp. 623–642.

11 Pages 134–135, van Hook, L. R. (1920). 'The exposure of infants at Athens'. *Transactions and Proceedings of the American Philological Association* 51, 134–145.

12 Van Hook (1920), 136.

13 Patterson (1985), 120.

14 Golden, M. (1981). 'Demography and the exposure of girls at Athens'. *Phoenix* 35(4), 316–331.

15 Longus, *Daphnis and Chloe*.

16 Bagnall, R. (1997). 'Missing females in Roman Egypt'. *Scripta Classica Israelica* 16, 121–138.

17 Page 6, Harris, W. V. (1994). 'Child-exposure in the Roman Empire'. *The Journal of Roman Studies* 84, 1–22.

18 Bennett, H. (1923). 'The exposure of infants in ancient Rome'. *The Classical Journal* 18(6), 341–351.

19 Page 143, Brunt, P. A. (1971). *Italian Manpower, 225 BC–AD 14*. Oxford: Oxford University Press.

20 Harris (1994), 1.

21 Vishwanath, L. S. (2001). 'Female foeticide and infanticide'. *Economic and Political Weekly* 36(35), 3411–3412.

22 Kobulsky, J. M., Dubowitz, H., and Xu, Y. (2020). 'The global challenge of the neglect of children'. *Child Abuse & Neglect* 110, 104296.

23 Kobulsky, Dubowitz. and Xu (2020), 2.

24 Linning, S. (2021). 'Parents sell Afghan baby girl for $500 to feed the rest of her starving siblings: Daughter was given to a stranger "who wants her to marry his son" - as country faces total collapse'. Mail Online. Available at www.dailymail.co.uk/femail/article-10131713/The-baby-sold-500-feed-family.html.

25 Pomeroy (1995), 85.

26 Page 105, Caldwell, L. (2015). *Roman Girlhood and the Fashioning of Femininity*. Cambridge: Cambridge University Press.

27 Caldwell (2015), 99.

28 Caldwell (2015), 94–100.

29 Bagnall (1997).

30 Pages 232–235, Everitt, A. (2001). *Cicero: A Turbulent Life*. London: John Murray.

31 Pomeroy (1995), xv.

32 Johnson, S. L. (2010). 'Nail this to your door: A disputation on the power, efficacy, and indulgent delusion of western scholarship that neglects the challenge of gender and women's history'. *Pacific Historical Review* 79: 605–617.

33 Stuttard, D. (2014). *A History of Ancient Greece in Fifty Lives*. London: Thames and Hudson.

34 Translation available at *Perseus Digital Library* at www.perseus.tufts.edu/hopper/text?doc=Perseus%3Atext%3A2008.01.0480%3Avolume%3D2%3Atext%3D22.

35 Page 52, Manne, K. (2018). *Down Girl: The Logic of Misogyny*. London: Penguin.

36 Manne (2018), 263.

37 Manne (2018), 90.

38 UNICEF (2005). *Female Genital Mutilation/Female Genital Cutting: A Statistical Report*. New York: UNICEF; UNICEF (2005). *Changing a Harmful Social Convention: Female Genital Mutilation/Cutting*. Florence: UNICEF.

39 Vivante, B. (1999). 'Introduction'. In Vivante, B. (ed.). *Women's Roles in Ancient Civilizations: A Reference Guide*. Westport: Greenwood Press, xi–xvii.

40 Pages 194–195, Meyers, C. (2013). *Rediscovering Eve: Ancient Israelite Women in Context*. Oxford: Oxford University Press.

41 Miller, P. (2017). *Patriarchy*. London: Routledge.
42 Page 1, Keuls, E. C. (1985). *The Reign of the Phallus. Sexual Politics in Ancient Athens*. Berkeley: University of California Press.
43 Smith, N. D. (1983). 'Plato and Aristotle on the nature of women'. *Journal of the History of Philosophy* 21(4), 467–478.
44 Page 45, Connell, S. (2021). *Aristotle on Women: Physiology, Psychology, and Politics*. Cambridge: Cambridge University Press.
45 Engel, D. M. (2003). 'Women's role in the home and the state: Stoic theory reconsidered'. *Harvard Studies in Classical Philology* 101, 267–288.
46 Pomeroy (1995), x.
47 Garland, L. (1999). *Byzantine Empresses: Women and Power in Byzantium, AD 527–1204*. London: Routledge.
48 Hölkeskamp, K.-L. (2014). 'Under Roman roofs: Family, house, and household'. In Flower, H. I. (ed.). *The Cambridge Companion to the Roman Republic*. 2nd ed., pp. 101–126.
49 Matić, U. (2016). 'Gender in ancient Egypt: Norms, ambiguities, and sensualities'. *Near Eastern Archaeology* 79(3), 174–183; Robins, G. (1999). 'Women in ancient Egypt'. In Vivante, B. (ed.). *Women's Roles in Ancient Civilizations: A Reference Guide*. Westport: Greenwood Press, pp. 154–187.
50 Gruber, M. I. (1999). 'Women in the ancient Levant'. In Vivante, B. (ed.). *Women's Roles in Ancient Civilizations: A Reference Guide*. Westport: Greenwood Press, pp. 115–152; Nemet-Nejat, K. R. (1999). 'Women in ancient Mesopotamia'. In Vivante, B. (ed.). *Women's Roles in Ancient Civilizations: A Reference Guide*. Westport: Greenwood Press, pp. 85–114; Bryce, T. R. (2016). 'The role and status of women in Hittite society'. In Budin, S. L., and Turfa, J. M. (eds.). *Women in Antiquity: Real Women across the Ancient Mediterranean*. London: Routledge, pp. 303–318.
51 Hawkes, J. (1968). *Dawn of the Gods*. London: Chatto and Windus.
52 Aranda-Jiménez, G., Montón-Subías, S., and Jiménez-Brobeil, S. (2009). 'Conflicting evidence? Weapons and skeletons in the Bronze Age of south-east Iberia'. *Antiquity* 83, 1038–1051.
53 Vince, G. (2019). 'Smashing the patriarchy: Why there's nothing natural about male supremacy'. *The Guardian*. Available at www.theguardian.com/books/2019/nov/02/smashing-the-patriarchy-why-theres-nothing-natural-about-male-supremacy.
54 Criado Perez, C. (2019). *Invisible Women: Exposing Data Bias in a World Designed for Men*. London: Penguin.
55 Pomeroy (1995), 230.
56 Fee, E. (1973). 'The sexual politics of Victorian social anthropology'. *Feminist Studies* 1(3/4), 23–39.
57 Page 41, Eller, C. (2011). *Gentlemen and Amazons: The Myth of Patriarchal Prehistory, 1861–1900*. Berkeley: University of California Press.
58 Eller (2011), 45.
59 Eller (2011), 46.
60 Eller (2011), 43.
61 Eller (2011), 60.
62 Page 92, Hutton, R. (1997). 'The Neolithic great goddess: A study in modern tradition'. *Antiquity* 71, 91–99.
63 Page 172, Ihm, S. (2015). 'Robert Graves's The Greek Myths and matriarchy'. In Gibson, A. G. (ed.). *Robert Graves and the Classical Tradition*. Oxford: Oxford University Press, pp. 165–180.
64 Hutton (1997), 93.
65 Eller, C. (2012). 'Two knights and a goddess: Sir Arthur Evans, Sir James George Frazer, and the invention of Minoan religion'. *Journal of Mediterranean Archaeology* 25(1): 75–98.
66 Gere, K. (2009). *Knossos and the Prophets of Modernism*. Chicago: The University of Chicago Press; Papadopoulos, J. K. (2005). 'Inventing the Minoans: Archaeology, modernity and the quest for European identity'. *Journal of Mediterranean Archaeology* 18(1): 87–149.
67 Gessner, G. C. (2011). 'A brief overview of the Halaf tradition'. In Steadman, S. L., and McMahon, G. (eds.). *The Oxford Handbook of Ancient Anatolia*. Oxford: Oxford University Press, pp. 777–795.
68 Pages 79–81, Mallowan, M. E. L., and Cruikshank Rose, J. (1935). 'Excavations at Tall Arpachiyah, 1933'. *Iraq* 2(1), i–xv, 1–178.
69 Mallowan and Cruikshank (1935), 81.
70 Quoted in Motz (1997), 5.
71 Quoted in Hutton (1997), 96.
72 Ihm (2015), 165.
73 Ihm (2015), 180.
74 Hawkes (1968), 90.

75 Hawkes (1968), 161.
76 Hawkes (1968), 26.
77 Pages 415–416, Hodder, I. (2015). 'James Mellaart Legates 1925–2012'. *Biographical Memoirs of Fellows of the British Academy* 14, 411–420; Mellaart (1967), 24.
78 Chapman, J. (1998). 'The impact of modern invasions and migrations on archaeological explanation: A biographical sketch of Marija Gimbutas'. In Diaz-Andreu, M., and Stig Sørensen, M. L. (eds.). *Excavating Women: A History of Women in European Archaeology.* London: Routledge, pp. 295–314; Elster, E. S. (2007). 'Marija Gimbutas: Setting the agenda'. In Hamilton, S., Whitehouse, R. D., and Wright, K. L. (eds.). *Archaeology and Women: Ancient and Modern Issues.* London: Routledge, pp. 83–120.
79 Gimbutas (1991), 352.
80 Repsiene, R. (2009). 'In pursuit of the goddess: How one woman defied the odds to restore the feminist principle'. Kultros Barai. Available at www.eurozine.com/in-pursuit-of-the-goddess/?pdf.
81 Page 3, Gimbutas, M. (1999). *The Living Goddesses.* Berkeley: University of California Press (edited and supplemented by Miriam Robbins Dexter). Çatalhöyük: pp. 8–9, 238–239, 255–256, Malta: pp. 172–181, 262–267, Gimbutas, M. (1991). *The Civilization of the Goddess: The World of Old Europe.* San Francisco: Harper Collins.
82 Bugeja, L. (2016). 'The Maltese Temple Period's unique religious significance'. *Times of Malta.* Available at www.timesofmalta.com/articles/view/20160228/life-features/The-Maltese-Temple-Period-s-unique-religious-significance.604050.
83 Page 8, Foxhall, L. (2013). *Studying Gender in Classical Antiquity.* Cambridge: Cambridge University Press.
84 McLeod, G. (1991). *Virtue and Venom. Catalogs of Women from Antiquity to the Renaissance.* Ann Arbor: The University of Michigan Press.
85 Page 85, Stevenson, J. (1998). 'Women and classical education in the early modern period'. In Too, Y. L., and Livingstone, N. (eds.). *Pedagogy and Power: Rhetorics of Classical Learning, Ideas in Context.* Cambridge: Cambridge University Press, pp. 83–109.
86 Hurst, I. (2006). *Victorian Women Writers and the Classics: The Feminine of Homer.* Oxford: Oxford University Press.
87 Pages 8–10, Donaldson, J. (1907). *Woman: Her Position and Influence in Ancient Greece and Rome, and Among the Early Christians.* London: Longmans, Green and Co.
88 Pages 3–4, Carroll, M. (1907). *Greek Women: Volume 1.* Philadelphia: George Barrie and Sons.
89 Sturgeon, M. C. (1914). *Women of the Classics.* London: Harrap.
90 Page 2, McClees, H. (1920). *A Study of Women in Attic Inscriptions.* New York: Columbia University Press.
91 Page 187, McManus, B. (2017). *The Drunken Duchess of Vassar: Grace Harriet Macurdy, Pioneering Feminist Classical Scholar.* Columbus: Ohio State University Press.
92 Garrod, D. A., Buxton, L. H., Smith, G. E., Bate, D. M., Spiller, R. C., Hinton, M. A., and Fischer, P. (1928). 'Excavation of a Mousterian rock-shelter at Devil's Tower, Gibraltar'. *The Journal of the Royal Anthropological Institute of Great Britain and Ireland* 58, 33–113; McManus (2017).
93 LeGates, M. (2001). *In Their Time: A History of Feminism in Western Society.* London: Routledge.
94 Pomeroy, S. B. (1973). 'Selected bibliography on women in antiquity'. *Arethusa* 6(1), 127–157.
95 Foxhall (2013), 7.
96 Pomeroy, S. B. (1991). 'The study of women in antiquity: Past, present, and future'. *The American Journal of Philology* 112(2), 263–268.
97 Pomeroy, S. B. (ed.). (1991). *Women's History and Ancient History.* Chapel Hill: The University of North Carolina Press.
98 Katz, M. A. (2000). 'Sappho and her sisters: Women in ancient Greece'. *Signs* 25(2), 505–531.
99 Conkey, M. W., and Spector, J. D. (1984). 'Archaeology and the study of gender'. *Advances in Archaeological Method and Theory* 7, 1–38.
100 Andersson, J., Elfwendahl, M., and Gustafson, G. et al. (2011). 'Visible men and elusive women'. *International Journal of Historical Archaeology* 15, 10–29.
101 Gilchrist, R. (1991). 'Women's archaeology? Political feminism, gender theory and historical revision'. *Antiquity* 65 (248), 495–501.
102 Page 31, Wylie, A. (1991). 'Gender theory and the archaeological record: Why is there no archaeology of gender?' In Gero, J. M., and

Conkey, M. W. (eds.). *Engendering Archaeology: Women and Prehistory*. Oxford: Blackwell, pp. 31–54.

103 Gero, J. M., and Conkey, M. W. (eds.). (1991). *Engendering Archaeology: Women and Prehistory*. Oxford: Blackwell.

104 Hays-Gilpin, K., and Whitley, D. S. (eds.). (1998). *Reader in Gender Archaeology*. London: Routledge.

105 Conkey, M. W. (2003). 'Has feminism changed archaeology?' *Signs* 28(3), 867–880.

106 Gilchrist, R. (2009). 'The archaeology of sex and gender'. In Cunliffe, B., Gosden, C., and Joyce, R. (eds.). *The Oxford Handbook of Archaeology*. Oxford: Oxford University Press, pp. 1029–1047.

107 James, S. L., and Dillon, S. (eds.). (2012). *A Companion to Women in the Ancient World*. Chichester: Wiley-Blackwell; Budin, S. L., and Turfa, J. M. (eds.). (2016). *Women in Antiquity. Real Women Across the Ancient World*. New York: Routledge.

108 Smith, B. G. (ed.). (2008). *The Oxford Encyclopedia of Women in World History*. Four volumes. Oxford: Oxford University Press; Tulloch, J. (2015). *A Cultural History of Women in Antiquity*. London: Bloomsbury [Volume 1 of A Cultural History of Women].

109 Budin and Turfa (2016), 1.

110 Gill, D. W. (2002). '"The passion of hazard": Women at the British School at Athens before the First World War'. *The Annual of the British School at Athens* 97, 491–510.

111 Lorimer, H. L. (1950). *Homer and the Monuments*. London: Macmillan.

112 Brown, T. B. (1952). 'Review of *Homer and the Monuments*, by H. L. Lorimer'. *The Journal of Hellenic Studies* 72, 152; Mylonas, G. E. (1953). 'Review of *Homer and the Monuments*, by H. L. Lorimer'. *The Classical Journal* 49(3), 142–143; Robinson, D. M. (1955). 'Review of *Homer and the Monuments*, by H. L. Lorimer'. *The American Journal of Philology* 76(4), 440–444.

113 Allsebrook, M. and Allsebrook, A. (2002). *Born to Rebel: The Life of Harriet Boyd Hawes*. Oxford: Oxbow Books.

114 Smith, P. J. (2000). 'Dorothy Garrod, first woman professor at Cambridge'. *Antiquity* 74 (283), 131–136.

115 *The New York Times* (1972). 'Gisela Richter, art curator dies'. *The New York Times* (26 December 1972), 27; Paglia, C. (2002). 'Gisela Richter'. In Carnes, M. (ed.). *Invisible Giants: Fifty Americans Who Shaped the Nation But Missed the History Books*. New York: Oxford University Press, pp. 235–239.

116 Taylor, H. (n.d.). 'Six groundbreaking female archaeologists'. *English Heritage*. Available at www.english-heritage.org.uk/learn/histories/women-in-history/six-groundbreaking-female-archaeologists/.

117 Voss, B. (2021). 'Documenting cultures of harassment in archaeology: A review and analysis of quantitative and qualitative research studies'. *American Antiquity* 86(2), 244–260.

118 Mead, R. (2014). 'The troll slayer'. *The New Yorker*. Available at: www.newyorker.com/magazine/2014/09/01/troll-slayer; Sherwin, A. (2020). 'Historian Bettany Hughes on academic sexism and the "Harvey Weinsteins of the ancient world"'. INews. Available at https://inews.co.uk/essentials/historian-bettany-hughes-academic-sexism-harvey-weinsteins-ancient-world-98827.

119 Pollock (1991).

120 Glazebrook A., and Tsakirgis, B. (eds.). (2016). *Houses of Ill Repute: The Archaeology of Brothels, Houses, and Taverns in the Greek World*. Philadelphia: University of Pennsylvania Press; Glazebrook, A., and Henry, M. M. (eds.). (2011). *Greek Prostitutes in the Ancient Mediterranean, 800 BCE–200 CE*. Madison: University of Wisconsin Press.

121 Abulafia, D. (2011). *The Great Sea: A Human History of the Mediterranean*. Oxford: Oxford University Press; Broodbank, C. (2015). *The Making of the Middle Sea: A History of the Mediterranean from the Beginnings to the Emergence of the Classical World*. London: Thames and Hudson.

PART I

1 Garcia-Castellanos, D., Micallef, A., Estrada, F., et al. (2020). 'The Zanclean megaflood of the Mediterranean – Searching for independent evidence'. *Earth-Science Reviews* 201, 103061.

2 Carbonell, E.. and Pedro Rodríguez, X. (2006). 'The first human settlement of Mediterranean Europe'. *Comptes Rendus Palevol* 5(1–2), 291–298.

3 Arzarell, M., Marcolini, F., Pavia, G., et al. (2007). 'Evidence of earliest human occurrence in Europe: The site of Pirro Nord (Southern

Italy)'. *Naturwissenschaften* 94, 107–112; Sahnouni, M., and de Heinzelin, J. (1998). 'The site of Ain Hanech revisited: New investigations at this Lower Pleistocene site in Northern Algeria'. *Journal of Archaeological Science* 25, 1083–1101.

4 Page 148, Pettit, P. (2009). 'The rise of modern humans'. In Scarre, C. (ed.). *The Human Past: World Prehistory & the Development of Human Societies*. London: Thames and Hudson, pp. 124–173.

5 Benito, B. M., Svenning, J.-C., Kellberg-Nielsen, T., et al. (2017). 'The ecological niche and distribution of Neanderthals during the Last Interglacial'. *Journal of Biogeography* 44, 51–61.

6 Bergström, A., Stringer, C. and Hajdinjak, M., et al. (2021). 'Origins of modern human ancestry'. *Nature* 590, 229–237; Higham, T., Compton, T., and Stringer, C., et al. (2011). 'The earliest evidence for anatomically modern humans in northwestern Europe'. *Nature* 479, 521–524; Pettit (2009), 152.

7 Bar-Yosef, O. (2002). 'The Upper Palaeolithic revolution'. *Annual Review of Anthropology* 31, 363–393.

8 Scott, J. C. *Against the Grain; A Deep History of the Earliest States*. New Haven: Yale University Press.

9 Watkins, T. (2010). 'New light on Neolithic revolution in south-west Asia'. *Antiquity* 84, 621–634.

10 Watkins (2010), 624.

11 Fairbairn, A., Martinolli, D., Butler, A. and Hillman, G. (2007). 'Wild plant seed storage at Neolithic Çatalhöyük east, Turkey'. *Vegetation History and Archaeobotany* 16, 467–479.

12 Page 660, Robb, J. (2013). 'Material culture, landscapes of action, and emergent causation: A new model for the origins of the European Neolithic'. *Current Anthropology* 54(6), 657–683.

13 Broodbank (2013), 184–188.

14 Broodbank, C. (2006). 'The origins and early development of Mediterranean maritime activity'. *Journal of Mediterranean Archaeology* 19(2), 199–230.

15 Broodbank (2013), 212.

16 Page 69, Trump, D. H. (2002). *Malta: Prehistory and Temples*. Malta: Midsea Books.

17 Trump (2002), 238–241.

CHAPTER 1

1 Pages 12–19, Bahn, P. G. (2016). *Images of the Ice Age*. Oxford: Oxford University Press; Pages 18–27, David, B. (2017). *Cave Art*. London: Thames and Hudson.

2 Saura Ramos, P. A., Muz̄quiz Perez-Seoane, M., and Beltran Martinez, A. (1999). *The Cave of Altamira*. New York: Harry Abrams; Pages 114–115, Sandars, N. K. (1985). *Prehistoric Art in Europe*. 2nd ed. New Haven: Yale University Press.

3 García-Diez, M., Hoffmann, D. L., Zilhão, J., de las Heras, C., Lasheras, J. A., Montes, R., and Pike, A. W. (2013). 'Uranium series dating reveals a long sequence of rock art at Altamira Cave (Santillana del Mar, Cantabria)'. *Journal of Archaeological Science* 40(11), 4098–4106; Schwarcz, H. P. (1992). 'Uranium-series dating and the origin of modern man'. *Philosophical Transactions of the Royal Society of London B* 337, 131–137.

4 Bahn (2016), 269–270.

5 Von Petzinger, G. (2016). *The First Signs: Unlocking the Mysteries of the World's Oldest Symbols*. New York: Atria Books.

6 Bahn (2016), 270.

7 Bahn (2016), 69.

8 Fritz, C., Tosello, G., and Conkey, M. W. (2016). 'Reflections on the identities and roles of the artists in European Paleolithic societies'. *Journal of Archaeological Method and Theory* 23, 1307–1332.

9 Pages 85–86, Hays-Gilpin, K. A. (2004). *Ambiguous Images: Gender and Rock Art*. Walnut Creek: Altamira Press.

10 Pages 323–324, Van Gelder, L., and Sharpe, K. (2009). 'Women and girls as Upper Palaeolithic cave "artists": Deciphering the sexes of finger fluters in Rouffignac cave'. *Oxford Journal of Archaeology*, 28, 323–333.

11 Guthrie, R. D. (2005). *The Nature of Paleolithic Art*. Chicago: University of Chicago Press; Guthrie, R. D. quoted in Fickling, D. (2006). 'Cave paintings are graffiti by prehistoric boys'. *Independent*. Available at www.independent.co.uk/news/science/cave-paintings-are-graffiti-prehistoric-yobs-6108231.html.

12 Page 292, Dunbar, R. (2014). *Human Evolution*. London: Pelican.

13 National Geographic. 'Prehistory 101: Cave art'. Available at www.youtube.com/watch?v=ZjejoT1gFOc.

14 Gurven, M., and Hill, K. (2009). 'Why do men hunt? A reevaluation of "man the hunter" and the sexual division of labour'. *Current Anthropology* 50(1), 51–74.
15 Bahn (2016), 277.
16 Bahn (2016), 279–282.
17 Hays-Gilpin (2004), 98–99.
18 Hays-Gilpin (2004), 91.
19 Bahn (2016), 276.
20 Haas, R., Watson, J., Buonasera, T. et al. (2020). 'Female hunters of the early Americas'. *Science Advances* 6(45), eabd0310.
21 Collado Giraldo, H., García Arranz, J. J., Fatás, P. et al. (2018). 'Cueva de Altamira'. In Collado Giraldo, H. (ed.). *Handpas: Manos del Pasado. Catálogo de representaciones de manos en el arte rupestre paleolítico de la península ibérica.* Mérida: Junta de Extremadura, pp. 93–118; EFE. (2019). 'Three new prehistoric hand prints found inside Altamira cave in Spain'. *El Pais.* Available at https://english.elpais.com/elpais/2019/01/30/inenglish/1548850297_888022.html.
22 Pettitt, P., Arias, P., García-Diez, M., Hoffmann, D., Maximiano Castillejo, A., Ontañon-Peredo, R., Pike, A., and Zilhão, J. (2015). 'Are hand stencils in European cave art older than we think? An evaluation of the existing data and their potential implications'. In Bueno-Ramírez, P. and Bahn, P. G. (eds.). *Prehistoric Art as Prehistoric Culture Studies in Honour of Professor Rodrigo de Balbín-Behrmann.* Oxford: Archaeopress, pp. 31–43.
23 Clottes, J., Beltrán, A., Courtin, J., and Cosquer, H. (1992). 'The Cosquer Cave on Cape Morgiou, Marseilles'. *Antiquity* 66(252), 583–598.
24 Valladas, H., Quiles, A., Delque-Kolic, M. et al. (2017). 'Radiocarbon dating of the decorated Cosquer Cave (France)'. *Radiocarbon* 59(2), 621–633.
25 Valladas et al. (2017), 621.
26 Clottes, J., Courtin, J., Collina-Girard, J. et al. (1997). 'News from Cosquer Cave: Climatic studies, recording, sampling, dates'. *Antiquity* 71(272), 321–326.
27 Clottes et al. (1992), 586–587.
28 Sharpe, K., and Van Gelder, l. (2006). 'The study of finger flutings'. *Cambridge Archaeological Journal* 16(3), 281–295.
29 Bahn (2016), 189–190; Etxepare, R., and Irurtzun, A. (2021). 'Gravettian hand stencils as sign language formatives'. *Philosophical Transactions of the Royal Society B.* 376, 20200205.
30 Bahn (1998), 112.
31 Page 126, Bahn, P. G. (1998). *The Cambridge Illustrated History of Prehistoric Art.* Cambridge: Cambridge University Press; Bahn (2016), 192–194.
32 Bahn (1998), 126.
33 Walker, J. W., Clinnick, D. T., and Pedersen, J. B. (2018). 'Profiled hands in Palaeolithic art: The first universally recognized symbol of the human form'. *World Art* 8(1), 1–19.
34 Bahn (1998), 115.
35 Page 71, Morgan, D. (2012). *The Embodied Eye: Religious Visual Culture and the Social Life of Feeling.* Berkely: University of California Press.
36 Guthrie (2005), 124.
37 Manning, J. T. (2002). *Digit Ratio.* New Brunswick: Rutgers University Press. Cited in Snow, D. R. (2006). 'Sexual dimorphism in Upper Palaeolithic hand stencils'. *Antiquity* 80, 390–404.
38 Snow (2006).
39 Snow, D. R. (2013). 'Sexual dimorphism in European Upper Palaeolithic cave art.' *American Antiquity* 78(4), 746–761.
40 Sharpe, K. and Van Gelder, L. (2006). 'Evidence for cave marking by Palaeolithic children'. *Antiquity* 80, 937–947; Van Gelder and Sharpe (2009), 323–333.
41 Van Gelder and Sharpe (2009), 326.
42 Nelson, E., Hall, J., Randolph-Quinney, P., and Sinclair, A. (2017). 'Beyond size: The potential of a geometric morphometric analysis of shape and form for the assessment of sex in hand stencils in rock art'. *Journal of Archaeological Science* 78, 202–213.
43 Galeta, P., Bruzek, J., and Láznicková-Galetová, M. (2014). 'Is sex estimation from handprints in prehistoric cave art reliable? A view from biological and forensic anthropology'. *Journal of Archaeological Science* 45, 141–149.
44 Bahn (2016), 254.
45 Pettitt et al. (2015), 40.

CHAPTER 2

1 Page 118, Haddow, S. D., Milella, M., Tibbetts, B., et al. (2017). 'Human remains'. In Haddow, S. D. (ed.). *Çatalhöyük 2017 Archive Report.* 101–142. Available at www.catalhoyuk.com/archive_reports/2017.

2 Page 31, Ayala, G., Wainwright, J., Walker, J., et al. (2017). 'Palaeoenvironmental reconstruction of the alluvial landscape of Neolithic Çatalhöyük, central southern Turkey: The implications for early agriculture and responses to environmental change'. *Journal of Archaeological Science* 87, 30e43.

3 Mellaart, J. (1964). 'A Neolithic city in Turkey'. *Scientific American* 210(4), 94–105; Mellaart, J. (1967). *Çatal Hüyük: A Neolithic Town in Anatolia*. London: Thames and Hudson; Mellaart, J. (1975). *The Neolithic of the Near East*. London: Thames and Hudson.

4 Bayliss, A., Brock, F., Farid, S., et al. (2015). 'Getting to the bottom of it all: A Bayesian approach to dating the start of Çatalhöyük'. *Journal of World Prehistory* 28, 1–26; Cessford, C. (2001). 'A new dating sequence for Çatalhöyük'. *Antiquity* 75(290), 717–725.

5 Hodder, I., and Pels, P. (2010) 'History houses'. In Hodder, I. (ed.). *Religion in the Emergence of Civilization: Çatalhöyük as a Case Study*. Cambridge: Cambridge University Press, pp. 163–186.

6 Hodder and Pels (2010), 178.

7 In 2018, six years after Mellaart's death, it became apparent that he had in fact forged some of the art from Çatalhöyük, amongst other things. Wall paintings that appear only in sketches and not in photographs may not be genuine. Figurines, however, have been found in number in subsequent excavations. See: Jarus, O. (2018). 'Famed archaeologist "discovered" his own fakes at 9,000-year-old settlement'. LiveScience. Available at www.livescience.com/61989-famed-archaeologist-created-fakes.html.

8 Hodder, I., and Gürlek, N. (2020). 'Creativity and innovation in the geometric wall paintings at Çatalhöyük'. In Hodder, I. (ed.). *Consciousness, Creativity, and Self at the Dawn of Settled Life*. Cambridge: Cambridge University Press, pp. 190–206.

9 Plate 18b, Mellaart, J. (1963). 'Excavations at Çatal Hüyük, 1962: Second preliminary report'. *Anatolian Studies* 13, 43–103; Mellaart (1964), 102.

10 Page 367, Last, J. (1998). 'A design for life: Interpreting the art of Çatalhöyük'. *Journal of Material Culture* 3(3), 355–378.

11 Çamurcuoğlu, D. S. (2015). 'The wall paintings of Çatalhöyük (Turkey): Materials, technologies and artists'. Unpublished PhD thesis. University College London. Available at https://discovery.ucl.ac.uk/id/eprint/1471163/1/Camurcuoglu_compressed.pdf.%20COMPLETE.pdf.

12 Hodder and Gürlek (2020), 190.

13 Mellaart (1967), 77; (1975), 108–109.

14 Page 322, Relke, J. (2007). 'Interpreting the bucrania of Çatalhöyük: James Mellaart, Dorothy Cameron, and beyond'. *Anthrozoös* 20(4), 317–328.

15 Relke (2007), 324–327.

16 Adams, R. L. (2005). 'Ethnoarchaeology in Indonesia illuminating the ancient past at Çatalhöyük?' *American Antiquity* 70(1), 181–188.

17 Pages 172–174, Morris, E. F. (2007). 'On the ownership of the Saqqara mastabas and the allotment of political and ideological power at the dawn of the state'. In Hawass, Z. A., and Richards, J. (eds.). *The Archaeology and Art of Ancient Egypt: Essays in Honor of David B. O'Connor. Volume II*. Cairo: Conseil Supreme des Antiquites de l'Egypte, pp. 171–190; Page 12, Watson, P. (1987). *Egyptian Pyramids and Mastaba Tombs*. Aylesbury: Shire.

18 Mellaart (1963), 93, 95.

19 Mellaart (1963), 95.

20 Mellaart (1964), 100–101; (1967), 202.

21 Nakamura, C., and Meskell, L. (2013). 'The Çatalhöyük burial assemblage', In Hodder, I. (ed.), *Humans and Landscapes of Çatalhöyük: Reports from the 2000–2008 Seasons*. London: British Institute at Ankara, pp. 441–446.

22 Andrews, P., Molleson, T., and Boz, B. (2005). 'The human burials at Çatalhöyük'. In Hodder, I. (ed.). *Inhabiting Çatalhöyük: Reports from the 1995–1999 Seasons*. Cambridge: McDonald Institute for Archaeological Research/British Institute of Archaeology at Ankara Monograph, pp. 261–278; Boz, B., and Hager, L. D. (2013). 'Living above the dead: Intramural burial practices at Çatalhöyük'. In Hodder, I. (ed.). *Humans and Landscapes of Çatalhöyük.: Reports from the 2000–2008 Seasons*. London: British Institute at Ankara, pp. 413–440.

23 Page 50, Hodder, I., and Matthews, R. (1998). 'Çatalhöyük: The 1990s seasons'. In Matthews, R. (ed.). *Ancient Anatolia: Fifty Years' Work by the British Institute of Archaeology at Ankara*. Ankara: British Institute of Archaeology at Ankara, pp. 43–52.

24 Haddow, Milella, and Tibbetts (2017), 118.

25 Nakamura and Meskell (2009), 206.
26 Andrews, Molleson, and Boz (2005), 275.
27 Pilloud, M. A., Haddow, S. D., Knüsel, C. J., and Larsen, C. S. (2016). 'A bioarchaeological and forensic re-assessment of vulture defleshing and mortuary practices at Neolithic Çatalhöyük'. *Journal of Archaeological Science: Reports* 10, 735–743.
28 Pilloud et al. (2016), 740–741.
29 Pilloud et al. (2016), 737–738.
30 Page 380, Meskell, L. (2008). 'The nature of the beast: Curating animals and ancestors at Çatalhöyük'. *World Archaeology* 40(3), 373–389.
31 Page 81, Hodder, I. (2004). 'Women and men at Çatalhöyük'. *Scientific American* 290(1), 76–83; Andrews, Molleson, and Boz (2005), 267–273.
32 Mellaart (1967), 221, 223–224.
33 Hillson, S. W., Larsen, C. S., Boz, B., et al. (2013). 'The human remains I: Interpreting community structure, health and diet in Neolithic Çatalhöyük'. In Hodder, I. (ed.), *Humans and Landscapes of Çatalhöyük: Reports from the 2000–2008 Seasons*. London: British Institute at Ankara, pp. 339–396; Larsen, Hillson, Boz, et al. (2015).
34 Atalay, S. and Hastorf, C. A. (2006). 'Food, meals, and daily activities: Food habitus at Neolithic Çatalhöyük'. *American Antiquity* 71 (2), 283–319.
35 Hodder (2004), 82.
36 Page 62, Mellaart, J. (1962). 'Excavations at Çatal Hüyük: First preliminary report, 1961'. *Anatolian Studies* 12, 41–65.
37 An interesting discussion is Gurven, M., and Hill, K. (2009). 'Why do men hunt? A reevaluation of "Man the Hunter" and the sexual division of labor'. *Current Anthropology* 50(1), 51–74.
38 Atalay and Hastorf (2006), 305–310.
39 Mellaart (1967), 215.
40 Atalay and Hastorf (2006), 292.
41 Atalay and Hastorf (2006), 308.
42 Atalay and Hastorf (2006), 310.
43 Leacock, E. (1993). 'Women in Samoan history: A further critique of Derek Freeman.' In Miller, B. D. (ed.). *Sex and Gender Hierarchies*. Cambridge: Cambridge University Press, pp. 351–365.
44 Andrews, Molleson, and Boz (2005), 277.
45 Larsen, Hillson, Boz, et al. (2015), 44; Molleson, T. (1994). 'The eloquent bones of Abu Hureyra', *Scientific American* 271(2), 70–75.
46 Hodder (2004), 81.

CHAPTER 3

1 Malone, C., Cutajar, N., McLaughlin, T. R. et al. (2019). 'Island questions: the chronology of the Brochtorff Circle at Xagħra, Gozo, and its significance for the Neolithic sequence on Malta.' *Archaeological and Anthropological Sciences*. https://doi.org/10.1007/s12520-019-00790-y
2 Pages 238–240, Trump, D. H. (2004). *Malta: Prehistory and Temples*. Malta: Midsea Books.
3 Malone, C., Stoddart, S., Bonnano, A. and Trump, D. with Gouder, T. and Pace, A. (eds.). (2009). *Mortuary Customs in Prehistoric Malta: Excavations at the Brochtorff Circle at Xagħra (1987–1994)*. Cambridge: McDonald Institute for Archaeological Research; Trump (2004), 176–181.
4 Page 315, Stoddart, S., Barber, G., Duhig, C., Mann, G., O'Connell, T., Lai, L., Redhouse, D., Tykot, R. H. and Malone, C. (2009a). 'The human and animal bones.' In Malone, C., Stoddart, S., Bonnano, A., and Trump, D. with Gouder, T. and Pace, A. (eds.). *Mortuary Customs in Prehistoric Malta: Excavations at the Brochtorff Circle at Xagħra (1987–1994)*. Cambridge: McDonald Institute for Archaeological Research, pp. 315–340.
5 Malone et al. (2019).
6 Trump (2004), 179.
7 Stoddart et al. (2009a), 325; Page 145, Stoddart, S. Malone, C., Mason, S., Trump, B. and Trump, T. (2009b). 'The Tarxien phase levels: Spatial and stratigraphic analysis and reconstruction.' In Malone, C., Stoddart, S., Bonnano, A., and Trump, D. with Gouder, T. and Pace, A. (eds.). *Mortuary Customs in Prehistoric Malta: Excavations at the Brochtorff Circle at Xagħra (1987–1994)*. Cambridge: McDonald Institute for Archaeological Research, pp. 109–205.
8 Stoddart et al. (2009a), 325.
9 Pages 78–79, Schwartz, J. H. (1997). *What the Bones Tell Us*. Tucson: The University of Arizona Press.
10 Molnar, P. (2011). 'Extramasticatory dental wear reflecting habitual behavior and health in past populations.' *Clinical Oral Investigations* 15(5), 681–689.
11 Malone, C. Bonanno, A., Trump, D., Dixon, J., Leighton, R., Pedley, M., Stoddart, S. and Schembri, P. J. (2009). 'Material culture.' In Malone, C., Stoddart, S., Bonnano, A. and Trump, D. with Gouder, T. and Pace,

A. (eds.). *Mortuary Customs in Prehistoric Malta: Excavations at the Brochtorff Circle at Xagħra (1987–1994).* Cambridge: McDonald Institute for Archaeological Research, pp. 219–313.

12 Stoddart et al. (2009b), 145.

13 Roebroeks, W., Sier, M. J., Nielsen, T. K., De Loecker, D., Parés, J. M., Arps, C. E. and Mücher, H. J. (2012). 'Use of red ochre by early Neandertals.' *Proceedings of the National Academy of Sciences* 109(6), 1889–1894.

14 Wreschner, E. E. (1980). 'Red ochre and human evolution: A case for discussion.' *Current Anthropology* 21(5), 631–644.

15 Roebroeks et al. (2012), 1889.

16 Richards, M. P., Hedges, R. E., Walton, I., Stoddart, S. and Malone, C. (2001). 'Neolithic diet at the Brochtorff Circle, Malta.' *European Journal of Archaeology* 4(2): 253–262; Stoddart et al. (2009a), 335–340.

17 Pages 28–29, Sagona, C. (2015). *The Archaeology of Malta: From the Neolithic through the Roman Period.* Cambridge: Cambridge University Press.

18 Richards et al. (2001); Stoddart et al. (2009a).

19 Barratt, R., Malone, C., McLaughlin, R., and Stoddart, S. (2018). 'Celebrations in prehistoric Malta.' *World Archaeology* 50(2), 271–284; Stoddart, S., Bonnano, A., Gouder, T., Malone, C. and Trump, D. (1993). 'Cult in an island society: Prehistoric Malta in the Tarxien period.' *Cambridge Archaeological Journal* 3(1), 3–19.

20 Barratt et al. (2018), 276.

21 Barratt et al. (2018), 277.

22 Barratt et al. (2018), 279.

23 Gregory, I. V. and Cilia, D. (2005). *The Human Form in Neolithic Malta.* Malta: Midsea Books.

24 Gregory and Cilia (2005), 9.

25 Gregory and Cilia (2005), 118–121; Trump (2004), 95–97.

26 Trump (2004), 94.

27 Stoddart et al. (1993), 10; Malone et al. (2009), 289–298.

28 Gregory and Cilia (2005), 56.

29 Malone, C. Bonanno, A., Trump, D. et al. (2009), 283–284.

30 Trump (2004), 103.

31 Barratt et al. (2018), 278.

PART II

1 Bard, K. A. (2015). *An Introduction to the Archaeology of Ancient Egypt.* Chichester: Wiley-Blackwell; Shaw, I. (ed.). (2000). *The Oxford History of Ancient Egypt.* Oxford: Oxford University Press; Wilkinson, T. (2010). *The Rise and Fall of Ancient Egypt: The History of a Civilisation from 3000 BC to Cleopatra.* London: Bloomsbury.

2 Bard, K. A. (2000). 'The emergence of the Egyptian state (c. 3200–2686 BC)'. In Shaw, I. (ed.). *The Oxford History of Ancient Egypt.* Oxford: Oxford University Press, pp. 57–82.

3 Liverani, M. (2014). *The Ancient Near East: History, Society and Economy.* Abingdon: Routledge; Van De Mieroop, M. (2008). *A History of the Ancient Near East, ca. 3000–323 BC.* 2nd ed. Oxford: Blackwell.

4 Callender, G. (2000). 'The Middle Kingdom renaissance (c. 2055–1650 BC)'. In Shaw, I. (ed.). *The Oxford History of Ancient Egypt.* Oxford: Oxford University Press, pp. 137–171.

5 Goren, Y., Bunimovitz, S., Finkelstein, I., and Na'Aman, N. (2003). 'The location of Alashiya: New evidence from petrographic investigation of Alashiyan tablets from El-Amarna and Ugarit'. *American Journal of Archaeology* 107(2), 233–255.

6 Fisher, K. D., Manning, S. W., and Urban, T. M. (2019). 'New approaches to Late Bronze Age urban landscapes on Cyprus: Investigations at Kalavasos-*Ayios Dhimitrios*, 2012–2016'. *American Journal of Archaeology* 123 (3), 473–507.

7 Bryce, T. (2005). *The Kingdom of the Hittites.* New ed. Oxford: Oxford University Press; Macqueen, J. G. (1986). *The Hittites and Their Contemporaries in Asia Minor.* Revised and enlarged ed. London: Thames and Hudson.

8 Fitton, J. L. (2002). *Minoans.* London: The British Museum Press; Watrous, L. V. (2021). *Minoan Crete: An Introduction.* Cambridge: Cambridge University Press.

9 Pages 118–120, Manning, S. W. (2008). 'Protopalatial Crete. Formation of the palaces'. In Shelmerdine, C. W. (ed.). *The Cambridge Companion to the Aegean Bronze Age.* Cambridge: Cambridge University Press, pp. 105–120.

10 Kelder J. M., Cole S. E., and Cline E. H. (2018). 'Memphis, Minos and Mycenae: Bronze Age contact between Egypt and the Aegean'. In Spier J., Potts T., and Cole S. (eds.). *Beyond the Nile: Egypt and the Classical World.* Los Angeles: Getty, pp. 9–17.

11 Chadwick, J. (1976). *The Mycenaean World.* Cambridge: Cambridge University Press;

Schofield, L. (2007). *The Mycenaeans*. London: The British Museum Press; Taylour, W. (1983). *The Mycenaeans*. Revised and enlarged ed. London: Thames and Hudson.

12 www.griffinwarrior.org/griffin-warrior-tomb/.

13 Aranda Jiménez, G., Montón-Subías, S., and Sánchez Romero, M. (2015). *The Archaeology of Bronze Age Iberia: Argaric Societies*. Abingdon: Routledge; Lull, V., Micó, R., Rihuete Herrada, C., and Risch, R. (2013). 'Bronze Age Iberia'. In Fokkens, H., and Harding, A. (eds.). *The Oxford Handbook of the European Bronze Age*. Oxford: Oxford University Press, pp. 594–616.

14 Lull, V., Micó, R., Rihuete Herrada, C., and Risch, R. (2013). 'Political collapse and social change at the end of El Argar'. In Meller, H., Bertemes, F., Bork, H.-R., and Risch, R. (eds.). *1600 – Cultural Change in the Shadow of the Thera-Eruption?* Halle: Landesmuseum für Vorgeschichte, pp. 283–302.

15 Cline, E. H. (2021). *1177 BC: The Year Civilization Collapsed*. Revised and updated. Princeton: Princeton University Press.

CHAPTER 4

1 Wilkinson, T. (2020). *A World Beneath the Sands: Adventurers and Archaeologists in the Golden Age of Egyptology*. London: Picador.

2 Millet, N. B. (1990). 'The Narmer macehead and related objects'. *Journal of the American Research Center in Egypt* 27, 53–59.

3 Pages 96–103, van Wetering, J. (2012). 'Relocating De Morgan's Royal Tomb at Naqada and identifying its occupant'. In Kabaciński, J., Chłodnicki, M., and Kobusiewicz, M. (eds.). *Prehistory of Northeastern Africa New Ideas and Discoveries*. Poznań: Archaeological Museum in Poznań, pp. 91–124.

4 Pages 24–26, Wilkinson T. A. (2000). 'What a king is this: Narmer and the concept of the ruler'. *The Journal of Egyptian Archaeology* 86 (1), 23–32.

5 Pages 26–27, Tyldesley, J. (2006). *Chronicle of the Queens of Ancient Egypt: From Early Dynastic Times to the Death of Cleopatra*. London: Thames and Hudson; Page 193, Tyldesley, J. (1994). *Daughters of Isis: Women of Ancient Egypt*. London: Penguin.

6 Pages 50–51, Bárta, M. (2011). *Journey to the West: The World of the Old Kingdom Tombs in Ancient Egypt*. Prague: Charles University Faculty of Arts; pages 153, 171–172, Snape, S. (2014). *The Complete Cities of Ancient Egypt*. London: Thames and Hudson.

7 Tyldesley (2006), 28–29; van Wetering (2012).

8 Bárta (2011), 54.

9 Bárta (2011), 63; Savage, S. H. (2001). 'Some recent trends in the archaeology of Predynastic Egypt'. *Journal of Archaeological Research* 9(2), 101–155.

10 Tyldesley (2006), 33–34.

11 Page 2, Petrie, W. M. F. (1900). *The Royal Tombs of the First Dynasty*. London: Egypt Exploration Society. Reprinted by Cambridge University Press, 2013.

12 Petrie (1900), 10–11.

13 Petrie (1900), 35–36.

14 '1st Dynasty Tomb is Found in Egypt'. *New York Times* 22 November 1946, p. 12.

15 Pages 128–138, Emery, W. B. (1954). *The Great Tombs of the First Dynasty*. Vol 2. London: Egypt Exploration Society.

16 Tyldesley (2006), 33–34.

17 Tyldesley (1994), 215.

18 Page 97, Kelly, S. (2019). 'Women's work in the Early Dynastic Period'. *Prague Egyptological Studies* 23, 92–105.

19 Emery (1954), 1.

20 Emery (1954), 4.

21 O'Connor, D. (1991). 'Boat graves and pyramid origins: New discoveries at Abydos, Egypt'. *Expedition* 33(3), 5–15; Page 182, Shaw, I. (2004). *Ancient Egypt: A Very Short Introduction*. Oxford: Oxford University Press.

22 Bard, K. A. (2017). 'Political economies of Predynastic Egypt and the formation of the early state'. *Journal of Archaeological Research* 25, 1–36.

23 Snape (2014), 153.

24 Emery (1954), 3.

25 Page 23, Kemp, B. J. (1967). 'The Egyptian 1st Dynasty royal cemetery'. *Antiquity* 41, 22–32.

26 Tyldesley (1994), 215.

27 Kemp (1967).

28 Page 46, Bestock, L. (2008). 'The Early Dynastic funerary enclosures of Abydos'. *Arche'o-Nil* 18, 42–59.

29 Snape (2011), 14.

30 Kemp (1967), 25.

31 Kemp (1967), 31–32.

32 O'Connor (1991).

33 O'Connor (1991), 10.

34 O'Connor, D. (2009). *Abydos: Egypt's First Pharaohs and the Cult of Osiris*. London: Thames and Hudson; Page 14, Snape, S. (2011). *Ancient Egyptian Tombs: The Culture of Life and Death*. Chichester: Wiley-Blackwell.

35 Morris, E. F. (2007). 'On the ownership of the Saqqara mastabas and the allotment of political and ideological power at the dawn of the state'. In Hawass, Z. A., and Richards, J. (eds.). *The Archaeology and Art of Ancient Egypt: Essays in Honor of David B. O'Connor. Volume II*. Cairo: Conseil Suprême des Antiquités de l'Égypte, pp. 171–190.

CHAPTER 5

1 Rider, K. V., and Swallow, A. (2016). 'Arranged marriage'. In Shehan, C. L. (ed.). *Encyclopedia of Family Studies*. Chichester: Wiley-Blackwell. Available at doi.org/10.1002/9781119085621.wbefs545.

2 Pande, R. (2014). 'Geographies of marriage and migration: Arranged marriages and South Asians in Britain'. *Geography Compass* 8, 75–86.

3 Watkins, J. (2017). *After Lavinia*. Ithaca: Cornell University Press.

4 Thomas, C. N. (2019). 'Gender and politics at Ugarit: The undoing of the daughter of the great lady'. *Journal of the American Oriental Society* 139(2), 287–305.

5 Schulman, A. (1979). 'Diplomatic marriage in the Egyptian New Kingdom'. *Journal of Near Eastern Studies,* 38(3), 177–193.

6 Pardee, D., and Glass, J. T. (1984). 'Literary sources for the history of Palestine and Syria: The Mari archives'. *The Biblical Archaeologist* 47 (2), 88–99; Sasson, J. M. (2015). *From the Mari Archives: An Anthology of Old Babylonian Letters*. Winona Lake: Pennsylvania State University Press.

7 Sasson, J. M. (1984). 'Zimri-Lim takes the Grand Tour'. *The Biblical Archaeologist* 47(4), 246–251.

8 Page 9, Batto, B. F. (1974). *Studies on Women at Mari*. Baltimore: Johns Hopkins University Press; Page 224, Melville, S. C. (2005). 'Royal women and the exercise of power in the ancient Near East'. In Snell, D. C. (ed.). *A Companion to the Ancient Near East*. Oxford: Blackwell, pp. 219–228.

9 Page 23, Stol, M. (2016). *Women in the Ancient Near East*. Boston: De Gruyter.

10 Stol (2016), 26.

11 Sabloff (2019), 61.

12 Page 456, Sasson, J. M. (1998). 'The king and I: A Mari king in changing perceptions'. *Journal of the American Oriental Society* 118(4), 453–470.

13 Page 70, Gates, M.-H. (1984). 'The palace of Zimri-Lim at Mari'. *The Biblical Archaeologist* 47 (2), 70–87.

14 Page 113, Margueron, J.-C. (2014). *Mari: Capital of Northern Mesopotamia in the Third Millennium. The Archaeology of Tell Hariri on the Euphrates*. Oxford: Oxbow.

15 Abram, M. (2011). 'A new look at the Mesopotamian rod and ring: Emblems of time and eternity'. *Studia Antiqua* 10(1), 15–36; Pages 104–112, Luciani, M. (2010). 'More than just landscapes of pleasure. The garden frame in the "Investiture" wall painting at Mari'. *Wiener Zeitschrift für die Kunde des Morgenlandes* 100, 99–118.

16 Stol (2016), 11. Also see: Bartash, V. (2015). 'Children in institutional households of Late Uruk Period Mesopotamia'. *Zeitschrift für Assyriologie und vorderasiatische Archäologie* 105 (2), 131–138; Joannès, F. (1997). 'La mention des enfants dans les textes néo-babyloniens: Enfance et éducation dans le Proche-Orient ancien'. *Ktèma* 22, 119–133.

17 Sasson (2015), 111–112.

18 Sasson (2015), 111 n. 223.

19 Sasson (2015), 113.

20 Sabloff, P. L. (2019). 'The political agency of royal women: A comparative analysis of eight premodern states according to societal rules and roles'. *Journal of Archaeological Research* 28, 53–97.

21 Sasson (2015), 115.

22 Sasson (2015), 114.

23 Sasson (2015), 113.

24 Sasson (2015), 115.

CHAPTER 6

1 Though: Chapman, R. (1990). *Emerging Complexity: The Later Prehistory of South-East Spain, Iberia and the West Mediterranean*. Cambridge: Cambridge University Press; and more recently Aranda Jiménez, G., Montón-Subías, S., and Sánchez Romero, M. (2015). *The Archaeology of Bronze Age Iberia: Argaric Societies*. Abingdon: Routledge and CWA. (2015). 'Rise and fall of the Argar'. *Current World Archaeology* 69, 16–22.

2 Gonzalo Ruis Zapatero in his foreword to Aranda Jiménez, Montón-Subías, and Sánchez Romero (2015), xiii.
3 Lull, V., Micó, R., Rihuete Herrada, C., and Risch, R. (2013). 'Political collapse and social change at the end of El Argar'. In Meller, H., Bertemes, F., Bork, H.-R., and Risch, R. (eds.). *1600 – Cultural change in the shadow of the Thera-Eruption?* Halle: Landesmuseum für Vorgeschichte, pp. 283–302.
4 Lull, V., Rihuete Herrada, C., Risch, R., et al. (2021). 'Emblems and spaces of power during the Argaric Bronze Age at La Almoloya, Murcia'. *Antiquity* doi.org/10.15184/aqy.2021.8.
5 Ng, K. (2021). 'Women may have ruled in bronze-age Spain, burial site suggests'. *The Independent* Available at www.independent.co.uk/news/science/archaeology/bronze-age-spain-women-rulers-archaeology-b1815736.html; *The New York Times* (2021). 'She was buried with a silver crown. Was she the one who held power? *The New York Times*. Available at www.nytimes.com/2021/03/11/science/bronze-age-tomb-women.html?surface=home-discovery-vi-prg&fellback=false&req_id=497380181&algo=identity&variant=no-exp&imp_id=300914443; Metcalfe, T. (2021). 'Ancient woman may have been powerful European leader, 4,000-year-old treasure suggests'. *National Geographic*. Available at www.nationalgeographic.com/history/article/ancient-woman-powerful-european-leader-4000-year-old-treasure-suggests.
6 CWA (2015). 'Rise and fall of the Argar'. *Current World Archaeology* 69, 16–22.
7 Lull et al. (2021).
8 Lull et al. (2021), 12.
9 Lull et al. (2021), 15–17.
10 Lull et al. (2021), 15.
11 Siret, H., and Siret, L. (1887). *Les Premiers âges du métal dans le Sud-Est de l'Espagne*. Louvain: Anvers.
12 Lull et al. (2013), 294–295; (2021), 3.
13 Aranda Jiménez, Montón-Subías, and Sánchez Romero (2015), 125, 156–158.
14 Quoted in Lull et al. (2021), 3.
15 Lull et al. (2021), 2.
16 Aranda Jiménez, G., Montón-Subías, S., and Sánchez Romero, M. (2015). *The Archaeology of Bronze Age Iberia: Argaric Societies*. Abingdon: Routledge; Lull, V., Micó, R., Rihuete Herrada, C., and Risch, R. (2013). 'Bronze Age Iberia.' In Fokkens, H., and Harding, A. (eds.). *The Oxford Handbook of the European Bronze Age*. Oxford: Oxford University Press, pp. 594–616; Siret and Siret (1887).
17 Lull et al. (2013), 285.
18 Pages 205–206, Chapman, R. (2008). 'Producing inequalities: Regional sequences in later prehistoric southern Spain'. *Journal of World Prehistory* 21, 195–260.
19 Lull, V., Micó, R., Rihuete Herrada, C., and Risch, R. (2014). 'The La Bastida fortification: new light and new questions on Early Bronze Age societies in the western Mediterranean'. *Antiquity* 88, 395–410; https://murciatoday.com/history-rewritten-4200-year-old-bronze-age-fortress-unveiled-at-la-bastida-totana_13379-a.html.
20 Lull et al. (2014), 399.
21 Lull et al. (2013), 602.
22 Cited in Aranda Jiménez, Montón-Subías, and Sánchez Romero (2015), 152.
23 Cited in Aranda Jiménez, Montón-Subías, and Sánchez Romero (2015), 153–154.
24 Aranda Jiménez, Montón-Subías, and Sánchez Romero (2015), 125–126.
25 Lull et al. (2021), 7; Delgado-Raack, S., Lull, V., Micó, R., Rihuete Herrada, C., and Risch, R. (2016). 'The silversmith's workshop of Tira del Lienzo (Totona, Murcia) in the context of Iberian Bronze Age metallurgy'. *Archaeometry* 58(5), 779–795.
26 Bartelheim, M., Contreras Cortés, F., Moreno Onorato, A., Murillo-Barroso, M., and Pernicka, E. (2012). 'The silver of the south Iberian El Argar culture: A first look at production and distribution'. *Trabajos de Prehistoria* 69 (2), 293–309.
27 Chapman (1990), chapter 2.
28 Lull et al. (2021), 17.
29 www.isleofman.com/parliament/the-sword-of-state/.

CHAPTER 7

1 Cain, C. D. (2001). 'Dancing in the dark: Deconstructing a narrative of epiphany on the Isopata ring'. *American Journal of Archaeology* 105 (1): 27–49; Rehak, P. (2000). 'The Isopata ring and the question of narrative in neopalatial glyptic'. In Müller, W. (ed.). *Minoisch-mykenische Glyptik: Stil, Ikonographie, Funktion*. Berlin: Mann, pp. 269–276.

2 Page 579, Younger, J. (2016). 'Minoan women'. In Budin, S. L., and Turfa, J. M. (eds.). *Women in Antiquity: Real Women Across the Ancient World*. London: Routledge, pp. 573–594.

3 Page 57, Evans, A. (1900/1901). 'The palace of Knossos'. *Annual of the British School at Athens* 7, 1–120; Pottier quoted on page 37 of Momigliano, N. (2013). 'Modern dance and the seduction of Minoan Crete'. In Morcilo, M. G., and Knippschild, S. (eds.). *Imagines II. Seduction and Power: Antiquity in the Visual and Performing Arts*. London: Bloomsbury Academic, pp. 35–55.

4 Papadopoulos, J. K. (2005). 'Inventing the Minoans: Archaeology, modernity and the quest for European identity'. *Journal of Mediterranean Archaeology* 18(1), 87–149.

5 Sakellarakis, Y., and Sapouna-Sakellaraki, E. (1981). 'Drama of death in a Minoan temple'. *National Geographic* 169, 204–222.

6 I rely on the excavators' precise descriptions and vivid interpretations in Sakellarakis, J., and Sakellarakis, E. (1991). *Archanes*. Athens: Ekdotike Athenon S. A., pp. 137–156. This edition is also very well illustrated and contains graphic reconstructions of the Anemospilia temple and the drama that unfolded there.

7 Shaw, J. W. (1978). 'Evidence for the Minoan tripartite shrine'. *American Journal of Archaeology* 82(4), 429–448.

8 Illustrated in Sakellarakis and Sakellarakis (1991), 144–145.

9 Shaw (1978), 441.

10 Page 563, Prag, J. (2016). 'From the Caves of the Winds to Mycenae rich in gold: The faces of Minoan and Mycenaean women'. In Budin, S. L., and Turfa, J. M. (eds.). *Women in Antiquity: Real Women Across the Ancient World*. London: Routledge, pp. 561–572.

11 Pages 97–100, Musgrave, J. H., Neave, R. A., Prag, A. J., Sakellarakis, E., and Sakellarakis, J. A. (1994). 'The priest and priestess from Archanes-Anemospilia: Reconstructing Minoan faces'. *Annual of the British School at Athens* 89, 89–100.

12 Younger (2016), 586.

13 NHS (2019). 'Thalassemia'. NHS. Available at www.nhs.uk/conditions/thalassaemia/.

14 Younger (2016), 579.

15 Musgrave et al. (1994); Prag (2016).

16 Prag (2016), 565.

17 Page 92, Eller, C. (2012). 'Two knights and a goddess: Sir Arthur Evans, Sir James George Frazer, and the invention of Minoan religion'. *Journal of Mediterranean Archaeology* 25(1), 75–98.

18 Pages 89–90, Gere, C. (2009). *Knossos and the Prophets of Modernism*. Chicago: The University of Chicago Press.

19 Quoted in Papadopoulos (2005), 122.

20 Hawkes, J. (1968). *Dawn of the Gods*. London: Chatto and Windus; Thomas, C. (1973). 'Matriarchy in early Greece: The Bronze and Dark ages'. *Arethusa* 6(2), 173–195.

21 Younger (2006), 587.

CHAPTER 8

1 Pages 230–231, Bryan, B. M. (2000). 'The Eighteenth Dynasty before the Amarna Period'. In Shaw, I. (ed.). *The Oxford History of Ancient Egypt*. Oxford: Oxford University Press, pp. 218–271. Page 92, Tyldesley, J. (2006). *Chronicle of the Queens of Egypt: From Early Dynastic Times to the Death of Cleopatra*. London: Thames and Hudson.

2 Quoted in Tyldesley (2006), 95.

3 Bryan (2000), 237.

4 The translations in this chapter are from Breasted, J. H. (1906). *Ancient Records of Egypt. Volume II*. Chicago: The University of Chicago Press, unless otherwise stated.

5 Tyldesley (2006), 95–96; Tyldesley, J. (1996). *Hatchepsut: The Female Pharaoh*. London: Penguin.

6 Tyldesley (1996), 97.

7 Bryan (2000), 237.

8 Tyldesley (1996), 177–209.

9 Phillips, J. (1997). 'Punt and Aksum: Egypt and the Horn of Africa'. *The Journal of African History* 38(3), 423–457.

10 Bryan (2000), 242; Shaw (2003), 142.

11 Tyldesley (2006), 100.

12 Wilkinson (2000), 175–176

13 Wicker, F. D. (1998). 'The road to Punt'. *The Geographical Journal* 164(2), 155–167; Wilkinson (2000), 177.

14 Bard, K. A., and Fattovich, R. (2011). 'The Middle Kingdom Red Sea harbour at Mersa/Wadi Gawasis'. *Journal of the American Research Center in Egypt* 47, 105–129; Phillips (1997), 427, 429; Shaw (2003), 141; Ward, C., and Zazzaro, C. (2010). 'Evidence for pharaonic seagoing ships at Mersa/Wadi Gawasis, Egypt'. *The International Journal of Nautical Archaeology* 39(1), 27–43.

15 Shaw (2003), 142–143.

16 I draw on Arnold, D. (2005). 'The temple of Hatshepsut at Deir el-Bahri'. In Roehrig, C. H. (ed.). *Hatshepsut: From Queen to Pharaoh*. New York: The Metropolitan Museum of Art, pp. 135–140; Pages 136–149, Shaw, I. (2003). *Exploring Ancient Egypt*. Oxford: Oxford University Press; pages 175–178, Wilkinson, R. H. (2000). *The Complete Temples of Ancient Egypt*. London: Thames and Hudson.
17 Arnold (2005), 135–136.
18 Bryan (2000), 242.
19 Tyldesley (2006), 99.
20 Bryan (2000), 239.
21 Bietak, M. (2005). 'Egypt and the Aegean: Cultural convergence in a Thutmoside palace at Avaris'. In Roehrig, C. H. (ed.). *Hatshepsut: From Queen to Pharaoh*. New York: The Metropolitan Museum of Art, pp. 75–81.
22 Bietak (2005), 80.
23 Tyldesley (2006), 99.
24 Tyldesley (2006), 106.
25 Tyldesley (2006), 107–109.

CHAPTER 9

1 Bryce, T. (2005). *The Kingdom of the Hittites*. 2nd ed. Oxford: Oxford University Press; Collins, B. J. (2007). *The Hittites and Their World*. Atlanta: Society of Biblical Literature.
2 Collins (2007), 37.
3 Seeher, J. (2011). *Hattusha Guide: A Day in the Hittite Capital*. Rev. ed. Istanbul: Ege Yayinlari.
4 Bryce (2005), 230–233.
5 Bryce (2005), 239.
6 Beckman, G. (2012). 'Hattusili III'. In Bagnall, R. S., Brodersen, K., Champion, C. B., Erskine, A., and Huebner, S. (eds.). *The Encyclopedia of Ancient History*. Oxford: Wiley-Blackwell. DOI: 10.1002/9781444338386.wbeah24096.
7 Bryce, T. (2014). 'Hittites and Anatolian ethnic diversity'. In McInerney, J. (ed.). *A Companion to Ethnicity in the Ancient Mediterranean*. Oxford: Wiley-Blackwell, pp. 127–141; von Dassow, E. (2013). 'Hurrian, Hurrians'. In Bagnall, R. S., Brodersen, K., Champion, C. B., Erskine, A., and Huebner, S. R. (eds.). *The Encyclopedia of Ancient History*. Oxford: Wiley-Blackwell, pp. 3345–3347.
8 Miller, J. L. (2013). 'Kizzuwatna'. In Bagnall, R. S., Brodersen, K., Champion, C. B., Erskine, A., and Huebner, S. (eds.). *The Encyclopedia of Ancient History*. Oxford: Wiley-Blackwell. DOI: 10.1002/9781444338386.wbeah24120.
9 Bryce (2005), 55–56, 175–178.
10 Collins (2007), 32.
11 Pages 134–135, Bryce, T. (2002). *Life and Society in the Hittite World*. Oxford: Oxford University Press.
12 Bryce (2005), 250–251.
13 Bryce (2002), 150; Hoffner, H. (1987). 'Ancient views of prophecy and fulfilment: Mesopotamia and Asia Minor'. *Journal of the Evangelical Theological Society* 30(3), 257–265.
14 Bryce (2005), 232.
15 Bryce (2005), 252–253; Collins (2007), 56–59.
16 Pages 97–105, Singer, I. (2002). *Hittite Prayers*. Atlanta: Society of Biblical Literature.
17 Beckman (2012).
18 Bryce, T. (2006). 'The "Eternal Treaty" from the Hittite perspective'. *BMSAES* 6: 1–11. Available at www.thebritishmuseum.ac.uk/bmsaes/issue6/bryce.html.
19 Page 174, Breasted, J. H. (1906). *Ancient Records of Egypt. Volume III: The Nineteenth Dynasty*. Chicago: The University of Chicago Press.
20 Bryce (2005), 286.
21 Pages 125–129, Beckman, G. M. and Hoffman, H. A. (1996). *Hittite Diplomatic Texts*. Atlanta: Scholars Press.
22 Pages 307–308, Bryce, T. (2016). 'The role and status of women in Hittite society'. In Budin, S. L., and Turfa, J. M. (eds.). *Women in Antiquity: Real Women across the Ancient World*. London: Routledge, pp. 303–318
23 Page 159, Tyldesley, J. (2006). *Chronicle of the Queens of Egypt: From Early Dynastic Times to the Death of Cleopatra*. London: Thames and Hudson.
24 Tyldesley (2006), 146.
25 Beckman and Hoffman (1996), 123.
26 Bryce (2005), 289; Page 123, Canby, J. V. (1989). 'Hittite Art'. *Biblical Archaeologist* 52(2/3): 109–129.
27 Silver, C. (2010). 'From priestess to princess'. *Archaeology*. Available at https://archive.archaeology.org/online/features/iron_ladies/puduhepa.html.
28 Bryce (2005), 288.
29 Bryce (2005), 288.
30 Bryce (2002), 137.
31 Singer (2002), 102.
32 Miller (2013); and Miller, J. L. (2012). 'Puduheba'. In Bagnall, R. S., Brodersen, K., Champion, C. B., and Erskine, A. (eds.). *The*

Encyclopedia of Ancient History. DOI: 10.1002/9781444338386.wbeah24168.

33 Silver (2010).
34 Bryce (2005), 286–287.
35 Bryce (2016), 306.
36 Silver (2010).
37 Bryce (2005), 289; (2016), 306.
38 Bryce (2016), 304–305.
39 Page 593, Beal, R. H. (2011). 'Hittite Anatolia: A political history'. In Steadman, S. R., and McMahon, G. (eds.). *The Oxford Handbook of Ancient Anatolia.* Oxford: Oxford University Press, pp. 579–603; Silver (2010);Bryce (2016), 306.

CHAPTER 10

1 Chadwick, J. (1967). *The Decipherment of Linear B.* 2nd ed. Cambridge: Cambridge University Press.
2 Nakassis, D. (2013). *Individuals and Society in Mycenaean Pylos.* Leiden: Brill; Olsen, B. A. (2014). *Women in Mycenaean Greece: The Linear B Tablets from Pylos and Knossos.* Abingdon: Routledge.
3 Olsen (2014), 95–100.
4 Page 256, Hoffner, H. A. (2009). *Letters from the Hittite Kingdom.* Atlanta: Society of Biblical Literature.
5 Olsen (2014), 69–89.
6 Kelder, J. M., and Poelwijk, M. (2016). 'The wanassa and the damokoro: A new interpretation of a Linear B text from Pylos'. *Greek, Roman, and Byzantine Studies* 56, 572–584.
7 Nakassis (2013), 244; Nakassis, D. (2012). 'Prestige and interest: Feasting and the king at Mycenaean Pylos'. *Hesperia* 81(1), 1–30.
8 Olsen (2014), 136.
9 Olsen (2014), 139.
10 Page 611, Boëlle-Weber, C. (2016). '*I-je-re-ja, ka-ra-wi-po-ro*, and others … women in Mycenaean religion'. In Budin, S. L., and Turfa, J. M. (eds.). *Women in Antiquity. Real Women across the Ancient World.* New York: Routledge, pp. 608–617; Olsen (2014), 143, 241.
11 Olsen (2014), 239–240.
12 Pages 89–96, Chadwick, J. (1976). *The Mycenaean World.* Cambridge: Cambridge University Press.
13 Olsen (2014), 136–137.
14 Olsen (2014), 135.
15 Page 366, Palaima, T. G. (2010). 'Linear B'. In Cline, E. H. (ed.). *The Oxford Handbook of the Aegean Bronze Age.* Oxford: Oxford University Press, pp. 356–372.
16 Page 16, Killen, J. T. (1995). 'Linear B as a source for social history'. In Powell, A. (ed.). *The Greek World.* London: Routledge, pp. 7–26; Pages 232–239, Ventris, M. and Chadwick, J. (1973). *Documents in Mycenaean Greek.* Cambridge: Cambridge University Press.
17 Olsen (2014), 223.
18 Lupack, S. (2011). 'Redistribution in Aegean palatial societies: A view from outside the palace: The sanctuary and the *damos* in Mycenaean economy and society'. *American Journal of Archaeology* 115(2), 207–217.
19 Boëlle-Weber (2016), 612.
20 Boëlle-Weber (2016), 612.
21 Boëlle-Weber (2016), 611.
22 Olsen (2014), 140.
23 Lupack, S. (2010). 'Mycenaean religion'. In Cline, E. H. (ed.). *The Oxford Handbook of the Aegean Bronze Age.* Oxford: Oxford University Press, pp. 263–276.
24 Cosmopoulos, M. B. (2014). 'Cult, continuity, and social memory: Mycenaean Eleusis and the transition to the Early Iron Age'. *American Journal of Archaeology* 118(3), 401–427.
25 Cosmopoulos, M. B., and Ruscillo, D. (2014). 'Mycenaean burnt animal sacrifice at Eleusis'. *Oxford Journal of Archaeology* 33(3), 257–273; Weilhartner, J. (2012). 'Religious offerings in the Linear B tablets: An attempt at their classification and some thoughts about their possible purpose'. *Faventia Supplementa 1. Actas del Simposio Internacional: 55 Años de Micenología (1952–2007)*, pp. 207–231.
26 Page 93, Connelly, J. B. (2007). *Portrait of a Priestess: Women and Ritual in Ancient Greece.* Princeton: Princeton University Press.
27 Connelly (2007), 92.

CHAPTER 11

1 Translated in Lichtheim, M. (2006). *Ancient Egyptian Literature: The New Kingdom. Volume II.* Berkeley: University of California Press, pp. 224–229.
2 Shaw, I. (2000). *The Oxford History of Ancient Egypt.* Oxford: Oxford University Press, p. 485
3 Taylor, J. (2000). 'The Third Intermediate Period (1069–664 BC)'. In Shaw, I. (ed.). *The*

Oxford History of Ancient Egypt. Oxford: Oxford University Press, pp. 324–363.

4 Sass, B. (2002). 'Wenamun and his Levant – 1075 BC or 925 BC?' *Egypt and the Levant* 12, 247–255.

5 Lichtheim (2006), 224; Page 317, Knapp, A. B. (2008). *Prehistoric and Protohistoric Cyprus: Identity, Insularity, and Connectivity*. Oxford: Oxford University Press.

6 Page 387, Steel, L. (2016). 'The social and economic roles played by the women of Alashiya'. In Budin, S. L., and Turfa, J. M. (eds.). *Women in Antiquity: Real Women across the Ancient World*. London: Routledge, pp. 386–398.

7 Fisher, K. D., Manning, S. W., and Urban, T. M. (2019). 'New approaches to Late Bronze Age urban landscapes on Cyprus: Investigations at Kalavasos-*Ayios Dhimitrios*, 2012–2016'. *American Journal of Archaeology* 123 (3), 473–507; South, A. K. (2012). 'A view from Cyprus.' *British School at Athens Studies* 20 *(Parallel Lives: Ancient Island Societies in Crete and Cyprus)*, 218–231.

8 South-Todd A. (2002). 'Late Bronze Age settlement patterns in Southern Cyprus: the first Kingdoms?' In *Cahiers du Centre d'Etudes Chypriotes. Volume 32. Hommage à Marguerite Yon. Actes du colloque international 'Le temps des royaumes de Chypre, XIIIe -IVe s. av. J.-C.' Lyon, 20–22 juin 2002*. pp. 59–72.

9 A plan and some photographs of the site can be seen here: https://kambe.cnrs.ubc.ca/the-sites/kalavasos-ayios-dhimitrios/.

10 Goring, E. (1989). 'Death in everyday life: Aspects of burial practice in the Late Bronze Age'. In Peltenburg, E. (ed.). *Early Society in Cyprus*. Edinburgh: Edinburgh University Press, pp. 95–105; Pages 353–354, Lorentz, K. O. (2016). 'Real bones, real women, real lives: Bioarchaeology and osteobiographies of women in ancient Cyprus'. In Budin, S. L., and Turfa, J. M. (eds.). *Women in Antiquity: Real Women across the Ancient World*. London: Routledge, pp. 349–360; Steel (2016), 393–394.

11 Goring (1989), 103–104.

12 Hirschfeld, N. (2010). 'Cypro-Minoan'. In Cline, E. H. (ed.). *The Oxford Handbook of The Bronze Age Aegean*. Oxford: Oxford University Press, pp. 373–384.

13 Steel (2016), 394.

14 Goren, Y., Bunimovitz, S., Finkelstein, I., and Na'Aman, N. (2003). 'The location of Alashiya: New evidence from petrographic investigation of Alashiyan tablets from El-Amarna and Ugarit'. *American Journal of Archaeology* 107(2), 233–255.

15 Moyer, J. (1989). 'Human skeletal remains'. In South, A., Russel, P., and Keswani, P. S. (eds.). *VVP 3: Kalavasos-Ayios Dhimitrios II: Ceramics, Objects, Tombs, Specialist Studies*. Goteborg: Paul Åströms Förlag, pp. 58–69.

PART III

1 Bryce, T. (2012). *The World of the Neo-Hittite Kingdoms: A Political and Military History*. Oxford: Oxford University Press; Middleton, G. D. (ed.) (2020). *Collapse and Transformation: The Late Bronze Age to Early Iron Age in the Aegean*. Oxford: Oxbow.

2 Van Dijk, J. (2000). 'The Amarna Period and the Later New Kingdom (c. 1352–1069 BC)'. In Shaw, I. (ed.). *The Oxford History of Ancient Egypt*. Oxford: Oxford University Press, pp. 265–307.

3 Dickinson, O. (2006). *The Aegean from Bronze Age to Iron Age: Continuity and Change between the Twelfth and Eighth Centuries BC*. London: Routledge; Lemos, I. S., and Kotsonas, A. (eds). (2020). *A Companion to the Archaeology of Early Greece and the Mediterranean*. Hoboken: Wiley-Blackwell.

4 Thomas, C. G., and Conant, C. (1999). *Citadel to City-State: The Transformation of Greece, 1200–700 BCE*. Bloomington: Indiana University Press.

5 Boardman, J. (1999). *The Greeks Overseas: Their Early Colonies and Trade*. London: Thames and Hudson.

6 Pages 48–63, Cunliffe, B. (1997). *The Ancient Celts*. Oxford: Oxford University Press.

7 Milcent, P.-Y. (2014). 'Hallstatt urban experience before the Celtic oppida in central and eastern Gaul. Two case-studies: Bourges and Vix'. In Fernández-Götz, M., Wendling, H. and Winger, K. (eds.). *Paths to Complexity: Centralisation and Urbanisation in Iron Age Europe*. Oxford: Oxbow, pp. 35–51.

8 Mayor, A. (2014). *The Amazons: Lives & Legends of Warrior Women across the Ancient World*. Princeton: Princeton University Press.

9 Brosius, M. (2006). *The Persians: An Introduction*. London: Routledge.

10 Holland, T. (2006). *Persian Fire: The First World Empire and the Battle for the West*. London: Abacus.

CHAPTER 12

1 Donker van Heel, K. (2016). *Mrs Naunakhte & Family: The Women of Ramesside Deir al-Medina.* Cairo: The American University in Cairo Press.
2 Translation – Pages 38–40, McDowell, A. G. (1999). *Village Life in Ancient Egypt.* Oxford: Oxford University Press.
3 Donker van Heel (2016), 89–91, 138.
4 Page 39, Tyldesley, J. (1994). *Daughters of Isis.* London: Penguin.
5 Tyldesley (1994), 41.
6 Page 248, Sweeney, D. (2016). 'Women at Deir el-Medina.' In Budin, S. L., and Turfa, J. M. (eds.). *Women in Antiquity: Real Women across the Ancient World.* London: Routledge, pp. 243–254.
7 Donker van Heel (2016), 21, 28.
8 UNICEF (2020). 'Child marriage around the world'. Available at www.unicef.org/stories/child-marriage-around-world.
9 Hampton T. (2010). 'Child marriage threatens girls' health'. *Journal of the American Medical Association* 304(5), 509–510.
10 Donker van Heel (2016), 91.
11 Pages 74–86, Snape, S. (2014). *The Complete Cities of Ancient Egypt.* London: Thames and Hudson.
12 Sweeney (2016), 243.
13 Page 22, Lesko, L. H. (1994). *Pharaoh's Workers: The Villagers of Deir el-Medina.* Ithaca: Cornell University Press.
14 Lesko (1994), 22.
15 Lesko (1994), 33.
16 Sweeney (2016), 246.
17 Sweeney (2016), 246.
18 Lesko (1994), 26.
19 Sweeney (2016), 249.
20 Snape (2014), 81.
21 Lesko (1994), 101.
22 Snape (2014), 80.
23 Donker van Heel (2016).
24 Donker van Heel (2016), 137–148.
25 Donker van Heel (2016), 96–101.
26 Donker van Heel (2016), 95–96.
27 Donker van Heel (2016), 102–103.
28 Snape (2014), 74.

CHAPTER 13

1 Smithson, E. L. (1968). 'The tomb of a rich Athenian lady, ca. 850 BC'. *Hesperia* 37(1), 77–116.
2 Page 35–40, Papadopoulos, J. K. (2021). 'The emergence of the *polis*'. In Neils, J., and Rogers, D. K. (eds.). *The Cambridge Companion to Ancient Athens.* Cambridge: Cambridge University Press, pp. 35–46.
3 Blegen, C. W. (1952). 'Two Athenian grave groups of about 900 BC'. *Hesperia: The Journal of the American School of Classical Studies at Athens* 21(4), 279–294.
4 Young, R. S. (1949). 'An early Geometric grave near the Athenian agora'. *Hesperia* 18(4), 275–297.
5 Pages 185–186, Dickinson, O. (2006). *The Aegean from Bronze Age to Iron Age: Continuity and Change between the Twelfth and Eighth Centuries BC.* London: Routledge.
6 Page 546, Wilson, J.-P. (2013). 'Literacy'. In Raaflaub, K. A., and van Wees, H. (eds.). *A Companion to Archaic Greece.* Chichester: Wiley-Blackwell, pp. 542–563.
7 Nakassis, D. (2020). 'The economy'. In Lemos, I. S., and Kotsonas, A. (eds.). *A Companion to the Archaeology of Early Greece and the Mediterranean.* Hoboken. Wiley-Blackwell, pp. 271–291.
8 Nakassis (2020), 285.
9 Thomas and Conant (1999), 66.
10 Pages 4–5, Harding, P. (1994). *Androtion and the Atthis.* Oxford: Oxford University Press.
11 Pages 56–62, Ehrenberg, V. (1973). *From Solon to Socrates: Greek History and Civilization during the 6th and 5th Centuries BC.* 2nd ed. London: Routledge; Osborne, R. (2002). 'Archaic Greek history'. In Bakker, E. J., de Jong, I. J., and van Wees, H. (eds.). *Brill's Companion to Herodotus.* Leiden: Brill, pp. 497–520.
12 Dickinson (2006), 185–186.
13 Page 366, Galanakis, Y. (2020). 'Death and burial'. In Lemos, I. S., and Kotsonas, A. (eds.). *A Companion to the Archaeology of Early Greece and the Mediterranean.* Hoboken. Wiley-Blackwell, pp. 349–374.
14 Page 15, Liston, M. A., and Papadopoulos, J. K. (2004). 'The 'Rich Athenian Lady' was pregnant: The anthropology of a Geometric tomb reconsidered'. *Hesperia* 73, 7–38.
15 Page 272, Musgrave, J. (1990). 'Dust and damn'd oblivion: A study of cremation in ancient Greece'. *The Annual of the British School at Athens* 85, 271–299.
16 Liston and Papadopoulos (2004), 16.
17 Page 256, Sørensen, T. F., and Bille, M. (2008). 'Flames of transformation: The role of fire in

cremation practices'. *World Archaeology* 40(2), 253–267.
18 Liston and Papadopoulos (2004), 15.
19 Smithson (1968), 93–97.
20 Smithson (1968), 83, 96.
21 Smithson (1968), 83; Harding (1994), 4–5.
22 Martelli, I. (2016). 'The tomb of a rich Athenian lady, ca. 850 BC: Honey and purple for a textile interpretation attempt'. *Pasiphae* 10, 117–144.
23 Pages 395–396, Coldstream, J. N. 'The Rich Lady of the Areopagus and her contemporaries: A tribute in memory of Evelyn Lord Smithson'. *Hesperia* 64(4), 391–403.
24 Smithson (1968), 83.
25 Smithson (1968), 81.
26 Coldstream (1995), 397–398.
27 Smithson (1968), 81 n. 18.
28 Liston and Papadopoulos (2004), 17.
29 Liston and Papadopoulos (2004), 17.
30 Liston and Papadopoulos (2004), 18.
31 Smithson (1968), 81 n. 18 and n. 19.
32 Liston and Papadopoulos (2004), 16, 19.
33 Liston and Papadopoulos (2004), 15.
34 Liston and Papadopoulos (2004), 20–22.
35 Page 408, Roussou, M., Ripanti, F., and Servi, K. (2017). 'Engaging visitors of archaeological sites through "emotive" storytelling experiences: A pilot at the ancient Agora of Athens'. *Archeologia e Calcolatori* 28(2), 405–420.
36 Roussou, Ripanti, and Servi (2017), 411.

CHAPTER 14

1 Pages 85–87, Mayor, A. (2014). *The Amazons: Lives and Legends of Warrior Women across the Ancient World*. Princeton: Princeton University Press.
2 Cunliffe, B. (2019). *The Scythians: Nomad Warriors of the Steppe*. Oxford: Oxford University Press; Rolle, R. (1989). *The World of the Scythians*. London: Batsford.
3 Mayor (2014), 235–237.
4 Cunliffe (2019), 35–39, 53–54.
5 Mayor (2014), 249–258.
6 Mayor (2014), 259–270.
7 Mayor (2014), 260.
8 Mayor (2014), 287–304.
9 Cunliffe (2019), 32.
10 Blok, J. H. (1996). 'A tale of many cities: Amazons in the mythical past of Greek cities in Asia Minor'. In Marchand, S., and Lunbeck, E. (eds.). *Proof and Persuasion: Essay on Authority, Objectivity, and Evidence*. Brussels: Brepols, pp. 81–99.
11 Mayor (2014), 272.
12 Mayor (2014), 283–285.
13 Pages 1–2 and Plate I 1a and b., von Bothmer, D. (1957). *Amazons in Greek Art*. Oxford: Oxford University Press.
14 Page 125, Carpenter, T. H. (1991). *Art and Myth in Ancient Greece*. London: Thames and Hudson.
15 Page 16, Man, J. (2017). *Amazons: The Real Warrior Women of the Ancient World*. London: Corgi.
16 Stewart, A. F. (2015). 'Phidias'. *Oxford Classical Dictionary*. https://oxfordre.com/classics/view/10.1093/acrefore/9780199381135.001.0001/acrefore-9780199381135-e-4954.
17 Carpenter (1991), 46–47; Harrison, E. B. (1966). 'The composition of the Amazonomachy on the shield of Athena Parthenos'. *Hesperia* 35(2), 107–133.
18 Pages 271, 275, Neer, R. T. (2012). *Art & Archaeology of the Greek World: A New History, c. 2500–c. 150 BCE*. London: Thames and Hudson.
19 Mayor (2014), 1–10. Mayor interviewed in Rothman, J. (2014). 'The real Amazons'. *The New Yorker*. Available at www.newyorker.com/books/joshua-rothman/real-amazons.
20 Mayor (2014).
21 Guliaev, V. I. (2003). 'Amazons in Scythia: New finds at the middle Don, southern Russia'. *World Archaeology* 35(1), 112–125; Morgunova, N. L., and Khoklova, O. S. (2006). 'Kurgans and nomads: New investigations of mound burial in the southern Urals'. *Antiquity* 80, 303–317.
22 Guliaev (2003), 114.
23 Rolle (1989), 88–89.
24 Rolle (1989), 88.
25 Machemer, T. (2019). 'Tomb containing three generations of warrior women unearthed in Russia'. *Smithsonian Magazine*. Available at www.smithsonianmag.com/smart-news/tomb-containing-three-generations-amazon-warrior-women-unearthed-russia-180973877/; Strickland, A. (2020). 'Three generations of ancient Amazon women warriors found in Russian tomb'. CNN. Available at https://edition.cnn.com/2020/01/06/world/scythian-amazon-burial-scn-intl-scli/index.html.
26 Khudaverdyan, A. Y., Yengibaryan, A. A., Khachatryan, H. H., and Hovhanesyan, A. A.

(2021). 'Warrior burial of the Late Bronze Age and Early Iron Age: The phenomenon of women warriors from the Jrapi cemetery (Shirak Province, Armenia)'. *International Journal of Osteoarchaeology*, 1–12. doi.org/10.1002/oa.3077.

27 Guliaev (2003), 120–121.

28 Mayor, A., Colarusso, J., and Saunders, D. (2014). 'Making sense of nonsense inscriptions associated with Amazons and Scythians on Athenian vases'. *Hesperia* 83(3), 447–493.

29 Mayor, Colarusso, and Saunders (2014), 471–472.

CHAPTER 15

1 Herodotus *Histories* 3.88, 7.2; Waters, M. (2014). *Ancient Persia: A Concise History of the Achaemenid Empire, 550–330 BCE.* Cambridge: Cambridge University Press.

2 McClure, L. (2006). 'Maternal authority and heroic disgrace in Aeschylus's "Persae"'. *Transactions of the American Philological Association* 136(1), 71–97.

3 Pages 141–146, Rosenbloom, D. (2006). *Aeschylus: Persians.* London: Duckworth.

4 *Iliad* 22.476.

5 Page 10, Heitman, R. (2005). *Taking Her Seriously: Penelope & the Plot of Homer's Odyssey.* Ann Arbor: The University of Michigan Press.

6 Herodotus *Histories* 3.129.

7 Herodotus *Histories* 3.132.

8 Herodotus *Histories* 3.133; Sandison, A. T. (1959). 'The first recorded case of inflammatory mastitis – Queen Atossa of Persia and the physician Democedes'. *Medical History* 3(4): 317–322.

9 Herodotus *Histories* 3.134.

10 Herodotus *Histories* 7.2.

11 Herodotus *Histories* 7.3.

12 Pages 25–27, Sancisi-Weerdenburg, H. (1993). 'Exit Atossa: Images of women in Greek historiography on Persia'. In Cameron, A., and Kuhrt, A. (eds.). *Images of Women in Antiquity.* Revised ed. London: Routledge, pp. 20–33.

13 Evans, J. (1968). 'Father of history or father of lies; The reputation of Herodotus'. *The Classical Journal* 64(1), 11–17; Griffiths, A. (2006). 'Stories and storytelling in the *Histories*'. In Dewald, C., and Marincola, J. (eds.). *The Cambridge Companion to Herodotus.* Cambridge: Cambridge University Press, pp. 130–144.

14 Page 39, Davies, M. (2010). 'From rags to riches: Democedes of Croton and the credibility of Herodotus'. *Bulletin of the Institute of Classical Studies* 52(2), 19–44.

15 Griffiths (2006), 137.

16 Kimball Armayor, O. (1978). 'Herodotus' catalogues of the Persian Empire in the light of the monuments and the Greek literary tradition'. *Transactions of the American Philological Association* 108, 1–9.

17 Dandamayev, M. (2002). 'Persepolis Elamite Tablets'. Available at www.iranicaonline.org/articles/persepolis-elamite-tablets.

18 Page 599, Lewis, D. M. 'Postscript'. In Burn, A. R. (1984). *Persia and the Greeks.* 2nd ed. London: Duckworth, pp. 587–612.

19 In Davies (2010), 42–44.

20 I rely on the account given by Brosius, M. (2016). 'No reason to hide: Women in the Neo-Elamite and Persian periods'. In Budin, S. L., and Turfa, J. M. (eds.). *Women in Antiquity: Real Women across the Ancient World.* London: Routledge, pp. 156–174, pages 160–161; and her earlier study: Brosius, M. (1996). *Women in Ancient Persia (559–331 BC).* Oxford: Oxford University Press.

21 Pages 63–64, Yoder, C. R. (2001). *Wisdom as a Woman of Substance: A Socio-Economic Reading of Proverbs 1–9 and 31:10–31.* Berlin: De Gruyter.

22 Herodotus *Histories* 7.69.

23 Brosius (2016), 161.

CHAPTER 16

1 Page 117, Van De Mieroop, M. (2005). 'The eastern Mediterranean in early antiquity'. In Harris, W. V. (ed.). *Rethinking the Mediterranean.* Oxford: Oxford University Press, pp. 117–140.

2 Milcent, P.-Y. (2014). 'Hallstatt urban experience before the Celtic oppida in central and eastern Gaul. Two case-studies: Bourges and Vix'. In Fernández-Götz, M., Wendling, H., and Winger, K. (eds.). *Paths to Complexity: Centralisation and Urbanisation in Iron Age Europe.* Oxford: Oxbow, pp. 35–51.

3 Page 57, Cunliffe, B. (1997). *The Ancient Celts.* Oxford: Oxford University Press; Pare, C. (1991). '*Fürstensitze,* Celts and the Mediterranean world: Developments in the West Hallstatt culture in the 6th and 5th centuries BC'. *Proceedings of the Prehistoric Society* 57 (2), 183–202.

4 Pages 157–158, Arnold, B. (1995). '"Honorary males" or women of substance? Gender, status, and power in Iron-Age Europe'. *Journal of European Archaeology* 3(2), 153–168.
5 Megaw, J. V. (1966). 'The Vix burial'. *Antiquity* 150, 38–44.
6 Page 283, Knüsel, C. (2002). 'More Circe than Cassandra: The Princess of Vix in ritualised social context'. *European Journal of Archaeology* 5(3), 275–308.
7 Joffroy, R. (1954). 'La tombe de Vix (Côte-d'Or)'. *Monuments et mémoires de la Fondation Eugène Piot* 48(1), 1–68.
8 Cunliffe (1997), 57–59. For the Lavau discovery, see Daly, J. (2017). 'Researchers analyse burial of ancient Celtic prince'. Smithsonian.com. Available at www.smithsonianmag.com/smart-news/researchers-analyze-burial-ancient-celtic-prince-180963515/; and Dubuis, B., Josset, D., Millet, E., and Villenave, C. (2015). 'La tombe princière du Ve siècle avant notre ère de Lavau "ZAC du Moutot" (Aube)'. *Bulletin de la Société préhistorique française* 112(2), 371–374.
9 Joffroy (1954), with Charles' comment in Appendix 3. Also Charles, R. P. (1954). 'Étude anthropologique de la "Dame de Vix"'. *Bulletin de la Société préhistorique de France* 51(11–12), 550–553.
10 Discussed on page 370, Arnold, B. (1991). 'The deposed Princess of Vix: The need for an engendered European prehistory'. In Walde, D., and Willows, N. D. (eds.). *The Archaeology of Gender*. Calgary: The University of Calgary, pp. 366–374; Knüsel (2002), 288–294.
11 E.g., Aldhouse-Green, M. (2016). 'Viragos and virgins: Women in the Celtic world'. In Budin, S. L., and Turfa, J. M. (eds.). *Women in Antiquity. Real Women across the Ancient World*. New York: Routledge, pp. 1008–1026; Arnold (1991), 370; and Knüsel (2002), 291.
12 Arnold (1991), 369.
13 Discussed in Arnold (1991); and Knüsel (2002).
14 Arnold (1991), 372.
15 Herodotus *Histories* 1.105, 4.67.
16 *Airs, Waters, Places* 22.
17 Arnold (1991), 373; (1995), 156; Shipley, L. (2015). 'Leaping to conclusions: Archaeology, gender and digital news media'. *Antiquity* 89, 472–477.
18 Aldhouse-Green (2016), 1011.
19 Aldhouse-Green (2016), 1012.
20 Milcent (2014), 42.
21 Cunliffe (1997), 57.
22 Crawford J. (2002). 'Cartimandua, Boudicca, and rebellion: British queens and Roman colonial views'. In Hunt T. L., and Lessard M. R. (eds.). *Women and the Colonial Gaze*. London: Palgrave Macmillan, pp. 17–28.
23 Tacitus *The Histories,* 3.45.
24 Tacitus *Agricola* 16.
25 Aldhouse-Green (2016), 1022.
26 Knüsel (2002), 289–294.
27 Aldhouse-Green (2016), 1012.
28 Formicola, V., Pontrandolfi, A., and Svoboda, J. (2001). 'The Upper Paleolithic triple burial of Dolní Vestonice: Pathology and funerary behavior'. *American Journal of Physical Anthropology* 115, 372–379; Grosman, L., Munro, N. D., and Belfer-Cohen, A. (2008). 'A 12,000-year-old shaman burial from the southern Levant (Israel)'. *Proceedings of the National Academy of Sciences* 105(46), 17665–17669.
29 Sered, S. (1997). 'Symbolic illnesses, real handprints, and other bodily marks: Autobiographies of Okinawan priestesses and shamans'. *Ethos* 25(4), 408–427.
30 Knüsel (2002), 298; Tacitus *The Histories* 4.61

CHAPTER 17

1 Scott, M. (2014). *Delphi: A History of the Centre of the World*. Princeton: Princeton University Press.
2 Maurizio, L. (2001). 'The voice at the center of the world: The Pythias' ambiguity and authority'. In Lardinois, A., and McClure, L. (eds.). *Making Silence Speak: Women's Voices in Greek Literature and Society*. Princeton: Princeton University Press, pp. 38–54.
3 Fontenrose, J. (1978). *The Delphic Oracle*. Berkeley: University of California Press; Lloyd-Jones, H. (1976). 'The Delphic oracle'. *Greece and Rome* 23(1), 60–73; Scott (2014), 31–42.
4 *Odyssey* 8.79; *Iliad* 9.404–405.
5 Hesiod *Theogony* 498ff.
6 Chappell, M. (2006). 'Delphi and the *Homeric Hymn to Apollo*'. *Classical Quarterly* 56(2), 331–348; Strolonga, P. (2011). 'The foundation of the oracle at Delphi in the *Homeric Hymn to Apollo*'. *Greek, Roman, and Byzantine Studies* 51, 529–551.
7 Scott (2014), 33.
8 Pages 308–309, Dietrich, B. C. (2016). *The Origins of Greek Religion*. Berlin: De Gruyter;

Page 33, Pomeroy, S. B. (1995). *Goddesses, Whores, Wives and Slaves: Women in Antiquity*. New York: Schocken Books.

9 Scott (2014), 45–47.

10 Page 73, Connelly, J. B. (2007). *Portrait of a Priestess: Women and Ritual in Ancient Greece*. Princeton: Princeton University Press.

11 Connelly (2007), 79.

12 Herodotus *Histories* 7.140–141.

13 Pages 250–251, Holland, T. (2006). *Persian Fire: The First World Empire and the Battle for the West*. London: Abacus.

14 Scott (2014), 114.

15 Scott (2014), 116.

16 Holland (2006), 250.

17 Herodotus *Histories* 7.143.

18 Holland (2006), 307–326.

19 Connelly (2007), 74–75.

20 Lucan *The Civil War* 5.67–236.

21 Herodotus *Histories* 6.66.

22 Diogenes Laertius *Pythagoras* 8.

23 Pausanias *Guide to Greece* 10.13.8.

24 Connelly (2007), 75.

25 Fontenrose (1978), 196.

26 Scott (2014), 20–21.

27 Littleton, C. (1986). 'The pneuma enthusiastikon: On the possibility of hallucinogenic "vapors" at Delphi and Dodona'. *Ethos* 14(1), 76–91.

28 De Boer, J. Z., and Hale, J. R. (2000). 'The geological origins of the oracle at Delphi, Greece'. *Geological Society, London, Special Publications* 171, 399–412.

29 National Academies Press (US) (2010). '2, Ethylene Oxide Acute Exposure Guideline Levels'. In *National Research Council (US) Committee on Acute Exposure Guideline Levels. Acute Exposure Guideline Levels for Selected Airborne Chemicals: Volume 9*. Available at www.ncbi.nlm.nih.gov/books/NBK208167/.

30 Foster, J., and Lehoux, D. (2007). 'The Delphic oracle and the ethylene-intoxication hypothesis'. *Clinical Toxicology* 14(1), 85–89.

31 Maurizio (2001), 38; Maurizio, L. (1995). 'Anthropology and spirit possession: A reconsideration of the Pythia's role at Delphi'. *Journal of Hellenic Studies* 115, 69–86.

CHAPTER 18

1 Miner, J. (2003). 'Courtesan, concubine, whore: Apollodorus' deliberate use of terms for prostitute'. *The American Journal of Philology* 124(1), 19–37.

2 Hamel, D. (2003). *Trying Neaira: The True Story of a Courtesan's Scandalous Life in Ancient Greece*. New Haven: Yale University Press.

3 Translations come from the Loeb Classical Library edition: Murray, A. T. (1939). *Demosthenes VI. Orations 50–59. Private Cases. In Neaeram*. Cambridge, MA: Harvard University Press. Sections are referred to using the § symbol.

4 Page 120, Blundell, S. (1995). *Women in Ancient Greece*. London: British Museum Press.

5 Page 140, Lindgren, M. (2013). 'Education and work'. In Tulloch, J. H. (ed.). *A Cultural History of Women in Antiquity*. London: Bloomsbury, pp. 125–145; Pages 6–7, McClure, L. K. (2006). 'Introduction'. In Faraone, C. A., and McClure, L. K. (eds.). *Prostitutes and Courtesans in the Ancient World*. Madison: The University of Wisconsin Press, pp. 3–18.

6 Page 145, Glazebrook, A. (2011). 'Prostitution'. In Golden, M., and Toohey, P. (eds.). *A Cultural History of Sexuality, Vol. I: In the Classical World (800 BCE–350 CE)*. Oxford: Berg, pp. 145–168; Hamel (2003), 6–7.

7 Lindgren (2013), 141.

8 McClure (2006), 7.

9 Ault, B. (2016). 'Building Z in the Athenian Kerameikos: House, Tavern, Inn, Brothel?' In Glazebrook A., and Tsakirgis, B. (eds.). *Houses of Ill Repute: The Archaeology of Brothels, Houses, and Taverns in the Greek World*. Philadelphia: University of Pennsylvania Press, pp. 75–102.

10 Page 184, Glazebrook, A. (2016), 184. 'Is there an archaeology of prostitution?' In Glazebrook, A., and Tsakirgis, B. (eds.). *Houses of Ill-Repute: The Archaeology of Brothels, Houses and Taverns in the Greek World*. Philadelphia: University of Pennsylvania Press, pp. 169–196.

11 Glazebrook (2016), 170.

12 On this discussion, see Budin, S. L. (2021). *Freewomen, Patriarchal Authority, and the Accusation of Prostitution*. Abingdon: Routledge. I thank the author for sending me her chapter on Neaira.

13 Glazebrook, A., and Henry, M. M. (eds.). (2011). *Greek Prostitutes in the Ancient Mediterranean, 800 BCE–200 CE*. Madison: University of Wisconsin Press.

14 Quoted in Hamel (2003), 36.

15 Harris, E. M. (2006). 'Did rape exist in classical Athens? Further reflections on the laws about sexual violence'. In Harris, E. M. (ed.).

Democracy and the Rule of Law in Classical Athens: Essays on Law, Society, and Politics. Cambridge: Cambridge University Press, pp. 297–332.

16 Page 54, Keuls, E. (1985). *The Reign of the Phallus: Sexual Politics in Ancient Athens*. Berkeley: University of California Press.

17 Page 102, Spatharas, D. (2009). 'Kinky stories from the rostrum: Storytelling in Apollodorus' *Against Neaira*'. *Ancient Narratives* 9, 99–120.

18 Page 74, Pomeroy, S. B. (1995). *Goddesses, Whores, Wives, and Slaves: Women in Classical Antiquity*. New York: Schocken. See also Tyrrell, W. B., and Bennett, L. J. (1999). 'Pericles' muting of women's voices in Thuc. 2.45.2'. *The Classical Journal* 95(1), 37–51.

19 Page 22, Kapparis, K. A. (1999). *Apollodoros: 'Against Neaira' [D 59]*. Berlin: Walter de Gruyter.

20 Plutarch *Pericles* 34, quoted in Pomeroy (1995), 89.

CHAPTER 19

1 Fox, R. L. (2020). *The Invention of Medicine: From Homer to Hippocrates*. London: Allen Lane; Pages 53–71, Nutton, V. (2013). *Ancient Medicine*. 2nd ed. London: Routledge.

2 Mattern, S. P. (2013). *The Prince of Medicine: Galen in the Roman Empire*. Oxford: Oxford University Press; Nutton (2013), 222–235.

3 Nutton (2013), 37–41.

4 *Odyssey* 4.219–234.

5 *Odyssey* 10.276–399.

6 Nutton (2013), 178–179.

7 Pomeroy, S. B. (1978). 'Plato and the female physician (Republic 454d2)'. *American Journal of Philology* 99: 496–500.

8 www.atticinscriptions.com/inscription/CEG2/569.

9 Nováková, L., and Pagáčová, M. (2016). 'Dexiosis: A meaningful gesture of the classical antiquity'. *ILIRIA International Review* 6(1), 207–222.

10 Though see Milnor, K. (2013). 'Public and private'. In Tulloch, J. H. (ed.). *A Cultural History of Women in Antiquity*. London: Bloomsbury, pp. 105–124.

11 Nováková and Pagáčová (2016), 219–220.

12 www.atticinscriptions.com/inscription/IGII34/700.

13 Xenophon *Economics* 7.37.

14 Nutton (2013), 1.

15 Plato *Theaetetus* 149a–150a.

16 Plato *Theaetetus* 150c.

17 Flemming (2007), 261.

18 Flemming (2007), 262.

19 Cole, S. G. (1981). 'Could Greek women read and write?' *Women's Studies: An Interdisciplinary Journal* 8(1–2), 129–155; Gould, J. (1980). 'Law, custom and myth: Aspects of the social position of women in Classical Athens'. *The Journal of Hellenic Studies* 100, 38–59.

20 Page 122, Parker, H. (2012). 'Women and medicine'. In James, S. L., and Dillon, S. (eds.). *A Companion to Women in the Ancient World*. Chichester: Wiley-Blackwell, pp. 107–124.

21 Dillon, M. P. (2013). 'Engendering the scroll: Girls' and women's literacy in Classical Greece'. In Evans Grubbs, J., and Parkin, T., with Bell, R. (eds.). *The Oxford Handbook of Childhood and Education in the Classical World*. Oxford: Oxford University Press, pp. 396–417.

22 Parker (2012), 123.

23 Parker (2012), 122.

24 Flemming (2007), 265.

25 Flemming (2007), 276–278.

26 Pages 101–103, Muir, S., and Totelin, L. (2013). 'Medicine and disease'. In Tulloch, J. H. (ed.). *A Cultural History of Women in Antiquity*. London: Bloomsbury, pp. 81–104.

27 Muir and Totelin (2013), 103.

28 Parker (2012), 122.

PART IV

1 Chaniotis, A. (2018). *Age of Conquests: The Greek World from Alexander to Hadrian, 336 BC–AD 138*. London: Profile; Erskine, A. (2009). *A Companion to the Hellenistic World*. Oxford: Wiley-Blackwell.

2 Waterfield, R. (2011). *Dividing the Spoils: The War for Alexander the Great's Empire*. Oxford: Oxford University Press.

3 Ameling, W. (2011). 'The rise of Carthage to 264 BC'. In Hoyos, D. (ed.). *A Companion to the Punic Wars*. Oxford: Wiley-Blackwell, pp. 39–57.

4 Ameling (2011), 55.

5 Page 76–77, Bradley, G. (2020). *Early Rome to 290 BC: The Beginnings of the City and the Rise of the Republic*. Edinburgh: Edinburgh University Press.

6 Hoyos, D. (ed.). (2011). *A Companion to the Punic Wars*. Oxford: Wiley-Blackwell; Miles,

R. (2010). *Carthage Must Be Destroyed: The Rise and Fall of an Ancient Civilization*. London: Penguin; Rosenstein, N. S. (2012). *Rome and the Mediterranean 290 to 146 BC: The Imperial Republic*. Edinburgh: Edinburgh University Press.

7 Steel, C. (2013). *The End of the Roman Republic, 146–44 BC: Conquest and Crisis*. Edinburgh: Edinburgh University Press.

8 Osgood, J. (2018). *Rome and the Making of a World State, 150 BCE–20 CE*. Cambridge: Cambridge University Press.

9 Syme, R. (1939). *The Roman Revolution*. Oxford: Oxford University Press.

10 Pages 53–54, Goodman, M. (2007). *Rome and Jerusalem: The Clash of Ancient Civilizations*. New York: Vintage.

CHAPTER 20

1 Meyer, E. (2015). 'Molossia and Epeiros'. In Beck, H., and Funke, P. (eds.). *Federalism in Greek Antiquity*. Cambridge: Cambridge University Press.

2 Pages 5–6, Carney, E. (2006). *Olympias: Mother of Alexander the Great*. New York: Routledge.

3 Plutarch *Alexander* 2.

4 Cole, S. G. (1984). *Theoi Megaloi: The Cult of the Great Gods at Samothrace*. Leiden: Brill.

5 Page 170, Carney, E. (1992). 'The politics of polygamy: Olympias, Alexander and the murder of Philip'. *Historia: Zeitschrift für Alte Geschichte* 41(H.2), 169–189.

6 Carney (2006), 21.

7 Carney (2006), 15–16.

8 Page 121, Pomeroy, S. B. (1995). *Goddesses, Whores, Wives, and Slaves*. New York: Schocken.

9 Carney (2006), 24.

10 Carney (2006), 24–25.

11 Carney (2006), 25, 101; Schultz, P. (2009). 'Divine images and royal ideology in the Philippeion at Olympia'. In Jensen, J. T., Hinge, G., Schultz, P., and Wickkiser, B. (eds.). *Aspects of Ancient Greek Cult: Context, Ritual, Iconography*. Aarhus: Aarhus University Press, pp. 125–194.

12 Pausanias *Guide to Greece* 5.20.8.

13 For other views of the monument, see Palagia, O. (2010). 'Philip's Eurydice in the Phillippeum at Olympia'. In Carney, E., and Ogden, D. (eds.). *Philip II and Alexander the Great: Father and Son, Lives and Afterlives*. Oxford: Oxford University Press, pp. 33–41.

14 Carney (2006), 33–36

15 Plutarch *Alexander* 10.

16 Carney (2006), 39.

17 Pausanias *Guide to Greece* 8.7.7.

18 Carney (2006), 44.

19 Carney (2006), 46.

20 Theodossiev, N. (1996). 'Cult clay figurines in ancient Thrace'. *Kernos* 9. Available at: http://journals.openedition.org/kernos/1169.

21 See 'Dionysus', 'ecstasy', and 'Orphism' in Hornblower, S., and Spawforth, A. (eds.) (2003). *The Oxford Classical Dictionary*. Revised 3rd ed. Oxford: Oxford University Press.

22 Carney (2006), 50.

23 Carney (2006), 51.

24 Carney (2006), 95–96.

25 Waterfield, R. (2011). *Dividing the Spoils: The War for Alexander the Great's Empire*. Oxford: Oxford University Press.

26 Carney (2006), 64.

27 Waterfield (2011), 23.

28 Carney (2006), 66.

29 Carney (2006), 68–70.

30 Carney (2006), 74–75.

31 Carney (2006), 75–77.

32 Loman, P. (2004). 'No woman no war: Women's participation in ancient Greek warfare'. *Greece and Rome* 51(1), 34–54.

33 Carney (2006), 82.

34 Edson, C. (1949). 'The Tomb of Olympias'. *Hesperia* 18(1), 84–95.

35 Lobell, J. A. (2015). 'Greece's biggest tomb'. *Archaeology* 68(1), 30; Pages 10–12, Morgan, C. (2013–2014). 'Archaeology in Greece 2013–2014'. *Archaeological Reports* 60, 4–12.

36 Chugg, A. (2014). 'Is the mother of Alexander the Great in the tomb at Amphipolis?' *Greek Reporter*. Part one: https://greece.greekreporter.com/2014/09/07/is-the-mother-of-alexander-the-great-in-the-tomb-at-amphipolis/; Part two: https://greece.greekreporter.com/2014/09/24/is-the-mother-of-alexander-the-great-in-the-tomb-at-amphipolis-part-2/.

CHAPTER 21

1 Mentink, H. J. (1967). 'The Etruscans'. *The Classical Outlook* 45(1), 8–10.

2 Agostiani, L. (2013). 'The Etruscan language'. In Turfa, J. M. (ed.). *The Etruscan World*. Abingdon: Routledge, pp. 457–477.

3 Athenaeus *Deipnosophistae* 12.517–518.
4 De Grummond, N. T. (2013). 'Haruspicy and augury: Sources and procedures'. In Turfa, J. M. (ed.). *The Etruscan World*. Abingdon: Routledge, pp. 539–556.
5 Page 18, Levick, B. (2001). *Claudius*. Abingdon: Routledge.
6 Page 2, Turfa, J. M. (2013). 'Introduction: Time to give the Etruscans their due'. In Turfa, J. M. (ed.). *The Etruscan World*. Abingdon: Routledge, pp. 1–7.
7 For example, Riva, C. (2021). *A Short History of the Etruscans*. London: Bloomsbury.
8 Swaddling, J., and Prag, J. (eds.). (2002). *Seianti Hanunia Tlesnasa: The Story of an Etruscan Noblewoman*. London: British Museum Press.
9 Swaddling, J. (2016). 'Seianti Hanunia Tlesnasa: An Etruscan aristocrat'. In Budin, S. L., and Turfa, J. M. (eds.). *Women in Antiquity: Real Women across the Ancient World*. London: Routledge, pp. 769–780.
10 Ginge, B. (2002). 'The sarcophagus, the tomb and the Seiante family in their archaeological context'. In Swaddling, J., and Prag, J. (eds.). *Seianti Hanunia Tlesnasa: The Story of an Etruscan Noblewoman*. London: British Museum Press, pp. 11–15.
11 Page 17, Becker, M. J. (2002). 'Seianti Hanunia Tlesnasa: A re-evaluation of her skeleton in the British Museum'. In Swaddling, J., and Prag, J. (eds.). *Seianti Hanunia Tlesnasa: The Story of an Etruscan Noblewoman*. London: British Museum Press, pp. 17–22.
12 Ginge (2002), 11.
13 Swaddling, J. (2002). 'The Seianti project'. In Swaddling, J., and Prag, J. (eds.). *Seianti Hanunia Tlesnasa: The Story of an Etruscan Noblewoman*. London: British Museum Press, p. 1.
14 Barlow, A., Barlow, M., Brodrick, A., and Quinton, J. (2002). 'A technical investigation of the life-sized painted terracotta figure'. In Swaddling, J., and Prag, J. (eds.). *Seianti Hanunia Tlesnasa: The Story of an Etruscan Noblewoman*. London: British Museum Press, pp. 41–48.
15 Page 5, Swaddling, J. (2002). 'The world Seianti knew'. In Swaddling, J., and Prag, J. (eds.). *Seianti Hanunia Tlesnasa: The Story of an Etruscan Noblewoman*. London: British Museum Press, pp. 3–6.
16 Joyner, L. (2002). 'Scientific examination of the pigments and ceramic fabric from the sarcophagus of Seianti Hanunia Tlesnasa'. In Swaddling, J., and Prag, J. (eds.). *Seianti Hanunia Tlesnasa: The Story of an Etruscan Noblewoman*. London: British Museum Press, pp. 49–51.
17 Stoddart, R. W. (2002). 'Remains from the sarcophagus of Seianti Hanunia Tlesnasa: Pathological evidence and its implications'. In Swaddling, J., and Prag, J. (eds.). *Seianti Hanunia Tlesnasa: The Story of an Etruscan Noblewoman*. London: British Museum Press, pp. 29–38.
18 Vellucci, K. B. (1985). 'Etruscan athletics'. *Expedition Magazine* 27(2), 22–29.
19 Livy *History of Rome* 1.35.
20 Root, M. C. (1973). 'An Etruscan horse race from Poggio Civitate'. *American Journal of Archaeology* 77(2), 121–137.
21 Stoddart (2002).
22 Lilley, J. D. (2002). 'Seianti Hanunia Tlesnasa: Some observations on the dental features'. In Swaddling, J., and Prag, J. (eds.). *Seianti Hanunia Tlesnasa: The Story of an Etruscan Noblewoman*. London: British Museum Press, pp. 23–26.
23 Lilley (2002), 25.
24 Lilley (2002), 26.
25 Page 37, Briquel, D. (2013). 'Etruscan origins and the ancient authors'. In Turfa, J. M. (ed.). *The Etruscan World*. Abingdon: Routledge, pp. 36–55.
26 Page 212, Bittarello, M. B. (2009). 'The construction of Etruscan "otherness" in Latin literature'. *Greece and Rome* 56(2), 211–233.
27 Izzet, V. (2012). 'Etruscan women: Towards a reappraisal'. In James, S. L., Dillon, S. (eds.). *A Companion to Women in the Ancient World*. Chichester: Wiley-Blackwell, pp. 66–77.
28 Pages 243–245, Warren, L. B. (1973a). 'Etruscan women: A question of interpretation'. *Archaeology* 26(4), 242–249; Page 92, Warren, L. B. (1973b). 'The women of Etruria'. *Arethusa* 6(1), 91–101.
29 Warren (1973a), 248.
30 Page 784, Bonfante, L. (2016). 'Motherhood in Etruria'. In Budin, S. L., and Turfa, J. M. (eds.). *Women in Antiquity: Real Women across the Ancient World*. London: Routledge, pp. 781–796.
31 Warren (1973a), 245.
32 Millender, E. G. (2017). 'Spartan women'. In Powell, A. (ed.). *A Companion to Sparta*. Chichester: Wiley-Blackwell, pp. 500–524.

33 Izzet, V. E. (2005). 'The mirror of Theopompus: Etruscan identity and Greek myth'. *Papers of the British School at Rome* 73, 1–22.

CHAPTER 22

1 Grebe, S. (2013). 'Terentia'. In Bagnall, R. S., Brodersen, K., Champion, C. B., Erskine, A., and Huebner, S. R. (eds.). *The Encyclopedia of Ancient History*. Oxford: Wiley-Blackwell, pp. 6607–6608.

2 Page 31, Treggiari, S. (2007). *Terentia, Tullia and Publilia: The Women of Cicero's Family*. London: Routledge.

3 Treggiari (2007), xi.

4 Page 51, Kraemer, R. S. (1992). *Her Share of the Blessings: Women's Religion Among Pagans, Jews, and Christians in the Greco-Roman World*. Oxford: Oxford University Press.

5 Pages 224–226, Phang, S. E. (2022). *Daily Life of Women in Ancient Rome*. Santa Barbara: ABC-Clio.

6 Pages 17–27, Caldwell, L. (2015). *Roman Girlhood and the Fashioning of Femininity*. Cambridge: Cambridge University Press.

7 Hallett, J. P. (2002). 'Women writing in Rome and Cornelia, Mother of the Gracchi'. In Churchill, L. J., Brown, P. R., and Jeffrey, J. E. (eds.). *Women Writing Latin in Roman Antiquity, Late Antiquity, and the Early Christian Era*. New York: Routledge, pp. 13–21.

8 Treggiari (2007), 19.

9 Caldwell (2014), 18–19.

10 Page 129, Culham, P. (2014). 'Women in the Roman Republic'. In Flower, H. (ed.). *The Cambridge Companion to the Roman Republic*. Cambridge: Cambridge University Press, pp. 127–148.

11 Pages 70–71, Salisbury, J. (2001). *Encyclopedia of Women in the Ancient World*. Santa Barbara: ABC-Clio.

12 Page 58, Dixon, S. (2007). *Cornelia: Mother of the Gracchi*. London: Routledge.

13 Treggiari (2007), 31.

14 Treggiari (2007), 37.

15 Treggiari (2007), 29.

16 Treggiari (2007), 36.

17 Plutarch *Cicero* 20.

18 Brennan (2012), 355.

19 Pages 230, 234–235, Potter, D. (2019). *The Origin of Empire: Rome from the Republic to Hadrian, 264 BC–AD 138*. London: Profile Books.

20 Treggiari (2007), 31.

21 Brennan, T. C. (2012). 'Perceptions of women's power in the Late Republic: Terentia, Fulvia, and the generation of 63 BC'. In James, S. L., and Dillon, S. (eds.). *A Companion to Women in the Ancient World*. Oxford: Wiley-Blackwell, pp. 354–366.

22 Plutarch *Cicero* 20.

23 Balsdon, J. P. V. D. (1966). 'Fabula Clodiana'. *Historia: Zeitschrift Für Alte Geschichte*, 15(1), 65–73.

24 Plutarch *Cicero* 28.

25 Page 137, Everitt, A. (2001). *A Turbulent Life: Cicero*. London: John Murray.

26 Plutarch *Cicero* 33; Treggiari (2007), 60.

27 Cicero *Letter* 14.4.

28 Cicero *Letter* 14.2.

29 Cicero *Letter* 14.1.

30 Cicero *Letter* 14.2.

31 Treggiari (2007), 65.

32 Cicero *Letter* 14.3.

33 Treggiari (2007), 91; Claassen, J.-M. (1996). 'Documents of a crumbling marriage: The case of Cicero and Terentia'. *Phoenix* 50(3/4), 208–232.

34 Everitt (2001), 205–210, 216–217.

35 Cicero *Letter* 14.7; Claassen (1996), 217.

36 Claassen (1996), 216.

37 Treggiari (2007), 128.

38 Plutarch *Cicero* 41.

39 Treggiari (2007), 129.

CHAPTER 23

1 Salisbury, J. (2001). *Encyclopedia of Women in the Ancient World*. Santa Barbara: ABC-Clio, pp. 208–209; Page vii, Valency, M. J. (1966). *The Tragedies of Herod & Mariamne*. New York: AMS Press.

2 Page 11, Rajak, T. (2002). *Josephus: The Historian and His Society*. London: Duckworth.

3 Chapman, H. H., and Rodgers, Z. (eds.). (2015). *A Companion to Josephus*. Chichester: Wiley-Blackwell.

4 Rajak (2002), 4–6; Curran, J. (2005). '"The long hesitation": Some reflections on the Romans in Judaea'. *Greece and Rome* 52(1), 70–98.

5 Josephus *The Jewish War* 1.241.

6 Bohak, G. (2009). 'The Jews'. In Erskine, A. (ed.). *A Companion to Ancient History*. Chichester: Wiley-Blackwell, pp. 201–212.

7 Pages 214–215, Ilan, T. (2016). 'Josephus on women'. In Chapman, H. H., and Rodgers,

Z. (eds.). *A Companion to Josephus*. Chichester: Wiley-Blackwell, pp. 210–221; Liebowitz, E. (2018). 'Female monarchical succession in Hellenistic and Jewish society in antiquity: Parallels and contrasts'. *Journal for the Study of Judaism* 49, 30–48.

8 Bohak (2009), 205.

9 Sterling, G. E. (2007). 'The Jewish appropriation of Hellenistic historiography'. In Marincola, J. (ed.). *A Companion to Greek and Roman Historiography*. Oxford: Blackwell, pp. 231–243.

10 Ilan, T. (1987). 'The Greek names of the Hasmoneans'. *The Jewish Quarterly Review* 78(1/2), 1–20.

11 Page 264, Gruen, E. S. (2003). 'Jews and Greeks'. In Erskine, A. (ed.). *A Companion to the Hellenistic World*. Oxford: Blackwell, pp. 264–279.

12 Josephus *Jewish War* 1.241

13 Page 241, van Henten, J. W. (2016). 'Herod the Great in Josephus'. In Chapman, H. H., and Rodgers, Z. (eds.). *A Companion to Josephus*. Chichester: Wiley-Blackwell, pp. 235–246.

14 Josephus *Jewish War* 1.431–1.444.

15 Josephus *Jewish Antiquities* 15.2.3.

16 Josephus *Jewish Antiquities* 15.3.3.

17 Josephus *Jewish Antiquities* 15.3.5.

18 Josephus *Jewish Antiquities* 15.3.6.

19 Josephus *Jewish Antiquities* 15.3.7.

20 Josephus *Jewish Antiquities* 15.3.9.

21 Josephus *Jewish Antiquities* 15.3.9.

22 Josephus *Jewish Antiquities* 15.3.9.

23 Josephus *Jewish Antiquities* 15.6.5

24 van Henten (2016), 241–242.

25 Josephus *Jewish Antiquities* 15.7.1.

26 Josephus *Jewish Antiquities* 15.7.2.

27 Josephus *Jewish Antiquities* 15.7.2.

28 Josephus *Jewish Antiquities* 15.7.4.

29 Josephus *Jewish Antiquities* 15.7.4.

30 Josephus *Jewish Antiquities* 15.7.6.

31 Bond, H. K. (2012). 'Josephus on Herod's domestic intrigue in the *Jewish War*'. *Journal for the Study of Judaism* 43, 295–314.

32 Valency (1966).

33 Goldhill, S. (2009). 'See Josephus: Viewing first-century sexual drama with Victorian eyes'. *Victorian Studies* 51(3), 470–479.

PART V

1 Beard, M. (2008). *Pompeii: The Life of a Roman Town*. London: Profile; Butterworth, A., and Laurence, R. (2005). *Pompeii: The Living City*. London: Phoenix.

2 Ando, C. (2012). *Imperial Rome AD 193 to 284: The Critical Century*. Edinburgh: Edinburgh University Press.

3 Pages 144–145, Brosius, M. (2006). *The Persians: An Introduction*. Abingdon: Routledge.

4 Page 2, Stoneman, R. (1992). *Palmyra and Its Empire: Zenobia's Revolt against Rome*. Ann Arbor: The University of Michigan Press.

5 Heather, P. (2005). *The Fall of the Roman Empire: A New History*. London: Pan.

6 Maas, M. (ed.) (2005). *The Cambridge Companion to the Age of Justinian*. Cambridge: Cambridge University Press.

CHAPTER 24

1 See chapter 1, Schiff, S. (2011). *Cleopatra: A Life*. London: Virgin; Pina Polo, F. (2013). 'The great seducer: Cleopatra, queen and sex symbol'. In Knippschild, S., and Garcia Morcillo, M. (eds.). *Seduction and Power: Antiquity in the Visual and Performing Arts*. London: Bloomsbury, pp. 183–196.

2 Key modern sources are Macurdy, G. H. (1932). *Hellenistic Queens: A Study of Woman-Power in Macedonia, Seleucid Syria, and Ptolemaic Egypt*. Westport: Greenwood Press; Roller, D. W. (2018). *Cleopatra's Daughter and Other Royal Women of the Augustan Era*. Oxford: Oxford University Press. See also: Draycott, J. (2018). 'Cleopatra's daughter'. History Today. Available at www.historytoday.com/miscellanies/cleopatras-daughter.

3 Chapter 11, Osgood, J. (2018). *Rome and the Making of a World State, 150 BCE–20 CE*. Cambridge: Cambridge University Press.

4 Page 165, Scullard, H. H. (1982). *From the Gracchi to Nero: A History of Rome 133 BC to AD 68*. 5th ed. London: Methuen.

5 Ager, S. L. (2013). 'Marriage or mirage? The phantom wedding of Cleopatra and Antony'. *Classical Philology* 108(2), 139–155.

6 Cassius Dio *Roman History* 49.41; Plutarch *Mark Antony* 54.

7 Draycott, J. (2012). 'The symbol of Cleopatra Selene: Reading crocodiles on coins in the Late Republic and Early Principate'. *Acta Classica* 55, 43–56.

8 Pages 161–162, Grant, M. (1972). *Cleopatra*. London: Phoenix.

9 Cassius Dio *Roman History* 51.21

10 Roller (2018), 32–33.

11 Advertised on coins and in his 'autobiography', the *Res Gestae divi Augusti;* see also chapters 1 and 2 of Dowling, M. B. (2006). *Clemency and Cruelty in the Roman World*. Ann Arbor: The University of Michigan Press.
12 Kleiner, D. E., and Buxton, B. (2008). 'Pledges of empire: The Ara Pacis and the Donations of Rome'. *American Journal of Archaeology* 112(1), 57–89.
13 Pages 38–41, Freisenbruch, A. (2010). *The First Ladies of Rome: The Women Behind the Caesars*. London: Vintage.
14 Freisenbruch (2010), 58–59.
15 Harders, A.-C. (2009). 'An imperial family man: Augustus as surrogate father to the children of Mark Antony'. In Huebner, S., and Ratzan, D. (eds.). *Growing Up Fatherless in Antiquity*. Cambridge: Cambridge University Press, pp. 217–240.
16 Freisenbruch (2010), 52–53.
17 Roller (2018), 33–34.
18 Quoted in Roller (2018), 35–36.
19 Roller (2018), 36.
20 Roller (2018), 39.
21 Draycott (2012).
22 Roller (2018), 38.
23 Archaeology Wiki (2012). 'The twins of Cleopatra and Mark Antony'. Available at www.archaeology.wiki/blog/2012/04/23/the-twins-of-cleopatra-and-mark-antony/; Lorenzi, R. (2012). 'Faces of Cleopatra and Antony's twin babies revealed'. LiveScience. Available at www.livescience.com/19838-antony-cleopatra-babies-sculpture.html.
24 Walker, S., and Higgs, P. (eds.). (2001). *Cleopatra of Egypt: From History to Myth*. London: The British Museum Press, p. 197.
25 Draycott, J. (2012). 'Dynastic politics, defeat, decadence and dining: Cleopatra Selene on the so-called "Africa" dish from the Villa Della Pisanella at Boscoreale'. *Papers of the British School at Rome* 80, 45–64.
26 Pages 54–55, Davies, P. J. E. (2004). *Death and the Emperor: Roman Imperial Funerary Monuments from Augustus to Marcus Aurelius*. Austin: University of Texas Press; Roller (2018), 48.
27 Roller (2018), 44–46.
28 Roller (2018), 45.
29 Roller (2018), 48.

CHAPTER 25

1 Pages 236–237, Beard, M. (2008). *Pompeii: The Life of a Roman Town*. London: Profile; Page 248, Knapp, R. (2011). *Invisible Romans: Prostitutes, Outlaws, Slaves, Gladiators, Ordinary Men and Women ... The Romans That History Forgot*. London: Profile Books.
2 Prostitution was not limited to male customer + female prostitute. Male/male prostitution also existed in the Roman world, see Williams, C. A. (1999). *Roman Homosexuality*. 2nd ed. Oxford: Oxford University Press, pp. 38–47, 83–86.
3 Descoeudres, J.-P. (2007). 'History and historical sources'. In Dobbins, J. J., and Foss, P. W. (eds.). *The World of Pompeii*. London: Routledge, pp. 9–27.
4 Knapp (2011), 244; McGinn, T. (2004). *The Economy of Prostitution in the Roman World: A Study of Social History and the Brothel*. Ann Arbor: University of Michigan Press.
5 Heikki Solin, cited on page 41, Levin-Richardson, S. (2019). *The Brothel of Pompeii: Sex, Class, and Gender at the Margins of Roman Society*. Cambridge: Cambridge University Press.
6 Quoted on page 95, Joshel, S. R. (2010). *Slavery in the Roman World*. Cambridge: Cambridge University Press.
7 Henry, M. M. (2011). 'The traffic in women: From Homer to Hipponax'. In Glazebrook, A., and Henry, M. M. (eds.). *Greek Prostitutes in the Ancient Mediterranean, 800 BCE–200 CE*. Madison: The University of Wisconsin Press, pp. 14–33; Thalmann, W. G. (1998). 'Female slaves in the *Odyssey*'. In Joshel, S. R., and Murnaghan, S. (eds.). *Women & Slaves in Greco-Roman Culture*. London: Routledge, pp. 22–34.
8 Pages 60–65, de Souza, P. (1999). *Piracy in the Graeco-Roman World*. Cambridge: Cambridge University Press; Trümper, M. (2009). *Graeco-Roman Slave Markets: Fact or Fiction?* Oxford: Oxbow.
9 Scheidel, W. (1997). 'Quantifying the sources of slavery in the early Roman Empire'. *The Journal of Roman Studies* 87, 156–169; Scheidel, W. (2005). 'Human mobility in Roman Italy, II: The slave population'. *The Journal of Roman Studies* 95, 64–79; Trümper (2009), 31.
10 Page 201, Pomeroy, S. B. (1995). *Goddesses, Whores, Wives, and Slaves*. New York: Schocken.

11 Page 103, Cohen, E. H. (2006). 'Free and unfree sexual work: An economic analysis of Athenian prostitution'. In Faraone, C. A., and McClure, L. K. (eds.). *Prostitutes & Courtesans in the Ancient World*. Cambridge: Cambridge University Press, pp. 95–124.
12 Page 139 n. 34, Hanses, M. (2020). *The Life of Comedy after the Death of Plautus and Terence*. Ann Arbor: University of Michigan Press.
13 Page 12, Joshel, S. R. (2010). *Slavery in the Roman World*. Cambridge: Cambridge University Press.
14 Bindel, J. (2017). 'The "sex worker" myth'. *The Spectator*. Available at www.spectator.co.uk/article/the-sex-worker-myth; Smyth C., and Estes Y. (2019). 'The myth of the happy hooker: Kantian moral reflections on a phenomenology of prostitution'. In Teays, W. (eds.). *Analyzing Violence against Women*. Cham: Springer, pp. 152–158.
15 Knapp (2011), 244.
16 Pages 454–455, Trimble, J. (2016). 'The Zoninus collar and the archaeology of Roman slavery'. *American Journal of Archaeology* 120(3), 447–472.
17 Beard (2008), 235.
18 Knapp (2011), 245.
19 Pomeroy (1995), 202.
20 Knapp (2011), 243.
21 Strong (2016), 42–43.
22 Ovid *Art of Love* 1.433–436; Strong (2016), 18.
23 Laurence, R. (1994). *Roman Pompeii: Space and Society*. London: Routledge; Wallace-Hadrill, A. (1995). 'Public honor and private shame: The urban texture of Pompeii'. In Cornell, T. J., and Lomas, K. (eds.). *Urban Society in Roman Italy*. London: Routledge, pp. 39–64.
24 Levin-Richardson, S. (2019). *The Brothel of Pompeii: Sex, Class, and Gender at the Margins of Roman Society*. Cambridge: Cambridge University Press.
25 McGinn, T. (2006). 'Zoning shame in the Roman city'. In Faraone, C. A., and McClure, L. K. (eds.). *Prostitutes and Courtesans in the Ancient World*. Cambridge: Cambridge University Press, pp. 161–176.
26 Page 543–544, Severy-Hoven, B. (2012). 'Master narratives and the wall painting of the House of the Vettii, Pompeii'. *Gender & History* 24(3), 540–580.
27 Pages 206–235, Clark, J. R. (1991). *The Houses of Roman Italy, 100 BC–AD 250: Ritual, Space, and Decoration*. Berkeley: University of California Press.
28 Clark (1991), 212.
29 Severy-Hoven (2012), 545.
30 Laetsch, K. (2015). 'Priapus is alive and well in cyberspace – the age-old art of trolling'. *The Conversation*. Available at https://theconversation.com/priapus-is-alive-and-well-in-cyberspace-the-age-old-art-of-trolling-44468.
31 For example, pages 28, 94 in Hooper, R. (1999). *The Priapus Poems: Erotic Epigrams from Ancient Rome*. Urbana: University Illinois Press.
32 McGinn (2004), 158.
33 Pages 125–128, Strong, A. K. (2016). *Prostitutes and Matrons in the Roman World*. Cambridge: Cambridge University Press.
34 Clark (1991), 221.
35 McGinn (2004), 295–296.

CHAPTER 26

1 Suetonius *Life of Domitian* 4.
2 Page 151, Dunkle, R. (2008). *Gladiators: Violence and Spectacle in Ancient Rome*. Abingdon: Routledge.
3 Page 407, Coleman, K. (1997). '"The contagion of the throng": Absorbing violence in the Roman world'. *European Review* 5, 401–417.
4 Petronius *Satyricon* 45.
5 Kanz, F., and Grossschmidt, K. (2006). 'Head injuries of Roman gladiators'. *Forensic Science International* 160, 207–216.
6 Kennedy, M. (2000). 'Roman grave believed to be female gladiator's'. *The Guardian*. Available at www.theguardian.com/culture/2000/sep/13/artsfeatures; but see pages 484–485, Brunet, S. (2014). 'Women with swords: Female gladiators in the Roman world'. In Christesen, P., and Kyle, D. G. (eds.). *A Companion to Sport and Spectacle in Greek and Roman Antiquity*. Chichester: Wiley-Blackwell, pp. 478–491.
7 Hargreaves, J. (1997). 'Women's boxing and related activities: Introducing images and meanings'. *Body and Society* 3(4), 33–49.
8 Manas, A. (2011). 'New evidence of female gladiators: The bronze statuette at the Museum für Kunst und Gewerbe of Hamburg'. *The International Journal of the History of Sport* 28(18), 2726–2752; McCullough, A. (2008). 'Female gladiators in

imperial Rome: Literary context and historical fact'. *The Classical World* 101(2), 197–209.

9 Calpurnius Flaccus *Declamations* 52.
10 Edwards, C. (1997). 'The unspeakable professions: Public performance and prostitution in ancient Rome'. In Hallett, J. P., and Skinner, M. P. (eds.). *Roman Sexualities.* Princeton: Princeton University Press, pp. 66–95; Barton, C. A. (1989). 'The scandal of the arena'. *Representations* 27(Summer), 1–36.
11 Tertullian *De Spectaculis* XXII
12 Page 14, Strauss, B. (2009). *The Spartacus War.* London: Phoenix.
13 Lewis, N., and Reinhold, M. (1990). *Roman Civilization: Selected Readings. Volume II: The Empire.* 3rd ed. New York: Columbia University Press, pp. 143–144; Levick, B. (1983). 'The senatus consultum from Larinum'. *The Journal of Roman Studies* 73, 97–115.
14 Brunet (2014), 482.
15 McCullough (2008), 208.
16 Brunet (2014), 486–487.
17 Satire 6 is discussed in Braund, S. H. (1992). 'Juvenal – Misogynist or Misogamist?' *The Journal of Roman Studies* 82, 71–86.
18 Juvenal *Satires* 6.246–268.
19 Page 75, Matyszak, P. (2011). *Gladiator: The Roman Fighter's (Unofficial) Manual.* London: Thames and Hudson.
20 Coloru, O. (2010). 'A marble relief representing the gladiator Dareios'. *Zeitschrift für Papyrologie und Epigraphik* 175, 161–163.
21 Matyszak (2011), 91–94.
22 Coleman, K. (2000). '*Missio* at Halicarnassus'. *Harvard Studies in Classical Philology* 100, 487–500.
23 Carter, M. J. (2015). 'Bloodbath: Artemidorus, apotomos combat, and Ps.-Quintilian's "The Gladiator"'. *Zeitschrift für Papyrologie und Epigraphik* 193, 39–52.
24 Page 272, Knapp, R. (2011). *Invisible Romans: Prostitutes, Outlaws, Slaves, Gladiators, Ordinary Men and Women ... The Romans that History Forgot.* London: Profile Books.
25 Dunkle (2008), 122.
26 Pages 182–183, Auguet, R. (1994). *Cruelty and Civilization: The Roman Games.* Abingdon: Routledge.
27 Page 407, Coleman, K. (1997). '"The contagion of the throng": Absorbing violence in the Roman world'. *European Review* 5, 401–417.
28 Knapp (2011), 275.
29 Dunkle (2008), 122.

CHAPTER 27

1 Gold, B. K. (2018). *Perpetua: Athlete of God.* Oxford: Oxford University Press; Heffernan, T. J. (2012). *The Passion of Perpetua and Felicity.* Oxford: Oxford University Press; Salisbury, J. E. (1997). *Perpetua's Passion: The Death and Memory of a Young Roman Woman.* London: Routledge.
2 Pages 432–433, Fox, R. L. (1986). *Pagans and Christians in the Mediterranean World from the Second Century AD to the Conversion of Constantine.* London: Penguin.
3 Wagemakers, B. A. (2010). 'Incest, infanticide, and cannibalism: Anti-Christian imputations in the Roman Empire'. *Greece and Rome* 57(2), 337–354.
4 Fox (1986), 287, 294.
5 Fox (1986), 419–420.
6 Pages 41–46, Chadwick, H. (2001). 'The early Christian community'. In McManners, J. (ed.). *The Oxford Illustrated History of Christianity.* Oxford: Oxford University Press, pp. 21–61.
7 Page 24, Bowersock, G. (1995). *Martyrdom and Rome.* Cambridge: Cambridge University Press.
8 Bowersock, (1995), 1.
9 Quoted in Bowersock, (1995), 2.
10 Pages 3–4, Shaw, B. (1993). 'The Passion of Perpetua'. *Past and Present* 139, 3–45.
11 All quotes from *The Passions* are from the translation of Heffernan, T. J. (2012). *The Passion of Perpetua and Felicity.* Oxford: Oxford University Press, chapter 5.
12 Gold (2018), 104; Salisbury (1997), 44.
13 Heffernan, T. J. (2016). 'The legacy of misidentification: Why the martyrs in the *Passio Sanctarum Perpetuae et Felicitatis* were not from Thuburbo Minus'. *Journal of Early Christian History* 6(3), 126–151.
14 Gold (2018), 68.
15 Gold (2018), 70.
16 Gold (2018), 88.
17 Attridge, H. W. (2021). 'Early Christianity'. In Johnston, S. I. (ed.). *Ancient Religions.* Cambridge, MA: Harvard University Press, pp. 233–240; Chadwick, H. (1993). *The Early Church.* Revised ed. London: Penguin.
18 Page 567, Becker, A. H. (2011). 'Christian society'. In Peachin, M. (ed.). *The Oxford Handbook of Social Relations in the Roman World.* Oxford: Oxford University Press, pp. 567–586.

19 Becker (2011), 572.
20 Pages 15–27, Caldwell, L. (2015). *Roman Girlhood and the Fashioning of Femininity.* Cambridge: Cambridge University Press.
21 Caldwell (2015), 107.
22 Caldwell (2015), 108.
23 Cooper (2013), 108–109.
24 Pages 125–128, Hillner, J. (2015). *Prison, Punishment and Penance in Late Antiquity.* Cambridge: Cambridge University Press.
25 Gold (2018), 15–18: Heffernan (2012), 5.
26 Page 6, Bremmer, J. N., and Formisano, M. (2012). 'Perpetua's Passions: A brief introduction'. In Bremmer, J. N., and Formisano, M. (eds.). *Perpetua's Passions: Multidisciplinary Approaches to the* Passio Perpetuae et Felicitatis. Oxford: Oxford University Press, pp. 1–13; Hunink, V. (2010). 'Did Perpetua write her prison account?' *Listy filologické/Folia philologica* 133(1/2), 147–155.

CHAPTER 28

1 Historia Augusta *Aurelian* 33.
2 Page 210, Andrade, N. J. (2018). *Zenobia: Shooting Star of Palmyra.* Oxford: Oxford University Press.
3 Page 1, Syme, R. (1971). *The Historia Augusta.* Bonn: Rudolf Habelt Verlag GmbH.
4 Page 2, Southern, P. (2008). *Empress Zenobia: Palmyra's Rebel Queen.* London: Continuum.
5 Southern (2008), 3–4; Page 112, Stoneman, R. (1992). *Palmyra and Its Empire: Zenobia's Revolt Against Rome.* Ann Arbor: The University of Michigan Press.
6 Stoneman (1992), 31–49.
7 Andrade (2018), 18.
8 Southern (2008), 4.
9 Andrade (2018), 100–101.
10 Historia Augusta *Aurelian* 30.
11 Historia Augusta *Tyranni Triginta* 27, 30.
12 Historia Augusta *Tyranni Triginta* 30.
13 Historia Augusta *Tyranni Triginta* 28, 30.
14 Southern (2008), 3.
15 Andrade (2018), 90–91.
16 Southern (2008), 3.
17 Historia Augusta *Tyranni Triginta* 30.
18 Andrade (2018), 112, 153, 235–236.
19 Southern (2008), 47–48.
20 Historia Augusta *The Two Gallieni* 3.
21 Southern (2008), 73–74.
22 Southern (2008), 75.
23 Andrade (2018), 143–152; Southern (2008), 76–81.
24 Andrade (2018), 153.
25 Southern (2008), 81.
26 Southern (2008), 80.
27 Zosimus *New History* 1.39.
28 Southern (2008), 88; Andrade (2018), 172.
29 Andrade (2018), 150–152, 172.
30 Pages 260–261, Potter, D. S. (2004). *The Roman Empire at Bay, AD 180–395.* London: Routledge.
31 Potter (2004), 280–290.
32 Andrade (2018), 176–178.
33 Southern (2008), 119; Andrade (2018), 191.
34 Southern (2008), 119; Andrade (2018), 195–196;. For illustrations of coins and a discussions, see Judith Weingarten's blog article 'My money on Zenobia' at http://judithweingarten.blogspot.com/2008/11/my-money-on-zenobia.html.
35 Zosimus *New History* 1.50.
36 Zosimus *New History* 1.56.
37 Zosimus *New History* 1.55.
38 Historia Augusta *Tyranni Triginta* 30.
39 Burgersdijk, D. (2004–2005). 'Zenobia's biography in the *Historia Augusta*'. *TAAANTA* 36/37, 139–151; Syme (1971).
40 Andrade (2018), 3.
41 White, P. (1967). 'The authorship of the *Historia Augusta*'. *The Journal of Roman Studies* 57(1/2), 115–133.
42 Pages 205–207, Syme, R. (1968). *Ammianus and the Historia Augusta.* Oxford: Clarendon Press; Rosebank, J. (2020). 'G. N. Clark and the Oxford School of Modern History, 1919–1922: Hidden origins of *1066 And All That*'. *The English Historical Review* 135(572), 127–156.
43 Burgersdijk (2004–2005); Cameron, A. D. E. (1964). 'Literary allusions in the *Historia Augusta*'. *Hermes* 92(3), 363–377.

CHAPTER 29

1 Socrates Scholasticus *The Ecclesiastical History* 7.15.
2 Page 113, Dzielska, M. (1995). *Hypatia of Alexandria.* Cambridge, MA: Harvard University Press.
3 Dzielska (1995), 102.
4 Bowersock, G. W. (2010). '*Parabalani:* A terrorist charity in Late Antiquity'. *Anabases* 12, 45–54; Page 136, Nixey, C. (2017). *The*

Darkening Age: The Christian Destruction of the Classical World. London: Pan.

5 See the reviews by Gray, M. W. (2014). '*Agora* by Alejandro Amenábar'. *The Mathematical Intelligencer* 36(4), 111–113; Mark, J. (2014). 'Historical accuracy in the film *Agora*'. In *Ancient History Encyclopedia*. Available at www.ancient.eu/article/656/historical-accuracy-in-the-film-agora/; Viney, D. W. (2013). 'Remembering and misremembering Hypatia: The lessons of *Agora*'. *Midwestern Quarterly* 54(4), 352–369.

6 Dzielska (1995), 2–3.

7 Pages 945–946, Gibbon, E. (1995 [1788]). *The History of the Decline and Fall of the Roman Empire. Volume II*. London: Penguin. (Volume 4, chapter 47.)

8 Dzielska (1995), 101.

9 Dzielska (1995), 4.

10 Pages 318–319, Kingsley, C. (1853). *Hypatia. Volume I*. London: John W. Parker and Son.

11 Pages 277–288, Kingsley, C. (1857). *Hypatia. Volume II*. Leipzig: Bernhard Tauchnitz.

12 Page 170, Richards, J. (2009). *The Ancient World on the Victorian and Edwardian Stage*. Basingstoke: Palgrave Macmillan.

13 Page 65, Downes, D. A. (1972). *The Temper of Victorian Belief: Studies in the Religious Novels of Pater, Kingsley and Newman*. New York: Twayne.

14 Richards (2009), 170–177.

15 Richards (2009), 175.

16 Dzielska (1995); Deakin, M. A. (2007). *Hypatia of Alexandria: Mathematician and Martyr*. New York: Prometheus Books; Watts, E. J. (2017). *Hypatia: The Life and Legend of an Ancient Philosopher*. Oxford: Oxford University Press.

17 Dzielska (1995), 113.

18 Pages 424–429, Bernard, A. (2000). 'The Alexandrian school. Theon of Alexandria and Hypatia'. In Gerson, L. (ed.). *The Cambridge History of Philosophy in Late Antiquity*. Cambridge: Cambridge University Press, pp. 417–436; Deakin, (2007), 88.

19 Ancient sources outlined by Dzielska (1995), 113–117 and translated in Deakin (2007), 137–159, to which I refer below.

20 Deakin (2007), 158.

21 Deakin, (2007), 138, 141.

22 Deakin (2007), 150–151.

23 Deakin (2007), 156.

24 Watts (2017), 74–75.

25 Alic, M. (1981). 'Women and technology in ancient Alexandria'. *Women's Studies International Quarterly* 4(3), 305–312.

26 Cameron, A. (1990). 'Isidore of Miletus and Hypatia: On the editing of mathematical texts'. *Greek, Roman, and Byzantine Studies* 31, 103–127.

27 Deakin (2007), 158.

28 Deakin (2007), 89.

29 Deakin (2007), 110.

30 Deakin (2007), 147.

31 Deakin (2007), 141–142.

32 Watts (2017), 79.

33 Deakin (2007), 147.

34 Deakin (2007), 142.

35 Deakin (2007), 148; Watts (2017), 46.

36 Page 22, Wider, K. (1986). 'Women philosophers in the ancient Greek world: Donning the mantle'. *Hypatia* 1(1), 21–62.

37 Watts (2017), 93.

38 Watts (2017), 94–97.

39 Dzielska (1995), 68; Watts (2017), 21.

40 Watts (2017), 56–60.

41 Watts (2017), 151, 155.

CHAPTER 30

1 Pages xvii, xix, Sarris, P. (2007). 'Introduction'. In Procopius. *Secret History*. London: Penguin, pp. vii–xx.

2 Page 3, Potter, D. (2015). *Theodora: Actress, Empress, Saint*. Oxford: Oxford University Press.

3 Pages 77–82, Greatrex, G. (2014). 'Perceptions of Procopius in recent scholarship'. *Histos* 8, 76–121.

4 Greatrex (2014), 91.

5 Procopius *Secret History* 9.

6 Potter (2015), 91.

7 Potter (2015), 97–98.

8 Procopius *Secret History* 9–10.

9 Procopius *Secret History* 10.

10 Page 101, Brubaker, L. (2004). 'Sex, lies, and intertextuality: The *Secret History* of Prokopios and the rhetoric of gender in sixth-century Byzantium.' In Brubaker, L., and Smith, J. M. (ed.). *Gender in the Early Medieval World, East and West, 300–900*. Cambridge: Cambridge University Press, pp. 83–101.

11 Pages 433–434, Brubaker, L. (2005). 'The age of Justinian: Gender and society'. In Maas, M. (ed.). *The Cambridge Companion to the Age of Justinian*. Cambridge: Cambridge University Press, pp. 427–447.

12 Page 141, Foss, C. (2002). 'The empress Theodora'. *Byzantion* 72(1), 141–176.

13 Greatrex, G. (1997). 'The Nika riot: A reappraisal'. *The Journal of Hellenic Studies* 117, 60–86.
14 Procopius *History of the Wars* 1.24.
15 Potter (2015), 153.
16 Marincola, J. (2007). 'Speeches in classical historiography'. In Marincola, J. (ed.). *A Companion to Greek and Roman Historiography. Volume 1*. Oxford: Blackwell, pp. 118–132; Page 570, Croke, B. (2007). 'Late Antique Historiography, 250–650 CE'. In Marincola, J. (ed.). *A Companion to Greek and Roman Historiography. Volume 2*. Oxford: Blackwell, pp. 568–581.
17 Pages 182–184, Lilie, R.-J. (2014). 'Reality and invention: Reflections on Byzantine historiography'. *Dumbarton Oaks Papers* 68, 157–210.
18 Meier, M. (2004). 'Zur Funktion der Theodora-Rede im Geschichtswerk Prokops (BP 1,24,33–37)'. *Rheinisches Museum für Philologie* 147, 88–104.
19 Foss (2002).
20 Foss (2002), 148.
21 Foss (2002) Foss (2002), 149.
22 Procopius *History of the Wars* 7.31.
23 Potter (2015), 182.
24 Foss (2002), 150.
25 Potter (2015), 207–208.
26 De Pizan, C. (1999). *The Book of the City of Ladies*. London: Penguin, pp. 99–100.
27 De Pizan (1999), 100.
28 De Pizan (1999), 101.
29 Naples, M. (2015). 'Saint Theodora'. *Classical Wisdom*. Available at https://classicalwisdom.com/people/saint-theodora/.
30 Potter (2015), 207.
31 Brubaker (2005), 435.

SELECT BIBLIOGRAPHY

In order to make the bibliography shorter and more accessible to a wide audience, I have divided it into general works, primary sources in translation, and then a list of books on women that I have used or referred to. I have not included general archaeological or historical works, edited works with individually relevant chapters, or journal articles; sources I have used are referred to in the endnotes.

Many archaeology and ancient history handbooks published by Cambridge and Oxford University Presses, Routledge, and Wiley-Blackwell have chapters on or related to 'women' in particular contexts or cultures and are well worth searching out – again, ones I have consulted are listed in the endnotes.

The *Oxford Classical Dictionary* and the *Encyclopedia of Ancient History* (URLs below) are both very useful works of reference on individuals and topics and can be searched online, though may require library access.

GENERAL WORKS

Budin, S. L., and Turfa, J. M. (eds.). (2016). *Women in Antiquity: Real Women across the Ancient Mediterranean*. London: Routledge.

James, S. L., and Dillon, S. (eds.). (2012). *A Companion to Women in the Ancient World*. Chichester: Wiley-Blackwell.

Salisbury, J. (2001). *Encyclopedia of Women in the Ancient World*. Santa Barbara: ABC-Clio.

Smith, B. G. (ed.). (2008). *The Oxford Encyclopedia of Women in World History*. Four volumes. Oxford: Oxford University Press.

Vivante, B. (ed.). (1999). *Women's Roles in Ancient Civilizations: A Reference Guide*. Westport: Greenwood Press.

WEBSITES

The Encyclopedia of Ancient History: https://onlinelibrary.wiley.com/doi/book/10.1002/9781444338386.

The Oxford Classical Dictionary: https://oxfordre.com/classics/.

PRIMARY SOURCES IN TRANSLATION

I have accessed classical sources via translations in Oxford World's Classics, Penguin Classics, the Loeb Classical Library, and others listed below. Many of the secondary works also contain their own translations either of lines, sections, or sometimes entire texts. Translations of many classical texts can be accessed free of charge via the Perseus Digital Library, www.perseus.tufts.edu/hopper/ and LacusCurtius, https://penelope.uchicago.edu/Thayer/E/Roman/home.html. I have used these for and in addition to works not listed below.

CLASSICAL WORKS

Aristotle. (1981). *The Politics*. Translated by T. A. Sinclair. Revised and re-presented by T. J. Saunders. London: Penguin.

Cicero. (1978). *Cicero's Letters to His Friends*. Two volumes. Translated by D. R. Shackleton-Bailey. Harmondsworth: Penguin.

Demosthenes. (2014). *Selected Speeches*. Translated by R. Waterfield. Oxford: Oxford University Press.

Herodotus. (1996). *The Histories*. Translated by A. de Sélincourt. Revised by J. Marincola. London: Penguin.

Hippocrates. (1978). *Hippocratic Writings*. Edited by G. E. R. Lloyd. Translated by J. Chadwick and W. N. Mann. London: Penguin.

Historia Augusta. (1932). *The Scriptores Historiae Augustae. Volume III*. Translated by D. Magie. Cambridge, MA: Harvard University Press.

Homer. (1999). *Iliad*. Two volumes. Translated by A. T. Murray. Revised by W. F. Wyatt. Cambridge, MA: Harvard University Press.

Homer. (1995). *Odyssey*. Two volumes. Translated by A. T. Murray. Revised by G. E. Dimock. Cambridge, MA: Harvard University Press.

Josephus. (1888). *The Works of Josephus: With a Life Written by Himself. Volumes I–2*. Translated by W. Whiston. New York: A. C. Armstrong & Son.

Josephus. (1981). *The Jewish War*. Translated by G. A. Williamson. Revised by M. Smallwood. Harmondsworth: Penguin.

Juvenal. (1991). *The Satires*. Translated by Niall Rudd. Oxford: Oxford University Press.

Perpetua. (2012). *The Passions of Perpetua and Felicity*. Translated by T. J. Heffernan in Heffernan, T. J. (2012). *The Passion of Perpetua and Felicity*. Oxford: Oxford University Press, chapter 5.

Petronius. (1999). *The Satyricon*. Translated by P. G. Walsh. Oxford: Oxford University Press.

Plato. (1987). *The Republic*. Translated by D. Lee. London: Penguin.

Plato. (1987). *Theaetaetus*. Translated by R. Waterfield. London: Penguin.

Plutarch. (1973). *The Age of Alexander*. Translated by I. Scott-Kilvert. Harmondsworth: Penguin.

Plutarch. (2006). *Fall of the Roman Empire*. Translated by R. Warner. Revised by R. Seager. London: Penguin.

Plutarch. (2010). *Rome in Crisis*. Translated by I. Scott-Kilvert and Christopher Pelling. London: Penguin.

Procopius. (2007). *The Secret History*. Translated by G. A. Williamson. Revised by P. Sarris. London: Penguin.

Socrates Scholasticus. (1853). *The Ecclesiastical History*. London: H. Bohn.

Soranus. (1991). *Gynecology*. Translated by O. Temkin. Baltimore: Johns Hopkins University Press.

Tacitus. (1997). *The Histories*. Translated by W. H. Fyfe. Revised and edited by D. S. Levene. Oxford: Oxford University Press.

Tacitus. (1999). *Agricola and Germany*. Translated by A. R. Birley. Oxford: Oxford University Press.

Tertullian. Minucius Felix. (1931). *Apology. De Spectaculis. Octavius*. Translated by T. R. Glover and G. H. Rendall. Cambridge, MA: Harvard University Press.

Xenophon. (1923). *Memorabilia. Oeconomicus. Symposium. Apology*. Translated by E. C. Marchant and O. J. Todd. Revised by Jeffrey Henderson. Cambridge. MA: Harvard University Press.

Zosimus. (1814). *The History of Count Zosimus, sometime Advocate and Chancellor of the Roman Empire*. Translated by W. Green and T. Chaplin. London: J. Davis.

COLLECTIONS OF OTHER PRIMARY TEXTS

Beckman, G. M., and Hoffman, H. A. (1996). *Hittite Diplomatic Texts*. Atlanta: Scholars Press.

Breasted, J. H. (1906). *Ancient Records of Egypt*. Volumes II and III. Chicago: The University of Chicago Press.

Hoffner, H. A. (2009). *Letters from the Hittite Kingdom*. Atlanta: Society of Biblical Literature.

Lichtheim, M. (2006). *Ancient Egyptian Literature: The New Kingdom*. Volume II. Berkeley: University of California Press.

Sasson, J. M. (2015). *From the Mari Archives: An Anthology of Old Babylonian Letters*. Winona Lake: Pennsylvania State University Press.

Ventris, M., and Chadwick, J. (1973). *Documents in Mycenaean Greek*. Cambridge: Cambridge University Press.

BOOKS ON WOMEN

Allsebrook, M., and Allsebrook, A. (2002). *Born to Rebel: The Life of Harriet Boyd Hawes*. Oxford: Oxbow Books.

Andrade, N. J. (2018). *Zenobia: Shooting Star of Palmyra*. Oxford: Oxford University Press.

Batto, B. F. (1974). *Studies on Women at Mari*. Baltimore: Johns Hopkins University.

Blundell, S. (1995). *Women in Ancient Greece*. London: British Museum Press.

Bremmer, J. N., and Formisano, M. (eds.). (2012). *Perpetua's Passions: Multidisciplinary Approaches to the Passio Perpetuae et Felicitatis*. Oxford: Oxford University Press.

Brosius, M. (1996). *Women in Ancient Persia (559–331 BC)*. Oxford: Oxford University Press.

Brown, V. (2003). *Boccaccio: Famous Women*. Cambridge, MA: Harvard University Press.

Brubaker, L., and Smith, J. M. (ed.). (2004). *Gender in the Early Medieval World, East and West, 300–900*. Cambridge: Cambridge University Press.

Budin, S. L. (2021). *Freewomen, Patriarchal Authority, and the Accusation of Prostitution*. Abingdon: Routledge.

Budin, S. L., and Turfa, J. M. (eds.). (2016). *Women in Antiquity: Real Women across the Ancient Mediterranean*. London: Routledge.

Caldwell, L. (2015). *Roman Girlhood and the Fashioning of Femininity*. Cambridge: Cambridge University Press.

Cameron, A., and Kuhrt, A. (eds.). (1993). *Images of Women in Antiquity*. Revised ed. London: Routledge.

Carney, E. (2006). *Olympias: Mother of Alexander the Great*. New York: Routledge.

Carroll, M. (1907). *Greek Women: Volume 1*. Philadelphia: George Barrie and Sons.

Churchill, L. J., Brown, P. R., and Jeffrey, J. E. (eds.). (2002). *Women Writing Latin in Roman Antiquity, Late Antiquity, and the Early Christian Era*. New York: Routledge.

Criado Perez, C. (2019). *Invisible Women: Exposing Data Bias in a World Designed for Men*. London: Penguin.

Connell, S. (2021). *Aristotle on Women: Physiology, Psychology, and Politics*. Cambridge: Cambridge University Press.

Connelly, J. B. (2007). *Portrait of a Priestess: Women and Ritual in Ancient Greece*. Princeton: Princeton University Press.

De Pizan, C. (1999). *The Book of the City of Ladies*. London: Penguin.

Deakin, M. A. (2007). *Hypatia of Alexandria: Mathematician and Martyr*. New York: Prometheus Books.

Diaz-Andreu, M., and Stig Sørensen, M. L. (eds.). (1998). *Excavating Women: A History of Women in European Archaeology*. London: Routledge.

Dixon, S. (2007). *Cornelia: Mother of the Gracchi*. London: Routledge.

Donaldson, J. (1907). *Woman: Her Position and Influence in Ancient Greece and Rome, and among the Early Christians*. London: Longmans, Green and Co.

Donker van Heel, K. (2016). *Mrs Naunakhte & Family: The Women of Ramesside Deir al-Medina*. Cairo: The American University in Cairo Press.

Dzielska, M. (1995). *Hypatia of Alexandria*. Cambridge, MA: Harvard University Press.

Eller, C. (2011). *Gentlemen and Amazons: The Myth of Patriarchal Prehistory, 1861–1900*. Berkeley: University of California Press.

Faraone, C. A., and McClure, L. K. (eds.). (2006). *Prostitutes and Courtesans in the Ancient World*. Madison: The University of Wisconsin Press.

Fontenrose, J. (1978). *The Delphic Oracle*. Berkeley: University of California Press.

Foxhall, L. (2013). *Studying Gender in Classical Antiquity*. Cambridge: Cambridge University Press.

Franklin, M. (2006). *Boccaccio's Heroines: Power and Virtue in Renaissance Society*. London: Routledge.

Freisenbruch, A. (2010). *The First Ladies of Rome: The Women Behind the Caesars*. London: Vintage.

Garland, L. (1999). *Byzantine Empresses: Women and Power in Byzantium, AD 527–1204*. London: Routledge.

Gero, J. M., and Conkey, M. W. (eds.). (1991). *Engendering Archaeology: Women and Prehistory*. Oxford: Blackwell.

Gimbutas, M. (1991). *The Civilization of the Goddess: The World of Old Europe*. San Francisco: Harper Collins.

Gimbutas, M. (1999). *The Living Goddesses*. Berkeley: University of California Press.

Glazebrook, A., and Henry, M. M. (eds.). (2011). *Greek Prostitutes in the Ancient Mediterranean, 800 BCE–200 CE*. Madison: University of Wisconsin Press.

Glazebrook A., and Tsakirgis, B. (eds.). (2016). *Houses of Ill Repute: The Archaeology of Brothels, Houses, and Taverns in the Greek World*. Pennsylvania: University of Pennsylvania Press.

Gold, B. K. (2018). *Perpetua: Athlete of God*. Oxford: Oxford University Press.

Golden, M., and Toohey, P. (eds.). (2011). *A Cultural History of Sexuality, Vol. I: In the Classical World (800 BCE–350 CE)*. Oxford: Berg.

Grant, M. (1972). *Cleopatra*. London: Phoenix.

Gregory, I. V., and Cilia, D. (2005). *The Human Form in Neolithic Malta*. Malta: Midsea Books.

Hallett, J. P., and Skinner, M. P. (eds.). *Roman Sexualities*. Princeton: Princeton University Press.

Hamel, D. (2003). *Trying Neaira: The True Story of a Courtesan's Scandalous Life in Ancient Greece*. New Haven: Yale University Press.

Hamilton, S., Whitehouse, R. D., and Wright, K. L. (eds.). (2007). *Archaeology and Women: Ancient and Modern Issues*. London: Routledge.

Hawkes, J. (1968). *Dawn of the Gods*. London: Chatto and Windus.

Hays-Gilpin, K. A. (2004). *Ambiguous Images: Gender and Rock Art*. Walnut Creek: Altamira Press.

Hays-Gilpin, K., and Whitley, D. S. (eds.). (1998). *Reader in Gender Archaeology*. London: Routledge.

Heffernan, T. J. (2012). *The Passion of Perpetua and Felicity*. Oxford: Oxford University Press.

Heitman, R. (2005). *Taking Her Seriously: Penelope & the Plot of Homer's Odyssey*. Ann Arbor: The University of Michigan Press.

Hooper, R. (1999). *The Priapus Poems: Erotic Epigrams from Ancient Rome*. Urbana: University Illinois Press.

Huebner, S., and Ratzan, D. (eds.). *Growing Up Fatherless in Antiquity*. Cambridge: Cambridge University Press.

Hunt T. L., and Lessard M. R. (eds.). (2002). *Women and the Colonial Gaze*. London: Palgrave Macmillan.

Hurst, I. (2006). *Victorian Women Writers and the Classics: The Feminine of Homer*. Oxford: Oxford University Press.

Joshel, S. R., and Murnaghan, S. (eds.). (1998). *Women & Slaves in Greco-Roman Culture*. London: Routledge.

Kapparis, K. A. (1999). *Apollodoros: 'Against Neaira' [D 59]*. Berlin: Walter de Gruyter.

Keuls, E. C. (1985). *The Reign of the Phallus: Sexual Politics in Ancient Athens*. Berkeley: University of California Press.

Kingsley, C. (1853). *Hypatia. Volume I*. London: John W. Parker and Son.

Knapp, R. (2011). *Invisible Romans: Prostitutes, Outlaws, Slaves, Gladiators, Ordinary Men and Women ... The Romans That History Forgot*. London: Profile Books.

Kraemer, R. S. (1992). *Her Share of the Blessings: Women's Religion among Pagans, Jews, and Christians in the Greco-Roman World*. Oxford: Oxford University Press.

Lardinois, A., and McClure, L. (eds.). (2001). *Making Silence Speak: Women's Voices in Greek Literature and Society*. Princeton: Princeton University Press.

Levin-Richardson, S. (2019). *The Brothel of Pompeii: Sex, Class, and Gender at the Margins of Roman Society*. Cambridge: Cambridge University Press.

Macurdy, G. H. (1932). *Hellenistic Queens: A Study of Woman-Power in Macedonia,*

Seleucid Syria, and Ptolemaic Egypt. Westport: Greenwood Press.

Man, J. (2017). *Amazons: The Real Warrior Women of the Ancient World*. London: Corgi.

Manne, K. (2018). *Down Girl: The Logic of Misogyny*. London: Penguin.

Mayor, A. (2014). *The Amazons: Lives & Legends of Warrior Women across the Ancient World*. Princeton: Princeton University Press.

McClees, H. (1920). *A Study of Women in Attic Inscriptions*. New York: Columbia University Press.

McGinn, T. (2004). *The Economy of Prostitution in the Roman World: A Study of Social History and the Brothel*. Ann Arbor: University of Michigan Press.

McLeod, G. (1991). *Virtue and Venoma: Catalogs of Women from Antiquity to the Renaissance*. Ann Arbor: The University of Michigan Press.

McManus, B. (2017). *The Drunken Duchess of Vassar: Grace Harriet Macurdy, Pioneering Feminist Classical Scholar*. Columbus: Ohio State University Press.

Meyers, C. (2013). *Rediscovering Eve: Ancient Israelite Women in Context*. Oxford: Oxford University Press.

Miller, B. D. (ed.). (1993). *Sex and Gender Hierarchies*. Cambridge: Cambridge University Press.

Olsen, B. A. (2014). *Women in Mycenaean Greece: The Linear B Tablets from Pylos and Knossos*. Abingdon: Routledge.

Phang, S. E. (2022). *Daily Life of Women in Ancient Rome*. Santa Barbara: ABC-Clio.

Pomeroy, S. B. (ed.). (1991). *Women's History and Ancient History*. Chapel Hill: The University of North Carolina Press.

Pomeroy, S. B. (1995). *Goddesses, Whores, Wives and Slaves*. New York: Schocken Books.

Potter, D. (2015). *Theodora: Actress, Empress, Saint*. Oxford: Oxford University Press.

Roehrig, C. H. (ed.). *Hatshepsut: From Queen to Pharaoh*. New York: The Metropolitan Museum of Art.

Roller, D. W. (2018). *Cleopatra's Daughter and Other Royal Women of the Augustan Era*. Oxford: Oxford University Press.

Salisbury, J. E. (1997). *Perpetua's Passion: The Death and Memory of a Young Roman Woman*. London: Routledge.

Schiff, S. (2011). *Cleopatra: A Life*. London: Virgin.

Southern, P. (2008). *Empress Zenobia: Palmyra's Rebel Queen*. London: Continuum.

Stol, M. (2016). *Women in the Ancient Near East*. Boston: De Gruyter.

Stoneman, R. (1992). *Palmyra and Its Empire: Zenobia's Revolt against Rome*. Ann Arbor: The University of Michigan Press.

Strong, A. K. (2016). *Prostitutes and Matrons in the Roman World*. Cambridge: Cambridge University Press.

Sturgeon, M. C. (1914). *Women of the Classics*. London: Harrap.

Swaddling, J., and Prag, J. (eds.). (2002). *Seianti Hanunia Tlesnasa: The Story of an Etruscan Noblewoman*. London: British Museum Press.

Treggiari, S. (2007). *Terentia, Tullia and Publilia: The Women of Cicero's Family*. London: Routledge.

Tyldesley, J. (1994). *Daughters of Isis: Women of Ancient Egypt*. London: Penguin.

Tyldesley, J. (1996). *Hatchepsut: The Female Pharaoh*. London: Penguin.

Tyldesley, J. (2006). *Chronicle of the Queens of Ancient Egypt: From Early Dynastic Times to the Death of Cleopatra*. London: Thames and Hudson.

Valency, M. J. (1966). *The Tragedies of Herod & Mariamne*. New York: AMS Press.

von Bothmer, D. (1957). *Amazons in Greek Art*. Oxford: Oxford University Press.

Walde, D., and Willows, N. D. (eds.). (1991). *The Archaeology of Gender*. Calgary: The University of Calgary.

Walker, S., and Higgs, P. (eds.). (2001). *Cleopatra of Egypt: From History to Myth*. London: The British Museum Press.

Watkins, J. (2017). *After Lavinia*. Ithaca: Cornell University Press.

Watts, E. J. (2017). *Hypatia: The Life and Legend of an Ancient Philosopher*. Oxford: Oxford University Press.

Yoder, C. R. (2001). *Wisdom as a Woman of Substance: A Socio-Economic Reading of Proverbs 1–9 and 31:10–31*. Berlin: De Gruyter.

INDEX

Abbamuš, 137
abortion, 1, 245
Abydos, 56–61
Acharnai, 156
Achillia, 212–218
Adea Eurydice, 168–170
Aeschylus, 132, 134, 144
Alashiya. *See* Cyprus/Alashiya
Alexander Helios, 200–201, 204
Alexander IV, 169–170
Alexander the Great, 161, 163, 165–171, 189, 199, 205
Alexandra, grandmother of Mariamne, 189
Alexandra, mother of Mariamne, 189, 191–192
Alexandria, 197, 200–201, 205, 221, 232, 236–242
Alma-Tadema, Lawrence, 238
Amazon (gladiator), 212–218
Amazon burials
  Akkermen, 129
  Jrapi, 130
  Scythia, 129
  Urals, 129
  Volga, 129
  Voronezh, 129
Amazonomachies, 128
Amazons, 125–131
Amazons in Greek culture, 125–129
Anemospilia, 52, 75–81
Antiochis of Tlos, 159
Antiope, 127
Antony, Mark, 186, 189, 191–192, 195, 199–202, 204–205
Apollodorus, 111
Apuleius, 208
Argaric awls, 70–71
Argaric culture, 9, 52, 68–74
Argaric silver diadems, 68, 70–74
Argaric sites
  Cerro de la Encina, 71
  El Argar, 52, 68, 71–73
  Fuente Álamo, 71
  Gatas, 71
  La Almoloya, 52
  La Bastida, 52, 71–73
Aristonice, 111, 143–148
Aristotle, 8, 120, 134, 239
Armenoi, 79
Arrhidaeus, 166, 169, *See* also Philip III
Arunta, 29
Aspasia (companion of Pericles), 151, 154
Aspasia (medical writer), 160
Atalanta, 129
Athenaeus, 166, 176, 178
Athens, 4, 8, 109–111, 119–124, 127–129, 133–134, 145–147, 149–160, 169, 180–182, 205, 207
Atossa, 111, 132–137
Audata, 170
Augustus, 8, 19, 176, 189, 195, 201–202, 205, 213, *See* also Octavian
Aurelian, 196, 227–230, 232–235

Bachofen, Johann Jakob, 9–10, 12
Balsdon, J. P. V. Dacre, 15
Bate, Dorothea, 18
Beard, Mary, 18
Beerbohm Tree, Max, 238
boat graves, Egyptian, 52, 58
Boccaccio, ix–xi, 14, 188
Bolger, Diane, 17
Boudica, 141
Brochtorff Circle. *See* Gozo/Malta, Xagħra
Budin, Stephanie Lynn, xii, 17
Byzantine Empire, 197, 243–250

Caesar, Julius, 162, 179, 183, 185, 195, 199, 201–202
Caesarea, 243
Caligula, 195, 205
Cambyses, 110, 132
Cameron, Dorothy, 36
Carroll, Lewis, 238
Carroll, Mitchell, 15
Carthage/Carthaginians, xix, 161–162, 181, 219–221
Cartimandua, 141
Cary, Elizabeth, 194
Çatalhöyük (Neolithic), 13, 24, 34–41
  'history houses', 35
  bucrania, 35–37
  burial, 37
  diet/food, 38–40
  figurines, 37

Çatalhöyük (Neolithic) (cont.)
goddess figurine, 37
heads, 38
paintings, 36, 38–39
cave art (Palaeolithic), 24, 27–33, 45
hands, 30–33
sexing, 32–33
caves, 24
Altamira, 27–28, 30
Cosquer, 30
Cueva de Ardales, 30
Cueva de la Pileta, 30
Devil's Tower, 18
Gargas, 30
Gorham's Cave, 30
Paglicci, 30
Celtic women, 141
Celts, xi, 73, 110, 138–142
children, xi, 1–5, 10, 29, 31–32, 36–37, 62–64, 67, 85, 90, 96, 105–107, 113–118, 120, 123, 126, 137, 144, 146, 153–154, 156–157, 166–167, 176, 181–187, 190, 195, 199–203, 205, 227, 234, 240
Christians/Christianity, xi, 196–197, 208, 213, 219–226, 235, 248–249
Cicero, 5, 7, 162, 179–187
Circe, 156
Classical Greece, 111, 132–137, 143–160
Claudius, 19, 172, 195
Claudius II, 232
Cleopatra (daughter of Olympias and Philip II), 168
Cleopatra (medical writer), 160
Cleopatra (niece of Attalus), 167–168
Cleopatra Selene, xi, 195, 199–205
tomb of, 205
Cleopatra VII, 55, 82, 160–161, 189, 191–192, 195, 199–201, 203–204, 230
Commodus, 213, 220
Conkey, Margaret, 16–17
Constantine, 197
Constantinople, 197, 238, 243–250
Corinth, 135, 150, 152, 154, 162
Cornelia, 181, 187
Crawford, Osbert Guy, 12
cremation, x, 109
cremation, Rich Athenian Lady, 119–121, 123
Cynnane, 170
Cypros, 191–192
Cyprus/Alashiya, xi, 51, 102–107
Cyril, 236–237, 241
Cyrus, 110, 132, 137, 216

Damascius, 240–241
Darius, 110, 132–137, 145, 216
de Pizan, Christine, ix–xi, 14, 248
de Sautuola, Marcelline Sanz, 27
de Sautuola, María Sanz, 28
Deir el-Bahri, 82–87
Deir el-Medina, 113–118
Delphi, 100, 110–111, 143–148, 169
gases/vapours, 147–148
Delphic oracle, 143–148
Demaratus, 135
Democedes, 135
Demosthenes, 111
Dido, 230
diet/food, xviii, 4–5, 17, 24, 29, 36, 38–40, 45, 47, 53, 77, 79, 97, 100, 116–117, 121, 142, 175, 224
Dillon, Sheila, xii, 17
Dio, Cassius, 200–202
Diocletian, 196, 233, 235
Diodorus Siculus, 170, 183
Diogenes Laertius, 147
Dionysus of Halicarnassus, 176
Domitian, 195–196, 212
Donaldson, James, 15
Donations of Alexandria, 200
Drusilla, 205

education, 4, 10, 14, 18, 65, 114, 159, 180, 202, 222, 229, 239
Egypt/Egyptians, xi, xviii, 3, 8, 15, 19, 21, 37, 49–53, 82–88, 91–92, 94, 102–104, 106–107, 113–118, 156, 161, 189, 197, 199–205, 232, 234, 236–242, 249
Emery, Walter, 58–60
Eritha, 95–101
Etruscan sites
Caere, 162
Cerveteri, 174
Chiusi, 162, 173
Poggio Cantarello, 173
Poggio Civitate, 175
Pyrgi, 162
Tarquinia, x, 174
Etruscans, xix, 138, 161–162, 172–178, 181
Eutychis, 206–211
Evans, Arthur, 11, 75, 79–80
evidence, archaeological and textual, 19–20
exposure (of babies), 1–4

Felicity, 219, 221–222, 225
female scholars of archaeology and ancient history (modern), 15–18
Flaccus, Calpurnius, 213
Flores, Pedro, 71
fluting. *See* cave art (Palaeolithic)
foetus, 2, 37, 44, 105, 123
France, ix, xi, 20–21, 30, 32, 110, 138–142
Frazer, James, 11–12
Fulvia, 182

Galen, 155, 160
Galla Placidia, 8
Gallienus, 231–232
Garrod, Dorothy, 18

gender, x, xii, 6–9, 12–13, 16–17, 19, 29, 39, 41, 70, 117, 130, 140, 176, 215, 237
Geometric Greece, 109, 119–124
Gerhard, Eduard, 11
Gero, Joan, 17
Geta, 221
Gilchrist, Roberta, 16–17
Gimbutas, Marija, 13
gladiators, 212–218, 225–226
  body of female gladiator from London, 213
  grave of in Ephesus, 213
Godward, John William, 133
Gozo/Malta, xi, 13, 20, 25, 47
  figurines and statues, 46
  Ggantija, 46
  Hal Saflieni, 43
  Tarxien, 14, 46
  Xagħra, 42–47
graffiti, 21, 28, 87, 115, 196, 206, 208, 210–211, 217
Graves, Robert, 12
Greco-Persian War, 110, 145–148
Greece/Greeks, xi
  Passim. *See also* Minoan Crete, Mycenaean Greece, Geometric Greece, Classical Greece, Hellenistic Greece

Halaf culture, 11–12
Halicarnassus, 215–217
Hall, Edith, 18
Hammurabi, 63
hand prints. *See* cave art (Palaeolithic)
hand stencils. *See* cave art (Palaeolithic)
Harrison, Jane Ellen, 11–12, 76–80
Hasmoneans, 163, 189–191, 193
Hatiba, 51, 102–107
Hatshepsut, 8, 50, 82–88
Hattusa (Boğazköy), 51, 89, 91–92
Hattusili III, 51, 89–94
Hawes, Harriet Boyd, 18
Hawkes, Jacquetta, 12
Haya-Sumu, 65–67
Hellanikos, 125
Hellenistic Greece, 161–163, 165–171
Hemelrijk, Emily, xii
Herennia Cervilla, 5
Herod, 163, 190–194
Herodotus, 120, 126, 129, 132, 135–137, 140, 145–147, 176
Hersilia, 180
Hesiod, 120, 143, 176
hetairai, 150–151, 154, 177
Hippocrates, 125, 140, 155
Hippolyte, 127–128
Historia Augusta, 227–235
Hittites, xi, 8, 19–20, 51, 53, 89–94, 96, 109
Homer
  Iliad, 73, 99, 125, 127, 134, 143, 207
  Odyssey, 134, 143, 155–156, 207

House of the Vettii, 206, 209–210
Hughes, Bettany, 18
human sacrifice, Anemospilia, 78
hunting, 24–25, 29, 36, 39, 45
Hurrian/Hurrians, 90, 93
Hypatia, 236–242
hypogea, 25, 42, 45

Iberia, xi, 9, 20, 30, 52, *See* also Spain
infanticide, 2, 4, 245, *See* also exposure (of babies)
inscriptions, xii, 15, 19, 49, 82, 85, 92, 105–106, 130, 147, 157–158, 170, 172–173, 196, 205–206, 208–209, 217, 229–231, 247
Iol-Caesarea, 203–205
Irdabama, 136–137
Irtašduna, 137
Isopata ring, 75–76, 81

James, Edwin Oliver, 12
James, Sharon L., xii, 17
jewellery, 24, 37, 44, 47, 65, 70–71, 105–106, 120, 122–123, 129, 139, 153, 174, 230
Jews, 188–194, 197, 241
Joffroy, René, 140
John of Nikiu, 241
Josephus, 188–194
Juba II, 195, 200, 202–203, 205
Judaea, 163, 188–194
Julia, 202
Julian, 236
Justinian, x, xviii, 20, 197, 235, 243–250
Juvenal, 214–215, 217, 234

Kalavasos-*Ayios Dhimitrios*, 51, 104–107
Karpathia, 95–101
Kingsley, Charles, 227, 238
Kirum, 50, 62–67
Kizzuwatna, 90–92, 94

La Almoloya, 68–74
La Parisienne, 76, 79, 81
Laïs, 152
Lais (medical writer), 160
Landor, Walter Savage, 151
Levant, xi, xix, 8, 20, 24, 49, 89, 104
Linear B, 95–101
literacy, 14, 50, 65, 115, 118, 159–160, 180, 202, 222, 229–230
Livia, 8, 195
Longus, 3
Lorimer, Hilda, 17
Lucan, 147

Macedonia, 165–171
Macurdy, Grace Harriet, 15–18
Mallowan, Max, 11
Mari, 49–50, 62–67
Mari tablets, 62–67

Mariamne, 163, 188–194
Marius, 233
marriage, 4–5, 9–10, 52–53, 91, 116, 126, 135, 149, 153, 178
  of Adea Eurydice, 169
  child, 115
  of Cleopatra Selene, 202
  of Hatshepsut, 82
  of Mariamne, 188–194
  of Naunakhte, 115, 118
  of Neithhotep, 51
  of Olympias, 165–171
  of Publilia, 186
  of Puduhepa, 90
  of Šimatum and Kirum, 62–67
  of Terentia, 179–187
  of Theodora, 244, 248–249
  of Tullia, 185
  of Zenobia, 229
Marseilles, 110, 138
martyrs/martyrdom, 219–226
matriarchy, prehistoric, 9–14
Mauretania, 195, 202–205
McLees, Helen, 15
McLennan, John, 10
medicine/doctors, 155–160
Mediterranean (unit of study), xviii–xix
Megara, 150, 153
Mellaart, James, 13, 34–36, 38–39
Memphis, 49, 103
Ménage, Gilles, 241
Merneith, 8, 49–53
Mesopotamia/Mesopotamians, xi, 8, 17, 20, 49–50, 62–67
Metrodora (medical writer), 160
midwifery, 2, 157–160
Mill, John Stuart, 9
Minoan Crete, 9, 11–12, 18, 50–52, 68, 75–81, 87, 95, 100, 105
misogyny, 1, 6–9, 18, 211
missing women, 1–6
Mitchell, Charles, 227, 238
Molossia, 165, 168–169
Morgan, Lewis Henry, 10, 56
Mother Goddess, 9–14, 79
Mycenaean Greece, 9, 12, 52–53, 95–101, 109, 119–120, 122

Naqada, 56
Narmer, 56–57
Naunakhte, 113–118
Neaira, 149–154
Neanderthals, 18, 23, 45
Nefertari, 92
neglect, 1, 4
Neil, Jennifer, xii
Neithhotep, 51, 59, 61
Neolithic Revolution, 24–25
Nepos, Cornelius, 180
Nero, 19, 195, 219
Neumann, Erich, 12
Nika riots, 246
Nikarete, 150, 152, 154

ochre, 37, 45, 47
Octavia, 202
Octavian, 192, 195, 204, *See* also Augustus
Odainathus, 196, 227–235
Ogilvie, G. Stuart, 238
Oltos painter, 130
Olympias, 165–171
  tomb of, 170–171
Orestes, 241
Orithyia, 127

Palaeolithic, 23–24
Palaeolithic Revolution, 23–24
Palmyra, 227–235
Pandrosion, 241
paterfamilias, 8, 180, 223
patriarchy, 1, 6–14, 80
Pausanias, 147, 166, 168, 170
Pausanias (lover of Philip II), 168
pelvis, 37, 43, 69, 122, 140, 175
Penthesileia, 127, 216
Perialla (Pythia), 147
Perpetua, 219–226
  baby son of, 224
  death of, 225–226
  relationship with father, 222–223
  visions of, 222, 224–225
Persepolis, 136–137
Persia/Persians, 20, 110–111, 120, 128, 132–137, 146–147, 168, 196, 227, 229, 231–232, 234, 243, 248
Petrie, Flinders, 57–59, 92
Petronius, 210, 212
Phainarete, 158
Phanostrate, 111, 155–160
Phemonoe (Pythia), 147
Philip II, 165–171
Philip III, 169, *See* also Arrhidaeus
Phoenicians, xix
Plato, xix, 2, 8, 111, 120, 156, 158, 239
Pliny the Elder, 160
Pliny the Younger, 3, 195, 219
Plutarch, 4, 137, 148, 154, 165, 167–168, 179, 182–186, 200, 202
Pomeroy, Sarah B., xii, 6, 8–9, 16, 144, 208
Pompeii, 195, 206–211, 217
Posidippus, 3
Postumus, 233
Pottier, Edmond, 76
Prag, John, 79
Priapus, 209
Princess of Vix, 138–142

Procopius, 197, 235, 243–250
prostitutes, 244–245
prostitution, 19, 148–154, 177, 206–211, 213, 244–245, 248
Ptolemy, 205
Publilia, 186
Puduhepa, 89–94
Punt, 84–86
Pylos, 95–101
Pythia, 143–148

radiocarbon dating, 69
Ramesses II, 50–51, 89–92, 113
rape, 8, 16, 127, 141, 144, 152–153, 210
Rich Lady of Athens, 119–124
Richter, Gisela, 18
rings, 11, 70–71, 75, 78, 81, 105–106, 122, 139, 174, 193, 248
Rives, Amélie, 194
Roman Empire, 188–197, 199–250
Roman Republic, 179–187
Rome/Romans
  Passim, x
Rose, Jon Cruikshank, 11
Roxane, 169–170
Rufus, Musonius, 180

Sakellarakis, John and Efi, 76–79, 81
Salisbury, Joyce, xii
Sallust, 182, 187
Salome (Herod's sister), 191–193
San Vitale (Ravenna), 220, 227, 249
Sanctuary of Philip (the Philippeion), 166–167
Sapor, 196, 231
Saqqara, 37, 57–61
Sarmatia/Sarmatians, 125–131
Scythia/Scythians, 125–131, 135, 140
  names, 130
Scythians
  police in Athens, 127
seals, 19, 58–59, 66, 75, 78–79, 91–92, 94, 105, 122, 137, 209
Seianti Hanunia Tlesnasa, 172–178
Seltman, Charles, 15
Semiramis, 230
Semonides of Amorgos, 6
Sempronia, 181
Sen, Amartya, 1–2, 4, 6
Senenmut, 84, 87
Septimius Severus, 213–214
Severus Alexander, 229
sexual relations, x, 6, 8, 16–17, 28, 67, 84, 149–154, 176–178, 190, 210, 244
Šimatum, 50, 62–67
Siret, Henri, 68
Siret, Louis, 68, 71
skeleton, x, 21, 40, 42–44, 69–70, 77–79, 105–106, 129–130, 139–142, 174–175, 208
skull, 18, 38, 44, 71, 78–79, 122–123, 129, 140, 142, 173
slave collar from Bulla Regia, 208
slave/slavery, 3, 7, 81, 97, 149–150, 152–154, 206–211, 214, 244
Socrates Scholasticus, 236, 238–241
Soranus, 2, 159
Spain, 23, 27, 30, 32, *See* also Iberia
Sparta, 2, 110, 128, 145, 178
Spartacus, 214
Spartan girls, 135, 217
  Spartan girls vs Roman girls, 5–21
Spartan women, 8, 178
Spector, Janet, 16–17
Sphagianes, 96–97, 99–100
Stratonike, 100
Sturgeon, Mary, 15

Tarhuntassa, 89
tawannana, 94
teeth, 6, 21, 29, 39, 44, 78–79, 105, 122, 130, 142, 175–176, 230
Tell el-Daba, Minoan frescoes, 87
Tennyson, Alfred, 238
Terentia, 5, 162, 179–187
Tertullian, 213, 220, 223
Tetricus I and II, 233
Theano, 99
Themistokleia (Pythia), 147
Theodora, x, xviii, 8, 20–21, 197, 243–250
Theodote (medical writer), 160
Theophilus, 242
Theopompus, 176–178
Thuburbo Minus, 221
Thutmose III, 82, 84, 87
Titus, 195–196
Toland, John, 237
Trajan, 219
Tringham, Ruth, xi
Tudhaliya IV, 89, 94
Tullia, 5, 7, 179, 181, 184–186
Turfa, Jean MacIntosh, xii, 17

Ugarit, 50, 63–64, 94, 106
uranium series dating, 27

Vaballathus, 229, 231–233
Valerian, 196, 231
Vedda, 29
Ventris, Michael, 95
Vespasian, 188, 195
Veturia, 180
Victorinus, 233
Vix krater, 138–139
Vix, France, 110, 138–142

Voltaire, 188, 194, 237
Volumnia, 180

Waterhouse, John William, 194
weapons, x, 24, 29, 70, 73, 78, 119, 126–131, 140, 145, 213, 216, 224
Wenamun, 51, 102–104, 107
Wetwang burial, 142
Wilamaya Patjxa burial, 29
women in antiquity, the study of, 14–18
Wylie, Alison, 16

Xenokleia (Pythia), 147
Xenophon, 4, 158–159
Xerxes, 132–133, 135, 145–146

Zabbai, 229, 231, 234
Zabdas, 231–233
Zenobia, 196, 227–235
Zimri-Lim, 50, 63–67
  palace, 63–64
Zosimus, 232–234